S0-AJE-712

Plant Health Care
for Woody Ornamentals

Issued in furtherance of Cooperative Extension Work, Acts of May 8 and June 30, 1914, in cooperation with the U.S. Department of Agriculture. Dennis R. Campion, Interim Director, Cooperative Extension Service, University of Illinois at Urbana-Champaign. The Cooperative Extension Service provides equal opportunities in programs and employment.

The information provided in this publication is for educational purposes only. References to commercial products or trade names do not constitute an endorsement by the University of Illinois and do not imply discrimination against other similar products.

College of Agricultural, Consumer and Environmental Sciences, University of Illinois at Urbana-Champaign

Cooperative Extension Service
University of Illinois at Urbana-Champaign
Helping You Put Knowledge to Work

Plant Health Care

for Woody Ornamentals

A Professional's Guide to Preventing and Managing Environmental Stresses and Pests

International Society of Arboriculture
Champaign, Illinois

Cooperative Extension Service
College of Agricultural, Consumer and Environmental Sciences
University of Illinois at Urbana-Champaign

Copyright © 1997 by University of Illinois Board of Trustees and the International Society of Arboriculture.

This manual may not be reproduced without the written permission of the International Society of Arboriculture and the University of Illinois. Permission may be granted for parts of this work to be reproduced for educational purposes, provided that copies are distributed at no cost; the authors(s), the publication, the International Society of Arboriculture, and the University of Illinois College of Agricultural, Consumer and Environmental Sciences are identified on each copy; and proper notice of copyright is affixed to each copy.

The primary author of each chapter has the right to first refusal for future revisions of this manual.

ISBN 1-883097-17-7

Printed in the United States of America
by Printec Press, Champaign, Illinois
10 9 8 7
8/05 RF 1000

Dedication

This book is dedicated to the landscapers, arborists, nurserymen, urban foresters, and horticulturists who make a living using ecologically sensitive maintenance and management techniques to maintain the plants in our environment.

—John Lloyd, Coordinating Author

Contents

Foreword

Tree care is an evolving field. Practices and techniques common 20 or 30 years ago have become more selectively applied, modified, or eliminated. Reduction in the use of calendar or cover sprays, soil amendments for planting, and pruning paints are just three of the many changes witnessed in our profession.

Along with updated practices and techniques, our philosophy of care has also changed. We once focused on managing parts, treating a leaf disease, adding nutrients for roots to absorb, or removing branches from the canopy. Each of these practices has ramifications far beyond the direct effect. By focusing on parts, however, we ignored the system.

Plant Health Care for Woody Ornamentals: A Professional's Guide to Preventing and Managing Environmental Stresses and Pests marks another step in the evolution of tree care. Plant Health Care (PHC) presents tree care as a study of a system rather than just its parts. A tree is a biological system of interdependent parts; managing only one part of the system may cause unexpected results. For example, fertilizing a tree may cause not only increased shoot growth, but increased (rather than decreased) susceptibility to certain pests, as well.

As a tree care practitioner, you may believe that Plant Health Care is just another name for Integrated Pest Management (IPM), or that the former replaces the latter. Neither statement could be further from the truth. PHC is a comprehensive approach to the care of all landscape plants. It incorporates an array of such practices as pruning, nutrient management, and Integrated Pest Management, among others, into an overall approach to the care of trees and other plants in the ornamental landscape.

Plant Health Care also brings the client into the management process. As tree care professionals, we strive to assist our clients, whether they are homeowners who hire us to prune the maple in their front yard or the citizens we serve as urban and community foresters. Consequently, although we take care of trees, our work is not performed in isolation. We work for someone whose tree and landscape-related needs and desires must be clearly understood before we begin our work.

Within these pages you will find the most complete and current information on a wide variety of tree care practices, all within the context of PHC. The lead author of this publication is John Lloyd, an Extension entomologist, who clearly recognized that pest management can be influenced by many variables—from planting techniques to fertilizer practices. His goal was to create a guide that explains tree care at the system level. He assembled a team of authors who emphasize the role of stress and pest management in the PHC system. John has admirably fulfilled this goal.

Plant Health Care for Woody Ornamentals makes a fine companion to the *Guide to the Plant Health Care Management System*, the International Society of Arboriculture's guide to implementing and managing a successful PHC business (developed with the support of the U.S. Forest Service, the National Arborist Association, and the ISA Research Trust).

I am confident this book will become a valuable resource in your endeavor to care for trees and the "green world" that is so important to our daily lives.

Bill Kruidenier, Executive Director
International Society of Arboriculture
Savoy, Illinois
January 1997

Preface

Plant Health Care for Woody Ornamentals: A Professional's Guide to Preventing and Managing Environmental Stresses and Pests attempts to organize and integrate information from specific disciplines to provide a complete perspective on Plant Health Care and Integrated Pest Management. It was developed to fill an information gap in resources for professionals in PHC-related industries, based upon feedback from a survey of landscape practitioners in the Midwestern United States.

Plant Health Care for Woody Ornamentals serves as a textbook for undergraduate-level courses in woody landscape maintenance and pest management and is the companion to the International Society of Arboriculture's (ISA) business guide to Plant Health Care, *A Guide to the Plant Health Care Management System*. It is also a reference manual and text for ISA's advanced training program in Plant Health Care.

Funding for development of this publication was provided by the United States Forest Service Urban Forestry Technology Transfer Grant Program, the University of Illinois Cooperative Extension Service, the Illinois Arborist Association, and the International Society of Arboriculture.

Chapters 1, 2, and 3 delve into the basics of Plant Health Care. Chapter 1 introduces the concepts that provide the foundation for Plant Health Care programs. Chapter 2 examines the basics of plant biology that are necessary to understand plant systems and responses. Chapter 3 provides a crucial look into the complexity of interactions that affect plant health, and should initiate critical thinking on the part of the reader to understand that Plant Health Care is not a cut-and-dried recipe, but a process that relies upon continual observation and examination of plant processes and environmental interactions, as well as an understanding of client expectations, to provide successful plant care. Chapter 3 also provides a transition to the plant and pest management chapters that follow.

Chapters 4 through 10 offer specific information on plant establishment, maintenance, and pest manage-

ment. Specific pests and management techniques are identified in these chapters to assist practitioners in diagnosing disorders and pest problems. Pests specifically identified in the chapters are those of importance to a broad geographical area in the Eastern and Midwestern United States. It is our intent to provide information on specific pest categories that will be of use to practitioners throughout the world when identifying pest "categories" and their associated damage. It is *not* our intent to mention every pest of woody ornamentals or to provide chemical management recommendations. Many reference materials are available that address pests for specific regions in the United States and Canada and on other continents. Many of these resources are referenced in the pest-specific chapters.

Concluding the guide in Chapter 11 is a discussion of dealing with people. This chapter discusses the most important and most overlooked aspect of Plant Health Care—working with clients and the public at large to communicate the positive effects of a PHC program.

If you have any comments, suggestions, or corrections for future editions of *Plant Health Care for Woody Ornamentals*, please forward them to:

Publications Coordinator
International Society of Arboriculture
Post Office Box GG
Savoy, IL 61874-9902 USA

John Lloyd
Extension Entomologist
Department of Natural Resources
& Environmental Sciences
University of Illinois at Urbana-Champaign

James Skiera
Associate Executive Director
International Society of Arboriculture

Acknowledgments

Editorial Staff

Peggy Currid, Nancy Nichols, and
  Terri Stone
Editorial Section
Information Services
College of Agricultural, Consumer
  and Environmental Sciences
University of Illinois at Urbana-
  Champaign

Production Staff

Cathy Murphy and
  John Wondrasek
Buerkett Marketing Consultants
Savoy, Illinois

Gretchen Wieshuber
Studio 2D
Champaign, Illinois

Nancy Komlanc
Publications Coordinator
International Society of
  Arboriculture
Savoy, Illinois

Reviewers

*The following persons generously
provided suggestions and reviewed
drafts of the manuscript*

Kim D. Coder
Professor of Forestry
Department of Forest Resources
University of Georgia

John Ball
Associate Professor of Forestry
Department of Landscape,
  Horticulture Forestry, and
  Parks
South Dakota State University

David J. Williams
Professor of Ornamental
  Horticulture
Department of Natural Resources
  and Environmental Sciences
University of Illinois at Urbana-
  Champaign

Antoine G. Endress
Professor of Horticulture
Department of Natural Resources
  and Environmental Sciences
University of Illinois at Urbana-
  Champaign

International Society of Arboriculture Editorial Board

Robert Miller
University of Wisconsin,
  Stevens Point
Stevens Point, WI

R. Dan Neely
Scott City, MO

Bonnie L. Appleton
Hampton Roads Agricultural
  Research and Extension Center
Virginia Beach, VA

William R. Chaney
Purdue University
West Lafayette, IN

James R. Clark
HortScience, Inc.
Pleasanton, CA

Jack Fisher
Bergen Community College
Paramus, NJ

Edward F. Gilman
University of Florida
Gainesville, FL

Larry Hall
Hendricksen The Care of Trees
Wheeling, IL

George Hudler
Cornell University
Ithaca, NY

Patrick Kelsey
The Morton Arboretum
Lisle, IL

Daniel F. Marion
Finger Lakes Community College
Canandaigua, NY

Tom Smiley
Bartlett Tree Research Laboratory
Charlotte, NC

Gary Watson
The Morton Arboretum
Lisle, IL

Michael Walterschiedt
Texas A&M University
College Station, TX

CHAPTER 1

Introduction to Plant Health Care

John Lloyd and Fredric Miller

The concept of Plant Heath Care (PHC) was developed in the 1980s as an enhancement of maintenance and management practices for landscape professionals. Plant Health Care evolved from the concept of "integrated pest management" (IPM), which has its roots in production agriculture. The predominant goal of IPM is to use a combination of management tactics (mechanical, cultural, biological, chemical, and regulatory) to reduce pest populations or maintain them at nondamaging levels. Levels of **damage** are identified by loss of yield and by an increase in expenditures. Damage past a certain level results in what is referred to as economic loss. Mathematical models based on pest biology and their influence on yield and the cost of management practices were developed for IPM agricultural commodity-based programs.

The basic premise of IPM is that pest populations will grow and may reach a level where damage to the commodity will result in economic loss. The level where economic loss occurs is the "economic **injury** level" (EIL). With a basic understanding of specific pest biologies, scientists are developing models to predict when a pest population will reach the EIL. This prediction is described as setting an "economic threshold" (ET). By determining when pest populations will reach a point where they might cause economic injury in the near future, treatments can be applied before damage occurs. The cost of treatment at the ET should not be prohibitive considering the decrease in profit that will occur if the pest reaches the EIL.

The IPM philosophy was carried into the landscape arena in the 1970s. Many ornamental pest control programs were and are still based on calendar date chemical treatments. The first goal of this version of landscape IPM was and is to get people to look before they treat. Pest management studies in the United States show reductions in pesticide use based on a simple program of scouting and monitoring (Olkowski and Olkowski 1978; Raupp 1985; Ball 1987). Scouting is the actual process of observing, recognizing, identifying, estimating, and recording problems in the landscape. The overall program of several episodes of scouting is referred to as "monitoring."

As IPM continued to make inroads in the landscape industry, additional studies began to examine the use of pesticides in the urban environment and the ability of landscape professionals to develop IPM programs (Holmes and Davidson 1984; Neely and Smith 1991; Neilsen 1986, 1989, 1990; Raupp and Noland 1984).One of the initial difficulties with the IPM concept in landscape situations is that the EIL and ET are not as identifiable as they are in agriculture. The level of damage on plant materials in the landscape, and materials produced for landscape use, cannot be easily classified across a broad spectrum with different client perceptions and expectations. Clients are defined as the people purchasing or who own the plant materials. Damage that is harmful to the plants can easily be recognized, but factors other than plant health are of concern to the majority of clients. What concerns most clients is the appearance or aesthetic quality of the plant materials (Ball 1994).

Aesthetics tend to be qualitative and as such are hard to quantify except in the form of generalizations and approximations. Many studies were developed to ascertain quantitative measures of "aesthetic thresholds" (AT) and "aesthetic injury levels" (AIL) across large groups of clientele (Ball and Marsan 1991; Coffelt and Schultz 1990; Raupp et al. 1988, 1989; Smith and Raupp 1986). In addition to these survey studies that attempt to determine clientele interpretations of injury, other methods such as expert approximations of pest density and injury potential and expert rankings to establish rating scales for specific plant materials and damage caused by specific stresses have been developed. All these methods of assessing aesthetic thresholds for injury help generalize the relation between specific landscape plants and aesthetic damage potential of their associated stresses (Sadof and Raupp 1997).

Few plants and stresses have been assessed for ATs and AILs. For those systems that have identified levels, the information can be used in scouting regimes to assist practitioners in maintenance and management. However, the fact remains that individual clients have different expectations for their landscape as a whole and for individual plants within their landscape. With the profusion of plant materials and stress problems associated with those plant materials in the landscape, it is unlikely that comprehensive lists of aesthetic thresholds and aesthetic injury levels will be available or of practical use in the near future.

Plant Health Care (PHC)

To address many of the plant vigor and pest management considerations that were identified in IPM programs for the landscape, a program of Plant Health Care was developed. Plant Health Care does not replace IPM, but refines many portions of the concept and incorporates them into a comprehensive program with a focus on the plant and the client.

Monitoring remains the mainstay of PHC programs, although PHC significantly strengthens the focus on problem prevention. By using the plant as the focus, a PHC program attempts to prevent problems through proper planting, site selection, and maintenance. If problems do occur, multiple management measures are used in an attempt to remedy them. A PHC program goes beyond just the plant and its potential stresses. It includes site inventories to identify key plants and key stresses in the environment and relies on client inter-

action to understand the history of the site and expectations of the client (Smith et al. 1995).

Ideally, a PHC program begins with the planning of the landscape and the planting of the plant materials. In many instances, landscape professionals are called in a time of crisis to remedy situations that were designed and developed without the PHC philosophy. In these situations, it is up to the client and the practitioner to come to an understanding of what the expectations are and to define a realistic avenue for meeting these expectations.

The Appropriate Response Process

Many processes are involved with developing and maintaining PHC programs. If PHC practitioners are fortunate enough to be involved in the development of the initial landscape, they must be involved in the plant selection and site selection process. If, as is more likely, they are called to work in situations with established plant materials, they must use other processes to determine appropriate actions. In the latter case, a **sign**, **symptom**, or event will initiate their contact with the client and begin the process that helps them determine if a response is needed in each distinct situation. This process is called the "appropriate response process" (ARP) and is represented in graphic form in Figure 1.1. As with most processes, ARP is not a set of instructions or a list of ingredients, but a collection of information ascertained through knowledge, expertise, experience, and informational resource materials that leads to a determination whether some form of management action is necessary. Some information may be irrelevant to the situation at hand, but it is up to the practitioner to determine what is necessary in each situation.

Client

The client is the key to any situation. Clients can be defined as broadly as the community for which a city forester has responsibilities or the individual homeowners for whom a landscaper or arborist works. It is the client's initial perception of the situation, expectations of the practitioner, and confidence in the practitioner that motivate and ultimately decide the outcome of any PHC program.

Client interaction, at some level, is necessary for a PHC program to be effective. The most informative avenue of interaction is one-on-one contact. It is an opportunity to discuss the clients' perceptions, inform them about situations, and influence their expectations.

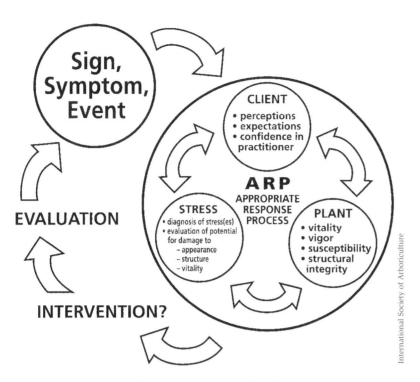

Figure 1.1 ▪ *The Appropriate Response Process (ARP) was developed to demonstrate how decisions are made in a PHC program. ARP enables the practitioner to determine an appropriate response by considering client expectations, plant health, and stress factors. If an intervention (treatment) occurs, a follow-up evaluation is made, and the process begins again.*

derstand its susceptibility to stresses (**abiotic** and **biotic**) and provides a physiological basis for determining the **vitality** and vigor of the plant. A basic knowledge of the growth response and physical qualities of the plant material also allows evaluations of the structural integrity of the species in question.

Stress

As with the plant, proper identification of **stress factors** is essential to making decisions. Stresses can be mechanical, physiological, biological, or a combination of factors in a stress **complex**. Identification of the stress factors through the process of diagnostics is integral to determining the type of stresses and their potential to damage the health or appearance of the plant.

The Diagnostic Process ▪ Diagnostics is a process of examination and investigation that leads to identifying the **causal agent** of a plant problem. Specific causal agents (stresses) and their signs and symptoms are discussed in detail in subsequent chapters. The process of diagnostics involves asking questions and relying on your knowledge and resources to determine the problem and its potential effect on the plant. Proper identification of the plant material is necessary for a proper **diagnosis** (Green, Maloy, and Capizzi 1995).

The first question that needs to be addressed is whether the plant is normal. Interior needle drop in the fall is normal for most conifers but may be mistaken as a **disorder** by uninformed clientele. The time of the occurrence is also important in this example. Symptoms (the plant's response to the causal agent) must also be investigated. Careful examination of the abnormal characteristics of the plant may provide information to identify the cause of the problem. Looking for patterns to symptom development within a landscape and within a plant will assist in determining whether the problem is caused by a living organism or by abiotic (nonliving) factors. Random patterns are for the most part suggestive of a biotic cause, whereas uniform, or nonrandom, symptoms tend to be abiotic.

The histories of the symptoms and affected plant materials are also very important in establishing potential cause. Living organisms tend to spread throughout a single plant and to adjacent plants, whereas nonliving damage tends not to spread to new growth. The cultural and environmental conditions of affected plant

International Society of Arboriculture

If this level of interaction is impossible, contact via reporting forms and other forms of educational paraphernalia is necessary. Even if clients do not read the information, it gives them something for their money and may enhance their confidence in the practitioner's expertise.

The expectations of the client are a primary component regardless of the plant materials or pests involved. Expectations will vary from client to client and will vary with individual clients as they become more informed. Expectations should be discussed and agreed upon prior to developing a program or resolving a problem. All the experience and knowledge of the practitioner should be involved in determining and defining the expectations. Information contained in other references and later in this manual will be useful in establishing realistic goals. The expectations of the client will need to be re-addressed on a continuing basis.

Plant

Proper plant identification is essential to the ARP process. To make an appropriate decision, PHC practitioners must be able to identify plants and have a basic understanding of their physiology. Identifying a plant to species and variety enables the practitioner to un-

materials before and after injury is observed are also important for diagnosis. Many times, events that initiate symptoms occur before practitioners are asked to make a diagnosis. It is therefore important to ask questions of the client to determine the conditions that may have contributed to the damage. Site history, pesticide history, weather conditions, cultural practices, and other factors are all important in determining potential causes of the problem.

Many diagnostic tools are available to assist practitioners in diagnosing plant problems. The most common tools are a hand lens, forceps, and other specimen sampling equipment. Soil probes help practitioners investigate soil characteristics in the landscape that reflect directly upon plant health. Insect traps and phenological models that correlate temperature with insect and plant development are also tools that can be used to predict and examine certain pest (stress) populations (Lloyd and Nixon 1996). Many of these tools and techniques are mentioned in the chapters that deal with specific stress and pest problems. Appendix A lists plant diagnostic clinics in the United States and Canada that can help with diagnosis of plant problems.

Intervention

The appropriate response process leads to a decision whether to initiate management techniques, to enhance maintenance procedures, or to do both. This action is based on all available information accumulated from resource materials, client expectations, and the practitioner's knowledge, experience, and foresight. Treatments applied merely at the request of a client, without any other justification, or as an insurance against unknown or possible stresses, are not a part of PHC programs.

If no action is deemed necessary, monitoring should continue until ARP needs to be initiated again. When action is appropriate, the extent and degree of the action, as well as the type of action, must be determined.

Management can be in the form of culturally modifying the environment, mechanically disrupting the stressor, chemically augmenting the plant, chemically disrupting a stressor, using other organisms to eat, parasitize, or out-compete the stressing organisms, and preventing the spread of stressors through the implementation of governmental regulation. General management techniques are discussed in further detail in the management sections of this manual. Additional information on management practices for specific stressors can be obtained from your local Cooperative Extension Service in the United States and universities' agriculture colleges and agriculture branches of governments throughout the world. Information on specific stressors can also be obtained through manuals, reference materials, and a user-friendly part of the Internet called the World Wide Web. The International Society of Arboriculture provides a good starting point for PHC information at its web site, Arboriculture On-Line (http://www.ag.uiuc.edu/~isa) (Lloyd 1996).

Evaluation

Assessing the results of the action is necessary to determine if the actions were successful or if ARP must be reinitiated. This determination can be made via continual diligent monitoring. Records based on evaluations and monitoring reports are essential to maintaining effective and evolving PHC programs.

Conclusion

In this chapter, we have tried to outline the processes involved with PHC and chart how they have evolved. In the remaining chapters, the authors will provide the basic information necessary to begin developing and maintaining profitable PHC programs. Plant Health Care continually evolves as more information becomes available for practitioners to use in their programs. Truly effective PHC practitioners must keep current with this new information via resources such as Arboriculture On-Line, various technical and scientific journals, and programs and workshops that address PHC-related issues.

John Lloyd
Extension Entomologist
University of Illinois

Fredric Miller
Extension Educator–Urban IPM
University of Illinois

References

Ball, J. 1987. Efficient monitoring for an urban IPM program. *J. Arboric.* 13:174–177.

Ball, J. 1994. Plant health care and the public. *J. Arboric.* 20:33–37.

Ball, J., and P. Marsan. 1991. Establishing monitoring routines and action thresholds for a landscape IPM service. *J. Arboric.* 17:88–93.

Coffelt, M.A., and P.B. Schultz. 1990. Development of an aesthetic injury level to decrease pesticide use against orange-striped oakworm (*Lepidoptera: Saturniidae*) in an urban pest management project. *J. Econ. Entomol.* 83:2044–2049.

Green, J.L., O. Maloy, and J. Capizzi. 1995. *A Systematic Approach to Diagnosing Plant Damage.* Oregon State Univ. Coop. Ext. Serv., Corvallis. 24 pp.

Holmes, J.J., and J.A. Davidson. 1984. Integrated pest management for arborists: Implementation of a pilot program. *J. Arboric.* 10:65–70.

Lloyd, J.E. 1996. Arboriculture On-Line. *Arborist News.* Vol. 4–5 (Continuing)

Lloyd, J.E. and P.L. Nixon. 1996. Managing insects and insect damage on woody ornamental plants. In *Illinois Urban Pest Management Handbook.* Univ. of Ill. Coop. Ext. Serv., Urbana-Champaign. pp. 49–57.

Neely, D., and G.R. Smith. 1991. IPM strategies used by arborists. *J. Arboric.* 17:8–12.

Nielsen, D.G. 1986. Planning and implementing a tree health care practice. *J. Arboric.* 12:265–268.

Nielsen, D.G. 1989. Integrated pest management in arboriculture: From theory to practice. *J. Arboric.* 15:25–30.

Nielsen, D.G. 1990. Landscape integrated pest management. *J. Arboric.* 16:253–259.

Olkowski, W., and H. Olkowski. 1978. Urban integrated pest management. *J. Arboric.* 4:241–246.

Raupp, M.J. 1985. Monitoring: An essential factor to managing pests of landscape trees and shrubs. *J. Arboric.* 11:349–354.

Raupp, M.J., J.A. Davidson, C.S. Koehler, C.S. Sadof, and K. Reichelderfer. 1988. Decision-making considerations for aesthetic damage caused by pests. *Bull. Entomol. Soc. Am.* 34:27–32.

Raupp, M.J., J.A. Davidson, C.S. Koehler, C.S. Sadof, and K. Reichelderfer. 1989. Economic and aesthetic injury levels and thresholds for insect pests of ornamental plants. *Fla. Entomol.* 72:403–407.

Raupp, M.J., and R.M. Noland. 1984. Implementing plant management programs in residential and institutional settings. *J. Arboric.* 10:161–169.

Sadof, C.S., and M.J. Raupp. 1997. Aesthetic thresholds and their development. Chapter 12 in L. Higley and L. Pedigo, eds. *Economic Thresholds for Pest Management.* Univ. Nebraska Press.

Smith, D.C., and M.J. Raupp. 1986. Economic and environmental assessment of an integrated pest management program for community owned landscape plants. *J. Econ. Entomol.* 79:162–165.

Smith, M.A.L., A.G. Endress, G.R. Smith, J.E. Lloyd, R.D. Neely, R.K. Stutman, J.J. Ball, K.D. Coder, and T.L. Wadley. 1995. *A Guide to the Plant Health Care Management System.* 2nd ed. Savoy, Illinois: International Society of Arboriculture. 148 pp.

CHAPTER 2

Basic Woody Plant Biology

Chris Starbuck

Woody plants are complex organisms. An understanding of how trees and shrubs are put together and how they function helps the landscape and tree-care professional develop management practices to keep such plants in good condition. The following information provides some background in plant anatomy and physiology.

Anatomy and Physiology

Cells and Tissues

Trees and shrubs are the giants of the plant kingdom. They are perennials, and some individual plants grow for thousands of years, reaching several hundred feet in height. Because of their relatively large size, trees and shrubs have evolved many specialized types of cells and tissues to support themselves and to transport materials from one part of the plant to another.

The cell is the basic building block of a plant (Figure 2.1). Cells of animals and plants have many things in common. Both have nuclei, containing the genetic information that determines the form and function of the organism. Both also have all of the machinery required for **respiration** so they can derive energy from food materials such as sugar and starch. In this process, oxygen is consumed and carbon dioxide released. In addition, both plant and animal cells are surrounded by a **cellular membrane** that regulates the movement of water, ions, and molecules in and out of the cell.

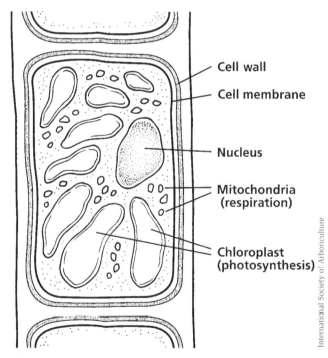

Figure 2.1 ▪ *The cell is the basic building block of a plant*

Despite the many similarities between plant and animal cells, plant cells have some features not found in animal cells. The most important of these is the **cell wall,** for this is what gives woody plants the strength to stand up and enables them to move water and nutrients over such large distances. The cell wall is made primarily of long, chainlike molecules of **cellulose.**

These are interwoven and crosslinked to give the cell wall great strength. The cell wall is further strengthened by materials called **lignin** and **hemicellulose.**

Another important feature of plant cells that is not present in animal cells is the **chloroplast.** This organelle contains the pigment **chlorophyll** that the plant uses to harvest light energy during **photosynthesis**.

Where Do Cells Come From?

All of the cells in a plant are descendants of the original cells found in the embryo of the seed, or in the cutting or bud from which the plant grew. During a process called **mitosis,** cells divide into identical daughter cells, each one taking with it a copy of the genetic information found in the nucleus of the dividing cell. Mitosis occurs in tissues called **meristems,** which are found at the very tips of the shoot and root (apical meristems) and under the bark (vascular **cambium**) (Figure 2.2).

Even though all of the cells formed during mitosis have the same genetic information, they do not all develop the same. As they mature, they form groups of cells called **tissues,** which work together to perform special functions in the plant. Cells produced by the vascular cambium develop into **xylem** and **phloem,** specializing in transport of water and nutrients, respectively. Cells formed in the shoot apical meristem may develop into epidermal tissue that protects the leaves and stem or into a tissue such as the **palisade parenchyma** in the leaf that specializes in photosynthesis (Figure 2.3).

How Woody Plants Grow

Plants increase in size by a combination of cell division and cell enlargement. If the plant has enough water and the temperature is warm enough, cells formed by division in the apical meristems enlarge until they reach their mature size. This cell enlargement is responsible for the growth of stems and branches between budbreak in the spring and the cessation of growth in summer or fall. Root elongation occurs in the same way whenever the soil temperature is high enough and there is enough soil moisture to allow growth.

Increase in stem diameter is due to enlargement of cells produced by the vascular cambium. The cambium forms a cylinder under the bark that is only a few cells thick. It increases in diameter each year, however, producing a layer of phloem to the outside and xylem toward the center of the tree. A nail driven into a tree trunk will never move farther from the ground, but it may be covered by xylem tissue as the tree increases in diameter. A piece of wire wrapped around a tree trunk will eventually **girdle** it, possibly killing the entire tree.

The Stem

In woody plants, the stem (Figure 2.4) is made primarily of xylem cells with very thick cell walls containing a lot of lignin. Cells toward the center of the stem are no longer living and make up the **heartwood.** Because an individual tree ring shows the xylem tissue formed during a single year, rings can be used to estimate the

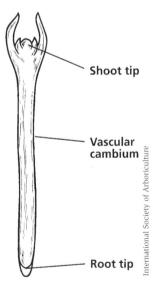

Figure 2.2 ▪ Meristems in plants

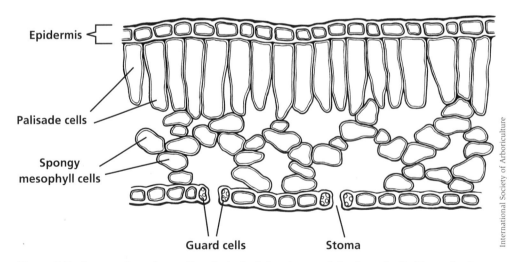

Figure 2.3 ▪ *Cross-section of a small part of a leaf showing specialization of cells. The palisade cells specialize in photosynthesis, the epidermis protects the leaf, and the guard cells regulate the movement of CO_2 and water into and out of the leaf. Spongy mesophyll cells are loosely arranged to allow diffusion of gases in the leaf.*

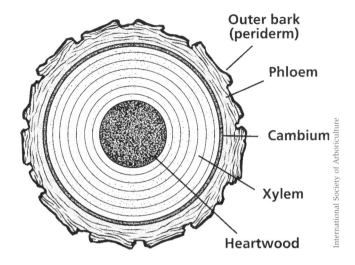

Outer bark (periderm)

Phloem

Cambium

Xylem

Heartwood

International Society of Arboriculture

Figure 2.4 ▪ *Cross-section of a woody plant stem*

age of a tree. Living, tubelike xylem cells near the cambium carry water and dissolved minerals from the roots to the leaves.

Just outside of the cambium is a thin layer of phloem tissue that functions to transport the plant sugars produced by photosynthesis in the leaves. The phloem does not form rings like the xylem. Phloem produced in previous years simply dies and sloughs off. When a tree is girdled, the xylem may still be functional, but the flow of sugars toward the roots through the phloem is interrupted, resulting in a gradual root "starvation." This is why it may take several years for a tree to die after it is girdled.

Outside of the phloem is the outer bark, or **periderm.** This is made of corky cells produced by a tissue called the **phellogen.** The periderm increases in diameter each year, forming a protective covering over the trunk. The outermost layers, however, cannot keep up with the expansion of the trunk; they develop cracks and plates, giving the bark the appearance characteristic of the tree species.

The outer bark of a woody plant is an effective barrier to the entry of insects, **bacteria**, and fungal organisms into the stem. Mechanical bark damage caused by lawn mowers, "string" trimmers, or vehicle bumping creates a direct opening for **pathogens** to enter the stem and cause decay. Seemingly minor bark damage is often the initial step leading to the decline and death of a tree.

Twig Characteristics

In most cases, the first step in diagnosing a plant problem is to identify the plant. This may be easy during the growing season but can be a challenge when a tree

or shrub has lost its leaves. A close look at the winter twigs reveals many characteristics that can be used for identification. For example, the green ash twig shown in Figure 2.5 has rounded, opposite buds with fuzzy, overlapping bud scales. The twig is easily distinguished from that of a red oak, which has alternate rather than opposite buds. The twig also has distinct, whitish pores called **lenticels.** The leaf scar, where the petiole was attached during the growing season, is straight on the top rather than U-shaped like that on a white ash. The terminal bud scar indicates where growth started during the previous growing season. This is useful in determining whether the tree put on a reasonable amount of growth during the growing season.

Leaves

The most important function of leaves is photosynthesis. This is the process in which carbon dioxide gas (CO_2) from the air is combined with water from the soil to form the sugars used as an energy source by plants. The energy driving this process is derived from solar radiation, which is absorbed by the pigment chlorophyll in the chloroplasts. The plant arranges its leaves in a pattern that is most effective in intercepting sunlight. Sugar produced during photosynthesis is translocated to other parts of the plant, where it is used directly as an energy source or stored in the form of starch in leaves, stems, or roots for future use. Sugars and starch are often referred to as **carbohydrates.** These are processed through respiration in the cells' **mitochondria** to release energy. Some of the sugar is also used to produce cellulose, fats, proteins, and other materials required as structural materials or chemical reactants by growing cells.

Damage to leaves from insect feeding, foliar diseases, or air

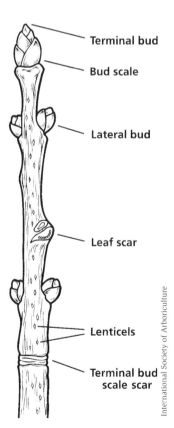

Terminal bud

Bud scale

Lateral bud

Leaf scar

Lenticels

Terminal bud scale scar

International Society of Arboriculture

Figure 2.5 ▪ *A winter twig reveals many characteristics that can be used for identification*

pollution can drastically reduce the rate of photosynthesis, as can excessive shading or stress. CO_2 is taken into the leaf through pores called **stomata** (Figure 2.3). If a plant is under drought stress, the stomata close, restricting the uptake of CO_2 and limiting photosynthesis. The net result of reduced photosynthesis is a reduction of sugars available for direct use or as storage reserves. This weakens the plant, making it more susceptible to stress and attack by pests.

Another important function of leaves is **transpiration.** This is the evaporation of water from the stomata. Transpiration has a cooling effect on the leaf. It also aids in the process of nutrient and water uptake from the soil.

Roots

The main functions of roots are to absorb water and nutrients, to anchor the plant, and to move water and minerals taken from the soil to the aerial parts of the plant. Roots also serve as storage organs for sugar, starch, and other materials translocated from the aboveground parts. Most of the **absorption** of materials by roots occurs very near the actively growing tips, where delicate structures called **root hairs** are found. These may last only a few days but are quickly replaced by new ones as the root tip elongates. Considerable water is also absorbed by older, suberized roots (covered with a waxy material called **suberin**).

Most of the water taken up by plants moves into the roots by a process called **passive absorption**, in which transpiration of water from the leaves acts like a wick, pulling water into the roots. As long as there is sufficient water available in the soil to meet this "transpirational demand," the plant can continue to grow normally. Once moisture becomes limiting, however, the stomata close to reduce water loss from the leaves. Further soil drying results in wilting of leaves and stems because cells lose their turgidity and shrink due to water loss. Loss of **cell turgor** also interferes with cell enlargement, so growth is limited.

Uptake of minerals from the soil by roots is a complex process. Some materials move into the root by diffusion, but a considerable amount simply moves in dissolved form in water taken up by passive absorption. Once the material is inside the root, certain cells have the ability to regulate which **ions** can actually enter the cells and which are left behind. Many woody plants have a beneficial association between their roots and fungal organisms (called **mycorhizae**) that greatly increases the effective surface area for root absorption of water and nutrients from the soil.

Just like stems and leaves, roots need oxygen to grow. Therefore, anything limiting the penetration of air into the soil will limit root growth. **Soil compaction**, paving, and poor soil drainage will promote shallow root growth, making a plant more susceptible to drought stress and **wind-throw**. These stresses also make roots susceptible to attack by fungal pathogens that cause root **rot**. Compaction can be reduced during construction by placing barriers around trees or putting a deep layer of **mulch** over the root system. Installing subsurface drain tiles or planting on a berm may be necessary when planting a species not adapted to poor soil drainage in a tight soil.

Contrary to popular belief, the root system of a tree is not a mirror image of the top. Most of the absorbing roots are found in the top 18 inches of the soil, but they may spread to a diameter five or six times that of the tree's dripline. Water and fertilizer should therefore be applied so that they move into this rooting zone. Frequent light applications may be taken up by turf roots before they reach the roots of trees and shrubs.

Control of Growth and Development

The form of a plant is determined to a large extent by a balance of growth-regulating chemicals within its tissues. A type of growth regulator called **auxin**, for example, is produced in actively growing shoot tips. This chemical moves downward in the plant, inhibiting the development of lateral buds below it. When a shoot tip is pruned off, the flow of auxin is interrupted, releasing the lateral buds from dominance and causing branching. Plants with a well-defined central stem, or leader, are said to have strong **apical dominance.** Growth regulators translocated from the roots can also act as chemical signals to the top of a plant. Under drought stress, a regulator called **abscisic acid**, formed in the roots, signals the stomata to close and slows top growth. Another type of growth regulator, called **cytokinin,** is translocated from the roots in the spring and promotes budbreak.

Dormancy and Winterhardiness

Most woody plants in temperate climates go through alternating periods of growth and rest. Toward the end of the growing season, shortening days and low temperatures induce plants to stop growing, to set buds, and, in the case of deciduous plants, to drop their leaves. By late fall, many plants will not resume growth even if they are moved to an environment favoring growth. They are **dormant.**

Associated with dormancy is the ability to withstand low temperatures. A Norway maple tree that withstands a temperature of –30°F when dormant may be severely damaged by a temperature just below freezing if this occurs during the growing season. Cultural practices such as late-summer fertilization and pruning, which encourage a plant to grow late in the season, may interfere with the development of cold tolerance.

As already noted, roots never really go dormant. They also cannot tolerate temperatures nearly as low as the above-ground part. Although the top of a boxwood shrub may be able to tolerate –10°F, the roots will probably be killed at 20°F. For this reason, **container-grown** nursery stock must be stored over the winter under conditions that will keep the roots from getting much below freezing. Roots of trees and shrubs permanently planted in large above-ground containers are also susceptible to freezing injury. Containers should be insulated and designed so that they conduct ground heat into the root zone.

Usually when a plant has gone dormant, it must be exposed to a period of cold (below 40°F) for buds to begin growth when conditions favorable for growth return. This means that dormant plants cannot simply be stored over the winter in a warm building.

How Woody Plants Die

Although some trees exist for thousands of years, most woody plants live for considerably less than a century. It is usually difficult to attribute the death of a plant to a single cause. Rather, mortality is most often the result of a combination or series of factors such as drought stress, defoliation, mechanical damage, or nutrient deficiency. Franklin et al. (1987) used the term **mortality spiral** to describe a series of interrelated events leading to the gradual death of a tree. Mortality can occur over a period of several months, as with Dutch elm disease or pine wilt disease. In most cases, however, the ultimate failure of a tree or shrub was initiated by an event that occurred several years before. During the mortality spiral, one stress predisposes the plant to another until the plant finally loses the ability to protect itself from even minor **stress factors**. At this point, opportunistic insects and decay organisms can quickly destroy the structural integrity of the stems, branches, and roots, causing mechanical failure.

When plant death is viewed as a mortality spiral, the importance of preventing stress becomes clear.

Overirrigation and poor soil drainage, for example, have been shown to predispose some trees to attack by Phytophthora root rot (Svihra 1991). Infection with this disease often seriously impairs the ability of a plant to take up water and nutrients from the soil, leading to a rapid decline. Defoliation by insects or diseases drastically reduces the amount of carbohydrates a plant is able to manufacture and store. With limited carbohydrate reserves, the plant has less energy available to defend itself from attack by other pests. In both of these cases, the beginning of a mortality spiral could be prevented by good cultural practices such as judicious watering and insect control.

Conclusion

Trees and shrubs are large, complex organisms with tissues and organs specializing in water uptake, food production, mechanical strengthening, protection from pathogens, and many other functions. Understanding the structure and function of these plants is the first step in using effective pest management and in developing cultural practices such as irrigation and fertilization to maximize their life spans. Seemingly minor damage can trigger a series of subsequent stresses that ultimately lead to plant death. For this reason, it is important to maintain trees and shrubs to prevent damage whenever possible.

Chris Starbuck
Associate Professor of Horticulture
University of Missouri

Selected References

Esau, K. 1977. *Anatomy of Seed Plants.* 2nd ed. New York: John Wiley & Sons.

Franklin, J., H. Shugart, and M. Harmon. 1987. Tree death as an ecological process. *BioScience* 37:550.

Kramer, P.J., and T.T. Kozlowski. 1979. *Physiology of Woody Plants.* Orlando, Florida: Academic Press.

Pirone, P.P. 1988. *Tree Maintenance,* 6th ed. New York: Oxford University Press.

Svihra, P. 1991. A practical guide for diagnosing root rot in ornamentals. *J. Arboric.* 17:294.

CHAPTER 3

Trees, Stress, and Pests

Daniel Herms and William Mattson

Many **abiotic** and **biotic** factors influence the health of trees. These factors, or stresses, rarely work alone and are often the result of either natural events in the environment or human activities. The purpose of this chapter is to describe these stresses and their relationship to each other and to provide information about how stresses can influence tree health and pest resistance. Examples of stress, stress **complexes**, and pest-resistance strategies are provided to help the reader better understand the concept of plant-stress-pest interactions. By no means, however, do these examples provide a complete representation of all stresses and stress complexes that exist for woody plants. Many disease, weed, and abiotic complexes and interactions will be discussed in later chapters that focus on specific tree problems.

It has become almost axiomatic that "healthy," rapidly growing trees are the most resistant to insects and diseases, and that stressed trees are most susceptible to pest attack. But is this always true? Although it clearly is true in certain cases, a large number of studies show that in many situations rapidly growing trees are less resistant to pests and less tolerant of stress. The very same cultural practices generally thought to enhance pest resistance—such as fertilization—often increase tree susceptibility to pests and other stresses.

This chapter includes a discussion of the effects of environmental stress on tree physiology, tree resistance to insects and other pests, and the implications for pest management in the low-maintenance landscape. We focus particularly on nutrient and drought stress because landscape managers can affect these stresses directly by means of cultural practices. Effective use of fertilization and irrigation in a low-maintenance tree health-care program requires a sound understanding of the physiological effects of, and tree responses to, changes in soil fertility and soil moisture.

This chapter also explains ways to reduce stress through selection of plant materials, proper planting techniques, and maintenance of plant materials to reduce these stresses.

Natural Defenses of Trees and Other Plants

The effects of stress on pest resistance may be revealed by answering two questions: (1) what are the traits that protect the plant from the pest, and (2) how does stress affect these traits?

Tree resistance to insects and disease results from the interaction of many physical and chemical defenses, including thorns and spines, foliar hairs, toughened cuticle, and indigestible structures such as **cellulose** and **lignin.** However, the toxic and deterrent effects of **allelochemicals** may be the primary reasons why plants are resistant to the vast majority of insects and other herbivores in their environment (reviews in Herms 1989, and Herms and Mattson 1992).

Allelochemicals are chemical substances produced by plants (and other organisms) that serve to protect them from their natural enemies. Thousands of such compounds have been isolated from plants, including tannins and other phenolic compounds; terpenes (for example, pine resins, the essential oils of mints, and the new anticancer compound taxol); alkaloids (for example, nicotine and morphine); cyanogenic compounds (cyanide-producing chemicals); and many others.

The defensive role of these compounds against insects, **pathogens**, and mammals is well documented. Several such compounds have been used as natural insecticides, such as nicotine, pyrethrin, rotenone, and pepper extracts. Others are commonly used as drugs, both legally and illegally.

Allelochemicals may also protect some plants from potential competitors. Some plants secrete allelochemical compounds that have a growth-suppressing effect on neighboring plants. This effect is called **allelopathy.** The phenolic compound juglone, secreted from the roots of black walnut, *Juglans nigra*, is responsible for the growth-suppressing effect that walnut has on many other plants.

The presence of allelochemicals in plants is the major reason most insects feed on only one plant or a few closely related plants. Insects possess special enzymes that allow them to detoxify the allelochemicals produced by their food plants. Some insects even use allelochemicals as cues for locating their food plants, or they accumulate and incorporate them into their own bodies for their own defense. For example, the monarch butterfly (*Danaus plexippus*) incorporates the toxic allelochemicals (cardenolides) of milkweed (*Asclepias* spp.) into its own body, rendering the insect unpalatable to predators such as birds. When the chemical defenses of plants are crossed in this manner, natural selection may lead to the evolution of even more toxic compounds in the plants, thereby escalating this coevolutionary arms race.

Even among insects that feed on many plants, chemical defenses remain important. Gypsy moth (*Lymantria dispar*), for example, feeds on many species of **deciduous** trees and is well adapted to the tannins and other phenolic compounds that dominate its hosts. However, gypsy moth prefers not to feed on host species containing alkaloids, including white ash (*Fraxinus americana*), red maple (*Acer rubrum*), and tuliptree (*Liriodendron tulipifera*) (Barbosa and Krischik 1987).

The nutritional quality of plants also plays a central role in their resistance to insects and other pests. Nitrogen, an essential component of protein, is a limiting nutrient for most, if not all, species of plants and animals, including humans in many developing countries (White 1993). The nitrogen content of insects ranges from about 7 percent to 14 percent dry weight, whereas that of plants averages about 2 percent. Because of this discrepancy, the growth and reproduction of plant-eating insects is frequently limited by the nutritional quality of their hosts and almost always increases as the nutrient content of the plant increases (Mattson 1980).

Many insect outbreaks have been correlated with stressful conditions, including drought and nutrient deficiency (Mattson and Haack 1987). These observations have led to the idea that stress increases the nutritional quality of plants, weakens the chemical defenses of plants, or both, thereby triggering population outbreaks of insects. However, there is little evidence to support this view (Larsson 1989). In fact, many studies have found that concentrations of allelochemicals and insect resistance actually increase in response to drought, nutrient limitation, and other stresses (Herms and Mattson 1992). Understanding how stress affects pest resistance requires a basic understanding of how plants respond physiologically to stress and how levels of allelochemicals in the tree are tied to these responses.

Just What Is Environmental Stress?

Through the process of **photosynthesis,** light energy is used to produce sugars from carbon dioxide obtained from the atmosphere. These simple sugars are then used to manufacture the complex **carbohydrates**, lipids, amino acids, proteins, allelochemicals, and all other biochemical building blocks of cells, leaves, bark, branches, and roots (Figure 3.1). All trees need the same basic resources to sustain photosynthesis: water, essential nutrients, and light.

Environmental stress can be defined as an external force, or **stress factor,** that limits the ability of the tree to acquire these essential resources from the environment. Stress occurs in two general ways: (1) when there are shortages of essential resources in the environment, including water during drought, nutrients in deficient soils, and light in the forest understory, and (2) when environmental factors limit the uptake of resources that are otherwise present in adequate supply. These factors include air pollution, which limits photosynthesis because of toxic effects on plant cells; soil pH, which can limit nutrient uptake for some species; and lack of soil oxygen, which can limit water and nutrient uptake on flooded soils.

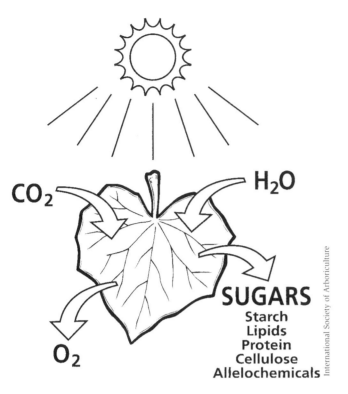

Figure 3.1 ▪ *Biochemical building blocks.* *The biochemicals that serve as building blocks from which plants are constructed are all manufactured directly from the simple sugars produced from carbon dioxide (CO₂) during photosynthesis.*

Under this definition, stress factors (for example, soil moisture, nutrient availability, pH, atmospheric ozone) and their effects (for example, decreased growth, photosynthesis) can be measured. Furthermore, in the same environment, one species may be stressed and another not. For example, bald cypress (*Taxodium distichum*) grows well on flooded sites where most other trees would not survive, and rhododendrons (*Rhododendron* spp.) experience nutrient deficiencies in alkaline soils where other species perform well. Flowering dogwood (*Cornus florida*) and sugar maple (*Acer saccharum*) exist quite well in the same shaded forest understory where the intolerant paper birch (*Betula papyrifera*) would rapidly decline.

Effects of Nutrient and Drought Stress

To obtain carbon from the atmosphere, a tree must intercept light from which it derives the energy necessary to drive photosynthesis. All other things being equal, the greater the total surface area of leaves on the tree (dependent on both the size and number of leaves), the more light the tree can intercept and the more carbon it can capture from the atmosphere dur-

ing photosynthesis. Indeed, many studies have shown that differences in growth rates among trees and other plants is due to differences in their total leaf area. Differences in photosynthetic rates also play a role, but to a lesser degree (Lambers and Poorter 1992).

The production of new leaf tissue requires a generous supply of nutrients; hence, growth is quite sensitive to nutrient stress. Nutrient stress decreases tree growth by decreasing both the number of leaves per tree and the area of individual leaves. Photosynthesis, which can continue in already existing leaves, is much less sensitive than growth to nutrient stress and does not become limited until stress becomes severe (Chapin 1980) (Figure 3.2). Severe nutrient deficiency limits photosynthesis because nitrogen is an essential element in the production of photosynthetic enzymes and **chlorophyll** (Linder and Rook 1984; Luxmore 1991).

Tree growth is also extremely sensitive to water stress because **turgor pressure** is necessary for cell expansion, and the presence of water is necessary for most if not all biochemical processes. Growth is limited by even mild water deficits, which can decrease both the number of leaves per plant and the size of individual leaves (Bradford and Hsiao 1982; Kozlowski 1982). Photosynthesis is much less sensitive to water stress than is growth. It becomes limited only when drought stress becomes moderate to severe (Luxmore 1991) (Figure 3.2). As water stress increases, photosynthesis becomes limited by closure of **stomata.** This process conserves water by decreasing **transpiration** but at the same time prevents uptake of carbon dioxide (CO₂) from the

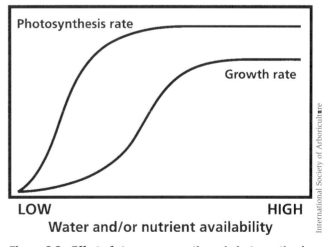

Figure 3.2 ▪ *Effect of stress on growth and photosynthesis.* *The growth of trees is quite sensitive to the availability of moisture and nutrients, and becomes limited by even mild deficiencies. Photosynthesis is much more resilient and does not become limited until nutrient and moisture deficits become more severe.*

atmosphere. Severe water stress can directly damage photosynthetic machinery, sometimes irreversibly (Kozlowski 1982).

Fertilization stimulates shoot growth to a greater degree than root growth, thus decreasing the root:shoot ratio of the tree (Linder and Rook 1984). In this way, fertilization can simultaneously increase tree water demands while decreasing the tree's ability to acquire water during drought. Hence, fertilized trees may be especially susceptible to drought stress. Indeed, a number of studies have shown fertilization to decrease tree resistance to drought stress (van den Driessche 1983; Etter 1969; Kleiner, Abrams, and Schultz 1992; Linder et al. 1987; Stewart and Lieffers 1993).

Tree Responses to Defoliation

Although trees tolerate mild defoliation with few noticeable effects, severe defoliation dramatically decreases the growth of trees (Kulman 1971). Tree energy reserves, rates of wound closure, and resistance to secondary pests such as wood borers, root **rot**, and canker **fungi** are also typically decreased. In severe situations, mortality occurs (Kulman 1971; Wargo 1978). Early season defoliation, just as leaves become fully expanded, is particularly damaging. In the early season, the tree is growing rapidly with maximum energy demands and little energy reserves (Wargo 1978). However, late-season defoliation can also decrease tree growth and energy reserves, thereby increasing tree mortality (Coffelt, Schultz, and Wolf 1993; Gregory and Wargo 1986).

Trees tolerate moderate defoliation quite well; less than 50 percent defoliation often has no detectable effect on growth (Wargo 1978). Trees can compensate for lost leaf area in several ways. Defoliation has been shown to increase photosynthesis in the remaining leaves, improve water balance within the plant, and increase shoot growth at the expense of root growth and carbohydrate storage (Welter 1989).

Deciduous trees often refoliate when defoliation exceeds 50 percent of the canopy. Although refoliation helps the tree recover from insect attack or foliar diseases, it also depletes stored energy reserves (Wargo 1978). But carbohydrates can be replenished, sometimes completely, by the new canopy following refoliation (Herms, Nielsen, and Sydnor 1987). Deciduous trees that are otherwise healthy can survive several successive years of complete defoliation, though they will be severely stressed.

Evergreen conifers, on the other hand, do not tolerate defoliation as well as deciduous trees and are fre-
quently killed by even one severe defoliation (Kulman 1971). Defoliation stresses conifers more than deciduous trees because conifers have much more invested in their canopies. The canopy of evergreen conifers holds several years' worth of foliage. Furthermore, conifers store a greater proportion of energy and nutrients in their canopy than do deciduous trees, which house a greater proportion of stored nutrients and energy in above-ground and underground woody tissue (Bryant, Tuomi, and Niemelä 1988). The loss of the canopy and its stores of nutrients and energy represents a severe stress for conifers.

Trees Adopt Best Strategy for Given Conditions

The physiological responses of plants to varying levels of soil fertility and moisture are shaped by their evolutionary history. In most natural forest ecosystems, tree growth is nutrient limited, and summer drought is a predictable fact of life. These stresses are a natural part of their existence, and trees are well adapted to dealing with them (Chapin et al. 1987; Chapin 1991, 1993).

Trees respond to stress in ways that minimize its negative effects. For example, as water stress develops, many tree species can maintain high turgor pressure in their leaves by increasing the concentration of certain dissolved substances in the cell, which causes more water to flow into the cell. By maintaining high turgor pressure through this process, called **osmotic adjustment,** wilting is prevented as stomata remain open, allowing water uptake and photosynthesis to continue as the soil dries (Abrams 1994). This response is generally stronger if water deficits develop gradually and if plants are preconditioned by previous exposure to drought. Moisture stress also increases root growth relative to shoot growth (Schulze 1986).

Plants also adjust to shortages of nutrients (Chapin 1980). For example, trees increase their root:shoot ratios in response to decreased nutrient availability, which decreases leaf area but increases nutrient uptake and the quantity of nutrients available for remaining foliage. Conversely, trees growing in nutrient-rich soil increase their shoot growth relative to root growth (Ericsson 1995; Harris 1992).

Light intercepted by leaves provides the energy with which photosynthetic enzymes convert carbon dioxide to sugars. Nitrogen is a major constituent of these enzymes. In fact, more than 50 percent of the nitrogen in a tree is involved directly in photosynthesis. Phosphorus, iron, manganese, and other nutrients also play critical roles. The greater the concentration of nutrients in the leaf, the higher the rate of photosynthesis possible, to a limit (Evans 1989).

Trees have a limited supply of nutrients they must budget across competing demands. Hence, they face a dilemma when deciding how to use their nutrients to produce leaves and photosynthetic enzymes. On the one hand, trees can spread their nutrients across many thin leaves, thereby maximizing total leaf area and the amount of light intercepted. On the other hand, because nutrients are diluted over a large area, the rate of photosynthesis by each leaf is lower than if nutrients were concentrated over a smaller area. Alternatively, trees can produce thicker, smaller leaves with more nutrients packed into a given area of a leaf. This allows each leaf to have higher levels of enzymes and thus higher rates of photosynthesis. Because total leaf area will be less, however, the tree will intercept less light but will be able to produce more photosynthate with the light that is captured (Figure 3.3).

Is it better to produce many leaves with a lower rate of photosynthesis or fewer leaves with a higher rate of

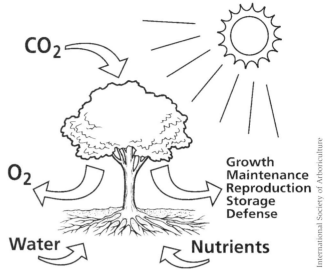

Figure 3.4 ▪ Resource allocation. *Trees carefully budget their limited supply of resources among the various processes that must be supported, including growth, maintenance, reproduction, storage, and defense. Not all processes can be supported fully at the same time.*

photosynthesis? Studies show that trees actively manage their nutrient supply, producing the best compromise for the current situation (McDonald 1990; Sinclair and Horie 1989). Under low-nutrient conditions, trees produce smaller, thicker leaves. They also increase root growth to increase nutrient uptake. As a result, high rates of photosynthesis are maintained, but growth is decreased because total leaf area is decreased. In fertile environments, trees increase their total leaf area and decrease root growth. The result is increased aboveground growth.

Trees Carefully Budget Limited Resources

Trees and other plants have limited resources to support their physiological processes. All requirements cannot be met simultaneously; therefore, trade-offs occur among growth, storage, reproduction, and defense (Bazzaz et al. 1987) (Figure 3.4). It has been widely observed that the shoot growth of trees is decreased in years of heavy fruiting and that significant root growth and accumulation of storage carbohydrates does not occur until shoot growth slows. An economic analogy is useful in understanding problems faced by trees in budgeting resources such as carbon and nutrients.

Carbon obtained through photosynthesis can be thought of as family income that must be budgeted across various functions. Just as a family must budget

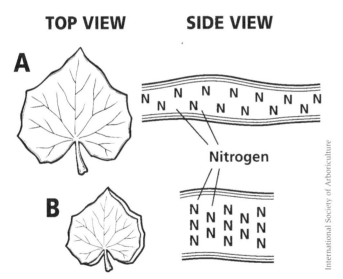

Figure 3.3 ▪ Relationship between photosynthetic rate and leaf characteristics. *Nutrients, especially nitrogen (N), are the building blocks of photosynthetic enzymes. These top and side views of a large and small leaf illustrate the dilemma faced by trees in deciding how to use their limited supply of nutrients. Trees can produce larger but thinner leaves that intercept more light (A). Such leaves will have a lower rate of photosynthesis because they have fewer photosynthetic enzymes in a given area of leaf. Alternatively, trees can produce smaller but thicker leaves that intercept less light (B). Such leaves will have higher rates of photosynthesis because they have more photosynthetic enzymes concentrated in a given area of leaf. Trees readily alter the size and thickness of their leaves in response to changing levels of nutrients in the soil, adopting the optimal strategy for current conditions.*

its limited income across food, clothing, shelter, and other essentials, a tree has limited income that must be budgeted across various competing processes such as growth, maintenance, reproduction, storage, and defense. If, for example, more income is allocated toward growth, then less income is available to support other processes, such as storage and defense (Figure 3.5). If, however, income can be increased by increasing photosynthesis, the additional income can be used to increase both growth and defense (Figure 3.6). Indeed, many studies have shown levels of allelochemicals and resistance to insects and disease to decrease in rapidly growing trees (Herms and Mattson 1992).

When nutrients, water, and light are plentiful, growth receives priority for plant resources. This is demonstrated in the extreme by the accelerated growth regimes sometimes used in nursery production. Trees are capable of extremely rapid growth when nutrients and water are present in optimal supplies. However, because the production of new biomass requires extremely

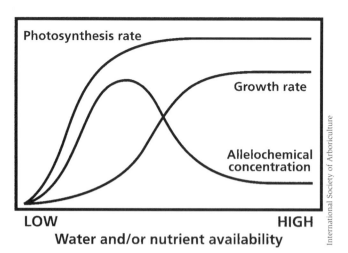

Figure 3.7 ▪ Benefits of moderate stress. *Moderately stressed trees are often most resistant to pests. Rapidly growing trees have few resources left over to support other processes, such as defense. Moderate nutrient and moisture stress does not impact photosynthesis but does limit growth, making carbohydrates available to support other processes such as the production of allelochemicals. Severe stress limits photosynthesis, and the tree has limited resources available to support growth or defense.*

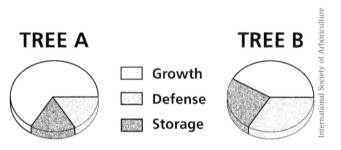

Figure 3.5 ▪ Different resource usages in trees with equal "incomes." *Trees have limited resources. Tree "A" is growing rapidly but is "spending" less on storage and defense. Tree "B," which is not growing as fast, can divert more "income" to storage and defense.*

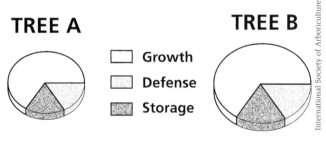

Figure 3.6 ▪ Resource usage in trees with unequal "incomes." *Photosynthesis in tree "A" is limited by severe nutrient or moisture stress, or a combination of the two, limiting the amount of "income" it has to "spend" on growth, storage, and defense. Fertilization of tree "B" has increased photosynthesis. As a result, it has more "income" and thus a bigger pie to divide. Growth, storage, and defense can all be increased.*

high levels of limited plant resources, rapidly growing trees have few resources available to devote to the production of structural support. Laden with succulent growth, such trees must be staked until growth slows and bark, lignin, and cellulose are produced; then the tree stiffens.

Moderate Stress Increases Resistance to Pests

Moderate stress generally increases tree resistance to **leaf-chewing** and **-sucking** insects (Herms and Mattson 1992). Why? As we have seen, photosynthesis is not as sensitive to stress as is growth (Figure 3.7). Thus, when moderate nutrient or drought stress limits growth, photosynthate cannot be diverted to growth processes, and carbohydrates accumulate in the plant. The carbohydrates can then be used to produce increased concentrations of allelochemicals (and storage compounds) that enhance tree resistance to insects (Herms and Mattson 1992) (Figure 3.7).

Fertilization and Insect Resistance

Numerous studies provide strong evidence showing that fertilization decreases tree resistance to insects. Fertilization of the willow (*Salix aquatica*) increased growth but decreased concentrations of starch, lignin, and tannins, as well as resistance to a leaf-feeding beetle (Larsson et al. 1986; Waring et al. 1985). Fertilization of birch (*Betula resinifera*) and quaking aspen (*Populus tremuloides*) also increased growth while decreasing concentrations of defensive compounds and resistance to snowshoe hares and leaf-feeding insects, respectively (Bryant et al. 1987a, 1987b). Fertilization of grand fir (*Abies grandis*) and loblolly pine (*Pinus taeda*) increased growth and decreased foliar phenolic concentrations (Muzika and Pregitzer 1992; Ross and Berisford 1990). In the case of loblolly pine, these fertilization-induced changes were accompanied by decreased resistance to the Nantucket pine tip moth (*Rhyacionia frustrana*). Fertilization also decreased the resistance of balsam fir (*Abies balsamea*) to the spruce budworm (*Choristoneura fumiferana*) (Shaw, Little, and Durzan 1978). Fertilization also generally increases tree susceptibility to sucking insects, including aphids, scales, leafhoppers, and psyllids, as well as spider mites (Larsson 1989).

Plant resistance to disease is also generally adversely affected by fertilization. Graham (1983), in a comprehensive review of the literature, concluded that fertilization generally increases plant susceptibility to disease by stimulating the production of disease-susceptible succulent new growth and by diverting resources away from chemical defense. However, this is not always the case. Fertilization increased walnut (*Juglans nigra*) resistance to anthracnose (*Gnomonia leptostyla*) (Neely 1986).

In two recent studies, however, fertilization of pine trees increased tree growth, concentrations of defensive compounds, and insect resistance (Björkman, Larsson, and Gref 1991; McCullough and Kulman 1991). However, both studies were conducted on extremely nutrient-deficient soils. In such sites, photosynthetic rates of conifers often increase in response to fertilization (Brix 1981; Linder and Rook 1984). If fertilization had increased photosynthesis, the "income" of the trees would have increased, and the increased pool of available photosynthate could have been used to increase both growth and defense (Figure 3.6). However, neither study measured the effects of fertilization on photosynthesis.

Drought Stress and Insect Resistance

A number of studies have shown drought stress to increase levels of allelochemicals and tree resistance to leaf-feeding insects. However, results of drought-stress studies have been more variable than those of fertilization studies. In some cases, drought stress had little

or no effect (for example, McCullough and Wagner 1987; Young and Hall 1986). Gypsy moth performance actually improved slightly on one paper birch clone experiencing drought stress, but there was no effect on another (Talhouk, Nielsen, and Montgomery 1990). Aphid and spider mite populations often increase during drought, perhaps because the higher temperatures often associated with drought allow these short-lived pests to grow and reproduce at a faster rate.

Shade Stress and Tree Resistance to Insects and Diseases

When sun-adapted trees are grown in shade, their photosynthesis rates decline dramatically, as do their concentrations of allelochemicals, probably because of decreased availability of carbon (Waterman and Mole 1989). As a result, insect and disease resistance of shade-stressed trees almost always declines. Shade has been shown to decrease tree resistance to bark beetles, browsing mammals, defoliating insects, and fungal pathogens (Herms and Mattson 1992).

Conversely, shade-adapted plants growing in the sun may also be stressed. Flowering dogwood (*Cornus florida*) is native to the forest understory and lacks the adaptations for tolerating the effects of midday water stress characteristic of trees adapted to full sun (Bahari, Pallardy, and Parker 1985). Probably for this reason, dogwoods planted in full sun are more susceptible to attack by dogwood borer (*Synanthedon scitula*) than those planted in at least partial shade (Potter and Timmons 1981).

Environmental Stress and Tree Resistance to Trunk Invaders

Bark beetles, wood borers, and trunk diseases are quite devastating to trees and deserve special attention. These organisms disrupt transport of water and nutrients in the **xylem** and **phloem,** often with fatal consequences. Bark beetles and wood borers such as the bronze birch borer (*Agrilus anxius*) feed on phloem tissue, **girdling** the tree. This disrupts the translocation of carbohydrates from the canopy to the roots, leading to root mortality, decreased nutrient and water uptake, and eventually death of the tree. If phloem damage is extensive, as in the case of mass attack by bark beetles, death can be rapid. **Vascular-wilt fungi,** associated with Dutch elm disease, interfere with xylem transport, disrupting water movement from the roots to the canopy and often rapidly killing the tree. The resistance of trees to stem-invading insects and pathogens is especially affected by stress. In particular, drought stress and defoliation have been shown to dramatically decrease tree resistance to these organisms (Kozlowski 1985; Schoeneweiss 1975; Wargo 1978; Wright, Berryman, and Wickman 1984).

Conifers resist bark beetles and pathogens by means of a wound-induced response. Cells damaged by insect feeding or pathogen infection accumulate allelochemicals toxic to the invading pests. This wound response requires a large expenditure of energy (Christiansen, Waring, and Berryman 1987). Many conifers also have a resin duct system containing terpene resins that repel colonizing beetles. Bark beetles can successfully colonize vigorous conifers only when they overwhelm the defenses of the tree by mass attack (Raffa and Berryman 1987).

As was the case with chemical defenses of foliage, there also appears to be a trade-off between growth and resin accumulation in the trunks of tree species using this defense system (Lorio 1986). Certain southern species of pines are heavily dependent on their resin system to resist bark beetles and may be susceptible to bark beetle colonization when they are rapidly growing as well as when they are severely stressed. Therefore, moderately stressed trees may be most resistant (Dunn and Lorio 1993; Lorio 1986). However, bark beetle resistance is generally decreased when stress is severe enough to decrease photosynthesis and subsequent movement of energy-containing carbohydrates to the trunk (Christiansen, Waring, and Berryman 1987).

Most deciduous trees lack the resin system of conifers and resist wood borers and trunk-infesting pathogens by producing allelochemicals that may slow the growth of invading organisms. They also produce **callus tissue** (wound periderms), which isolates the wound, inhibits the spread of colonizing organisms, and reestablishes **cambium** integrity (Bostock and Stermer 1989; Mullick 1977). Resistance is due in large part to rapid callus formation and isolation of damaged wood via compartmentalization. Compartmentalization occurs when the tree produces specific allelochemicals that attempt to block a pest, usually a pathogen, from moving further into the living tissues of the tree (Shigo 1984).

Rapid callus formation is associated with vigorous cambial activity and trunk growth (Neely 1983). As with tree growth in general, callus growth is extremely sensitive to stress (Herms 1991; Puritch and Mullick 1975). In particular, drought and defoliation stress slow callus growth and decrease tree resistance to wood borers. Examples include oak (*Quercus* spp.) resistance to twolined chestnut borer (*Agrilus bilineatus*) (Dunn,

Potter, and Kimmerer 1990; Wargo 1978) and birch (*Betula papyrifera*) resistance to bronze birch borer (*Agrilus anxius*) (Herms 1991).

Nutrient stress and fertilization, on the other hand, have had little effect on tree resistance to wood borers or bark beetles in the few available studies (Herms 1991; Waring and Pitman 1985).

Summarizing the Effects of Stress on Pest Resistance

Fertilization generally decreases the resistance of trees to foliage insect and disease pests by increasing tree growth and thereby diverting photosynthate from the production of defensive compounds. When trees are growing in soils that are severely deficient in nutrients, fertilization may increase both growth and insect resistance by increasing rates of photosynthesis and, thus, the pool of carbon available to support both growth and defense.

Drought stress and defoliation can dramatically decrease tree resistance to often-fatal trunk invaders, such as wood borers, bark beetles, canker, and **vascular tissue**–infesting disease organisms. Any positive effect of drought stress on resistance to leaf-feeding insects is far outweighed by the risk of attack by trunk invaders posed by drought.

The few available studies suggest fertilization has little direct effect on tree resistance to bark beetles or wood borers. However, a number of studies have found that fertilization increases the susceptibility of trees to drought stress, probably by increasing shoot:root ratios. If so, fertilizing trees that will not be irrigated during droughts may predispose them to attack by devastating trunk-invading pathogens and wood borers.

Implications for Cultural Practices in the Landscape and Nursery

A major challenge facing the "green industry" is defining, measuring, and maintaining tree "health." Traditional views have equated rapid growth with tree vitality. As a result, cultural recommendations have emphasized fertilization and other practices that maximize growth rate.

As discussed in this chapter, however, in many cases fast-growing trees are more susceptible to stress and less resistant to insects and diseases. As a result, fertilized trees may require regular irrigation and pesticide applications.

In some high-maintenance landscapes such as estates and golf courses, rapid growth may be desirable, and the high levels of inputs (and their associated expenses) necessary to maintain the health and aesthetic quality of rapidly growing trees are acceptable. These inputs include regular irrigation and pesticide applications.

However, the widespread use of fertilization as a cultural practice in the landscape needs to be reexamined. Fast growth may not be consistent with long-term health and survival of trees in the low-maintenance landscape. Moderately "stressed" trees make more efficient use of available water and nutrients, and have more extensive root systems, higher levels of stored carbohydrates, and higher concentrations of defensive chemicals (Chapin 1991, 1993). In short, such trees are more insect- and disease-resistant as well as more stress-tolerant.

Cultural practices used in nursery production of landscape trees should also be reexamined. Rapid growth is desirable to shorten the time required to produce marketable trees. However, cultural practices designed to maximize growth can lead to decreased performance and survival of the trees once they reach the landscape (Hamilton, Graca, and Verkade 1981). In one study, snowshoe hares greatly preferred nursery-grown white spruce (*Picea glauca*) over naturally regenerating seedlings (Rodgers et al. 1993). The more rapidly growing nursery plants had higher nutrient and lower allelochemical concentrations. In another study, cultural practices that decreased the growth of pine trees in the nursery by imposing moderate drought stress also enhanced tree survival once the trees were planted in the forest (van den Driessche 1991a, 1991b).

The environmental impact of fertilizer applications must also be considered. Urban and suburban landscapes represent a major source of fertilizer use and, consequently, fertilizer runoff in the United States (Bormann, Balmori, and Geballe 1993). Fertilizer runoff is a major cause of "nonpoint source" pollution and has a number of adverse ecological effects, including decreased quality of wetlands, lakes, and ponds. More judicious use of fertilizers in the landscape will decrease nutrient runoff and subsequent contamination of groundwater and surface water.

Before the beneficial effects of cultural practices can be fully exploited, detailed studies must be conducted on the effects of fertilization and irrigation on tree growth, photosynthesis, and pest resistance in the urban environment. Nonetheless, it is clear that stress tolerance and pest resistance of trees can be enhanced through proper cultural practices. The most effective use of cultural practices to manage pests and abiotic stress requires a sound understanding of the physiological responses of plants to environmental factors.

A Recommendation Based on Understanding Plant-Stress-Pest Complex

Consider two trees, one fertilized, the other not. The first tree is in a landscape that is regularly fertilized but seldom irrigated. It will produce vigorous shoot growth in the spring when soil moisture is plentiful, but at the expense of root growth and the production of defensive chemicals. The unfertilized tree with more conservative growth will have a more extensive root system, more resistance to pests, and more tolerance of summer drought. With higher levels of stored carbohydrates, it will also be in a better position to recover from a pest outbreak, should one occur.

Which tree is "healthier"? It is time to shift from the paradigm that rapid growth equals a healthy tree and recognize that rapid growth can also have negative consequences, and that moderate stress has its benefits.

Fertilization programs should be used only with an understanding of potential consequences for pest resistance and stress tolerance, and only when soil and foliar tests confirm that trees will respond to increased nutrient availability in the desired manner. Unless trees are showing visible symptoms of nutrient deficiency, fertilization generally will increase growth without increasing photosynthesis. The effect will be to decrease pest resistance and stress tolerance.

Studies have shown that even tree growth is not always increased by fertilization, indicating that nutrient availability is not always the growth-limiting factor (see Neely 1980; Stanturf, Stone, and McKittrick 1989). In a long-term study (fifteen years), fertilization had no effect on the growth of sugar maple (*Acer saccharum* 'Monumentale') and Snowdrift crabapple (*Malus* 'Snowdrift') (Smith and Treaster 1987). In the same study, fertilization did increase the growth of linden (*Tilia cordata* 'Select').

In the low-maintenance landscape, the long-term health of trees may best be maximized by the judicious use of fertilizers only when foliage shows clear signs of nutrient deficiency. Even when the plant is visibly nutrient deficient, fertilizers should be used only after foliar and soil testing reveal (1) which essential nutrient is causing the deficiency symptom and (2) that the deficiency is caused by an actual shortage of the nutrient in the environment rather than by another environmental factor (including soil pH, soil temperature, soil moisture, and interactions among nutrients present in excess) that is preventing the tree from taking up nutrients present in adequate supply.

Drought stress and defoliation, however, can dramatically decrease tree resistance to trunk-invading organisms such as wood borers as well as to canker and vascular wilt diseases. Irrigation during periods of severe drought and management of defoliating insects are absolutely critical to maintaining tree resistance to these often-lethal pests.

It is useful to consider the natural environment and how trees respond to it. The growth of trees in natural ecosystems is generally nutrient limited, midsummer moisture stress is a regular occurrence, and plant-eating insects and mammals are always present. Trees are well adapted to dealing with these stresses: their growth is slow to moderate, and they produce high concentrations of defensive chemicals, storage carbohydrates, and extensive root systems.

Conclusion

We end by quoting the eminent arborist Richard W. Harris (1992), who noted that native trees, though never fertilized, almost always have dark-green foliage: "I now look at native stands of trees with awe and new respect, knowing it should be possible to have good leaf color, low to moderate growth, and trees in balance with their surroundings with little or no fertilization needed."

When reading the following chapters, keep in mind that you, as a Plant Health Care practitioner, are attempting to provide an environment that is conducive to maintaining healthy and attractive trees. Many times in our efforts to maintain a healthy landscape we may jeopardize the long-term health of the tree or associated plant materials for short-term aesthetic appearance. Once a problem happens—whether it is abiotic or biotic—it may predispose the plants to a complex of stresses and pests that may initiate a **mortality spiral**. When problems arise, we also need to be aware that the situation may have been initiated by other factors that are the underlying cause of concern.

Daniel Herms
Assistant Professor of Entomology
Ohio Agricultural Research and Development Center
The Ohio State University

William Mattson
USDA Forest Service
North Central Forest Experiment Station
East Lansing, Michigan

References

Abrams, M.D. 1994. Genotypic and phenotypic variation as stress adaptations in temperate tree species: a review of several case studies. *Tree Physiol.* 14:833–842.

Bahari, Z.A., S.G. Pallardy, and W.C. Parker. 1985. Photosynthesis, water relations, and drought adaptation in six woody species of oak-hickory forests in central Missouri. *For. Sci.* 31:557–569.

Barbosa, P., and V.A. Krischik. 1987. Influence of alkaloids on feeding preference of eastern deciduous forest trees by the gypsy moth. *Am. Nat.* 130:53–69.

Bazzaz, F.A., N.R. Chiariello, P.D. Coley, and L.F. Pitelka. 1987. Allocating resources to reproduction and defense. *BioScience* 37:58–67.

Björkman, C., S. Larsson, and R. Gref. 1991. Effects of nitrogen fertilization on pine needle chemistry and sawfly performance. *Oecologia* 86:202–209.

Bormann, H.F., D. Balmori, G.T. Geballe. 1993. *Redesigning the American Lawn: A Search for Environmental Harmony.* New Haven, Connecticut: Yale University Press.

Bostock, R.M., and B.A. Stermer. 1989. Perspectives on wound healing in resistance to pathogens. *Annu. Rev. Phytopathol.* 27:343–371.

Bradford, K.J., and T.C. Hsiao. 1982. Physiological responses to moderate water stress. In *Physiological Plant Ecology II: Water Relations and Carbon Assimilation,* ed. O.L. Lange, P.S. Nobel, C.B. Osmond, and H. Ziegler, 263–324. Berlin: Springer-Verlag.

Brix, H. 1981. Effects of nitrogen fertilizer source and application rates on foliar nitrogen concentration, photosynthesis, and growth of Douglas fir. *Can. J. For. Res.* 11:755–780.

Bryant, J.P., F.S. Chapin, III, P. Reichardt, and T. Clausen. 1987a. Response of winter chemical defense in Alaska paper birch and green alder to manipulation of plant carbon/nutrient balance. *Oecologia* 72:510–514.

Bryant, J.P., T.P. Clausen, P.B. Reichardt, M.C. McCarthy, and R.A. Werner. 1987b. Effect of nitrogen fertilization upon the secondary chemistry and nutritional value of quaking aspen (*Populus tremuloides* Michx.) leaves for the large aspen tortrix (*Choristoneura conflictana* [Walker]). *Oecologia* 73:513–517.

Bryant, J.P., J. Tuomi, and P. Niemelä. 1988. Environmental constraint of constitutive and long-term inducible defenses in woody plants. In *Chemical Mediation of Coevolution,* ed. K.C. Spencer, 367–389. San Diego: Academic Press.

Chapin, F.S., III. 1980. The mineral nutrition of wild plants. *Annu. Rev. Ecol. Syst.* 11:233–260.

———. 1991. Integrated responses of plants to stress: A centralized system of physiological responses. *BioScience* 41:29–36.

———. 1993. Evolution of suites of traits in response to environmental stress. *Am. Nat.* 142:S78–S92.

Chapin, F.S., III, A.J. Bloom, C.B. Field, and R.H. Waring. 1987. Plant responses to multiple environmental factors. *BioScience* 37:49–57.

Christiansen, E., R.H. Waring, and A.A. Berryman. 1987. Resistance of conifers to bark beetle attack: Searching for general relationships. *For. Ecol. Manage.* 22:89–106.

Coffelt, M.A., P.B. Schultz, and D.D. Wolf. 1993. Impact of late-season orangestriped oakworm (Lepidoptera: Saturniidae) defoliation on oak growth and vigor. *Environ. Entomol.* 22:1318–1324.

van den Driessche, R. 1983. Growth, survival, and physiology of Douglas fir following root wrenching and fertilization. *Can. J. For. Res.* 13:270–278.

———. 1991a. Influence of container nursery regimes on drought resistance of seedlings following planting. Part I: Survival and growth. *Can. J. For. Res.* 21:555–565.

———. 1991b. Influence of container nursery regimes on drought resistance of seedlings following planting. Part II: Stomatal conductance, specific leaf area, and root growth capacity. *Can. J. For. Res.* 21:566–572.

Dunn, J.P., and P.L. Lorio, Jr. 1993. Modified water regimes affect photosynthesis, xylem water potential, cambial growth, and resistance of juvenile *Pinus taeda* L. to *Dedroctonus frontalis* (Coleoptera: Scolytidae). *Environ. Entomol.* 22:948–957.

Dunn, J.P., D.A. Potter, and T.W. Kimmerer. 1990. Carbohydrate reserves, radial growth, and mechanisms of resistance of oak trees to phloem-boring insects. *Oecologia* 83:458–468.

Ericsson, T. 1995. Growth and shoot:root ratio of seedlings in relation to nutrient availability. *Plant and Soil* 168–9:205–214.

Etter, H.M. 1969. Growth, metabolic components and drought survival of lodgepole pine seedlings at three nitrate levels. *Can. J. Plant Sci.* 49:393–402.

Evans, J.R. 1989. Photosynthesis and nitrogen relationships in leaves of C3 plants. *Oecologia* 78:9–19.

Graham, R.D. 1983. Effects of nutrient stress on susceptibility of plants to disease with particular reference to the trace elements. *Adv. Bot. Res.* 10:222–276.

Gregory, R.A., and P.M. Wargo. 1986. Timing of defoliation and its effect on bud development, starch reserves, and sap sugar concentration in sugar maple. *Can. J. For. Res.* 16:10–17.

Hamilton, D.F., M.E.C. Graca, and S.D. Verkade. 1981. Critical effects of fertility on root and shoot growth of selected landscape plants. *J. Arboric.* 7:281–290.

Harris, R.W. 1992. Root-shoot ratios. *J. Arboric.* 18:39–42.

Herms, D.A. 1989. Plants vs. herbivores: nature's arms race. *Amer. Nurseryman* 170(5):64–80.

———. 1991. "Variation in the Resource Allocation Patterns of Paper Birch: Trade-offs Among Growth, Reproduction, and Defense." Ph.D. diss., East Lansing: Michigan State University.

Herms, D.A., and W.J. Mattson. 1992. The dilemma of plants: To grow or defend. *Quarterly Review of Biology* 67(3):283–335.

Herms, D.A., D.G. Nielsen, and T.D. Sydnor. 1987. Impact of honeylocust plant bug (Heteroptera: Miridae) on ornamental honeylocust and associated adult buprestids. *Environ. Entomol.* 16:996–1000.

Kleiner, K.W., M.D. Abrams, and J.C. Schultz. 1992. The impact of water and nutrient deficiencies on the growth, gas exchange and water relations of red oak and chestnut oak. *Tree Physiol.* 11:271–287.

Kozlowski, T.T. 1982. Water supply and tree growth. Part I: Water deficits. *For. Abstr.* 43:57–95.

———. 1985. Tree growth in response to environmental stresses. *J. Arboric.* 11:97–111.

Kulman, H.M. 1971. Effects of insect defoliation on growth and mortality of trees. *Annu. Rev. Entomol.* 16:289–324.

Lambers, H., and H. Poorter. 1992. Inherent variation in growth rate between higher plants: A search for physiological causes and ecological consequences. *Adv. Ecol. Res.* 23:187–261.

Larsson, S. 1989. Stressful times for the plant stress–insect performance hypothesis. *Oikos* 56:277–283.

Larsson, S., A. Wiren, L. Lundgren, and T. Ericsson. 1986. Effects of light and nutrient stress on leaf phenolic chemistry in *Salix dasyclados* and susceptibility to *Galerucella lineola* (Coleoptera). *Oikos* 47:205–210.

Linder, S., M.L. Benson, B.J. Myers, and R.J. Raison. 1987. Canopy dynamics and growth of *Pinus radiata.* I. Effects of irrigation and fertilization during a drought. *Can. J. For. Res.* 17:1157–1165.

Linder, S., and D.A. Rook. 1984. Effects of mineral nutrition on carbon dioxide exchange and partitioning of carbon in trees. In *Nutrition of Plantation Trees,* ed. G.D. Bowen and E.K.S. Nambiar, 211–236. London: Academic Press.

Lorio, P.L., Jr. 1986. Growth-differentiation balance: A basis for understanding southern pine beetle-tree interactions. *For. Ecol. Manage.* 14:259–273.

Luxmore, R.J. 1991. A source-sink framework for coupling water, carbon, and nutrient dynamics of vegetation. *Tree Physiol.* 9:267–280.

Mattson, W.J. 1980. Herbivory in relation to plant nitrogen content. *Annu. Rev. Ecol. Syst.* 11:119–161.

Mattson, W.J., and R.A. Haack. 1987. The role of plant water deficits in provoking outbreaks of phytophagous insects. In *Insect Outbreaks: Ecological and Evolutionary Perspectives,* ed. P. Barbosa and J.C. Schultz, 365–407. New York: Academic Press.

McCullough, D.G., and H.M. Kulman. 1991. Effects of nitrogen fertilization on young jack pine (*Pinus banksiana*) and on its suitability as a host for jack pine budworm (*Choristoneura pinus*) (*Lepidoptera: Tortricidae*). *Can. J. For. Res.* 21:1447–1458.

McCullough, D.G., and M.R. Wagner. 1987. Influence of watering and trenching ponderosa pine on a pine sawfly. *Oecologia* 71:382–387.

McDonald, A.J.S. 1990. Phenotypic variation in growth rate as affected by N-supply: Its effects on net assimilation rate (NAR), leaf weight ratio (LWR) and specific leaf area (SLA). In *Causes and Consequences of Variation in Growth Rate and Productivity of Higher Plants,* ed. H. Lambers, M.L. Cambridge, H. Konings, and T.L. Pons, 35–44. The Hague, Netherlands: SPB Publishing.

Mullick, D.B. 1977. The non-specific nature of defense in bark and wood during wounding, insect and pathogen attack. *Rec. Adv. Phytochem.* 11:395–441.

Muzika, R.M., and K.S. Pregitzer. 1992. Effect of nitrogen fertilization on leaf phenolic production of grand fir seedlings. *Trees* 6:241–244.

Neely, D. 1980. Tree fertilization trials in Illinois. *J. Arboric.* 6:271–273.

———. 1983. Tree trunk growth and wound closure. *HortScience* 18:99–100.

———. 1986. Total leaf nitrogen correlated with walnut anthracnose resistance. *J. Arboric.* 12:312–315.

Potter, D.A., and G.M. Timmons. 1981. Factors affecting predisposition of flowering dogwood trees to attack by the dogwood borer. *HortScience* 16:677–679.

Puritch, G.S., and D.B. Mullick. 1975. Effect of water stress on the rate of non-suberized impervious tissue formation following wounding in *Abies grandis*. *J. Exper. Bot.* 26:903–910.

Raffa, K.F., and A.A. Berryman. 1987. Interacting selective pressures in conifer-bark beetle systems: A basis for reciprocal adaptations? *Am. Nat.* 129:234–262.

Rodgers, A.R., D. Williams, A.R.E. Sinclair, T.P. Sullivan, and R.J. Andersen. 1993. Does nursery production reduce antiherbivore defences of white spruce? Evidence from feeding experiments with snowshoe hares. *Can. J. For. Res.* 23:2358–2361.

Ross, D.W., and C.W. Berisford. 1990. Nantucket pine tip moth (Lepidoptera: Tortricidae) response to water and nutrient status of loblolly pine. *For. Sci.* 36:719–733.

Schoeneweiss, D.F. 1975. Predisposition, stress, and plant disease. *Annu. Rev. Phytopathol.* 13:193–211.

Schulze, E-D. 1986. Whole-plant responses to drought. *Aust. J. Plant Physiol.* 13:127–141.

Shaw, G.G., C.H.A. Little, and D.J. Durzan. 1978. Effect of fertilization of balsam fir trees on spruce budworm nutrition and development. *Can. J. For. Res.* 8:364–374.

Shigo, A.L. 1984. Compartmentalization: A conceptual framework for understanding how trees grow and defend themselves. *Annu. Rev. Phytopathol.* 22:189–214.

Sinclair, T.R., and T. Horie. 1989. Leaf nitrogen, photosynthesis, and crop radiation use efficiency: A review. *Crop Sci.* 29:90–98.

Smith, E.M., and S.A. Treaster. 1987. Fertilizing trees in the landscape: A 15-year evaluation. In *Ornamental Plants 1987: A Summary of Research*, Ohio Agric. Res. Dev. Cen. circular 291, 8–10.

Stanturf, J.A., E.L. Stone, Jr., and R.C. McKittrick. 1989. Effects of added nitrogen on growth of hardwood trees in southern New York. *Can. J. For. Res.* 19:279–284.

Stewart, J.D., and V.J. Lieffers. 1993. Preconditioning effects of nitrogen relative addition rate and drought stress on container-grown lodgepole pine seedlings. *Can. J. For. Res.* 23:1663–1671.

Talhouk, S.N., D.G. Nielsen, and M.E. Montgomery. 1990. Water deficit, defoliation, and birch clones: Short-term effect on gypsy moth (Lepidoptera: Lymantriidae) performance. *Environ. Entomol.* 19:937–942.

Wargo, P.M. 1978. Insects have defoliated my tree—now what's going to happen? *J. Arboric.* 4:169–175.

Waring, R.H., A.J.S. McDonald, S. Larsson, T. Ericsson, A. Wiren, E. Arwidsson, A. Ericsson, and T. Lohammar. 1985. Differences in chemical composition of plants grown at constant relative growth rates with stable mineral nutrition. *Oecologia* 66:157–160.

Waring, R.H., and G.B. Pitman. 1985. Modifying lodgepole pine stands to change susceptibility to mountain pine beetle attack. *Ecology* 66:889–897.

Waterman, P.G., and S. Mole. 1989. Extrinsic factors influencing production of secondary metabolites in plants. In *Insect-Plant Interactions,* Vol. 1, ed. E.A. Bernays, 107–134. Boca Raton, Florida: CRC Press.

Welter, S.C. 1989. Arthropod impact on plant gas exchange. In *Insect-Plant Interactions,* Vol. 1, ed. E.A. Bernays, 135–150. Boca Raton, Florida: CRC Press.

White, T.C.R. 1993. *The Inadequate Environment: Nitrogen and the Abundance of Animals.* Berlin: Springer-Verlag.

Wright, L.C., A.A. Berryman, and B.E. Wickman. 1984. Abundance of the fir engraver, *Scolytus ventralis,* and the douglas-fir beetle, *Dedroctonus pseudotsugae,* following tree defoliation by the douglas-fir tussock moth, *Orgyia pseudotsugata. Can. Entomol.* 116:293–305.

Young, C.E., and R.W. Hall. 1986. Factors influencing suitability of elms for elm leaf beetle *Xanthogaleruca luteola* (Coleoptera: Chrysomelidae). *Environ. Entomol.* 15:843–849.

CHAPTER 4

Tree Selection: Matching the Tree to the Site

Robert Argent

Relationship Between Site and Success of Planting

There are many reasons for planting a tree—as a memorial or gift, for privacy, to reduce soil erosion, for a winter windbreak, for summer cooling, to increase property value, to reduce air pollution, for fall color or spring bloom, for wildlife habitat, or as barrier against unwanted views or sounds.

Before you decide to plant a tree, you must consider the influence of site selection on the tree's health and longevity. If a tree is expected to reach its normal size and age and to remain healthy enough to satisfy the reasons for planting, then the tree you select should be appropriate for the conditions at the planting site. A poor match between tree requirements and site conditions commonly leads to early tree mortality or a high level of maintenance.

Evaluating the Site

Sometimes the function of the tree will dictate its general location. But even within that general location, the individual planting site must be evaluated. When evaluating a site for tree planting, you must consider both the growing space and the **microclimate**. Other site constraints may also be imposed due to aesthetic or legal precedents, such as ordinances that ban the use of silver maples near public sidewalks and curbs.

Growing Space

Constraints on space may include utilities (both above-ground and underground), structures, and surface covers. Above-ground utilities impose limits on a tree's height. It is much better to select a species that has a mature height less than the overhead limits than to select a taller species with the intent of pruning later to maintain an acceptable height. Underground lines become restrictive during tree planting, and it is imperative to be aware of underground utilities before digging starts. Regular maintenance of buried utilities or planned replacement and expansion of buried utilities should be considered before developing the planting scheme. If the planting area is a city boulevard or utility right-of-way and utility replacement is planned for the near future, either the decision to plant in that area or the timing of planting could be a mistake. Nothing is gained by planting a tree that will be severely injured when utilities are expanded or installed. Get in

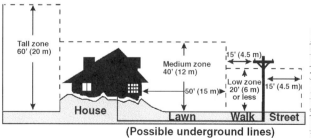

Figure 4.1 ▪ *Approximate location and heights of planting*

International Society of Arboriculture

27

touch with the local utility service for line information and location. The illustration in Figure 4.1 indicates the recommended location and size of trees to be planted near utility lines.

Tree spread and shape must also be considered when selecting a tree site. Structures such as buildings, fences, and roads will limit the amount of horizontal space available for tree crowns. Vehicular as well as pedestrian traffic will influence the height of the lowest branches in the tree crown. For example, trees hanging over boulevards may require pruning so that the lowest branches are at least 14 feet above the street grade to allow for the safe passage of commercial trucks. Likewise, trees hanging over sidewalks should have branches no lower than 6½ feet above the sidewalk grade. Mature tree crown spread should also be considered when determining plant spacing. Trees of identical or closely related species planted too close together may transmit diseases more readily through root grafts, and long-term maintenance costs could increase as trees start to shade each other, causing branch **dieback** in the lower crown. This doesn't mean that trees of the same (or closely related) species cannot be used to landscape a street or neighborhood. However, it is certainly not advisable to plant a single species throughout an entire community.

Spacing of trees will also be dictated by local ordinances. Typical setbacks established by ordinance are 30 feet from intersections, 15 feet from driveways and alleys, and 10 feet from hydrants and utility poles (Miller 1988). Most ordinances are based on vehicular traffic safety standards and will vary based on traffic loads for specific streets. The city of Milwaukee, for example, requires setbacks of 40 feet for approach intersections and 20 feet for nonapproach intersections. The city also requires a 5-foot setback for gas and water main shutoff boxes.

Communities may also prohibit planting trees in lawns less than a certain width. For example, Milwaukee requires a 6-foot border width. Some cities also set communitywide standards for spacing between trees, regardless of the species. Other cities set standards related to mature tree height, requiring more space between taller species and less space between smaller species. The National Arbor Day Foundation recommends spacing of 6 feet to 15 feet for trees less than 30 feet tall, 30 feet to 40 feet for trees 30 feet to 70 feet tall, and 40 feet to 50 feet for trees 70 feet or more in height.

The underground space a tree needs is more difficult to determine than the above-ground space. Different species of trees have different root forms and growth habits. Horizontal and vertical root spread is determined by the genetics of the tree species as well as the soil porosity. Most branch roots and fine roots occur within 18 inches of the soil surface. The horizontal spread of the roots is determined by plant density, root **competition**, and subsurface conditions that are favorable for root expansion. Roots are opportunistic and can grow laterally 10 feet or more per year in good soil that is free from competition. The more horizontal soil space a tree has, the better it will do. Research on selected species has revealed that tree root spread may be as much as two to four times the height of the tree in normal growing conditions.

The depth of good soil needed for optimum tree growth and health is 20 inches to 30 inches. Soil rooting depths that are thin due to a high **water table** or impenetrable soil layer are less productive than deeper soils. Conversely, water and minerals are quickly lost from soils that are too coarse in texture or too deep. According to Perry (1994), fair tree growth can be sustained on soils that are as thin as 10 inches, and good growth can be sustained on 16 inches of soil. But best tree growth occurs in 20 inches to 30 inches of soil.

Perry (1994) compared publications on soil volumes required for tree growth and noted that the resource requirements for trees is an exponential function of their diameters. Table 4.1 summarizes his results. In effect, if you want a tree to reach 10 inches in diameter, you would need 200 cubic feet of good soil 2 feet deep. This soil volume formula assumes that the soil surface area is exposed to the atmosphere and is not under an impenetrable layer such as asphalt or concrete, or that there is adequate air that can reach the soil through layers of coarse stone or geotextile fabrics under any pavement.

The less soil area given a tree, the quicker it will decline and need replacement. Urban (1992) looked at several studies relating tree growth to soil volume and suggested that a greater amount of soil is necessary for

Table 4.1 ▪ *Soil volume required for good tree root development*

Tree caliper size (dbh inches)	Exposed soil surface area (ft²)	Soil volume, 2-ft depth (ft³)
5	25 (5' x 5')	50
10	100 (10' x 10')	200
20	400 (20' x 20')	800
30	841 (29' x 29')	1,688
40	1,444 (38' x 38')	2,888

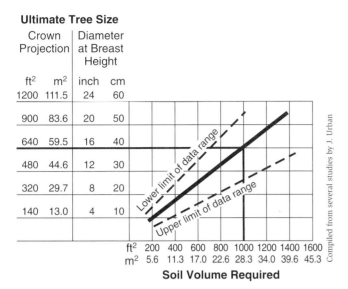

Figure 4.2 ▪ *Relationship between tree growth and soil volume*

good tree growth. His data are represented in Figure 4.2. It must be understood that the soil volumes are of good soil—something rare in urban settings. The characteristics of soil are discussed later in this chapter.

Climate

Aside from space consideration, factors such as temperature, light, moisture, wind, and air quality should be considered when selecting a site.

Temperature ▪ Most plant material is rated according to plant **hardiness zones**, described later in this chapter. The zones are delineated by the lowest temperatures that can be expected in that area based on the average annual minimum temperatures in that zone. Hardiness zones are large, and local variables can influence planting site temperature.

Urban areas are usually warmer in the winter than surrounding areas, a phenomenon known as the **heat island effect.** The probability of frost damage to plants is increased when the planting site is set in low-lying areas surrounded by hills. Cold air will flow down the slope and accumulate in the lower area, creating a frost pocket. Extremely low soil temperatures can kill tree roots; **containerized**, elevated plantings expose the roots even more to lower temperatures and increase the possibility of damage. Local temperatures may be moderated by the proximity of large bodies of water and heat re-radiated by asphalt and concrete structures heated by day. Roots under asphalt or other dark-colored material in full sun sites will also experience elevated daytime temperatures.

Injury from high temperature primarily takes the form of leaf desiccation. Planting-site air temperature

can be increased by highly reflective surfaces such as light-colored masonry structures and sidewalks. Enclosed planting areas such as courtyards can limit air flow and increase air temperatures. Stress caused by heat can be exacerbated if moisture is limited. Care should be taken to place planting sites away from external heat sources such as open sewers and air-conditioner exhaust vents.

Light ▪ Light is essential for photosynthesis to take place. The intensity, duration, quality (wavelengths), and sources of light can be influenced by the site. Shade moderates light intensity and quality. Tall structures and other plants can increase shade to the point that shade **tolerance** of a tree may become a factor. Artificial light of low intensity will have little effect on photosynthesis.

Moisture ▪ Many landscaped areas limit the availability of water to plants. Impermeable surfaces such as paved areas, compacted soils, and buildings can decrease the amount of water reaching the root zone. If these same structures radiate heat, **transpiration** might be increased, worsening the water deficit. Conversely, planting sites in low-lying areas might be flooded due to excessive runoff if surrounded by impermeable surfaces. Soil might be eroded away by this process, or plants could be buried by sediment. Plants could also die due to waterlogged soil. Proper draining of the planting site or redirection of runoff might be necessary.

Wind ▪ Catastrophic winds such as tornados and hurricanes can destroy a landscape regardless of how well the site was selected. Urbanization tends to decrease winds. In cities with long avenues of tall structures, however, winds commonly are accelerated due to a **wind-tunnel effect.**

In areas where there is a strong prevailing wind, a tree will need a large soil area for anchorage. Trees planted in groups will be better able to withstand winds; however, **wind-throw** and blowdown of remaining trees is common when some trees in the protective group are removed. A site exposed to strong prevailing winds can also lose soil moisture because of increased transpiration of the plants and a higher evaporation rate for water in the soil. With certain species, such as sugar maple, this often leads to scorched or tattered leaves.

Air quality ▪ Wherever possible, planting sites should be selected to avoid areas contaminated by pollutants. Sites should be well protected from deicing salts in soil, but more importantly from salt spray. Sometimes an elevated planting site might be required to protect plants from salt spray due to passing vehicles and deicing salt. Airborne pollutants such as ozone, sulfur dioxide, and deicing salt spray can adversely affect a tree regardless of the site; therefore, factors to consider when selecting the species to plant include the species' tolerance to air pollution.

Other factors ▪ Other site factors to consider include competition from other plants and lawns, landscape aesthetics, functionality of the site, and pedestrian traffic.

Tree roots grow in the top 18 inches of soil and compete directly with lawns and other plants for available nutrients. Proper mulching will help alleviate competition and is discussed in Chapter 10 of this manual. Sometimes a site will not be desirable due to the aesthetic consideration of the landscaper. Trees might be too small or large in proportion to the area, or they might block a view.

The intended function of the planting might be the overriding concern when selecting location and placement. Such concerns might include control or channeling of pedestrian traffic, planting for screening, and planting for windbreaks.

Soil Characteristics

Soil management in the urban landscape has typically been limited to fertility considerations. But good management needs to go further, taking into account that soil is a complex system of chemical, biological, and physical components that affect plant growth. Water, nutrients, oxygen, and root anchorage are all provided by the soil.

An ideal volume of soil is 50 percent solids and 50 percent pore space, the solid space being 1 percent to 5 percent organic material and the remainder mineral materials. The pore space will contain oxygen and water. Urban clay soils, however, typically contain 10 percent to 20 percent pore space and very little organic matter.

Bulk density ▪ This is a measurement of the mass of soil per unit volume (usually grams per cubic centimeter). It is an indirect indicator of soil pore space and is commonly used as an indicator of **soil compaction**, which is a physical resistance to root penetration.

Densities greater than 1.8 in fine-textured soils such as clay indicate compacted, poorly drained soils that are difficult for roots and water to penetrate. Typically, bulk densities between 1.0 and 1.4 optimize root growth. Higher densities in clay soils (1.5 to 1.8) reduce root growth and, subsequently, tree health. Bulk density usually ranges from 1.0 to 2.0 for mineral soils.

Soil texture ▪ Soil texture is the size distribution of soil particles. The characteristics are determined by the ratio of particle sizes (sand, silt, clay) found in the soil. Textures can be estimated by kneading the soil between the thumb and forefinger. Sand particles feel gritty, whereas silt feels like flour, and clay is sticky. A more accurate textural analysis would include a classification of the soil sample by particle size. A soil is usually described by its dominant particle size as indicated by the texture triangle in Figure 4.3.

The texture triangle reveals that a soil must be more than 45 percent sand to be considered "sandy" or 40 percent silt to be considered "silt." Because of clay's dominant characteristics, only 20 percent clay content will lead to a "clay" classification.

Soils that exhibit intermediate characteristics are called "loam" soils and are usually suited for growing a wide range of plants.

Soil structure ▪ Soil structure is a term used to indicate the degree to which soil particles are **aggregated**. It refers to the size and shape of soil held together by a complex of electrical and chemical bonds, plant roots, and microorganisms. The structure of the soil controls its permeability and gas exchange capacity.

Because composted organic matter aids in the development and stability of soil aggregates, the incorporation of composted grass clippings, leaves, peat moss, and other organic material will sometimes lessen permeability problems. Saline soils amended with gypsum and organic matter may improve aggregation, but the ability of gypsum to improve the structure of fine-textured soils has not been documented.

Permeability ▪ This is a measure of the ability of water, gases, and plant roots to move through the soil

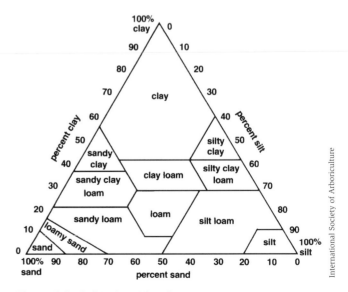

Figure 4.3 ▪ *Soil texture triangle*

International Society of Arboriculture

over a period of time. It is a function of soil texture, structure, and pore space. Soils with coarse texture are more permeable than fine-textured soils. Large pores transmit water and gases more rapidly than small pores. It should be noted that a highly permeable soil is not necessarily a well-drained one; it may be resting on a high water table or an impenetrable soil layer.

Compaction can destroy a soil's permeability and gas exchange capacity. In cases of severe compaction, however, the destroyed soil structure might not be able to reaggregate. There is no quick fix for this problem. Soil aggregates are easily destroyed by soil compaction or chemical dispersion (as in high-sodium soils).

Water-holding capacity ▪ A soil's ability to hold moisture is closely related to its texture. A fine-textured soil will hold more water than a coarse (sandy) soil because of a greater microscopic surface area available to hold water. Texture, along with structure, determines soil porosity. Although fine-textured soils contain a large surface area for holding water, such soils also hold the water tightly, sometimes leaving little water available for the plant. Soils high in silt-sized particles have the largest capacity to hold water for use by plants. Common ranges in total and available water-holding capacities are shown in Table 4.2.

The amount of water a soil can hold is determined by the total surface area of the particles (texture) and the amount and size of the pores. Water that will drain from the soil under the force of gravity is known as **gravitational water.** Once the gravitational water has drained away, the soil is said to be at **field capacity.** When enough water is lost from the soil that a plant's roots can no longer extract it, the soil is said to have reached the **wilting point.** Figure 4.4 illustrates this relationship.

Soil drainage ▪ Water movement in the soil depends primarily on the amount of water added, permeability of the soil, and the soil's initial water content. Water

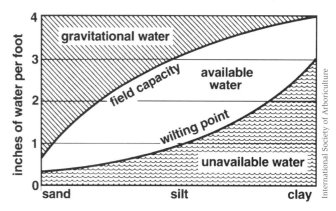

Figure 4.4 ▪ *Water-holding capacity of soil*

will moisten the surface of the soil to field capacity before it will infiltrate lower soil layers. This **infiltration** can be restricted by soil compaction or by layers of soils with differing textures.

A coarse layer of soil above a fine-textured layer will have water accumulate above the lower layer until it can be more slowly absorbed. The inverse of this situation—a fine soil layer above a coarse one—is equally serious. Water will not move from the fine-textured soil to the coarse soil below until it has completely saturated the top layer. Soil above the interface will remain saturated even after drainage has been completed. Figure 4.5 illustrates this point.

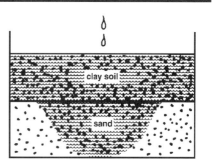

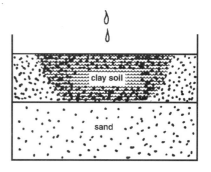

Figure 4.5 ▪ *Demonstration of water infiltration through a layer of fine-textured soil into sand. Upper layer must become saturated before water drains into lower layer.*

Table 4.2 ▪ *Inches of water-holding capacity per inch of soil*

Soil texture group	Total inches	Available inches
Fine (clay)	.40 to .50	.15 to .20
Moderately fine	.30 to .45	.20 to .25
Medium (silt)	.25 to .35	.20 to .30
Moderately coarse	.15 to .25	.10 to .20
Coarse (sand)	< .15	< .10

Care must be taken when amending soil as to the impact of differing soil textures. If a tree is planted in a clay soil and the planting hole is amended with coarse soil, then the hole will retain water until the water can seep into the clay soil. Paving gravel at the bottom of a container or planting hole will not improve drainage because the fine-textured soil will retain moisture until it is saturated.

Soil nutrients ▪ Organic matter and mineral particles provide thirteen of the sixteen elements essential to plant growth. These elements and the form of their availability are presented in Table 4.3, adapted from Harris (1992).

Essential elements in a water solution are absorbed by the plant through its roots. While in solution, these elements become positively charged ions called **cations.** Soil particles are negatively charged and attract these cations. This capacity of soil to absorb cations is known as the **cation exchange capacity** (CEC) and serves as a measure of the soil's attraction, retention, and exchange of cations. The more fine-textured clay a soil contains, the greater its cation exchange capacity. The attraction between soil particles and cations minimizes the tendency of elements to **leach** or wash out of a soil. Because of this, fine-textured soils are usually more "fertile" than coarse-textured ones.

Although elements may be in the soil, they may be unavailable to the plant. One important factor for the availability of minerals to the plant is **soil pH**. Soil pH refers to the soil's acidity or alkalinity. Low **pH** is acidic and high pH alkaline, with a pH of 7.0 considered neutral. Because pH is a logarithmic function, a one-unit change in pH indicates a tenfold change in acidic/alkaline concentration; a two-unit change indicates a hundredfold change in concentration. Although variable for different tree species, a pH range between 6.0 and 6.5 is most favorable for growth.

Highly acidic soils may limit the amount of phosphorus, whereas manganese and aluminum—elements required in only very small amounts—can reach toxic levels. Inversely, highly alkaline soils limit both iron and manganese. The relative availability of essential elements at different pH levels for mineral soils is illustrated in Figure 4.6.

Depending on their optimum pH ranges, trees react differently to pH extremes and subsequent element deficiencies or excesses. There are several symptoms that are common to pH extremes, especially at higher pH levels:

- Leaf **chlorosis** (pale green to yellow), especially interveinal chlorosis (green veins, yellow blades)
- Stunted growth, exhibited as reduced annual twig growth or size of foliage
- Reduced root growth
- Reduced winterhardiness, which is most commonly exhibited as increased twig dieback
- Increased vulnerability to problems such as insect damage
- **Scorch** and/or discoloration (other than chlorosis) of foliage

Soluble salts ▪ Soil salinity can be a problem in areas with arid

Table 4.3 ▪ *Essential elements for plant growth and their available form*

Source	Element	Symbol	Form available to plants	
Air and Water	Carbon	C		CO_2
	Oxygen	O		O_2, H_2O
	Hydrogen	H		H_2O
Soil	**Macronutrients**			
	Nitrogen	N	Nitrate	NO_3
			Ammonium	NH_4^+
	Phosphorus	P	Phosphate	$H_2PO_4^-$
	Potassium	K	Potassium	K^+
	Calcium	Ca	Calcium	Ca^{++}
	Sulfur	S	Sulfate	$SO_4^=$
	Magnesium	Mg	Magnesium	Mg^{++}
	Micronutrients			
	Manganese	Mn	Manganese	Mn^{++}
	Zinc	Zn	Zinc	Zn^{++}
	Boron	B	Borate	$H_2BO_3^-$
	Copper	Cu	Copper	Cu^{++}
	Iron	Fe	Iron	Fe^{+++}
	Molybdenum	Mo	Molybdate	$MoO_4^=$
	Chlorine	Cl	Chloride	Cl^-

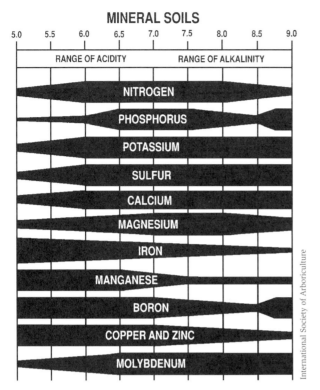

MINERAL SOILS

International Society of Arboriculture

Figure 4.6 ▪ *Relative availability of essential elements to plant growth at different pH levels for mineral soils*

conditions of less than 30 inches of rainfall per year. Deicing salt and excessive fertilizer salt can also lead to soil salinity problems. Salinity can decrease the growth of sensitive plants and can cause leaf burn (scorch), leaf drop, and even plant death. Excessive salt (sodium chloride) can adversely affect soil structure. The availability of water may also be decreased as a result of excessive soil salinity. A suggested caution level for salt in the soil is 600 parts per million (0.00857 dS/m). For unadapted plants, a soil salinity level of 1,000 ppm (0.01429 dS/m) or higher is dangerous. Plants vary in their tolerance to salt levels. For instance, Ohio buckeye and Norway maples are reasonably tolerant to higher salt concentrations, but serviceberry and maackia are very sensitive.

Urban soils ▪ These soils typically have been disturbed in some way that modifies the soil properties. They are frequently compacted, which can destroy soil structure, increase bulk density, and lower pore space. The reduction of pore space can lead to decreased aeration and drainage. Water-holding capacity and root penetration normally are also decreased.

Urban soils also hinder plant growth by containing less organic matter and exhibiting reduced nutrient cycling. Additionally, urban soils can become contaminated by pesticides and heavy-metal salts, which can

be toxic to plants. Soil structure is disturbed by waste products in fill. Fill soil can contain high amounts of material such as masonry, wood, glass, plastic, concrete, asphalt, paper, and metal. Synthetic materials in fill soil can impede root growth and change the chemical composition of the soil. It is not uncommon for disturbed urban soils to have dramatically different soil pHs from nearby undisturbed soils.

Urban soils typically need to be modified in order to support plant life successfully. Healthy trees need a soil with a low bulk density and a good distribution of soil pores, minerals that are accessible to the plant, adequate organic matter, and workable depth of at least 2 feet. The book *Urban Soil in Landscape Design* by P.J. Craul (1992) extensively addresses urban soils.

Selection of Hardy/Resistant Woody Plants

All too often, homeowners go to the nursery or garden center and choose a tree that looks "nice" or sounds familiar. This can lead to choosing a specific plant and then attempting to modify the site to fit the specimen— not a good idea. Instead, trees should be chosen with a specific site in mind. The environment and location should be the primary factors in tree selection.

Hardiness

Temperatures vary from state to state and within state boundaries. Although it may be easy to lump people of the Midwest into a group for economic, social, and political reasons, it's next to impossible to do the same for plants. Trees suited to southern regions may do poorly in more northern areas. Specimens in western regions face climatic conditions not found in eastern areas. Likewise, a plant that thrives in the comfort of river bottoms may die on the flatlands during August heat. Trees selected with a specific site in mind tend to provide the fastest growth and are better able to withstand adversity from climate changes and pests.

One environmental factor that we cannot regulate is temperature. The wide range of temperatures in the Midwest—down to –20° F in winter and up to 100° F in summer—can wreak havoc on trees. Excessive cold can freeze plant cells, causing them to crack and rupture. High summer temperatures place stress on the root system, causing root death or **leaf scorching**. Therefore, it is essential to choose the correct plant for the hardiness zone in which it will live.

The U.S. Department of Agriculture has recently updated its hardiness zone map, which provides some guidelines for determining whether a specific plant is adapted to a particular location. The warmer the climate, the higher the hardiness zone number. Most of the Midwest lies within hardiness zones 5 and 6, with the exception of some northern states in zone 4. Many plants listed as zone 5 will survive in zone 6 with little or no problems. Those adapted to zone 6, however, are likely to decline in zone 5 without special care. Examples include peaches and Japanese maples. Most plants listed as "zone 3 to 4 adaptable" are generally considered hardy throughout much of the Midwest.

The average annual minimum temperature is between –20° and –30°F in zone 4; between –10° and –20°F in zone 5; and between 0° and –10°F in zone 6. Plants may suffer due to "not how cold it gets but how it gets cold." Rapid fluctuations of temperatures can cause cells to rupture and plants to die back. Most trees can withstand lower temperatures if the temperature declines slowly, remains cold stably, and gradually gets warmer in late winter or early spring.

Exceptions to the hardiness zone rule—including higher elevations, slopes, and windy exposures—can lower the hardiness zone a half point or more. Placing specimens in windbreaks or near heated structures might shelter the plant enough so that it can be raised in an environment not generally considered favorable.

Plants can be harmed by winter temperatures in different ways, such as stem cracking, sun scalding of foliage and bark, root death, cambial death, or bud death. Some of the more common symptoms of winter injury include

- Twig dieback—from a few inches of branch tips to entire branches
- Frost cracking or bark splitting of stems or branches
- Dead, dried buds—vegetative or floral
- Scorching or shriveling and dying of newly emerged foliage on all or part of the tree
- Scorching of evergreen foliage
- Stunted annual twig growth or stunted foliage size
- Death of entire plant, which may not occur until late spring or early summer (most common when the root system has been severely damaged)

Although the hardiness zone considers primarily low winter temperatures, high summer temperatures can be just as important. For example, Colorado blue spruce, eastern white pine, and Norway maple are able to withstand winter temperatures but may decline under summer heat. Physiological scorch conditions may indicate a plant is located in the wrong place.

It is possible for younger, smaller plants to adapt to a particular climatic environment due to a less severe **transplant shock** period. Many plants may appear adapted to a site, only to die following temperature extremes. Don't be in a rush to remove plants following winter injury. Some plants may resprout from the roots and could be eventually pruned into desirable forms.

Aesthetics—Tree Characteristics

After evaluating the environmental characteristics of an area, determine the tree's purpose. It's impossible to find a tree that possesses all of the best characteristics, including fragrance; showy flowers during the spring; attractive, nonmessy fruit; good branching habits; stunning fall color; fast growth; disease and insect resistance; and leaves that disappear after dropping. But if a tree can't give you everything, it can give you some of the main characteristics you desire.

The following paragraphs describe several key aspects to consider when selecting a tree.

Shade ▪ Most people choose trees to provide shade. **Deciduous** trees block sun during the summer months and allow rays to penetrate in winter. Trees also transpire, or lose moisture, through their leaves, providing a cooling effect on the surrounding air. Trees that provide the best shade are tall with a wide crown or branch structure. Maples, oaks, sycamores, ashes, elms, and lindens provide excellent shade.

Evergreen trees retain their foliage throughout the winter and can block warm winter sunrays. Pines, firs, spruces, and hemlocks are common species. Allow ample room for growth because most evergreen trees retain their wide, lower branches for much of their lives. Evergreen windbreaks can reduce winter snow and wind; however, the windbreak needs to be designed carefully for maximum effect.

Form ▪ A tree's form is its shape. Tree shapes include weeping (willow), pyramidal (pin oak), round (sugar maple), columnar (poplar), and oval (hickory).

Choose a form suitable for the location. Trees such as the hackberry and the few remaining American elms make excellent street trees because their branch structure is vase-shaped, thus shading the sides of the street. High-branched trees generally require less pruning to remove safety conflicts and visual barriers, compared with pyramidal, round, or weeping tree forms.

Weeping and pyramidal trees are generally better for open landscapes than for street locations. Weeping and pyramidal trees must be pruned more often than higher branched trees to avoid safety conflicts such as branches hitting pedestrians on sidewalks; overhanging branches hitting trucks in streets; or low, dense branches blocking drivers' views at intersections.

But what makes a tree a nuisance in some situations can make it a blessing in other situations. Pyramidal, round, or weeping tree forms are excellent for blocking undesirable views, screening noise, or reducing winds. If the space allows, these trees can be used effectively for a number of benefits.

Size ▪ It's hard to keep in mind that plants grow up and out. What looks nice and small this year may look "ratty" and out of proportion in five years. It's even more difficult to envision something 20 or 50 years in the future. Oaks can reach 80 to 100 feet in height but are planted as 8- to 10-foot specimens. Problems occur when a large tree is planted in a small area where horizontal or vertical space is limited. Sidewalks and driveways can be cracked and lifted. Power lines can present an obstacle, resulting in indiscriminate pruning by some utility companies. It might be more practical to remove a large tree completely and replant it with a smaller species instead of yearly pruning. Large trees can shade gardens or block windows or scenic views. Roots can interfere with sewer lines or infringe on the neighbor's yard.

Along with height, tree width should be considered. It's important to space trees properly to allow for air circulation and proper development. Generally, trees less than 30 feet tall should be spaced 6 to 15 feet apart, trees 30 to 70 feet in height should be spaced 30 to 40 feet apart, and trees 70 or more feet in height should be spaced 40 to 50 feet apart.

Finally, consider how fast the tree will grow. The ideal growth for most trees is between 1 and 2 feet of new growth per year once the specimen is established. Plants advertised to grow 8 feet per year are more prone to wind, ice, and snow injury, usually due to poor branch attachment.

Flowers ▪ Although most trees produce flowers, some are showier than others. Crabapples, redbuds, dogwoods, and magnolias provide spectacular spring blooms. Blossom colors range from lavender, to red, to pink, to white. Many flowers appear in clusters, giving the tree the appearance of one massive flower. Most trees bloom in the spring, but a few bloom at other times. Golden-rain tree produces yellow blossoms in the summer. Common witchhazel blooms after the leaves have dropped in the fall; vernal witchhazel blooms in late winter or early spring.

Although a tree's "season of flowering" may be the most aesthetic addition to the urban forest, flowering should never be considered as the sole reason for selecting a tree. Unfortunately, varieties of flowering crabapples often are planted solely for their blossoms, with no consideration for their disease tolerance or maintenance requirements. Two weeks of glorious flowering will not compensate for an apple scab problem that **defoliates** the tree by midsummer.

Fruit ▪ Many trees produce a seed, fruit, or pod that ends up annoying homeowners. Sticky sweet-gum balls are a nuisance in lawns and on sidewalks. Horsechestnut pods, besides being large, are also poisonous. Ginkgo fruits produced on the female tree carry an unpleasant odor. Maples, poplars, and elms generate an abundance of seeds that germinate freely. Additionally, locust, plum, and sumacs sprout from roots, creating havoc in the lawn.

On the other hand, many tree fruits provide food for birds and animals. Hawthorns, crabapples, cherries, and dogwoods supply winter foods to migrating and overwintering birds. The nuts of walnuts, pecans, and hickories are winter food for squirrels. As a rule, birds and animals are more likely to eat smaller rather than larger fruit and seeds.

Many trees are bred or propagated to be either sterile or male varieties. These specimens may cost more, but savings might be recuperated in less maintenance and liability.

Color ▪ Leaf color is another characteristic to consider. Most are green through the spring and summer. Some trees, such as the copper beech, crimson king Norway maple, and purple leaf plum have leaves of different color. A few trees are variegated with two or more colors.

Fall colors vary among plants. Red maples provide an intense red, whereas sugar maples range from yellow, to orange, to red. Sour gum or black tupelo has a deep burgundy to purple color. Ashes range from bright yellow to a light purple. Hackberries are yellow. Sweet gums range from yellow, to red, to purple. Oaks run the gamut from yellow, to orange, to red, to russet.

Native Plants Versus Introduced Plants

Serious debate currently centers on using native plants as opposed to introduced specimens. But the issue is not black and white. The terms *native* and *naturalized* are not synonymous; the latter indicates a group of plants that escaped cultivation to become established in the wild. *Native* plants generally indicate plants that were present prior to settlement by Europeans in the 1500s. The definition can be flexible enough to include a group of plants growing over a large geographic area but with some genetic or race variability, such as flowering dogwood.

Native plants generally are thought to be more adapted to a particular locale in terms of their suitability for the soil type and environmental conditions as well as their resistance to local pest species. But that doesn't mean a native plant will do well in all situations in a particular location. Sugar maples will probably not thrive in an urban-altered, "basement-clay" soil even though they are native to the area. Pin oaks native to acidic river bottoms won't thrive 5 miles away in the alkaline soils of the uplands or in residential developments where construction techniques or maintenance practices have dramatically increased the soil pH.

It has taken thousands of years for native plants to adapt to their particular environment. Floods, droughts, temperature extremes, storms, and other climatic conditions have stabilized the plants' genetic makeup. Diseases and insect pests have eliminated less-resistant specimens. Native specimens usually have relatively few insect or disease susceptibilities that pose serious problems.

Introduced plants aren't necessarily bad. They have increased the diversity of plant materials within the landscape, expanding the palette of fall colors, bark textures, heights, forms, and flowering habits. Many introduced plants have succeeded in locations where native plants failed. Plants from Asia with a similar hardiness zone appear to thrive in the central United States with relatively few problems. However, introduced plants haven't experienced the diversity associated with the Midwest. Plants might grow perfectly well for several years or decades before experiencing weather extremes or pest problems. And some non-native species have developed into weedy pests, such as tree-of-heaven (*Ailanthus altissima*), which can choke out more desirable species.

New Varieties and Cultivars

Plant selection and breeding is expanding the variety of plants available. Columnar and dwarf forms can increase the number of potential sites for a specific type. For example, columnar red maples produce more vertical growth than horizontal plant forms, allowing for placement in narrow locations. The number of **cultivars** (cultivated varieties) is rapidly increasing the available range of plant material. Plant breeders are crossing plants and selecting desirable characteristics from the

seedlings. Plant breeders are also evaluating individual specimens or stands of trees, looking for improved traits that might conform to a particular landscape site or show resistance to pests.

Selecting Woody Plants

Trees are sold as three primary types: **bare-root**, **balled-and-burlapped**, and **container-grown**. Plant material can be obtained from many sources, including retail and wholesale nurseries, municipal nurseries, mail-order businesses, and forestry or conservation groups. Most states have nursery grower associations or related associations that can provide a complete listing of material suppliers available in your area.

It should be noted that even though a nursery is local, that does not necessarily mean that the stock is local. Make sure you check the origin of the stock you buy to be sure that it will be hardy at your intended planting site. When possible, also check for the seed source used to propagate the trees, especially for species with a wide natural range. For instance, red maples are native in forests from Minnesota to the Gulf Coast. Seed collected from southern stock will produce trees that often fail to be fully winterhardy in the northern states. Many of the winter tree damage problems in the northern states can be attributed to trees grown from southern U.S. seed sources.

Generally Desirable Characteristics of Nursery Stock

The following characteristics are what to look for in nursery stock:

- Strong, well-developed leader (or leaders in a multiple-leader plant); no **included bark** if multiple-leadered
- Bright, healthy bark
- Trunk and limbs free of insect or mechanical injury
- Branches well distributed around trunk
- Adequate vertical spacing between branches (10 inches to 18 inches for most species)
- Good trunk taper
- Wide-angle, U-shaped crotches of branches for strength
- Healthy buds
- Foliage evenly distributed on the upper two-thirds of the tree

When selecting nursery stock, remember to remove any tree wrap to check for hidden damage or problems.

Bare-Root Stock

This type of stock is usually sold as a small tree with roots bare or in a moisture-holding medium such as peat or moss. Take the following precautions when choosing this stock:

- Check for abundant root growth
- Check for fibrous and numerous small roots
- Check for good color of roots and bark (with cream- or tan-colored roots)
- Make sure roots have been kept moist
- Prune roots that are injured or diseased

Advantages of bare-root stock include the following:

- Least expensive of the three major types of stock
- Roots adapt to soil better than balled-and-burlapped stock
- Easy to transport to planting site
- Large-scale plantings possible and more economical

Disadvantages of bare-root stock include the following:

- Not practical for large plants
- Roots dry out easily without materials or facilities to keep them moist
- Small size makes them vulnerable to animal browsing and foot traffic from animals and humans
- Must be handled when dormant

Balled-and-Burlapped Stock

Trees can be quite large when they are sold. With this type of stock, a tree's roots are contained in a ball of soil—the larger the tree the larger the soil ball. The ball of soil is usually wrapped in burlap, cloth, or wire.

Take these precautions when selecting from balled-and-burlapped stock:

- Select only trees that have been dug with an adequate-sized soil ball—refer to American Association of Nurserymen standards
- Check for firm **root ball**
- Do not select plant with a broken ball or a dried out soil ball
- Always carry plant by the ball, never the trunk, stem, or branches
- Always remove twine from the soil ball
- Remove, score, or cut the burlap before planting, taking care not to break the root ball

- Open the burlap at the top of the soil ball and make sure the **root collar flare** is at or near the surface of the soil ball

Advantages of this type of stock include the following:

- Better survival rate than bare-root for larger plants, conifers, and selected species
- Large specimens provide instant visual effect

Disadvantages of this type of stock include the following:

- Harder to handle because of size and weight of the tree ball
- Availability may be seasonal
- Root ball can dry out if its soil is different than soil in planting hole

Container Stock

Trees are sold in containers (usually plastic pots) that are numbered according to size: #1, #5, #15, and so forth. The size of the container is often referred to as gallons, though the amount of soil volume may be less than the gallon designation. When specifications for plantings are made, avoid use of gallon specifications and refer to numbered container size.

Take these precautions when selecting from container stock:

- Avoid trees that are **root-bound**
- Avoid trees with **girdling roots**
- Remove container before planting
- Make sure roots are light in color; dark-brown or black roots could indicate a problem

Advantages of this type of stock include the following:

- Somewhat easier to handle than balled-and-burlapped stock
- Better survival rate than bare-root stock
- Continuous availability
- Reasonable price

Disadvantages of this type of stock include:

- Harder to handle than bare-root stock
- Possible root problems (encircling roots, root-bound)

Robert Argent
Urban Forestry Consultant
Chicago, Illinois

Selected References

Craul, P.J. 1992. *Urban Soil in Landscape Design.* New York: John Wiley and Sons.

Dirr, M.A. 1990. *Manual of Woody Landscape Plants: Their Identification, Ornamental Characteristics, Culture, Propagation and Uses.* 4th ed. Champaign, Illinois: Stipes Publishing Company.

Flint, H.L. 1983. *Landscape Plants for Eastern North America.* New York: Wiley Interscience.

Gerhold, H.D., and W.N. Wandell, eds. 1993. *Street Tree Fact Sheets.* University Park, Pennsylvania: The Pennsylvania State University.

Grey, G.W., and F.J. Deneke. 1986. *Urban Forestry.* 2d ed. New York: John Wiley and Sons.

Harris, R.W. 1992. *Arboriculture: Integrated Management of Landscape Trees, Shrubs, and Vines.* 2d ed. Englewood Cliffs, New Jersey: Prentice-Hall. 674 pp.

Hightshoe, G.L. 1988. *Native Trees, Shrubs and Vines for Urban and Rural America.* New York: Van Nostrand Reinhold.

Hille, D. 1980. *Fundamentals of Soil Physics.* New York: John Wiley and Sons.

Neely, D., ed. 1993. *Arborists' Certification Study Guide.* Savoy, Illinois: International Society of Arboriculture.

Miller, R.W. 1988. *Urban Forestry: Planning and Managing Urban Green Spaces.* Englewood Cliffs, New Jersey: Prentice-Hall.

Perry, T.O. 1994. Size, design and management of tree planting sites. In *The Landscape Below Ground: Proceedings of an International Workshop on Tree Root Development in Urban Soils.* ed. G.W. Watson and D. Neely. Savoy, Illinois: International Society of Arboriculture.

Sternberg, G., and J. Wilson. 1995. *Landscaping with Native Plants.* Shelburne, Vermont: Chapters Publishing.

Urban, J. 1992. Bringing order to the technical dysfunction within the urban forest. *J. Arbor.* 18:85–90.

Watson, G.W., and D. Neely, eds. 1994. *The Landscape Below Ground: Proceedings of an International Workshop on Tree Root Development in Urban Soils.* Savoy, Illinois: International Society of Arboriculture.

CHAPTER 5

Planting and Maintenance of Woody Ornamental Plants

John Ball, David Williams, and Patrick Weicherding

Plant Health Care begins with proper site design, plant selection, and planting technique. Careful consideration of these factors will help reduce or avoid **stress factors** that cause decline in trees and shrubs. Many problems that arborists and other landscape maintenance providers deal with, however, are only short-term or contributing factors in a plant's decline. Managing only these factors does not address the underlying, long-term stresses.

Long-term stresses leading to plant death or failure to thrive are usually the result of one or more underlying primary factors: a poor match of the plant to the site, selection of unhealthy planting stock, improper planting technique, and lack of post-transplant care. This chapter describes the proper methods of site evaluation, plant selection, planting techniques, and post-transplant care and maintenance.

Matching Plant Environmental Requirements to the Site

A primary reason for plant failure is poor adaptation to site conditions. Plants have evolved to tolerate and even thrive in most regions of the world, from the tundra to deserts to alpine meadows and even the ocean floor. Although plants inhabit most of the earth's surfaces, individual species are generally found within a narrow range of environmental conditions. Some species, considered site-sensitive, thrive only in relatively specific site conditions. For example, tuliptree (*Liriodendron tulipifera*) achieves optimum development on moist, well-drained soil of moderate fertility and will become the dominant tree at such sites. Tuliptree rapidly declines in **vitality** as site conditions become less favorable and it is outcompeted by other species.

Other tree species, known as site-insensitive, are found on a wide range of sites. Site insensitivity should be viewed as a tolerance of a wide range of conditions rather than a preference. For example, Virginia pine (*Pinus virginiana*) will grow in many site conditions, from dry to slightly wet. It performs best on moist, well-drained soils of moderate fertility, yet rarely thrives in such locations because it is outcompeted by tuliptree.

The first step in Plant Health Care, then, is matching the planting site conditions to the environmental requirements of the plant. The planting site encompasses the entire space that the plant will occupy at maturity. Too often installers focus attention on the planting hole—which may support the root system for only a single growing season or less. A thorough evaluation means assessing the climate and soil condition at a planting site and then limiting the selection of plants to those that are genetically adapted to the environmental conditions. The more costly alternative is to modify the planting site conditions to meet the environmental requirements of a particular plant.

Matching plant requirements to site conditions is complicated by the fact that most urban trees are actually two trees. Most ornamental trees are grafted, with the **scion** of one species type joined to the stock of another (Figure 5.1). Hundreds of such **cultivars** are available. The popularity of cultivars over seed-grown plant material is due to the uniformity of form, mature size, maintenance requirements, and environmental adaptation of cultivars. The influence of the stock on the performance of the scion has long been recognized by fruit breeders. (The same evaluation and categorizing of stock has not been available for ornamental trees.) Fruit growers can select not only the cultivar of a particular apple they wish to grow, for example, but also the stock, depending upon the mature size they want the tree to achieve, the soil characteristics of the site, and the presence of certain **diseases**. It is impossible to truly know how a particular cultivar will perform unless the capabilities of the rootstock are known.

Selecting Healthy Plants

Only healthy plants are worth the investment of time and effort in planting. The three primary criteria for selecting healthy plants are vigor, vitality, and structure. Vigor is the inherent capacity of a plant to resist strain (Shigo 1986). A plant's vigor cannot be modified by cultural practices. It can only be altered by plant breeders who select for high vigor as one of the requirements for cultivar release.

Vitality is the ability of a plant to thrive in its environment (Shigo 1986). A dynamic property, vitality can be modified by cultural practices in the nursery and the landscape. No single measure of vitality exists, so it is a difficult property to measure when selecting plants for installation. Nonetheless, one measure of vitality is annual shoot growth (Figure 5.2). Plants should exhibit normal growth for the particular species and cultivar. Many young trees maintain anywhere from 3 to 20 inches of annual shoot extension. Starch levels have also been suggested as a means to assess nursery plant vitality and predict transplant success. Root starch levels—while relatively easy to test—are fairly difficult to interpret. Also, this test has not been proven to be an accurate indicator for timing of transplanting (Witherspoon and Lumis 1986).

Structure should also be inspected when selecting plants for installation. Both above- and below-ground structural problems may create future maintenance problems. The above-ground structures that should be inspected are branch spacing, branch attachment, and stem taper.

The spacing of both the temporary and permanent branches should be evaluated. Temporary branches are those that will not become part of the permanent structure of the tree. The first branches for many ornamental and street trees begin anywhere from 6 to 15 feet from the ground. The spacing of lower branches is not critical because they will be removed before they become one to two inches in diameter. Ideally, lower branches should be maintained as long as possible because they contribute to good taper and reduce the need for staking.

The branches that will become part of the permanent structure of the tree must be inspected carefully. Some nurseries "head" trees, particularly small flowering trees such as crabapples and cherries, to create a denser canopy. This practice results in many weakly attached branches forming at short intervals along the stem. Trees pruned in this manner should be avoided because they will require much corrective pruning to improve their structure. The permanent branches on small-maturing trees should be spaced approximately 6 to 12 inches apart, while the permanent branches on large-maturing trees should be spaced 12 to 18 inches apart, sometimes even more. Closer spacing may result in branches crowding one another as they grow.

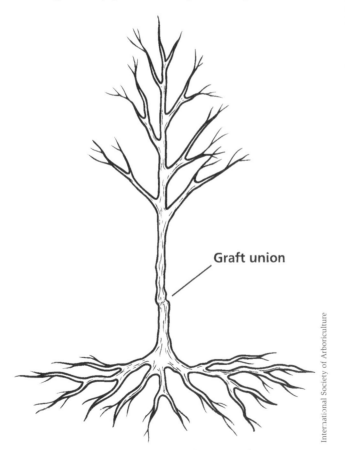

Graft union

Figure 5.1 ▪ Location of the bud union on cultivars. The bud union is usually two to three inches above the trunk flare.

International Society of Arboriculture

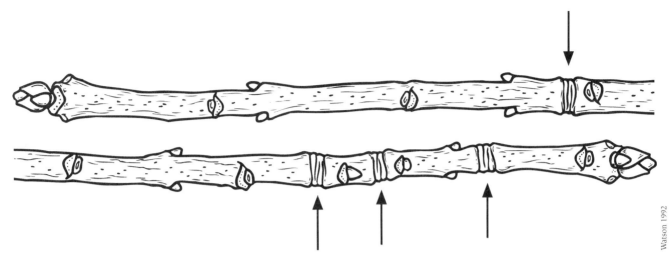

Figure 5.2 ▪ **Bud scale scar**. *These scars, indicated by the arrows, show where twig growth stops each year.*

Watson 1992

These general spacing recommendations must be consistent with the natural branching pattern and landscape function of the cultivar. Some will require closer spacing, others greater.

Many planting guides suggest that branches should diverge from the trunk at wide angles. This is based upon the mistaken notion that branch angle is an indication of strength. A better assessment of branch strength can be determined by examining the **branch bark ridges**. The ridges should be clearly visible. Inward curving bark is a possible indicator of **included bark** formation and future branch failure.

Stem taper is another above-ground structure characteristic to inspect. Taper is an important stability requirement for trees. If the tree stem lacks the necessary taper, it is more likely to snap during strong winds. Two practices that contribute to poor taper are removing lower branches too soon and staking a tree too tightly and for too long.

The tree stem should also be inspected for cracks, tears, **cankers**, and signs of borers. These defects can be hidden by kraft paper or other wrapping material, so landscapers and arborists should avoid purchasing trees that have their trunks wrapped. (This precaution does not apply to temporary wrapping placed on the tree trunk during shipping. Such wrap protects the trunk from **injury** as it is being moved. However, the wrap should be removed and the trunk inspected before delivery is accepted.)

Encircling and severed roots are two below-ground structural defects to check for. Such an inspection requires removing the plant from the container or pulling the burlap back from the soil ball. However, it is better to inspect for these defects while in the nursery than when the plant is being installed.

Roots that circle more than halfway around the circumference of the container are a major concern to landscape installers. These **encircling roots** in time may become **girdling roots** and contribute to the decline of the plant. Girdling root problems are difficult to correct once the tree has matured in the landscape and the treatment—excising the problem root or roots—is not always successful (Watson and Clark 1993). It is much better to avoid selecting plants with this defect.

Encircling roots are most common in round, rigid plastic containers, but the nursery industry has developed many new container designs to reduce this problem. Plants in polybags, porous-walled containers, and in-ground fabric containers have been shown to reduce encircling roots (Appleton 1993). Regardless of the container design, however, if the plant is grown in the same container for too long, encircling roots will occur.

Girdling roots are not exclusively related to container production. They may also begin from lateral roots that form after a primary root is severed during **balled-and-burlapped** (B&B) harvest (Watson, Clark, and Johnson 1990). Trees and shrubs transplanted B&B have been grown in field soil and are dug in this same soil. Regardless of the harvesting method, the majority of the roots are removed in B&B transplanting. When the tree is replanted, rooting beyond the soil ball occurs from roots captured in the ball and from roots generated from severed roots.

Soil ball sizes should follow the size requirements set by the American National Standards Institute (1986). Undersizing the ball may reduce the number of roots necessary to sustain the tree as it begins to recover. It may also result in severing roots at a larger diameter. Severed roots that are one inch in diameter or less generate more roots than those that are larger. Thus, undersizing the ball may reduce the number of roots generated from the cut roots. The soil ball should also be checked for dryness. If the ball remains dry for too long, the severed roots may dry out and fewer roots will be generated.

When inspecting plant material for transplanting, make sure that the plant has not been placed too low in the container or the burlapped soil ball. Tree cultivars are generally budded (grafted) onto the rootstock approximately two to three inches above the ground. The characteristic "crook" that signifies the connection between the rootstock and the scion should be visible above the container soil or the B&B soil ball (Figure 5.1). When a tree is placed too deeply in the container, the bud union is likely to be covered during cultivation or harvesting of B&B stock (Figure 5.3). If this error is not detected and corrected in the planting process, the tree will be planted too deeply.

The roots of container plants should also be inspected. Container culture can be very stressful for plants. The soil may dry out or be poorly drained. Temperature extremes are common, with container soils reaching temperatures below 10°F or above 104°F. Both extremes are fatal to roots. High temperatures often eliminate roots on the south and west side of an exposed container (Ingram 1981). If the container is moved to a garden center or installation site and another side is exposed, the plant may lose a significant portion of its roots.

An additional health concern is plant size. Transplanting large trees is not a new practice, but its popularity has increased primarily because of the development of tree-moving machines. The increase in the size of the trees being transplanted has also increased the period of establishment for many plantings. A transplanted tree is considered established when it restores its former root:shoot ratio. Because more than 90 percent of the root system is lost during field harvest of nursery stock, it may take years for the plant to recover its root mass and assume its former root:shoot ratio.

The general rule of one year for establishment for every inch of caliper means that increasing the size of the tree will dramatically increase the time period for post-transplant care (Watson 1985). A two-inch caliper tree will become established in two growing seasons. An eight-inch caliper tree will take eight years to become established, considerably lengthening the period during which the tree is stressed by the transplant operation and is susceptible to other short-term and contributing stresses. Thus, the increase in transplanting size may only provide short-term gains. Within a short time—five to ten years—a properly transplanted three-

Is trunk flare showing?

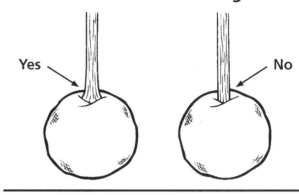

If trunk flare is not showing, open the burlap to find the flare. If the flare is buried in the soil ball, you will have to plant the tree higher in the hole.

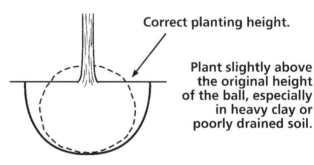

Correct planting height.

Plant slightly above the original height of the ball, especially in heavy clay or poorly drained soil.

Figure 5.3 ▪ Location of the trunk flare on a balled-and-burlapped plant. The trunk flare should be clearly visible at the top of the ball.

International Society of Arboriculture

or four-inch caliper tree may reach a size similar to that of a larger diameter tree planted at the same time.

Transplanting Methods

Planting appears to be a relatively easy and uncomplicated task. Most people have planted a tree or shrub at some time and had it live for at least the growing season—a common but misleading measure of success. Planting, while not extremely complicated, does require attention to detail to ensure the plant thrives for decades. Plant decline, even years after transplanting, can be traced back to improper installation.

Proper planting involves more than just construction of the planting site. While preparing the site is critical to the success of the transplant, two other steps are equally important: storage of the plant material prior to planting and transporting the material to the site. The four common transplanting techniques each have their own requirements for storage, delivery, and installation. A summary of each will be given.

The four common methods used for transplanting are **bare-root**, **container**, balled-and-burlapped, and tree spade. Bare-root plants are grown in the field, then harvested, transported, and installed without soil around the roots. The material may be stored and transported with the root system enclosed in a plastic bag. The bag may also contain moisture-retaining material such as sphagnum moss, shredded newsprint, or shingletow. Bare-root plants with the roots enclosed are referred to as "packaged bare-root."

Container plants are sold with the root system confined to a container. This is the most common method for shrubs and small trees. Container plants may be **container-grown**, **containerized**, or field potted. Container-grown plants are grown in a container throughout their entire production cycle. Generally, plants are transferred to increasingly larger containers during production, but the roots are always growing in a container and remain confined. Containerized plants are grown in the field, harvested bare-root, and placed in a container for sale. Field-potted plants are grown in the field, harvested along with the field soil, and placed in a container (usually biodegradable) for sale. Container-grown and containerized plants are placed in a wide variety of containers—from rigid plastic to polybags. Another type of container is the fabric container (also called "grow bag"). The fabric container is placed in the soil and the plant is grown under field conditions. The fabric limits the size of the roots that can penetrate the surrounding soil. As explained previously, this technique reduces the number of encircling roots and creates a more compact root system. The fabric bag must be removed before planting.

Balled-and-burlapped plants are grown in the field and harvested with the field soil. The soil ball is supported by burlap pulled tight with pinning nails and laced with twine; large soil balls are given additional support with a wire basket. The B&B method is usually used with larger shrubs and trees, but is also used for plants such as yews (*Taxus* spp.) that do not adapt well to containers. The plant is installed with the burlap, and often the wire basket, still in place. Problems can occur if the burlap has been treated to resist decay or is made of plastic. Plant failures have also been traced to the use of plastic twine that was not removed during planting. The use of wire baskets has also been a concern (this issue will be addressed in the section on planting specifications).

Sometimes bare-root plants have soil placed around their roots and the soil is held by burlap. This is called a manufactured ball. These plants should be avoided because the soil is held too loosely for proper root development.

Tree spades have become very popular in the last decade, due to the desire on the part of many landscape clients for "instant shade." Tree spades (or tree-moving machines) use hydraulically or screw-driven blades to harvest and move a tree with a soil plug intact. Spades come in a wide variety of sizes—from 24-inch-diameter clamshells that can be attached to bobcats, to self-propelled machines with blades capable of digging holes 16 feet in diameter and 5 feet deep. Trees moved by a tree spade either have been field grown in a nursery or are already established in a landscape. Occasionally trees are moved from a forest site.

Although tree spades are an excellent means of transplanting plants, they are not problem free. Generally less than four percent of the original root system is retained in the plug. Most tree spades are capable of lifting a larger plant than can be successfully moved with an adequate root volume retained in the soil plug. Problems may also occur when trees are moved from an established landscape rather than a nursery. These trees may not have a defined root system, or may not have been otherwise prepared for the transplant operation. Additional limitations will be covered in the section on planting specifications.

Holding and Planting Specifications for Bare-Root Plants

Bare-root plants must be stored in a controlled environment. Because of their inability to absorb water, desiccation can be a major problem. Plants are stored **dormant** and at temperatures slightly above or below freezing, but should not be permitted to continuously freeze and thaw. Storage at subfreezing temperatures (28° F) appears to improve transplant success for many species and helps reduce mold problems (Englert, Fuchigami, and Chen 1993). Relative humidity should generally be kept above 95 percent to further reduce moisture loss. As much as possible, these conditions should be maintained during delivery and handling. Most nurseries ship bare-root plants in wax-coated boxes with roots covered in a moisture-holding material and enclosed in plastic. Except for a brief inspection, the plants should remain in the box until planting.

Bare-root plants should be planted while dormant. In the southern regions of the United States, bare-root plants can be installed from late autumn to early spring. Winter conditions are often favorable for some root growth. Bare-root planting is limited to the early spring in northern sections of the United States and most of Canada. In addition, some plants such as birch (*Betula* spp.) and oak (*Quercus* spp.) require sweating before being planted. Sweating forces the buds to begin expanding. If the buds do not expand, root growth is delayed and survival is decreased.

The roots of bare-root plants must be kept moist during installation. If the root system dries during that time, the plant may not survive. Roots may be coated with a mud slurry to protect them during the time from the box to the planting site. A number of commercial products are also available to reduce moisture loss from the root system.

The planting hole should already be prepared so as to reduce the amount of time that the plant's roots are exposed. The hole should be at least three times the diameter of the root system and as deep or slightly shallower. If the plant contains one exceptionally long root, it is much better to cut the root cleanly than bend it to fit the hole. The plant should be positioned so that the trunk flare is slightly above ground level. The soil should be placed around the roots and water applied when about one-third of the backfill has been added (Figure 5.4)(Ball and Graper 1993a).

Holding and Planting Specifications for Container Plants

Container plants should be given more care during holding than they usually receive. Unless the plant is in a pot-in-the-pot system or an above-ground-system (AGS) container, the container soil will be exposed to extremes in temperature. If the south side of the container is exposed to the sun, the soil on that side may reach lethal temperatures (above 104° F). If the container is continually rotated as it moves from the wholesale nursery to the re-wholesaler to the landscape site, many of the roots may be killed. Containers should be held in an area away from exposure to direct summer sun.

If the plant is in a biodegradable container that has not been treated with a copper compound to reduce encircling roots, the container itself may be planted. All other types of containers should be removed just before installa-

tion. However, it is usually better to remove even biodegradable containers because the material may interfere with movement of moisture from the surrounding soil into the container.

Because the entire root system is retained, container plants may be planted throughout the growing season. There are a few guidelines, however. Containerized plant materials are best planted from summer to autumn. If the bare-root plant was placed in the container in early spring, it may not be established in the container until mid-season. Container evergreens planted during mid-autumn may experience significant winter injury (Ball 1987). If the plants are transplanted late in the growing season, planting stress may reduce their winterhardiness.

A common recommendation is to slice off or tease out the peripheral roots of a container soil ball. This is done to eliminate encircling roots (Swanson et al. 1989). However, slicing or teasing the roots does not always increase root growth and may even decrease it in some instances (Blessing and Dana 1988). The planting hole should be at least three times the diameter of the container and as deep or slightly shallower (Figure 5.5) (Ball and Graper 1993b).

Holding and Planting Specifications for Balled-and-Burlapped Plants

Balled-and-burlapped plants should be stored with the soil balls covered by wood chips or other porous material. If soil balls are exposed, the soil will dry out and be subject to temperature extremes. Such exposure may

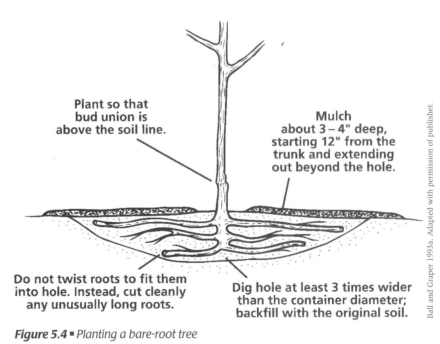

Plant so that bud union is above the soil line.

Mulch about 3 – 4" deep, starting 12" from the trunk and extending out beyond the hole.

Do not twist roots to fit them into hole. Instead, cut cleanly any unusually long roots.

Dig hole at least 3 times wider than the container diameter; backfill with the original soil.

Figure 5.4 ▪ *Planting a bare-root tree*

Ball and Graper 1993a. Adapted with permission of publisher.

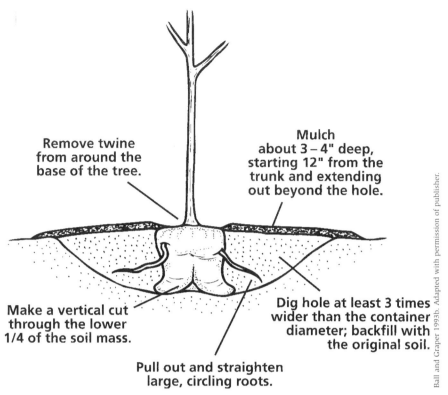

Remove twine from around the base of the tree.

Mulch about 3 – 4" deep, starting 12" from the trunk and extending out beyond the hole.

Make a vertical cut through the lower 1/4 of the soil mass.

Dig hole at least 3 times wider than the container diameter; backfill with the original soil.

Pull out and straighten large, circling roots.

Ball and Graper 1993b. Adapted with permission of publisher.

Figure 5.5 ▪ *Planting a container tree*

result in a reduction in new roots generated from the severed roots—which may delay establishment. When transporting the B&B stock from storage to the site, protect the tree canopies from the wind. This is usually done by covering the plant or shipping it in a climate-controlled truck. Storage conditions at the site should be similar to those at the nursery, with the soil balls covered if the material is not installed that same day. If the planting is delayed for more than one day, the canopies should be untied.

Balled-and-burlapped plants are generally harvested in the spring until budbreak, with harvest resuming after budset. They can be planted throughout the growing season, although there are some species considerations. Ideally, transplanting would be timed to the period of rapid root growth for a species. The optimum time for transplanting varies among species. For example, yews (*Taxus* spp.) generate the most roots in the spring (Lathrop and Mecklenburg 1971). Ponderosa pine (*Pinus ponderosa*) initiates new roots only in the spring, although root elongation occurs during most of the growing season (Stone and Schubert 1959). Many **deciduous** trees have reduced survival rates if moved just prior to budbreak (Farmer 1975).

Balled-and-burlapped plants should be planted in a hole at least three times the diameter of the soil ball

and as deep as or slightly shallower than the ball. The top of the ball should be carefully examined for the trunk flare and, in the case of budded trees, the bud union should be clearly visible above the ball (Figure 5.3). If the trunk flare and bud union are not visible, the tree may be placed too low in the ball. Some guides advocate removing the wire basket during the planting operation because of concern that the wire will remain for many years and possibly **girdle** the expanding roots (Feucht 1986). While it is true that wire baskets may remain intact for a decade or more, and roots do grow into the wire, there is little evidence that this significantly harms the plant (Goodwin and Lumis 1992). However, there are no advantages to keeping the wire basket once the plant is placed into the hole, so many planting guides suggest removing part or all of the basket. If removing just part of the basket, cut away the upper part of the basket because this is where many of the roots will be generated. To provide stability, the basket must not be removed or cut away until the plant is placed in the hole.

Regardless of how much of the basket is removed, the burlap should be pulled back from the top of the soil ball because burlap can interfere with water movement. The burlap along the sides and base of the ball may be left on; this usually decays within the first growing season. The only exception is treated or synthetic burlap, which must always be completely removed because it does not deteriorate and will prevent root expansion and water movement. All twine (natural or synthetic) should be removed from around the base of the plant. Otherwise, it may girdle the stem (Figure 5.6)(Ball and Graper 1993c).

Holding and Planting Specifications for Tree-Spaded Plants

Tree-spaded plants cannot be easily stored, so they are harvested and planted as one operation. Sometimes trees are tagged a year before transplanting and are root pruned with the spade in preparation for the transplanting. If the spade used to root prune is the same size as the one that will be used to harvest, then root pruning

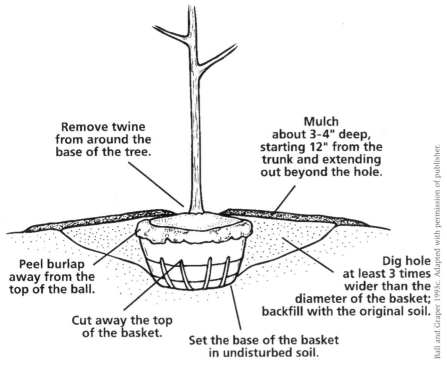

Remove twine from around the base of the tree.

Mulch about 3-4" deep, starting 12" from the trunk and extending out beyond the hole.

Peel burlap away from the top of the ball.

Cut away the top of the basket.

Set the base of the basket in undisturbed soil.

Dig hole at least 3 times wider than the diameter of the basket; backfill with the original soil.

Ball and Graper 1993c. Adapted with permission of publisher.

Figure 5.6 ▪ *Planting a balled-and-burlapped tree*

is not beneficial and can even be detrimental to the transplanting. After root pruning, new roots generate near the end of the severed root (Watson and Himelick 1983). Root pruning and transplanting with the same size of spade means that the newer roots are severed by the transplant operation. Therefore, it is better to root prune several years before transplanting and do so with a smaller spade, or not root prune at all.

Tree spades can be used to transplant trees throughout the growing season. Trees moved in the spring have a higher survival rate than autumn transplants (Walvatne 1983). Summer transplanting can also be difficult due to the increased moisture stress. However, many trees are successfully moved during this time. As already discussed under balled-and-burlapped holding and planting specifications, there are species differences in the optimum time for transplanting.

Most spaded trees are planted in a hole dug by the spade, but there are two potential problems with this practice. First, in clay soils, the sides of the hole may become glazed and less permeable for root penetration from the plug. Second, air gaps may occur between the plug and the sides of the hole because the plug and hole dimensions rarely are an exact match— even if the same machine is used. These problems can be avoided by excavating the hole with a backhoe or trencher rather than with a tree spade. However, it is

usually much quicker to use the spade to dig the hole. To reduce the problems occurring with a spade-dug hole, the sides of the hole should be roughed and a slurry of water and soil placed in the gap between the plug and the surrounding soil as the spade blades are retracted.

It is difficult to dig a planting hole three times the size of the transplanted root system of a large tree, so the area around the hole is sometimes broken up with a rototiller to ease root penetration. The plug should always be positioned so it is slightly above the surrounding soil (Figure 5.7)(Ball and Graper 1993d).

General Planting Specifications

Certain practices are common, regardless of the method of transplanting. The planting hole should always be larger than the present root system, and the sides of the hole should be sloped rather than vertical. The plant should also be set so the trunk flare is slightly higher than the surrounding soil. This is a major change from the recommendations in many planting guides in which the planting hole is shown deeper than the root system but not much wider. The primary purpose for the creation of a larger planting hole is to provide a medium that is more porous, which will increase the oxygen diffusion rate and reduce mechanical resistance. The sloped sides will direct roots that are not able to penetrate into the undisturbed soil (Watson, Kupkowski, and von der Heide-Spravka 1992). The soil removed from the planting hole should be put back into the hole after the plant is placed. It was once a common recommendation to fill the planting hole with a mix of **soil amendments** such as topsoil, sphagnum peat, leaf compost, finely shredded bark, composted manure, or sand. Research has not shown any significant benefit to this practice (Hummel and Johnson 1985; Smalley and Wood 1995; Watson, Kupkowski, and von der Heide-Spravka 1993). The use of amendments may even be detrimental in certain circumstances, decreasing drainage caused by textural differences between the amendments and the surrounding soil (Whitcomb 1987) or producing nitrogen deficiencies as the organic amendments decompose (Wood et al. 1994).

It was also a common practice to create a "saucer" around the edge of the planting hole. This was done to hold moisture near the base of the plant. While this practice provides some benefits for the first week or two after planting, the roots will soon expand into the surrounding soil, requiring the irrigation area to be expanded if the benefits are to continue. In addition, retaining water near the base of the plant may increase disease problems. Therefore, saucers should not be used, or left for a short time only.

Mulching

All plants benefit from mulching. The forest floor is usually covered with a layer of litter rather than the grass typically found at most planting sites. **Mulches** help conserve soil moisture, increase **infiltration** of water, and moderate soil temperatures. They also reduce **competition** with **herbaceous** plants and the possibility of lower-trunk injury from mowers and string-trimmers. Although mulches should be a part of most plantings, they can create problems. They can increase the air temperature above the surface (Einert, Guidry, and Huneycutt 1975); they can also keep soils too cool, create a favorable habitat for rodents, and increase fire hazard.

The best mulches are organic, leaf, and shredded bark compost because they provide nutrients as they decompose. The concern that organic mulches may slow nitrification appears to be unfounded (Greenly and Rakow 1995). Organic mulches, however, do not appear to reduce **soil pH**. Shredded hardwood and pine mulches did not lower pH in the upper two inches of soil over a two-year period (Greenly and Rakow 1995; Watson and Kupkowski 1991).

Mulch should be maintained at a depth of three to four inches. The depth may increase over the years because mulch is often replenished at a faster rate than it decomposes. This buildup of mulch to eight or ten inches generally is due to the desire of the client to have the mulch appear "fresh" and to suffocate **weeds**. This buildup does not significantly reduce soil oxygen levels (Watson and Kupkowski 1991), but it can slow the warming of the soil in the spring—thereby reducing root growth (Greenly and Rakow 1995). A mulch-free area should be maintained within six inches of the stem to discourage rodents and allow the trunk flare to dry. The mulch area should extend at least one or two feet beyond the planting hole because the roots may expand that far or farther within the first growing season. The increased area of mulch provides favorable conditions for continued root expansion and establishment.

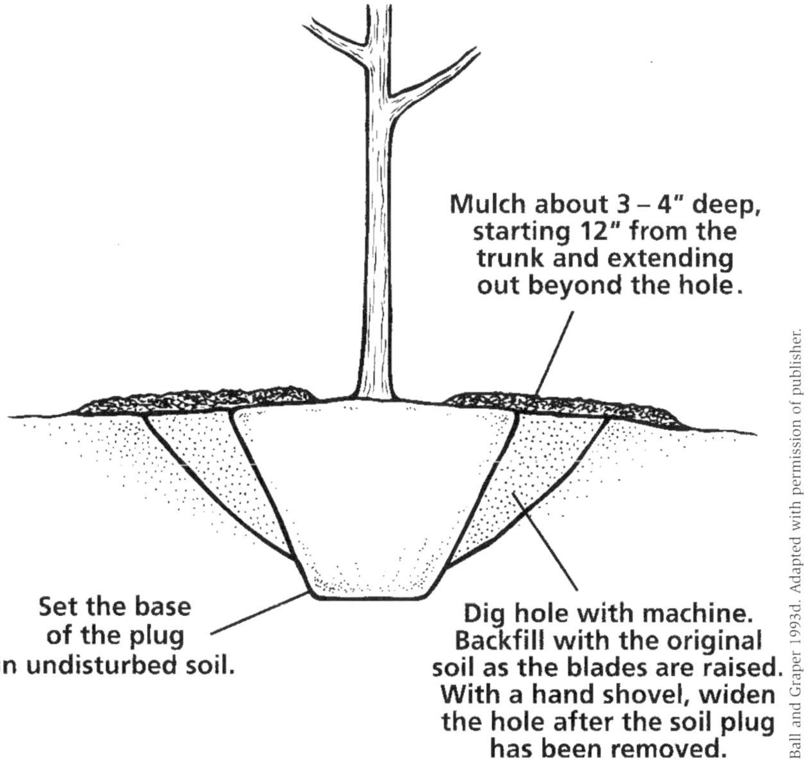

Tree Staking

Staking is a necessary part of many transplanting operations, but it can also retard the development of stem taper and can girdle the stem. Stakes should be used only as a temporary measure and be removed within the first year. The only exception to this general rule is the extended need to support large transplanted trees with guying.

The two most important considerations are staking height and material. The ideal height is between one-third and two-thirds the height of the stem (Leiser and Kemper 1968). Support at two-thirds the height or higher will retard the development of proper taper, thus reducing future stability of the stem and increasing the likelihood that the upper stem and crown will snap off

Mulch about 3 – 4" deep, starting 12" from the trunk and extending out beyond the hole.

Set the base of the plug in undisturbed soil.

Dig hole with machine. Backfill with the original soil as the blades are raised. With a hand shovel, widen the hole after the soil plug has been removed.

Ball and Graper 1993d. Adapted with permission of publisher.

Figure 5.7 ▪ *Planting a tree with a tree-moving machine*

because the entire stem cannot move with the wind. The second concern is the material used to support the tree. Wooden stakes are preferred to metal stakes. Although the choice of material does not affect tree establishment, if the stake is broken off, a metal base may interfere with future removal of the tree and stump grinding.

Two stakes should be used to prevent the stem from rubbing against a single stake. The most common support material is wire covered with a rubber hose. This material, however, can support the tree too tightly, interfering with normal stem formation and girdling the stem if left on for more than a growing season (Feucht and Butler 1988). A better choice is a cloth strip about two inches wide. This provides a wider surface to support the tree, and the material is more flexible—which allows for more movement. Also, a cloth strip will deteriorate over time, thereby eliminating the problems caused by leaving the tree staked for too long.

Tree Wrapping

Wrapping the stem of young trees after transplanting is not recommended. Wrapping has not been proven to reduce **sunscald** or **frost cracks**, the two most common reasons given for this practice (Litzow and Pellett 1983). In fact, wrapping has been shown to create two problems. First, most young stems contain **chlorophyll** and make a minor contribution to **photosynthate** production. Wrapping eliminates this source of photosynthates. Second, wrapping provides a favorable environment for insects (particularly borers) and several diseases. The only real benefit to wrapping is winter protection from rodents. If wrapping is used for this purpose, it should be in place only during the dormant season.

Post-Transplant Care and Maintenance

Until the plant becomes established, it will benefit from additional care. Too often transplanting is viewed as a single operation that ends when the plant is in the ground. The transplant operation does not truly end until the plant becomes established. The three most common post-transplant and establishment care operations are irrigation, fertilization, and pruning.

Irrigation

Irrigation is often necessary during establishment, when the root system is not sufficient to support the canopy without supplemental watering. Container-grown plants may have only a one- or two-day supply of water in the container medium. Such plants will need frequent irrigation after transplanting. After the growing season, almost half the roots may still remain in the container medium (Gilman 1990). Consequently, for many container-grown plants, the need to carefully monitor watering may continue for more than two growing seasons. Field-grown plants (bare-root, B&B, and tree-spaded) retain between two and eight percent of their original root system. These plants will be under moisture stress until they become established. Root growth for many trees and shrubs is approximately $1\frac{1}{2}$ to $3\frac{1}{2}$ feet per year (Gilman 1990). Post-transplant irrigation provided in an expanding zone around the plant will ensure adequate moisture to support root elongation. Drought conditions may necessitate irrigation for established plants.

Fertilization

Manipulating the availability of organic and inorganic minerals to enhance plant growth and appearance has been a long-accepted practice in plant care and arboriculture. Numerous products available in commercial and homeowner markets purport to make plants healthy by "feeding" them many different mineral compounds via soil application, foliar sprays, or direct injection into the xylem of the woody plant materials. The term "feeding" is a significant misnomer. Mineral nutrients enhance the well being of plants but do not serve as a direct source of energy. Plants use light and carbon dioxide to create the photosynthate they use as food. Mineral nutrients for plants are more analogous to the use of vitamins by humans. Vitamins supplement our diets, allowing us to use the energy contained within our food for growth, maintenance, and repair. Fertilization can enhance the well being of plants if mineral nutrients are limited or unavailable in their environments.

As discussed in Chapter 4, the **essential elements** for tree growth are hydrogen, carbon, oxygen, nitrogen, phosphorus, potassium, calcium, sulfur, magnesium, copper, manganese, iron, boron, chlorine, zinc, and molybdenum. Hydrogen and oxygen are supplied by water, and carbon and oxygen are supplied by air. The other elements for plant growth are absorbed from the soil by the tree's roots. Trees need relatively large amounts of the **macronutrients** (major elements) nitrogen, phosphorus, potassium, calcium, sulfur, and magnesium. Trees require relatively smaller amounts of the micronutrients (trace elements) copper, manganese, iron, boron, chlorine, zinc, and molybdenum.

Depending on what particular mineral is deficient, **chlorosis**, **stunting**, or **necrosis** of plant tissue can occur. Leaves of poorly nourished plants may be smaller or discolored, or may prematurely drop; fruits may abort or not form; and vegetative and root growth may be reduced. Generally, nutrient deficiencies of mobile elements (i.e., elements that can be translocated from one tissue to another) such as nitrogen, phosphorus, magnesium, and potassium appear in older leaves first, whereas nonmobile mineral deficiencies are first seen in younger leaves (Kozlowski, Kramer, and Pallardy 1991).

Trees in native forests (where they grow naturally from seed) survive well without additional fertilization. In fact, research has shown that moderate nitrogen limitation is the normal condition for forest trees (Chapin 1980), the growth of which often increases in response to nitrogen fertilization (Auchmoody 1982; McCullough and Kulman 1991; Van Cleve and Oliver 1982). It is interesting to note that these native trees germinated, established, and competed quite successfully in their environments without fertilization.

When considering fertilization in the frame of plant health in landscape situations, complex issues arise. Is rapid growth always correlated with good plant health? Fertilization increased the growth of trees in the example above, but does increased growth equate to increased plant health? Until recently, answers to these questions were assumed to be self-evident. Anyone could tell that a lush, rapidly growing plant was healthy. New research is providing insight into whether this statement is entirely accurate. Increasing the growth of otherwise healthy trees often increases their susceptibility to insect and disease problems and decreases their tolerance to stress (see Chapter 3).

We fertilize in the landscape to enhance the appearance and promote the health of plants. However, to most effectively incorporate fertilization into a Plant Health Care program, we must fully understand the impact of fertilization on whole plant physiology. The plant, stress, and pest **complex** issues discussed in Chapter 3 illustrate the complexity of the issues surrounding cultural manipulation and its influence on plant health.

In many cases, plants in the urban environment grow under much less than ideal conditions, and fertilization is warranted. Topsoil is often removed from planting sites, and the remaining subsoil is frequently low in **organic matter** and nutrient content. Furthermore, the natural cycling of nutrients that occurs in the forest as leaf litter accumulates and subsequently decomposes is interrupted in landscapes as grass clippings, leaves, and other detritus are collected and removed from the planting site.

The information that follows can serve as a base for Plant Health Care practitioners, with the understanding that each situation is unique. Blanket fertilization cannot be part of an effective Plant Health Care program. Only after the need for fertilization is determined through proper **diagnosis** should the appropriate treatment be prescribed and administered. Many of the plant clinics and universities listed in Appendix A can test for nutrient deficiencies or excesses. Contact your local university, Cooperative Extension office, or government department of agriculture if a clinic is not listed for your region.

Symbiotic relationships and tree nutrition ▪ A number of tree species (including *Alnus, Cercis, Cladrastis, Gleditsia, Gymnocladus, Robinia,* and *Sophora*) are legumes and thus have a symbiotic relationship with naturally occurring **bacteria**. The bacteria, which form nodules on the fine roots of the plants, collect nitrogen from the atmosphere and convert it into plant-usable forms. These symbiotic bacteria allow the trees to survive and flourish in nitrogen-poor environments; hence, some of these species are commonly used in land reclamation projects (Salisbury and Ross 1985).

Trees also have mutualistic relationships with fungi called **mycorhizae**. Mycorhizae are soil-borne fungi that surround and penetrate root tissues. The fungi are nourished by sugars produced by the plants, and in turn help the plant absorb water and nutrients—especially nutrients that are immobile in the soil, particularly phosphorus (Koide 1991). All tree species in natural systems maintain relationships with mycorhizae (Iyer, Corey, and Wilde 1980).

The potential use of mycorhizae in disturbed soils was discussed by Marx and Schenk (1983) as far back as the early 1980s. Recent studies have examined the impact of mycorhizae on trees planted in disturbed urban soils. These studies have shown that mycorhizae may also enhance uptake of micronutrients such as iron (Hauer and Dawson 1996). Other studies have examined the potential of inoculating disturbed urban soils with mycorhizae to alleviate nutrient-limiting conditions (Smiley, Marx, and Fraedrich 1997). The results are promising. However, long-term assessment is still needed to ascertain the effectiveness and potential effects that inoculations may have upon plants and native mycorhizae.

Determining fertilizer needs ▪ The need for tree fertilization can be determined by several methods. The most common is visual observation of plant vitality.

An awareness of what constitutes normal leaf size and color, as well as an understanding of the growth rate of the particular species, is critical. Many factors can result in deviations from the norm, including nutrient deficiencies. However, compacted and/or waterlogged soil, drought, temperature extremes, air pollution, excessive salts in the root zone, insects, and diseases can all produce **symptoms** that may be confused with nutrient deficiency. Proper diagnosis is the first step in developing an appropriate treatment strategy. If a factor other than nutrient availability is causing the symptoms, then plants in the landscape will not respond to fertilization (Neely 1980; Perry and Hickman 1992).

Soil and foliar testing ▪ Testing soil nutrients is another method to determine tree fertilizer needs. Standard soil tests conducted by commercial laboratories and those at many land-grant universities provide soil pH, available phosphorus and potash levels, and **cation exchange capacity** (CEC). Many labs will also test for micronutrients, soil organic matter, **soil structure**, bulk density, and other soil characteristics for an additional fee when a more detailed knowledge of the soil is required.

Results of soil tests are helpful in selecting tree species appropriate for a particular site. (Appendix B contains tree selection guidelines based on soil pH and other site conditions). This is especially significant because adjusting soil pH is extremely difficult. If soil adjustment in existing plantings is desired, applications of lime to raise the pH or sulfur to lower the pH can be attempted. Specialized fertilizer formulations are available for use in adverse soil pH conditions.

Foliar testing is a very effective technique to diagnose the nutrient status of a tree. While soil testing provides information about the presence and availability of nutrients in the soil, tissue analysis provides information about which nutrients the plant has been able to absorb and which nutrients are actually deficient. Together, soil and foliar analyses are powerful diagnostic tools. They provide information to determine the exact nature of the nutrient deficiency and whether the deficiency is due to limited concentrations of the nutrients in the soil, or to environmental factors (for example, high pH) that may prevent the plant from acquiring nutrients that are otherwise present in adequate amounts. This information is critical for determining the correct course of action to correct the deficiency (Kopinga and van den Burg 1995).

The interpretation of tissue tests depends on the species tested, the season of sampling, and tissue position within the canopy, as well as the age of the leaf tissue being tested. Furthermore, deficiencies of some nutrients may be obvious only in immature leaves (e.g., manganese deficiency in sugar maple), while deficiencies of other elements (e.g., nitrogen and magnesium) show up in older leaves first. Comparing the results of the analysis of symptomatic tissue with those from analysis of "control" foliage collected at the same time and in the same manner from a normal tree can greatly aid in the interpretation of results. Many laboratories that perform soil tests are also equipped to handle foliar analysis.

As with any recommendations, a local branch of the Cooperative Extension Service or government departments of agriculture can provide additional information on fertilizer formulations appropriate for specific sites, once a diagnosis or determination of fertilizer need is made.

Nutrient availability and fertilization ▪ Most soils are not deficient in phosphorus. The phosphorus content of soils routinely exceeds 200 pounds per acre. Application of phosphorus is recommended if soil testing indicates less than 60 pounds of P_2O_5 (phosphoric acid) per acre. Four pounds of P_2O_5 per acre is necessary to increase phosphorus content by one pound per acre.

Likewise, most soils are not deficient in potassium, which routinely exceeds 300 pounds per acre. Plants may respond to potassium fertilization if soil testing indicates that potash levels are below 156 pounds of K_2O (potash) per acre. An application of nine pounds of K_2O per acre is necessary to increase potassium content by one pound per acre.

Nitrogen is the most common element in the atmosphere, but is unavailable to plants in this form. Decomposing organic matter is the primary source of nitrogen for trees growing in natural ecosystems. Urban soils are often low in organic matter, and thus may require supplemental applications of nitrogen. Studies at The Ohio State University indicate that three pounds of nitrogen per 1,000 square feet of treated area is adequate to maintain tree health in most landscape situations. On extremely nitrogen-deficient soils, the rate can be increased to five to six pounds per 1,000 square feet per year (Smith and Gilliam 1978).

Trees should be fertilized only when naturally occurring nutrient levels are limiting to tree growth and vitality. Unnecessary or excessive applications of fertilizer can cause problems. Root damage, possible contamination of ground and surface waters, and pond or lake **eutrification** are some of the most common problems associated with the excess application of fertilizer. Trees growing on sites with intensive lawn care programs are likely receiving between four and six pounds of nitrogen per 1,000 square feet per year, and generally will not require additional fertilization.

Fertilizer selection ▪ Fertilizers are classified as inorganic, natural organic, and synthetic organic. Inorganic fertilizers originate from nonliving sources, such as rock and mineral deposits, or they may be chemically produced. Natural organic fertilizers originate in animals and plants. Synthetic organic fertilizers are carbon-based, manufactured chemicals.

Perhaps the most commonly cited difference between classes of fertilizers is their effect on the physical properties of soils. Organic fertilizers are **humus** forming and, as such, improve a soil's **aeration**, **water-holding capacity**, and **friability**. Such improvements in soil physical properties are favorable for tree growth. Inorganic fertilizers do not appreciably change soil physical properties.

The nutrients in inorganic fertilizers readily dissociate into their ionic forms when placed in water. This means that immediately or shortly after application, the nutrients are absorbed and used by plants or bind to soil particles. The presence of organic matter and clay increases the ability of the soil to bind nutrients and thus prevent their loss through **leaching**.

Fertilizers with readily available nutrients are considered "hot," which means there is potential for fertilizer burn to the roots if excessive amounts are applied. Natural organic fertilizers usually release nutrients slowly, which reduces the chance of fertilizer burn. Synthetic organic fertilizers can be formulated for slow or fast release of nutrients.

Fertilizer grade refers to the guaranteed percentage of mineral nutrients in a fertilizer. Single-grade fertilizers contain just one nutrient. Examples of single grade fertilizers are urea (44-0-0), ammonium nitrate (33-0-0), superphosphate (0-20-0), and muriate of potash (0-0-60). Mixed-grade fertilizers provide more than one nutrient. Examples are potassium phosphate (0-15-40) and diammonium phosphate (20-53-0).

Complete fertilizers contain all three primary nutrients: nitrogen, phosphorus, and potassium. Examples of complete fertilizers are 10-6-4, 12-12-12, and 5-10-5. A fertilizer with a grade of 10-20-10 contains 10 percent nitrogen, 20 percent phosphorus, and 10 percent potassium by weight. A 100-pound bag of 10-20-10 fertilizer contains 40 pounds of the primary nutrients.

Fertilizer ratio is the relative proportion of the primary macronutrients to each other. A 10-10-10 fertilizer has a ratio of 1:1:1, and a 5-10-5 fertilizer has a ratio of 1:2:1. Fertilizer ratio is important when customizing a fertilizer application based on soil test results. For example, if a soil test indicates the need for nitrogen, phosphorus, and potassium in a proportion of 2:1:1, fertilizers with such grades as 30-15-15, 20-10-10, or 10-5-5 will provide appropriate combinations of nutrients.

Fertilizer efficiency refers to the proportion of nutrients applied that are actually available, absorbed, and used by plants. Fertilizer efficiency is affected by environmental conditions, soil chemistry, volatilization, leaching, and **fixation**. Volatilization is an important factor with some nitrogen sources. Ammonium fertilizers will **volatilize** into ammonia gas at high temperatures, thus reducing their effectiveness as fertilizers. Leaching is another factor that must be considered before using fertilizer in some soils. Leaching results when dissolved nutrients are moved through the soil and out of the root zone by water, making the nutrient unavailable for tree utilization. Leached nutrients frequently contaminate ground and surface water.

Leaching is affected by a soil's cation exchange capacity. [The CEC is a measure of the soil's ability to bind nutrients in particular cations (positively charged ions) such as magnesium, calcium, potassium, iron, and manganese.] Ammonium nitrogen carries a positive charge and is thus less susceptible to leaching than is nitrate nitrogen. Soils with low CECs are more susceptible to nutrient leaching [CEC values less than 10 meq (milliequivalents) are considered low, and values more than 25 meq are high]. Coarse-textured (sandy) soils have low CECs, and nutrients in these soils are subject to leaching. Soils with high levels of clay or organic matter have higher CECs and are much less susceptible to leaching. A soil's CEC should be considered when selecting a fertilizer. Slow- or controlled-release fertilizers that release nitrogen in ammonium form are recommended for use on soils with a low cation exchange capacities.

The number of commercially available controlled-release fertilizers has increased. Differences in the release characteristics of the various products allow them to be categorized into three classes: coated water-**soluble** materials, inorganic materials of low water solubility, and organic materials of low water solubility that are decomposed by chemical hydrolysis and/or biological activity.

The mechanism for the release of the nitrogen varies between each class, and responses differ with soil conditions, such as pH, moisture, and temperature. Physical properties of the fertilizers, such as particle size and coating thickness, also influence the release mechanism.

Timing of fertilizer application ▪ Nutrients are absorbed by plants during times of root growth. Roots can grow and function even when the tops of the plants appear dormant. Although roots can absorb nutrients in the fall and winter months as long as the soil is not frozen, the uptake of nutrients is affected by soil temperature: the lower the soil temperature, the slower the nutrient uptake. The uptake of nutrients by trees is also reduced when soil temperatures exceed 104° F.

Soil conditions and plant growth patterns indicate that late summer and early fall applications of fertilizer are often more efficient than early spring applications. Spring applications are subject to excessive leaching by rain. Research indicates that early spring growth is due to accumulated and stored nutrients (Kozlowski 1971). Spring and early summer applications of fertilizer will not increase the growth of woody plants with determinate growth, which is regulated by the embryonic shoots in their buds. However, on deficient soils, fertilizing may improve leaf color and overall plant appearance, as well as growth the following year.

The relationship between the time of nutrient **absorption** and plant growth patterns can vary among species (Hershey and Paul 1983; Weinbaum, Merwin, and Muraoka 1978). It is also important to remember that fertilizer formulation affects the pattern of nutrient uptake.

Fertilizer application methods and precautions ▪ Fertilizers should be applied where tree roots are present, which can extend several feet beyond the dripline of the tree (Figure 5.8). The area of application should be extended farther out from the dripline for trees with upright growth habits or trees growing in areas with heavy root competition from surrounding trees.

Nitrogen, potassium, boron, **chelated** micronutrients, and molybdenum can be effectively applied directly to the soil surface. Dry fertilizers may be applied by broadcasting by hand, or with drop or rotary fertilizer spreaders. Liquid formulations can be sprayed over the surface. Avoid uneven fertilizer distribution by dividing the fertilizer to be applied into two equal parts and applying them separately. Be sure to wash fertilizer from foliage to prevent fertilizer burn. When making surface applications, do not apply more than three pounds of actual nitrogen per 1,000 square feet. Higher **concentrations** can injure turf. When turf is present and fertilizers are applied by surface application, irrigate the treated area immediately after application.

Phosphorus and other nutrients that do not readily move through the soil should be applied by methods that **incorporate** them into the root zone. This can be done by making holes in the soil with a punch bar or auger and filling them with dry fertilizers or injecting water-soluble fertilizers or **suspensions** of fertilizer into

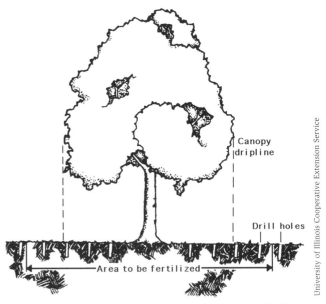

Figure 5.8 ▪ *Apply fertilizers several feet beyond the dripline of the tree*

the soil with the aid of high-pressure equipment. Begin the holes at least two feet from the tree trunk and place them in a grid pattern two to three feet apart extending to three feet beyond the dripline (Figure 5.9). The holes should be 12 to 18 inches deep and at a slight angle. In many cases, phosphorus and other immobile nutrients are not deficient, and this technique offers no nutritional benefits relative to surface applications. However, research has shown that trees growing on compacted, poorly drained soils can benefit from the increased aeration resulting from the holes augered in the soil with this method even if fertilizers are not applied (Smith and Reisch 1975).

Soluble fertilizers are usually applied by liquid injection methods; however, less soluble forms can be used if the application equipment has constant **agitation** that keeps the fertilizer in the storage tank in suspension. Because soluble fertilizers are readily available for plant use, trees respond relatively quickly. Suspensions of less soluble forms of fertilizer, although not immediately available for plant growth, provide plant nutrition over a longer time. A combination of soluble and slow-release forms of fertilizers provides both fast plant response and longer residual activity.

Foliar application of liquid fertilizers is a good way to apply chelated micronutrients such as iron. Because plants respond quickly to foliar application, its results are visible sooner than soil applications of the same fertilizer. However, this method is temporary.

Trunk implantation, also a temporary method, is another way arborists apply fertilizer. This method is used mainly to correct micronutrient deficiencies (iron, manganese, zinc) resulting from decreased uptake of micronutrients due to alkaline soil pH. Many arborists do not like to use this method because it involves drilling holes into otherwise healthy tree trunks, but research has shown that the holes close at the surface of the tree trunk and that trees respond well to this form of micronutrient application (Neely 1976). Practitioners must balance the value of the treatment with potential problems brought about by creating open wounds. Continued injections or implantations over long periods of time can eventually create problems by killing enough plant tissue to cause wounds to coalesce.

Before making a final decision on which fertilizer to obtain and how to apply it, arborists and landscape managers should determine:

- What species are to be fertilized?
- What nutrients are deficient in the plant?
- Why are these nutrients deficient?
- Is the nutrient content of the soil low or is some environmental factor preventing nutrient uptake?
- What are the environmental implications of the application of fertilizer?
- How will the fertilizer application affect overall tree health, including pest resistance and stress tolerance?
- How often will the fertilizer be applied?
- What type of fertilizer application equipment is available?
- What type of fertilizer is available and how much does it cost?

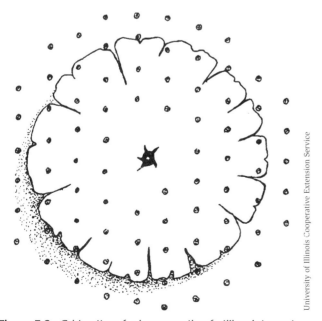

Figure 5.9 ▪ *Grid pattern for incorporating fertilizer into root zone*

University of Illinois Cooperative Extension Service

Answers to these questions will help tree care professionals make the intelligent and workable decisions necessary to fully integrate fertilization into an overall Plant Health Care program.

Pruning

Pruning is one of the least understood and most abused cultural practices. It is also probably the practice that can do the most harm to tree health if the physiology of tree growth is not taken into consideration. Pruning is more than the indiscriminate cutting of limbs and branches. It requires an understanding of the function of the parts of the tree and their impact on overall tree structure. If pruning is done properly, it can improve tree vitality, appearance, and fruitfulness, and will preserve structural integrity. Improper pruning often results in poor plant vitality, unnatural and unsightly tree appearance, and hazardous tree conditions. As with any PHC practice, a proper diagnosis is necessary before pruning should be initiated. This section discusses current pruning philosophies and provides a background on the concepts and principles of pruning as they relate to Plant Health Care. For more specific guidelines and pruning procedures, refer to *Tree-Pruning Guidelines* and the *Arborists' Certification Study Guide* (both published by the International Society of Arboriculture), as well as the American National Standards Institute's A300 Pruning Standard.

Pruning and tree health ▪ Mature trees in natural stands of deciduous and coniferous forests rarely have low branches. Competition for sunlight among trees limits light to only the highest branches, resulting in natural **dieback** and removal of lower, unproductive limbs. A limiting factor on tree vitality in landscape situations (where distances between planting spaces are sufficient to avoid competition among trees) is the shade a tree casts upon itself. Depending upon the species, foliage in the outer canopy may receive a higher light intensity than necessary. Beneath this layer, another layer of foliage may receive adequate light for optimum photosynthesis and, farther into the canopy, a third layer may receive insufficient light for photosynthesis (Chapman and Gower 1991). Branches in this interior layer may begin to decline in vitality as the **light compensation point** is reached. Additionally, high humidity and low light conditions caused by a dense canopy are favorable to the growth of fungi and bacteria that are **causal agents** of many **biotic** tree diseases. Pruning practices that result in a less dense tree canopy will provide increased light and air flow through the canopy. These improvements release some of the branches from competition and provide less favorable conditions for microorganism growth and development.

Trees are healthiest and most beautiful when planted in favorable site conditions and allowed to develop their natural habit. Limited space and poor landscape design often result in plants that are too large or otherwise out of scale for the planting site. In many cases, pruning is often used to solve problems created by poor planning. The best Plant Health Care solution is proper plant selection, not pruning. Nonetheless, even "good" trees that are properly sited will require occasional pruning. In these situations, trees should be selectively pruned, when necessary, to maintain their natural form or habit.

Pruning can be used to achieve a special appearance in the landscape. Examples of appearance-based pruning include **espalier**, formal hedges, **topiary**, **pollarding**, and **bonsai**. Many plants can be maintained with pruning in these specialized forms for many years. However, it is important to realize that plant forms and design effects that use these specialized pruning techniques require extensive and continuing maintenance.

Reasons for pruning ▪ Trees with narrow crotch angles may develop included bark between the branches and the trunk. As these branches increase in diameter, a crack develops along the sides of the tree below the crotch. Trees that develop narrow crotch angles are also more susceptible to mechanical **damage** during ice and wind storms. Some species of trees, such as silver maple (*Acer saccharinum*), have a natural tendency to develop narrow crotch angles. Trees with this characteristic are not recommended for use as street trees or near structures where they can cause damage if broken. The wood of some tree species is inherently weak regardless of the angles between branches. Young trees should be pruned to develop a strong framework—one with properly spaced primary scaffold branches.

Another reason for pruning is to remove undesirable plant parts such as dead wood, insect- or disease-infested wood, **suckers** or **watersprouts**, limbs that have been mechanically damaged, rubbing or crossing branches, and girdling roots. Dead wood is a potential source of disease and decay and should be removed. Pruning can help control, and often eliminate, some minor infestations of insects and diseases, such as scale and fire **blight**, without the use of pesticides. Watersprouts around old pruning wounds or along the branches from **adventitious** or **latent buds** destroy the natural shape of the tree. When clustered together, watersprouts form **witches' brooms**, which serve as a site for snow and ice accumulation and make the tree

more susceptible to mechanical damage. Branches that rub against each other or against a nearby structure develop abrasion wounds that can be a site of disease infestation and subsequent decay. Branches that are already rubbing or appear as if they will rub together should be removed. Girdling roots can limit normal growth and be life threatening to a tree.

Most cultivars of shade and flowering trees are propagated by budding and grafting. Trees produced by these methods have a tendency to develop shoots, called suckers, from below the bud or graft union. Suckering is one sign of graft incompatibility and can be life threatening to the tree. Suckers are genetically identical to the root understock and do not have the desirable characteristics of the selected cultivar. To maintain the cultivar, it is necessary to prune suckers from below the graft union. Suckering and the subsequent need for pruning can be reduced by planting trees that are propagated on their own roots.

It has long been recommended that the tops of transplanted trees be pruned to maintain the root:shoot ratio that was present before transplanting and to decrease water stress of transplanted trees. It has been suggested that, when regular irrigation is possible, pruning the top of a tree may not necessarily improve a plant's ability to survive or recover from **transplant shock** (Whitcomb 1987). Leaves produce **carbohydrates**, which are needed for new root development; therefore, extensive pruning of newly transplanted trees may actually reduce the ability of the plant to regenerate roots.

Plants dug and transplanted after they have leafed out may need pruning, but trees dug during the dormant season may not. There is a physiological relationship between the root system and the new vegetative growth of the tree. The initial new vegetative growth that develops on trees dug when they were dormant is regulated by the remaining root system and its carbohydrate supplies. The new vegetative growth that develops on a tree prior to digging is the result of an intact root system, carbohydrate reserves, and water-supplying ability. Consequently, the amount of new growth that existed at the time of digging for nondormant plants does not have a physiological relationship to the newly reduced root system.

Pruning can also impact the flowering and fruiting of woody plants. In general, pruning delays flowering. Plants that flower on lateral current-season growth will have increased flowering when terminal shoots are removed. Plants that flower terminally will have increased flower size and/or flower clusters on remaining terminal shoots when the number of terminal shoots is reduced. Practices that either increase or decrease flowering will have a subsequent effect on fruiting.

For many professionals, the primary reason for pruning is to create a safer environment. Tree canopies may be raised to provide clearance for pedestrians, lawn care personnel, and vehicles. The pruning or removal of trees in rights-of-way and around utility lines is also important for protection of power supplies and reducing utility line hazards. Whatever the reason for pruning (appearance, disease, or physical necessity), its impact on plant health should be taken into consideration.

When to prune ▪ There is an old saying: "You can prune a tree any time the saw is sharp." It should be stressed that the proper time to prune depends on the type of plant, the plant's condition, and the intended results of the pruning.

The dormant season is a good time to prune deciduous plants because leaves are not present. Without the presence of leaves, it is easier to see the branching structure of the plant and make better decisions about which limbs to remove.

Trees such as elms, birches, American yellowwood, and maples have a tendency to ooze sap when pruned (Brown 1972). Although the oozing of sap from pruning wounds is not analogous to the loss of blood from lacerations on animals, it can have negative effects on trees. Heavy oozing of sap can damage the **cambium** beneath the pruning wound, interfering with the development of **callus** (Neely 1970). The presence of oozing sap is also believed to attract some insect and animals pests and can support the growth of nonpathogenic fungi, which can mar the appearance of the plants. Tree oozing can be avoided by pruning in early winter and at other times when sap is not flowing throughout the canopy of the tree.

Pruning immediately after flowering is the best way to maximize flower display the following year in woody plants. This might be an important factor for plants that were chosen primarily for their flowers.

Needled evergreens should be pruned in late spring after the flush of new growth has begun to harden off. In the midwestern and northeastern United States, this occurs sometime in late May or June. Pruning the new growth of pines is recommended during the **candle stage** after extension growth has stopped, but before the new wood becomes **lignified**. Large limbs should be removed from conifers in the dormant season.

When increased canopy density is the desired effect, broadleaf evergreens should be pruned just before their most rapid growth is expected—usually immediately after flowering for spring-flowering plants such as rhododendrons and azaleas (Harris 1992). The time of pruning will vary by species and in some cases by cultivar. The dormant season is also an appropriate time to prune large limbs of broadleaf evergreens.

The time of pruning can affect the spread and extent of some diseases. Fire blight, Dutch elm disease, and oak **wilt** are examples of diseases that can be spread or initiated by pruning practices. Fire blight cankers should be removed during dry weather to minimize the possibility of spreading the bacterium with pruning tools. Fresh pruning wounds attract the beetles that spread Dutch elm disease and oak wilt. For this reason, it is best to avoid pruning most oaks and elms during the growing season. A knowledge of insect and disease life cycles enables tree care professionals to time pruning operations to periods that are conducive to plant health.

Types of pruning cuts ▪ Heading is the removal of a portion of the stem back to a bud or cutting an older

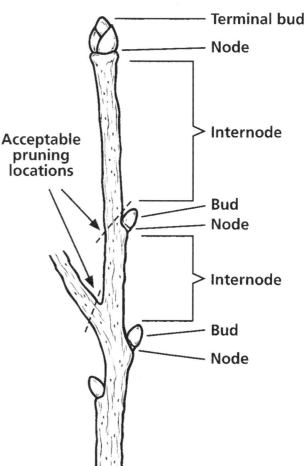

Figure 5.10 ▪ *Proper pruning locations. Always prune just above a node or tissue-connection zone. Never prune along internode areas.*

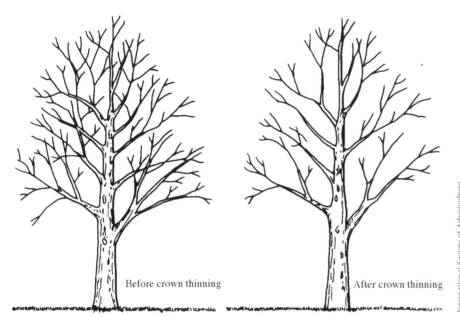

Before crown thinning   After crown thinning

International Society of Arboriculture

Figure 5.11 ▪ *Crown thinning.* *When a mature tree becomes densely branched, it can cast too much shade and be susceptible to wind damage. Thinning the branches allows more light to filter to the ground and improves air flow through the foliage.*

branch back to a stub. Heading cuts should be made above the branch bark ridge, leaving just a small piece of stem above the cut. Cutting too closely to the bud or at too sharp an angle behind the bud may injure the bud, possibly causing it to **desiccate** and die. Small branches or stems should not be headed back in such a way that a section of stem internode remains above a bud (Figure 5.10). Heading will release lateral buds from **apical dominance** and result in the formation of more lateral branches and a denser canopy.

Thinning is the removal of a branch or limb by cutting it back to a crotch. A lateral branch should be cut back to a branch or trunk that is at least ¹/₃ to ¹/₂ the diameter of the cut being made. Thinning can be used to reduce the height of a tree or to make the canopy less dense (Figure 5.11).

Dehorning and stubbing are terms describing the improper pruning technique of leaving a stub of wood where a limb is cut between two crotches, but not at a crotch. (Figure 5.12).

For **crown-reduction pruning**, the cut should begin close to, but outside the branch bark ridge (Figure 5.13) The cut should be angled away from the main trunk so that there is no danger of cutting into the cambium of the main trunk. The cut should not be made flush to the trunk. **Flush cuts** leave gaping wounds that take a long time to form callus and provide an avenue for decay in the trunk of the tree. As pruning wounds close, a callus roll forms in a ring from the division of cambial cells. Eventually the callus com-

pletely covers the pruning wound, with new bark forming over the **callus tissue**. If pruning is done properly and the tree is in good condition, the pruning wound will be "compartmentalized" or sealed off. A section of decayed wood may remain buried within the tree for the rest of its life, but compartmentalization will prevent the decay from spreading.

Natural target pruning suggests that the cut be angled from outside the branch bark ridge but not through the **branch collar** in such a way as to make the smallest wound possible. Pruning wounds that cut through the branch collar make it difficult for the tree to compartmentalize. It is impossible for a stub to callus over, so pruning should not leave stubs (a section of decayed wood remains, leaving an open invitation for decay to spread into the trunk) (Shigo 1983). Another accepted form of pruning, conventional pruning, maintains that cutting through the branch collar will not hurt the tree if the collar area is not removed entirely by the pruning (Neely 1988). In either case, the branch bark ridge should not be violated. Which method is used is not as important as which branches are removed. It is very important not to leave stubs and to have wounds that close rapidly and uniformly.

Large limbs should be removed using a three-cut procedure (Figure 5.13). The first cut should be made on the underside of the limb approximately 20 to 30 percent through. This will prevent stripping of the bark down the main trunk when the limb is removed. A second cut should be made a short distance outside of the first cut all the way through

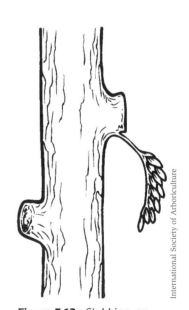

International Society of Arboriculture

Figure 5.12 ▪ *Stubbing, an improper pruning technique*

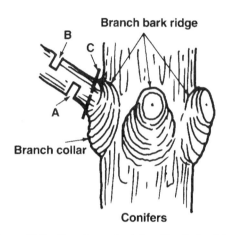

Hardwoods

Conifers

Figure 5.13 ▪ ***Pruning principles.*** *The first cut (A) undercuts the limb. The second cut (B) removes the limb. The final cut (C) should be just outside the branch collar to remove the resulting stub.*

International Society of Arboriculture

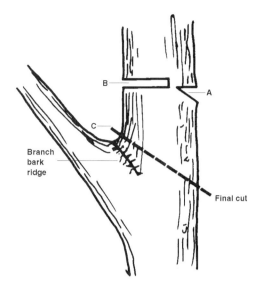

Figure 5.14 ▪ *Cutting back a limb to a major lateral*

International Society of Arboriculture

until the limb is removed. A third cut is made outside the branch bark ridge using either the natural target or conventional pruning method. Branches with V-shaped crotches should be removed using a similar three-cut procedure (Figure 5.14). The exact location of the third cut will vary from crotch to crotch.

Branches that have a dead stub should be removed by cutting through the dead stub without cutting into the live limb.

Treatment of pruning wounds ▪ Pruning paints are still being sold and used, although they are very rarely recommended. Rather than protect the tree wounds, asphalt and other watertight paints often provide a moist environment for wood-rotting fungi. The use of paints in combination with fungicides and other compounds is being studied as a way to manage some canker diseases. For cases in which pruning is required when disease-transmitting insects are active and may

be attracted to fresh wounds, the use of pruning paint might be considered as a way to reduce the attractiveness of the wound. **Plant growth regulators** can reduce the formation of watersprouts and their subsequent growth. Utility arborists occasionally apply plant growth regulators to pruning wounds to increase the period of time between pruning cycles.

Pruning and PHC ▪ Pruning, when viewed from a Plant Health Care perspective, can increase the vitality of most trees. Improper pruning (without an understanding of the physiological and physical requirements of the tree) can result in unsightly and unhealthy trees, as well as dangerous conditions for the surrounding area.

Acknowledgments

The authors are grateful to Chris Starbuck, University of Missouri, and Daniel Herms, The Ohio State University, for their comments and advice on this chapter.

John Ball
Associate Professor of Forestry
South Dakota State University

David Williams
Professor of Horticulture
University of Illinois

Patrick Weicherding
Urban Forestry Consultant
North St. Paul, MN

References

American National Standards Institute. 1986. *American Standard for Nursery Stock.* Washington, D.C.: ANSI.

Appleton, B.L. 1993. Nursery production alternatives for reduction or elimination of circling roots. *J. Arboric.* 19:383–388.

Auchmoody, L.R. 1982. Response of young black cherry stands to fertilization. *Can. J. For. Res.* 12:319–325.

Ball, J. 1987. Influence of fall planting date on the survival and growth of *Taxus, Thuja* and *Viburnum* species. *HortScience* 22:1289–1290.

Ball, J., and D. Graper. 1993a. *Planting a Bare-Root Tree.* ExEx 6018. Brookings: Cooperative Extension Service, South Dakota State University.

Ball, J., and D. Graper. 1993b. *Planting a Container Tree.* ExEx 6019. Brookings: Cooperative Extension Service, South Dakota State University.

Ball, J., and D. Graper. 1993c. *Planting a Balled-and-Burlapped Tree.* ExEx 6020. Brookings: Cooperative Extension Service, South Dakota State University.

Ball, J., and D. Graper. 1993d. *Planting a Tree with a Tree-Moving Machine.* ExEx 6021. Brookings: Cooperative Extension Service, South Dakota State University.

Blessing, S.C., and M.N. Dana. 1988. Post-transplant root system expansion in *Juniperus chinensis* as influenced by production system, mechanical root disruption, and soil type. *J. Environ. Hort.* 5:155–158.

Brown, G.E. 1972. *The Pruning of Trees, Shrubs, and Conifers.* London: Faber and Faber.

Chapin, F.S., III. 1980. The mineral nutrition of wild plants. *Annu. Rev. Ecol. and Systemat.* 11:233–260.

Chapman, J.W., and S.T. Gower. 1991. Aboveground production and canopy dynamics in sugar maple and red oak trees in southwestern Wisconsin. *Can. J. For. Res.* 21:1533–1543.

Einert, A.E., R. Guidry, and H. Huneycutt. 1975. Permanent mulches for landscape plantings of dwarf crape myrtles. *Amer. Nurseryman* 141(9):62–65.

Englert, J.M., L.H. Fuchigami, and T.H.H. Chen. 1993. Effects of storage temperatures and duration on the performance of bare-root deciduous hardwood trees. *J. Arboric.* 19:106–112.

Farmer, R.E. 1975. Dormancy and root regeneration of northern red oak. *Can. J. For. Res.* 5:176–185.

Feucht, J.R. 1986. Wire baskets can be slow killers of trees. *Amer. Nurseryman* 163(6):156–158.

Feucht, J.R., and J.D. Butler. 1988. *Landscape Management.* New York: Van Nostrand Reinhold.

Gilman, E.F. 1990. Tree root growth and development II. Response to culture, management and planting. *J. Environ. Hort.* 8:220–227.

Goodwin, C., and G. Lumis. 1992. Embedded wire in tree roots: Implications for tree growth and root function. *J. Arboric.* 18:115–123.

Greenly, K.M., and D.A. Rakow. 1995. The effect of wood mulch type and depth on weed and tree growth and certain soil parameters. *J. Arboric.* 21:225–232.

Harris, R.W. 1992. *Arboriculture: Integrated Management of Landscape Trees, Shrubs and Vines.* 2nd ed. Englewood Cliffs, New Jersey: Prentice-Hall. 674 pp.

Hauer, R.J., and J.O. Dawson. 1996. Growth and iron sequestering of pin oak (*Quercus palustris*) seedlings inoculated with soil containing ectomycorrihzal fungi. *J. Arboric.* 22:122–130.

Hershey, D.R., and J.J. Paul. 1983. Ion absorption by a woody plant with episodic growth. *HortScience* 18:357–359.

Hummel, R.L., and C.R. Johnson. 1985. Amended backfills: Their cost and effect on transplant growth and survival. *J. Environ. Hort.* 3:76–79.

Ingram, D.L. 1981. Characteristics of temperature fluctuations and woody plant growth in white poly bags and conventional black containers. *HortScience* 16:762–763.

Iyer, J.G., R.B. Corey, and S.A. Wilde. 1980. Mycorrhizae: Facts and fallacies. *J. Arboric.* 6:213–220.

Koide, R.T. 1991. Nutrient supply, nutrient demand and plant response to mycorrhizal infection. *New Phytologist* 117:365–386.

Kopinga, J., and J. van den Burg. 1995. Using soil and foliar analysis to diagnose the nutritional status of urban trees. *J. Arboric.* 21:17–24.

Kozlowski, T.T., ed. 1971. *Growth and Development of Trees,* Vol. 1. San Diego: Academic Press.

Kozlowski, T.T., P.J. Kramer, and S.G. Pallardy. 1991. *Physiological Ecology of Woody Plants.* San Diego: Academic Press. 657 pp.

Lathrop, J.K., and R.A. Mecklenburg. 1971. Root regeneration and root dormancy in *Taxus* spp. *J. Amer. Soc. Hort. Sci.* 96:111–114.

Leiser, A.T., and J.D. Kemper. 1968. A theoretical analysis of a critical height of staking landscape trees. *J. Amer. Soc. Hort. Sci.* 92:713–720.

Litzow, M., and H. Pellett. 1983. Materials for potential use in sunscald protection. *J. Arboric.* 9: 35–38.

Marx, D.H., and N.C. Schenk. 1983. Potential of mycorrhizal symbiosis in agriculture and forest productivity. In *Challenging Problems in Plant Health,* eds. T. Kommedahl and P.H. Williams, 334–347. St. Paul, Minnesota: American Phytopathological Society.

McCullough, D.G., and H.M. Kulman. 1991. Effects of nitrogen fertilization on young jack pine (*Pinus banksiana*) and on its suitability as a host for jack pine budworm (*Choristoneura pinus*) (Lepidoptera: Tortricidae). *Can. J. For. Res.* 21:1447–1458.

Neely, D. 1970. Healing of wounds on trees. *J. Amer. Soc. Hort. Sci.* 95:536–540.

Neely, D. 1976. Iron deficiency chlorosis of shade trees. *J. Arboric.* 2:128–130.

Neely, D. 1980. Tree fertilization trials in Illinois. *J. Arboric.* 6:271–273.

Neely, D. 1988. Wound closure rates on trees. *J. Arboric.* 14:250–254.

Perry, E., and G.W. Hickman. 1992. Growth response of newly planted valley oak trees to supplemental fertilizers. *J. Environ. Hort.* 10:242–244.

Salisbury, F.B., and C.W. Ross. 1985. *Plant Physiology.* 3rd ed. Belmont, California: Wadsworth. 540 pp.

Shigo, A.L. 1983. Targets for proper tree care. *J. Arboric.* 9: 285–294.

Shigo, A.L. 1986. *A New Tree Biology Dictionary.* Durham, New Hampshire: Shigo and Trees, Associates.

Smalley, T.J., and C.B. Wood. 1995. Effect of backfill amendment on growth of red maple. *J. Arboric.* 21:247–249.

Smiley, E.T., D.H. Marx, and B.R. Fraedrich. 1997. Ectomycorrhizal fungus inoculations of established residential trees. *J. Arboric.* 23:113–115.

Smith, E.M., and C.H. Gilliam. 1978. *Fertilizing Landscape and Field Grown Nursery Crops.* Bulletin 650. Columbus: Cooperative Extension Service, The Ohio State University.

Smith E.M., and K.W. Reisch. 1975. Fertilizing trees in the landscape: Progress report. *J. Arboric.* 1:77.

Stone, E.C., and G.H. Schubert. 1959. Root regeneration by ponderosa pine seedlings lifted at different times of the year. *For. Sci.* 5:322–332.

Swanson, B.T., J.B. Calkins, P.J. Rudquist, and S. Shimek. 1989. *Planting and Transplanting Trees and Shrubs.* AG-FO-3825. St. Paul, Minnesota: Minnesota Extension Service, University of Minnesota.

Van Cleve, K., and L.K. Oliver. 1982. Growth response of postfire quaking aspen (*Populus tremuloides* Michx.) to N, P, and K fertilization. *Can. J. For. Res.* 12:160–165.

Walvatne, P.G.A. 1983. Large tree moving results on Minnesota transportation projects. Misc. Rept., St. Paul, Minnesota: Minnesota Department of Transportation.

Watson, G.W. 1985. Tree size affects root regeneration and top growth after transplanting. *J. Arboric.* 11:37–40.

Watson, G.W. 1992. *Selecting and Planting Trees.* Lisle, Illinois: The Morton Arboretum.

Watson, G.W., and S. Clark. 1993. Regeneration of girdling roots after removal. *J. Arboric.* 19:278–280.

Watson, G.W., S. Clark, and K. Johnson. 1990. Formation of girdling roots. *J. Arboric.* 16:197–202.

Watson, G.W., and E.B. Himelick. 1983. Root regeneration of shade trees following transplanting. *J. Environ. Hort.* 1:52–54.

Watson, G.W., and G. Kupkowski. 1991. Effects of a deep layer of mulch on the soil environment and tree root growth. *J. Arboric.* 17:242–245.

Watson, G.W., G. Kupkowski, and K.G. von der Heide-Spravka. 1992. The effect of backfill soil texture and plant hole shape on root regeneration of transplanted green ash. *J. Arboric.* 18:130–135.

Watson, G.W., G. Kupkowski, and K.G. von der Heide-Spravka. 1993. Influence of backfill amendments on establishment of container-grown shrubs. *HortTechnology* 3:188–189.

Weinbaum, S.A., M.L. Merwin, and T.T. Muraoka. 1978. Season variation in nitrate uptake efficiency and distribution of absorbed nitrogen in non-bearing prune trees. *J. Amer. Soc. Hort. Sci.* 103:516–519.

Whitcomb, C.E. 1987. *Establishment and Maintenance of Landscape Plants.* Stillwater, Oklahoma: Lacebark Publications.

Witherspoon, W.R., and G.P. Lumis. 1986. Root regeneration, starch content, and root promoting activity in *Tilia cordata* cultivars at three different digging-planting times. *J. Environ. Hort.* 4: 76–79.

Wood, C.B., T.J. Smalley, M. Rieger, and D.E. Radcliffe. 1994. Growth and drought tolerance of *Viburnum plicatum* var. *tomentosum* 'Mariesii' in pine bark–amended soil. *J. Amer. Soc. Hort. Sci.* 119:687–692.

Suggested Readings

American National Standards Institute.1995. *Standard Practices for Tree, Shrub, and Other Woody Plant Maintenance.* ANSI A300. Washington, D.C.: ANSI.

ISA Performance Guidelines Committee. 1995. *Tree-Pruning Guidelines.* Savoy, Illinois: International Society of Arboriculture. 14pp.

Lilly, S.J. 1991. *Arborists' Certification Study Guide.* 1991. Savoy, Illinois: International Society of Arboriculture.

CHAPTER 6

Diagnosing Tree Disorders

Gary Johnson

This chapter focuses on tree **disorders** and how to accurately diagnose them. Tree **diseases** are the focus of Chapter 7.

Tree disorders and diseases have something in common. Both interrupt normal metabolic processes such as water and nutrient movement, **photosynthesis**, and respiration, and both produce characteristic **symptoms**. But disorders and diseases also differ. Diseases are caused by **biotic** (living) agents such as **bacteria**, **viruses**, **fungi**, and **phytoplasmas**, whereas disorders are caused by **abiotic** (nonliving) agents such as pesticides, **soluble** salts, compacted clay soils, and water and temperature extremes.

When discussing tree problems, the term *symptom* refers to plant reactions to either biotic or abiotic agents that disrupt normal plant processes. A **sign** is the physical evidence of the **causal agent** and is usually used to describe **pathogens** (biotic causal agents).

Common symptoms of tree disorders include **wilt, leaf scorch,** leaf **blotch,** stem **cankers, stunt,** and death. Common signs include **conks** or other "**fruiting structures,**" **spores**, **mycelium**, and **rhizomorphs**. Theoretically, abiotic disorders could have signs also: the string-trimmer striking the tree stem, the backhoe digging up roots a foot away from the tree trunk, **mulch** piled 24 inches up against the stem of a newly planted tree, or the **root collar flare** buried a foot lower than the landscape grade.

The difficulty with diagnosing tree disorders is twofold. The first difficulty is that pathogens, abiotic agents, and some insects produce similar disorder symptoms. The second difficulty is that signs are usually not obvious. Diagnosing problems, therefore, involves recognizing the disorder symptoms, determining which agents characteristically produce those symptoms, and identifying which agents are present (looking or testing for signs or conducting a site analysis).

Correctly diagnosing problems is not always easy; most tree problems in the landscape or streetscape are **complexes,** or combinations of causal agents. These combinations commonly involve multiple abiotic causal agents, or complexes with both biotic and abiotic agents. The Eutypella canker may be obvious on the stem of the Norway maple, producing the characteristic symptoms and maybe even signs, but it often starts with **sunscalded** or cracked bark that provided an entry wound for the fungus.

The most critical part of the diagnostic process is to determine what caused the problem.[1] The cause is what is ultimately sought, for that discovery provides the basis for control tactics. Often, control tactics are too late for the plant being diagnosed but may be used to prevent problems with other trees.

The following information is not inclusive, nor is it solely focused on abiotic problems. It is a process and a closer analysis of some **chronic** abiotic disorders. On

---

[1]Appendix A contains a list of soil testing and plant diagnostic clinics in the U.S. and Canada.

paper, the process for diagnosing plant problems is simple:

1. Identify the plant.
2. Determine what is abnormal about the plant—that is, determine which symptoms are present.
3. Get as much information as possible—information about the plant, the site, the weather, any activities that have occurred in the area, and maintenance practices.
4. Consult references—determine which problems are common or possible, given the site and the symptoms they produce.
5. Finally, match the symptoms you have observed, the site conditions, and the plant to the problem.

Identifying the plant and determining what is abnormal about the plant actually go hand in hand. Himalayan pine (*Pinus wallichiana*) always looks wilted; that is part of its character. Excelsior ash (*Fraxinus excelsior* 'Aurea') normally has a yellow, or **chlorotic,** appearance, especially the young shoots. Kentucky coffeetree (*Gymnocladus dioicus*) normally leafs out very late in the spring, and sumacs (*Rhus* spp.) normally develop bright-red foliage before anything else, usually in late summer. Sometimes what appears to be a problem is actually normal or at least not damaging for the region or particular site. For example, a fir (*Abies*) tree may look dangerously stunted even though its condition could be normal for the elevation or latitude where it is located.

Finally, some problems seem to be chronic everywhere. The last section of this chapter covers some of these problems in more detail, itemizing not only the common symptoms they produce but also how or why they cause problems (see Chronic Tree Disorders later in this chapter). The relative value of learning and using this process and becoming familiar with the chronic problems is that it forces the diagnostician to slow down, look closer, consider many causes, and not jump to quick and easy conclusions. In the end, it helps the treatment process become more effective and helps us maintain a healthier urban forest.

The Diagnostic Process

Step 1. Identify the Plant

As a minimum, identify to the **genus** level. In many instances, it will be more useful to identify to the species and, if possible, the **cultivar** level, to recognize unique plant characteristics.

Step 2. Determine What Is Abnormal: Identify the Symptoms

Determine normal characteristics for the species as well as for the situation in which the tree is growing. Appearances commonly change from full-sun sites to shady sites. For example, in shady situations the leaves are normally thinner and larger, and variegated plants are sometimes less variegated.

Symptoms—how the plant reacts to a problem—can include any one or more of the characteristics described below.

Overall stunt
- Abnormally reduced growth.
- Abnormally small leaves.
- Abnormally small flowers or few flowers.
- Abnormally reduced root growth.

Foliar (leaves)
- Abnormal wilting. This may mean that the plant appears to be wilting for no reason, that the wilting is chronic, or that the tree does not recover after irrigation.
- Scorching (browning of the leaf edge).
- Blotching (random dead areas throughout the leaves).
- Abnormal nongreen color of leaves: yellowing, reddening, purpling.
- Early leaf coloration—substantially early (three to four weeks) as compared to previous years or similar species in the area.
- Uneven leaf coloration (appears on one side of the tree before the other).
- Early leaf fall—substantially early (three to four weeks) as compared to previous years or similar species in the area.
- Uneven leaf fall (a distinct portion of the tree **defoliates** before the rest of the tree).
- Blackened leaves.
- Abnormally twisted or malformed leaves.

Stems and twigs
- Single branches wilting.
- **Flagging** (leaves wilt on a branch, turn brown, and hang on).
- **Stagheading** (branches without leaves, with loose bark, or with no bark).
- Cankers (open wounds that don't seal over; sometimes may be sunken areas under the bark).
- Abnormally loose bark. Abnormal as opposed to normal peeling such as with birches. Bark when tapped with a hammer sounds hollow and is often abnormal.

- Missing bark.
- Cracks.
- **Dieback.**
- **Witches' brooming** (many shoots arising from what seems like a single point).
- Buds dry, flaky, or dead.
- Normal trunk taper (**basal flare**) absent. Most trees, such as American elm, develop broad basal flares where the trunk meets the soil line.

Decay

- Decay starts at a pruning wound or other wound.
- Decay is all interior with no opening to the outside.
- Decay is at the soil line.
- Decay has an opening to the outside of the bark.

Step 3. Do Your History Lesson!

Search planting records for when the trees were planted, how they were transplanted (**bare-root, balled-and-burlapped,** container), the species and cultivars, which nursery supplied the trees, scheduled and actual maintenance, and any activities that may have occurred prior to or after the planting that may affect the tree's health.

Weather characteristics

- Unusual precipitation patterns? Very wet, very dry, normal rainfall but all at once, very little snow cover?
- Prevailing winter or summer wind direction?
- Lightning storms?
- Heavy wind storms?
- Hail?
- Constant summer winds?
- Constant winter winds?
- Late spring frosts?
- Early autumn frosts?
- Mild autumn, late winter?

Soil characteristics

- **Soil pH** unusually high (greater than 7.3 to 7.5)? Unusually low (less than 5.5)?
- Drainage problems? Soils for most trees should drain at a rate of 24 inches in 24 hours.
- Nutrient levels? Selected sites may have **macro-** or **micronutrient** deficiencies or toxicities that the area soils do not.
- Organic-matter level? Ideally, it should be at 3 percent to 5 percent for most trees.
- Compaction? For most urban clay soils, the **bulk density** should not be above 1.5 g/cm^3.
- Soil pollutants? For instance, deicing salts, concrete truck clean-out, solvents.

- Soil depth? For most shrubs, consider 24 inches as a minimum; for trees, 30 to 36 inches is recommended.
- Soil volume? For average-sized trees to grow normally, a minimum volume of 300 cubic feet is recommended.

Cultural practices

- Fertilization practices, types of fertilizers, amounts?
- Irrigation: Set up for turf? Amount? Time of year?
- Pesticides used—in particular, **herbicides**?
- String-trimmer or mower-deck damage to stems/trunks?
- Was pruning done? How much? What time of year? Was it done correctly (good pruning cuts)?
- Was the plant mulched? Type of mulch? Depth of mulch? Was black plastic placed under the mulch over heavy clay soil?
- Planting: How were the plants handled prior to planting? What was the planting depth? How big was the planting hole? Was the tree staked or guyed? How were the wires attached? Where were the wires attached? Was the trunk wrapped? When was it wrapped? When were the wires and wrapping taken off? What type of wrapping was used? What time of year was the planting/transplanting done?
- Is there turf up to the tree or shrub trunk/stem? Are annuals planted over the tree or shrub's root system?

Genetic characteristics

- Is the species hardy for the area or "borderline" hardy?
- Where was the plant grown?
- Where did the seed come from (what area of the country)?

Other factors

- Have there been any construction activities that have severed roots, changed water drainage patterns, piled soil over root systems, wounded roots or stems?
- Any campfires or charcoal fires over the roots or near the trunk and foliage?
- Excessive dust in the air that coated the leaves?
- New traffic patterns (foot, landscape equipment, vehicles)?
- Is the area used more during times of the year when the soil is wetter than normal? For instance, heavy use of parks during the spring can severely compact clay soils.

Step 4: Refer to a List of Common Problems and Common Culprits

Very common
- Soil problems (drainage, **pH**, compaction).
- Root damage (construction activities, cutting, filling).
- Improper planting (letting roots dry out, planting too deep).
- Improper cultural activities (too much mulch, string-trimmer or mower damage to stems, turf competition, poor pruning).
- **Transplant shock.**

Common
- Poor nursery stock (**root-bound**, poor root system, wounds).
- Weather extremes (drought, heavy winds, extreme temperatures, frosts).
- Too much or too little irrigation.
- Problem-prone plants: box elder, silver maple, willows.

Occasional
- Species not hardy to area or "borderline" in **hardiness**.
- Vandalism (intentional or not).
- Late summer fertilization—initiating vegetative growth that doesn't acclimate sufficiently for winter temperatures.
- Late, continual irrigation—initiating vegetative growth that doesn't acclimate sufficiently for winter temperatures.
- Deicing salt (spray and runoff).
- Animal damage.
- Girdling from wires, tags, ropes, tape.
- **Girdling root syndrome (GRS).**
- Herbicides.
- Plants grown from a southern seed source.

Tree Problems and Their Symptoms

Tables 6.1, 6.2, and 6.3 list tree problems and their symptoms according to how commonly they occur.

Chronic Tree Disorders

Tree Installation Problems

Depth ▪ Much urban tree decline or mortality can be attributed to installation or harvesting practices that place the root collar area of newly planted trees several inches below the landscape grade. This is more of a problem when trees are planted in clay soils or heavily compacted soils but can be aggravated by surface mulches, exposed sites, or turf covering the entire root system right to the stem of the tree.

Causes
- Trees planted with the root collar area 6 inches or more below the landscape grade.
- Balled-and-burlapped or machine-dug trees harvested with excessive amounts of soil over the root collar area (a result of "hilling-up" cultivation practices that smother weeds in the field).
- Burying the graft union—treating trees as some gardeners treat hybrid tea rose bushes.
- Planting holes dug extra deep, with loosened soil "cones" constructed in the hole center. Trees (especially balled-and-burlapped or machine-dug trees) planted on these "cones" eventually settle too much and, in effect, plant themselves too deep.
- Annual accumulations of mulch—in particular, fine-textured mulches.

Damage
- Restriction of water and oxygen to the fine-root systems.
- Higher incidence of stem cankers and decay due to water-saturated bark conditions.
- Poor root system regeneration of transplanted trees.
- Gradual death of original root system.
- Extended period of transplant shock.
- Lower tree **vitality** and reserve of energy.
- Increased vulnerability to biotic problems and environmental extremes.
- Death.

Symptoms
- Nutrient deficiency symptoms.
- Scorch.
- Wilt.
- Tip dieback.
- Stagheading.
- Stunt of foliage and annual growth rates.
- **Adventitious** rooting on many species.
- Early fall coloration and leaf fall.
- Decline in vitality, commonly slow and progressive. This may progress for five to ten years.
- Leaning.
- Chronic **wind-throw**.
- Death.

Interface penetration ▪ Trees planted in small planting holes, especially in soils that are severely compacted,

Table 6.1 ■ *Very common tree problems and symptoms*

S Y M P T O M S

PROBLEM	Wilt	Scorch	Blotch/ spots	Leaf drop[a]	Early color[b]	Off color[c]	Die-back	Failure[d]	Flagging	Stag-heading	Wind-throw	Witches' broom	Leaning	Stem cracking	Abnor-malities[e]	Tissue missing[f]	Decay
Soil problems (drainage, pH, compaction)	•	•		•	•	•	•	•		•	•		•	•			
Root damage (construction activities, cutting, filling)	•	•		•	•	•	•	•	•	•	•		•				•
Improper planting (letting roots dry out, planting too deep)	•	•		•	•	•	•	•		•	•		•	•			
Improper maintenance (too much mulch, string-trimmer or mower damage to stems, turf competition, poor pruning)	•			•	•	•	•	•		•				•	•	•	•
Transplant shock	•	•		•	•	•	•	•	•	•			•	•			

[a]Sudden or abnormally early leaf drop.

[b]Trees turn to their autumn foliage color abnormally early.

[c]Foliage is yellow, light green, reddish, blackened, or bleached.

[d]May be defined as tree death, or sudden breaking of the stem or branches.

[e]May include galls, cankers, or swollen areas of the stem or lack of basal flare or curling and other distortions of the foliage.

[f]May include missing leaf tissues, missing bark (outer), missing cambium.

Table 6.2 ▪ *Common tree problems and symptoms*

SYMPTOMS

PROBLEM	Wilt	Scorch	Blotch/ spots[a]	Leaf drop[a]	Early color[b]	Off color[c]	Die-back	Failure[d]	Flagging	Stag-heading	Wind-throw	Witches' broom	Leaning	Stem cracking	Abnor-malities[e]	Tissue missing[f]	Decay
Poor nursery stock (root-bound, poor root system, wounds)	•																
Weather extremes (drought, heavy winds, extreme temperatures, frosts)	•	•	•	•	•	•	•	•	•	•	•		•	•	•	•	•
Too much or too little irrigation water	•	•	•	•	•	•	•	•	•	•	•		•	•	•		•
Problem-prone plants: boxelder, silver maple, willows		•		•	•	•	•	•	•	•	•		•	•	•	•	•
Leaf spots			•	•	•	•	•									•	
Wilts	•	•		•		•	•	•	•	•							
Shoot blights	•	•	•			•	•		•								
Root rots	•	•	•	•	•	•	•	•	•	•	•		•				•
Cankers		•					•	•	•	•				•	•	•	•
Phytoplasmas		•			•	•	•	•	•	•	•	•			•		
Powdery mildews	•			•		•									•		
Viruses			•			•	•								•		
Rusts			•	•		•	•					•		•	•		

[a]Sudden or abnormally early leaf drop.
[b]Trees turn to their autumn foliage color abnormally early.
[c]Foliage is yellow, light green, reddish, blackened, or bleached.
[d]May be defined as tree death, or sudden breaking of the stem or branches.
[e]May include galls, cankers, or swollen areas of the stem or lack of basal flare or curling and other distortions of the foliage.
[f]May include missing leaf tissues, missing bark (outer), missing cambium.

Table 6.3 ▪ *Occasional tree problems and symptoms*

SYMPTOMS

PROBLEM	Wilt	Scorch	Blotch/ spots	Leaf drop[a]	Early color[b]	Off color[c]	Die-back	Failure[d]	Flagging	Stag-heading	Wind-throw	Witches' broom	Leaning	Stem cracking	Abnormalities[e]	Tissue missing[f]	Decay
Species not hardy to the area		•			•	•								•	•		
Vandalism (intentional and unintentional)							•	•	•	•			•			•	•
Late fertilization							•							•			
Late irrigation							•							•			
Deicing salt (spray and runoff)	•	•	•	•	•	•	•	•		•		•		•			
Animal damage	•	•	•	•	•	•	•	•	•	•					•	•	•
Girdling from wires, tags, ropes, tape	•	•		•	•	•	•	•	•	•					•		•
Girdling root syndrome (GRS)	•	•		•	•	•	•	•	•	•	•		•	•	•		•
Herbicides	•	•		•	•	•	•	•	•	•		•		•	•	•	•
Plants grown from a southern seed source	•	•		•	•	•	•	•	•	•	•		•	•		•	•

[a]Sudden or abnormally early leaf drop.
[b]Trees turn to their autumn foliage color abnormally early.
[c]Foliage is yellow, light green, reddish, blackened, or bleached.
[d]May be defined as tree death, or sudden breaking of the stem or branches.
[e]May include galls, cankers, or swollen areas of the stem or lack of basal flare or curling and other distortions of the foliage.
[f]May include missing leaf tissues, missing bark (outer), missing cambium.

commonly exhibit transplant shock symptoms for unusually long periods. Sometimes they never recover completely and languish their entire lives. Roots can eventually penetrate the **interface** of the planting hole, that is, the point at which the existing soil meets the prepared planting hole soil. However, when the existing soil is a very compacted clay, it may take several years for the new roots to penetrate extensively enough to support "normal" stem and canopy growth. Often roots never penetrate the existing soil adequately, and the trees never look "normal."

Causes

- Existing soils are primarily clays and might have very shallow organic horizons.
- Existing soils have been stripped of topsoil and compacted to meet engineering standards for construction.
- Existing soils are primarily clays and were subjected to extensive traffic compaction, especially during times of year when the soils were wet.
- Trees have been moved with a tree spade directly into clay or compacted soils. Planting holes have been dug with the tree spade and not modified or enlarged prior to insertion of the transplanted tree.
- Planting holes have been dug with vertical sides and only large enough to insert the soil ball (root system) of the new tree.

Damage

- Reduced (as compared to normal) fine-root surface area and **critical root zone**.
- Extended transplant shock period.
- Lengthy period of low vitality.
- **Encircling roots** (occasionally).
- Increased vulnerability to biotic problems and environmental extremes.
- Reduced root:shoot ratio.
- Shorter life span.

Symptoms

- Chronic annual scorching and wilting.
- Nutrient deficiency symptoms.
- Tip dieback. This may appear as chronic winter damage.
- Increased stem cracking (**frost cracks**) during winters, especially in colder regions.
- Slower sealing over of pruning wounds.
- **Decline syndrome.**
- Stagheading.
- **Epicormic sprouting.**
- Chronic wind-throw and leaning.
- **Girdling roots.**

Transplant shock ▪ Transplant shock is unavoidable; transplant shock that continues for years and years is unacceptable yet unfortunately very common. Trees that have had their roots severed during the harvesting process must reestablish an adequate root system before the entire plant can begin normal growth. During this period of system shock, it is normal to observe stress symptoms. Often, field-grown trees that are balled-and-burlapped or machine-harvested retain only 5 percent to 10 percent of their original root system in the soil ball. As a general rule, the transplant shock period lasts one year for each one inch of **stem caliper**.

Even trees that have been **container-grown** and theoretically retain 100 percent of their root system suffer some transplant shock. They have been grown under intensive cultural conditions of regular irrigation and fertilization and now have been thrust into the much harsher environment of the open landscape.

Bare-root harvested trees usually have a higher percentage of their roots dug with the plants and therefore should experience a milder form of transplant shock. Sometimes this happens. Unfortunately, bare-root trees are often improperly handled prior to planting, causing the more extensive root system to dry out and die.

Causes

- Removal of as much as 90 percent to 95 percent of the root system as a result of the harvesting process.
- Container-grown plants are transplanted from uniquely optimal conditions to the suboptimal conditions found in most landscapes.
- Plants are improperly handled following harvest: roots allowed to dry out and heavy soil balls dropped and rolled to planting sites instead of carted.

Damage

- Reduced ability to take up water and nutrients due to a reduced root volume.
- Increased vulnerability to biotic problems and environmental extremes.
- Reduced photosynthesis and accumulation of **energy reserves.**
- Reduced growth.
- Excessively high shoot:root ratio makes a tree more vulnerable to total failure.

Symptoms

- Overall stunt: leaves, annual shoot growth, caliper growth.

- Wilt, scorch.
- Early leaf coloration; early leaf fall.
- **Suckering** and/or epicormic sprouting.
- Reduced flowering or quality of flowers.
- Abnormally high amount of winter-killed twigs or buds.

Girdling wires ▪ Wires, synthetic ropes, and synthetic plant name tags left on trees and shrubs do not usually result in high mortality rates, though it does happen. More commonly, the items cause **girdled** branches or stems that disfigure the plant. Any synthetic material left on plant branches or stems may sooner or later cause **phloem girdling** at the least, and branch or stem failure or death at the worst. Often wires become embedded in the **sapwood** of a branch or stem and the plant appears to have overcome the obstruction. Unfortunately, this is a weak spot that frequently is the point of structural failure during wind storms and ice storms or after heavy and wet snows.

Girdling from wires and other synthetic materials is a particular and early problem on plants that are in ideal growing environments. When provided with good soils and care, young plants can begin putting on stem and branch caliper relatively soon after planting. It is not uncommon to see girdling damage after only one season in the landscape when the growing conditions are superior and the plants are vigorously growing. More commonly, however, girdling from these materials takes two or more years to finally cause noticeable damage, when it is usually too late to correct the problem.

Causes
- Synthetic materials that do not break down rapidly in natural light have not been removed at planting.
- Natural materials such as **jute rope** that have been wound around tree trunks and left exposed to sunlight and drying air might not break down fast enough to avoid compression of the new stem sapwood.
- Synthetic ropes that have been used to tie up soil balls on balled-and-burlapped plants or machine-dug plants might eventually cause girdling or sapwood compression when the stem caliper of the tree expands enough. Many times this does not occur until ten to fifteen years after planting.
- Trees that have been staked or guyed at planting and have had the attachment wires secured too tightly around the tree stem, even if the wires have been inserted through lengths of hose.

Damage
- Phloem girdling, sapwood compression; restriction of **photosynthates** flowing down.
- Death of branches or stems and canopy above the girdled point.
- Reduced root generation and stem caliper growth below the girdled point.
- Failure (breakage) of the branch or stem at the girdled/compressed point.
- Potential loss of the natural form of **excurrent** trees if the stem was girdled or compressed.

Symptoms
- Pinched appearance to the stem or branch at the point of constriction.
- Swollen appearance above the point of constriction.
- Leaf scorch, wilting, stunt.
- Flagging of branches or canopies, tip dieback, stagheading.
- Epicormic sprouting or excessive suckering below the point of constriction.
- If branches or stems break at the compressed or girdled point, breaks appear clean rather than torn or ragged.

Mulch ▪ Damage from incorrect mulch applications around trees and shrubs is becoming more common as homeowners and professionals recognize the many benefits of mulching plants. Problems may arise, however, under certain circumstances such as excessively deep applications of fine-textured organic mulches; organic mulches piled up against the trunk of young or thin-barked trees and shrubs; or plastic groundcovers applied before the topdressed mulch, especially when the plastic is in contact with heavy clay soils.

Causes
- Deep applications of fine-textured mulches over the fine-root system can restrict soil oxygen and water.
- Plastic groundcovers on heavy clay soils to prevent weeds from growing up through the mulch can create "glazed" interfaces (soil/plastic interface). The soil near the plastic commonly becomes water-saturated, which restricts soil oxygen.
- Organic mulches piled up against the trunks or stems of young or smooth-barked trees and shrubs retain unusually high amounts of moisture, do not allow the bark to dry out, and restrict natural light from the trunk or stem.

Damage
- Inadequate **oxygen-diffusion rates.**

- Fine-root mortality. Loss of part or all of the original branch root system.
- Excessive formation of adventitious roots off stems covered by mulches.
- Unusually large and "corky" **lenticels** where the trunks or stems are covered by mulches.
- **Mulch girdling**—a phenomenon in which the stem caliper grows normally above the mulch line, but grows abnormally slow below the mulch line.
- Some species are more prone to girdling root formation under deep mulch conditions.
- Under plastic groundcovers on heavy clay soils, many trees and shrubs produce extremely shallow and large branch roots.
- Reduced fine-root development.
- Increased vulnerability to stem canker pathogens and decay.

Symptoms

- Blackened roots.
- Scorch, wilt, nutrient deficiency, early fall color, early leaf drop, chronic and excessive tip dieback, flagging, stagheading.
- Overall stunt; decline.
- Mulch-girdled stems. Little to no stem caliper growth below the mulch line.
- Unstable trees or shrubs; poorly anchored, they lean or wind-throw more commonly than others.
- Excessive adventitious rooting on stems below the mulch line.

Soil Problems

pH ▪ Natural soils vary widely in their natural pH. Urban soils are just as variable and more unpredictable. It is not unusual for a soil pH to range from 6.5 to 8.5 within a neighborhood. This is due primarily to buried construction or other materials, such as wood ash, and is common in new developments where certain areas were used as clean-out sites for concrete trucks, plastering equipment, and masonry cleaners.

Causes

- Natural variability in soils due to parent materials.
- In urban areas, the burial or deposition of foreign materials and chemicals.

Damage

- Some soil minerals become unavailable for plant uptake.
- Reduced plant vitality; reduction of photosynthates.

- Increased vulnerability to biotic problems and environmental extremes.
- Occasional toxicity damage.

Symptoms

- Specific nutrient deficiency symptoms, ranging from off-colored leaves, to lack of flowering and fruit production, to foliar scorching, to malformed leaves, to poor growth habits.
- Overall stunt.
- Chronic problems with biotic pathogens and insects.
- Decline.
- Prolonged transplant shock periods.
- Chronic winter damage (especially dieback).

Drainage ▪ Poor soil drainage is one of the primary causes of low plant vitality and high mortality rates of urban trees. With urban soils, poor drainage is a chronic condition, especially in public areas and new construction sites.

Causes

- High water tables—either natural, periodic, or induced from alterations of watersheds.
- Natural **hardpans** or induced hardpans from cultivation techniques.
- Compacted subsoils to meet engineering standards for construction.
- Poor plant-to-site decisions.

Damage

- Low plant vitality, reduced photosynthesis, reduced energy reserve levels.
- Increased vulnerability to problems from biotic agents or environmental extremes, and poor recovery.
- Extensive root loss.
- Loss of stability.
- Death.

Symptoms

- Scorch, wilt, early leaf coloration, early leaf fall, nutrient deficiency symptoms.
- Excessive winter damage: frost cracking, twig dieback.
- Blackened roots.
- Flagging; stagheading.
- Higher incidence of wind-throw or leaning.
- Higher incidence of girdling roots.
- Death.

Compaction ▪ **Soil compaction**, especially with clay soils in urban areas, is a common condition that results in chronic problems of low tree vitality and secondary problems. Clay soils (clays, clay-loams) experience the most problems with compaction. Sandy and organic soils usually do not compact as severely or for as long; therefore, there are fewer problems with trees grown in these soils even if they have been subjected to compaction.

Compacted clay soils cause plant problems in three ways: (1) reduced soil oxygen, (2) reduced soil moisture, and (3) increased resistance to fine-root penetration. When sandy and organic soils are compacted, the structure of those soils allows roots to penetrate nevertheless, even when bulk-density measurements are fairly high. **Bulk density** is a measurement of soil compaction that is commonly used and commonly misinterpreted. Clay soils with a bulk-density value of 1.55 g/cm³ or greater are almost impenetrable by fine roots. Sandy soils with bulk-density values of 1.75 g/cm³ are not root-restrictive.

Bulk-density values do provide a clue when diagnosing tree problems, however. In particular with clay soils, higher bulk-density values are associated with lower oxygen-diffusion rates. Low oxygen-diffusion rates have been shown to directly relate to low plant vitality and might be a better measurement of a soil's ability to support plant life. Low oxygen-diffusion rates are not just associated with compacted clay soils. Even sandy soils—if saturated—have low oxygen-diffusion rates and will not support the majority of trees and shrubs used in the urban landscape.

Causes
- Stripping of organic topsoils to clay layers and compacting the subsoil to engineering standards (95 percent) to support foundations and road bases.
- Repeated equipment use over a common traffic pattern. This can occur on a construction site or in an agricultural field where tractors use the same paths periodically.
- High levels of foot traffic, such as in parks or schools, especially on clay soils at times of the year when the soil is very moist.
- Very fine landscape grading of clay soils.

Damage
- Reduced soil oxygen and moisture.
- Increased resistance to new fine-root penetration.
- Extended periods of transplant shock.
- Lowering of plant vitality and ability to store energy reserves.
- Increased vulnerability to biotic problems and environmental extremes.

Symptoms
- Scorch, wilt, nutrient deficiency symptoms, early fall coloration, early leaf drop.
- Excessive winter damage, twig dieback, stag-heading.
- Overall stunt.
- Decline, death.
- Chronic problematic infections and infestations.

Volumes ▪ Trees grown in planters, pots, or below-ground pits (sometimes referred to as "tree coffins") rarely are in rooting environments that are adequate in volume. Research has shown that most landscape trees need 300 to 1,000 cubic feet of soil for normal growing conditions. The larger the tree when it matures (maples, oaks, lindens), the more volume required.

The reality of most tree containers is an average soil volume of 75 to 100 cubic feet, or enough to support a forsythia shrub. Low soil volumes compound all of the soil problems previously mentioned by adding another stress to the trees once they have filled the volumes with roots.

Causes
- Inadequate soil volumes provided in containers and tree pits for survival of medium and large tree species.
- Poor plant selection for these 75 to 100 cubic foot "plant coffins." Trees and shrubs naturally small in stature (such as crabapples) do not normally require very large volumes of soil (greater than 500 cubic feet).

Damage
- Limited carrying capacity for supporting plant life. A volume of soil has a limit to its nutrient- and **water-holding capacity**.
- Smaller volumes are more vulnerable to environmental extremes, such as quick and deep freezes and excessively high summer soil temperatures.
- Trees normally medium to large in size eventually fill the volumes with roots and cannot expand anymore, and above-ground plant parts are stressed due to the limited moisture and nutrient uptake capabilities.
- Trees slowly decline in vitality.

Symptoms
- For trees normally medium to large in stature, leaf scorch, chronic wilting, and nutrient deficiency symptoms.
- For trees grown in sidewalk-level street tree pits that are near major streets or parking areas, in-

creased deicing salt symptoms from snow-melt runoff.

- Higher incidences of stem cracking, frost cracks, winter damage as twig dieback.
- Flagging, stagheading.
- Increased vulnerability to biotic problems and environmental extremes.
- Excessive suckering and epicormic sprouting.
- Decline and death.

Girdling Root Syndrome (GRS)

Genetically induced ▪ Certain trees chronically experience problematic girdling roots and are theorized to be genetically prone to this condition, known as girdling root syndrome. Topping the list are the maples, especially Norway maples. Other species include American beech, poplars, and the small-leaf linden cultivar 'Greenspire'.

Not all girdling roots are problematic. Only those that occur at the root collar area or above are considered chronically dangerous. Girdling roots that occur below the root collar area are not normally a threat to the tree's health or stability. It is also nearly impossible to look at a developing girdling root and predict that it will cause problems for the tree. If a tree has girdling roots, however, it is more likely to have problems than if it does not have girdling roots.

Culturally induced ▪ Any tree can develop root systems that could eventually result in girdling root problems, depending on how it was grown or planted. Root-bound plants often develop girdling roots if the roots are not pruned at planting time. Girdling roots can develop from poor planting techniques such as "twirling" a bare-root system into a planting hole that is too small for the roots, planting too deep, and planting in inadequate soil volumes.

Causes
- For genetically GRS-prone plants, simply cutting the branch roots during harvesting operations may result in girdling roots. Most plants generate roots at acute angles off the branch roots. Trees such as Norway maples commonly generate roots that run tangential to the tree trunk and later become girdling roots.
- For culturally induced girdling, poor growing practices (allowing plants to become root-bound) or poor planting techniques (no root pruning of root-bound plants, planting too deeply, "twirling" roots into small planting holes).

- Roots that girdle at the root collar area or above compress sapwood and restrict the flow of photosynthates to the root system.
- Declining root systems—insufficient root systems for supplying water and nutrients to the tree and supporting it physically.

Damage
- Restriction of photosynthates to the root system.
- Root death.
- Loss of anchorage system.
- Creation of weak points in the stem at or above the root collar flare.

Symptoms
- Scorch, early fall coloration, early leaf drop, localized damage symptoms.
- Excessive twig dieback, stagheading.
- Thin appearance to crown, overall stunt.
- Little to no stem taper (buttressing) at ground level, or one-sided taper.
- Leaning.
- Vulnerability to other biotic problems and environmental extremes.

Deicing Salt

Runoff salt ▪ Snow melt from deicing salts, especially sodium chloride, can become problematic in sidewalk planting pits, edges of parking lots and sidewalks, and drainage ditches. High levels of soluble salts can accumulate, causing long-term decline of plant health. All forms of plants are affected by deicing salts—from turfgrass to trees and shrubs.

Spray or drift salt ▪ Road-salt spray or drift poses a more chronic threat to tree and shrub health than runoff salt. Most damage occurs within 65 feet of high-traffic, high-speed roads; however, damage is not uncommon for distances of 150 feet or more from high-speed roads. Most trees and shrubs are susceptible to deicing-salt spray damage.

Causes
- Sodium chloride heavily used as deicing agent.
- Runoff (melt-off) salt elevates soluble salt levels in soils.
- Heavy accumulations of runoff salt breaks down the structure of soils.
- Spray salt can create high levels of soluble salts in the soil.
- Spray-salt drift causes deposits of sodium chloride on buds and growing points of deciduous plants and on foliage of conifers; these deposits are toxic to plant materials.

Damage

- Disruption of water movement from soil to plant roots.
- Death of buds, growing points, and foliage from direct chemical toxicity.
- Reduction in plant vitality.
- Breakdown of soils, leaving them more susceptible to drainage problems and reduced soil-oxygen levels.

Symptoms

- Witches' brooming, increased suckering, and epicormic sprouting.
- Scorch, wilt, early fall coloration, early leaf fall, twig dieback.
- Overall stunt, decline.
- Increased vulnerability to other biotic problems and environmental extremes.

Weather Extremes

Winter stem damage ▪ Winter stem damage is usually labeled as frost cracking, bark splitting, or bark scalding. Most damage occurs in parts of the country where winters are characterized by long periods of snow cover with subsequent increased light reflection.

Causes

- Trees grown in exposed sites such as boulevards, parking-lot planting pits, or new landscapes.
- Poor plant selection. Trees selected for boulevards are commonly native to forested areas, not normally exposed to full sunlight.
- Plants entering winter under water stress are more vulnerable.
- Plants more prone to stem damage suffer more if they enter winter in any stressed condition.
- Warm winter sunlight warms up the southern and southwestern sides of young or smooth-barked trees. When the cold night temperatures cool the bark down to ambient temperatures, splitting of the bark occurs.
- Warm winter sunlight warms up tender, smooth bark, which eventually dehydrates it and results in scalding.

Damage

- Opening of wounds on tree stems.
- Wounds must compartmentalize and seal over, which draws from the tree's energy reservoir.
- Wounded areas disrupt flow of materials in the phloem.
- Decay commonly results from wounded areas.

- Secondary infections commonly enter through wounds.

Symptoms

- Open splits or cracks on tree stems, especially on young trees or smooth-barked trees. Cracks might also occur on older trees that have been previously cracked.
- Sunken, dead areas on stem.
- Secondary canker infections.
- Stem decay.
- Excessive epicormic sprouting.
- Overall stunt.

Mechanical Damage

Mower or string-trimmer damage ▪ This is a chronic and insidious landscape-tree problem. Repeated damage from mowers banging into tree trunks or tearing off bark with wheels and mowing decks often occurs on a weekly basis during the growing season. Mowers do not need to tear off bark to cause damage; simply banging into tender young bark and **cambium** may eventually kill the cambium or even girdle the stem. String-trimmers are just as damaging. Damage is particularly severe during the weeks of the early growing season and on thin, smooth-barked trees. Older, thick-barked trees are less vulnerable to this problem.

Causes

- Crushing of the cambium from banging equipment into trunks.
- Tearing off bark and cambium with equipment.

Damage

- Wounding of the cambium and sapwood.
- Subsequent decay, interruption of the sapwood and **heartwood**.
- Open wounds and decay drastically increase the strength loss percentage and create hazard trees.
- Open wounds provide openings for secondary, canker-causing pathogens.
- Interruption of the flow of photosynthates to the root system.
- In some cases, girdling of the stem and complete restriction of photosynthates.
- Constant sealing over of wounds drains the energy reserve systems of trees.

Symptoms

- Swollen, wounded areas from repeated wounding and callusing.
- Leaf scorch, thin appearance to canopy, uneven fall coloring, and leaf drop.

- Basal decay.
- Under girdling conditions, overall stunt, wilt, scorch, dieback.
- Tree failure during windy weather.
- Excessive suckering and epicormic sprouting.

Construction Damage

Construction damage usually includes several assaults on a tree or forest system; many of the causes, damage, and symptoms of damage have already been discussed. Two types of construction damage should be considered: (1) damage to trees and forest systems during the development of homes or business parks near previously undisturbed trees, and (2) damage to boulevard trees from street, sidewalk, or curb reconstruction projects. Both types of construction damage have similarities, but boulevard trees present a different problem because their root systems usually are not characteristically symmetrical. Because of their planting locations (confined between curbs and sidewalks, or against streets and curbs), they have a tendency to develop linear root systems in these confined spaces. Therefore, damaging one side of their root system can produce more severe results than similar damage in a previously open area.

Causes

- Trees that have been grown in forest systems have part of that system damaged or removed; for example, removal of the litter layer, topsoil, or understory shrubbery and wildflowers. The removal of these components alters the entire system.
- Trees that have been grown in forest systems have spent their entire lives as part of these systems and have adjusted their roots, stems, and crowns to function within that environment.
- Urbanization of forest systems commonly introduces foreign competition, such as turfgrass, to the individual trees.
- Root systems are commonly severely damaged during construction and development.
- Tree stems and branches are often wounded from mechanized equipment used to develop the site.
- Soil grades are often altered, either by cutting or filling over root systems.
- Soil is commonly compacted, especially clay soils.
- Soil chemistry, especially pH, is commonly altered when foreign materials (asphalt) or solutions (concrete truck clean-out slurries) are added to the soils.
- Water-drainage rates and patterns are often adversely altered.

Damage

- Trees are exposed to temperature and water extremes, vastly different from what they had been growing in. Water stresses are common.
- Nutrient deficiencies are not unusual when the nutrient recycling capacity has been removed (loss of litter layer) and the nutrient-rich topsoil has been removed.
- Root loss further exaggerates the water-stress and nutrient-deficiency problems by lessening the ability of trees to absorb water and minerals.
- Photosynthetic rates commonly decline due to water and nutrient stresses.
- Respiration rates decline due to compacted or poorly drained soils.
- Recovery rates decline due to compacted soils and poor root regeneration and penetration.
- Energy reserves are reduced due to energy used to compartmentalize and seal over wounds.
- Bark cracking and sunscalding commonly occur on trees that were previously shaded by forests and are now fully exposed.
- Trees are more vulnerable to insect and disease problems.

Symptoms

- Long-term decline in overall vitality.
- Branch dieback and stagheading.
- Chlorotic foliage.
- Foliage appears to be growing in clumps rather than uniformly distributed.
- Decay is common, especially near the ground line.
- Wind-throw is common, especially where boulevard trees suffer root damage from reconstruction projects.
- Chronic wilting.
- Foliage may have a blue-silver-green hue instead of a normal medium- to dark-green color.
- Epicormic sprouting and suckering become common.
- No trunk flare is obvious where grades have been elevated.
- Bark may become loosened, sounding hollow when tapped with a small hammer.

Gary Johnson
Extension Educator and Associate Professor
Extension Service/Department of Forest Resources
University of Minnesota

Selected References

d'Ambrosio, R.P. 1990. Crown density and its correlation to girdling root syndrome. *J. Arboric.* 16(6):153–157.

Craul, P.J. 1994. Soil compaction on heavily used sites. *J. Arboric.* 20(2):69–74.

Cregg, B. 1995. Plant moisture stress of green ash trees in contrasting urban sites. *J. Arboric.* 21(6):271–276.

Day, S.D., and N.L. Bassuk. 1994. Effects of soil compaction and amelioration treatments on landscape plants. *J. Arboric.* 20(1):9–17.

Derr, J., and B.L. Appleton. *1988. Herbicide Injury to Trees and Shrubs: A Pictorial Guide to Symptom Diagnosis.* Virginia Beach, Virginia: Blue Crab Press. 72 pp.

Goodwin, C., and G. Lumis. 1992. Embedded wire in tree roots: Implications for tree growth and root function. *J. Arboric.* 18(3):115–123.

Green, J.L., O. Maloy, and J. Capizzi. *A Systematic Approach to Diagnosing Plant Problems.* Corvallis: Oregon State University. pp. 7–11.

Hamilton, W.D. 1988. Significance of root severance on performance of established trees. *J. Arboric.* 14(12):288–292.

Harris, R.W. 1992. *Arboriculture: Integrated Management of Landscape Trees, Shrubs, and Vines.* 2d ed. Englewood Cliffs, New Jersey: Prentice-Hall. 674 pp.

Hauer, R.J., W. Wang, and J.O. Dawson. 1993. Ice storm damage to urban trees. *J. Arboric.* 19(4):187–194.

Hickey, K.R., and M. Castonguay. 1995. A diagnostic guide. *Arbor Age* 15(1):10–12.

Kriett, K. 1995. Coping with stress in urban settings. *Arbor Age* 15(7):10–13.

Lesser, L.M. 1995. Drought stress in trees: Getting to the roots of the problem. *Arbor Age* 15(6):18–22.

Matheny, N.P., and J.R. Clark. 1991. *A Photographic Guide to the Evaluation of Hazard Trees in Urban Areas.* Savoy, Illinois: International Society of Arboriculture. 72 pp.

Myers, M.K., and H.C. Harrison. 1988. Evaluation of container plantings in an urban environment. *J. Arboric.* 14(12):293–297.

Peterson, C., R. Heatley, G. Adams, D. Smitley, D. Roberts, and M. Cameron. 1987. *Diagnosing Problems of Ornamental Landscape Plants.* East Lansing: Michigan State University, Cooperative Extension Service. Bulletin E-2024. 4 pp.

Sinclair, W.A., H.H. Lyon, and W.T. Johnson. 1987. *Diseases of Trees and Shrubs.* Ithaca, New York: Cornell University Press. 574 pp.

Stone, H.M. 1993. Girdling tree roots: The hidden cause of tree failure. *Arbor Age* 13(10):8–12.

Tate, R.L. 1981. Characteristics of girdling roots on urban Norway maples. *J. Arboric.* 7(10):268–270.

Watson, G., G. Kupkowski, and K.G. von der Heide-Spravka. 1992. The effect of backfill soil texture and planting hole shape on root regeneration of transplanted green ash. *J. Arboric.* 18(3):130–135.

CHAPTER 7

Managing Infectious Plant Diseases

Karen Rane and Nancy Pataky

Plant **disease** can be defined as any disturbance of a plant that interferes with its normal structure, function, or economic value. Disease has a negative impact on the health and vigor of plants. In addition, disease often has an adverse effect on a plant's appearance, which is an important quality influencing the value of landscape ornamentals.

Many different factors can hinder the growth and development of trees and shrubs. Disease-causing agents can be divided into two groups, based on whether they are living or nonliving. Nonliving disease-causing agents (referred to as **abiotic** or **noninfectious**) include such factors as environmental stress, nutritional deficiencies and toxicities, and injury from chemicals such as pesticides and deicing salts. The term **disorder** is often used to describe problems caused by nonliving agents. Noninfectious disorders, which are common in landscape ornamentals, are described in more detail in Chapter 6.

In this chapter, we will discuss diseases caused by living agents (**biotic** or **infectious** agents)— microorganisms such as **fungi, bacteria, viruses,** and **nematodes.** Microorganisms that cause disease in plants are called **pathogens.** Unlike abiotic agents, plant pathogens are able to spread from plant to plant, resulting in an increase in diseased plants over time. Infectious plant diseases are often grouped into categories based on the part of the plant infected, such as foliar, root, or stem diseases.

Diagnosing Infectious Disease[1]

We recognize disease in plants by the presence of **symptoms**. A symptom is the plant's response to one or more disease-causing agents. Symptoms differentiate diseased plants from their healthy counterparts. Symptoms can occur on any part of a diseased plant and can be characteristic for a specific causal agent. More often, however, the same type of symptom can be induced by more than one agent. Some common symptom types include:

- **Leaf spots:** Small discolored areas on foliage.
- **Blight:** Large dead areas on leaves, shoots, or flowers—often occurring rapidly.
- **Mosaic:** Intermingling patches of yellow and green tissue on a leaf.
- **Stunting:** Abnormally small size of entire plant or plant part.
- **Chlorosis:** Yellowish-green coloration in normally green tissues, such as leaves.
- **Marginal necrosis:** Brown, dead tissue around the edges of leaves.
- **Distortion:** Twisting or abnormally shaped leaves and shoots.
- **Wilt:** Flaccid, limp condition of leaves or nonwoody shoots resulting from water deficit.

---

[1]Appendix A contains a list of soil testing and plant diagnostic clinics in the U.S. and Canada.

- **Canker:** A localized, often sunken, dead area on a twig, branch, or stem.
- **Gall:** Abnormal swelling of a portion of a branch, leaf, root or bud; a tumor.
- **Rot:** Tissue breakdown or decay.
- **Witches' brooming:** Twig growth resulting from a lack of **apical dominance** causing side shoots to elongate equally, forming a dense cluster or broomlike mass of twigs.
- **Dieback:** Gradual death of individual branch or groups of branches.

Symptoms can develop in specific plant tissues invaded by a plant pathogen, or they can develop in plant parts far removed from the actual site of pathogen invasion. For example, symptoms of infectious root diseases include wilting of leaves and branches, even though root pathogens invade only root tissues. Symptoms can also change over time so that the first symptoms of a disease are quite different from symptoms associated with later stages.

Some plant pathogens produce structures that are visible on diseased plants. These structures or growths are called **signs** and are direct evidence of a pathogen's presence. **Conks, mushrooms,** bacterial **ooze,** and **mildews** are prominent signs of plant disease.

Infectious Plant-Disease Agents

Fungi

A fungus is a small (usually microscopic) organism made of filaments called **hyphae**. The body of the fungus, made up of many hyphae, is called the **mycelium** (mycelia). Fungi are similar to plants in many ways, but they do not contain chlorophyll and thus cannot produce sugars from carbon dioxide and water. Fungi must obtain all of their nutrients from organic matter. Most fungi use nonliving plant or animal material for nutrients and serve an important role in recycling organic matter in the environment. There is a small group of fungi, however, that obtains its nutrition from living plants, resulting in plant disease. The most numerous and destructive of all infectious plant diseases are caused by fungi. Some plant pathogenic fungi are able to attack many different plant species. Others are host-specific, that is, they are able to invade only one or a few closely related plants.

Fungi reproduce by means of **spores**. These microscopic units are often compared to seeds in flowering plants. Although individual hyphae require moisture and a relatively narrow range of temperatures to survive, spores can withstand environmental extremes.

Spores can be formed as the result of genetic recombination in a sexual process or can be formed asexually from fragments of hyphae that develop thickened cell walls and separate from the mycelium.

The terms "perfect" and "imperfect" are used to describe sexual and asexual fungal stages, respectively. An asexual fungal spore is called a **conidium** (conidia). Some fungi can produce both sexual spores and conidia, that is, they have both perfect and imperfect stages. Others have no sexual stage and produce only conidia.

Spores are often produced in specialized structures called **fruiting structures,** or **fruiting bodies**. Mushrooms and conks are some of the largest fungal fruiting structures; most fruiting structures are much smaller and visible only with a hand lens or microscope. To the unaided eye, fruiting structures of many plant-pathogenic fungi look like tiny dots in leaf spots or cankered stem tissue. These structures are classified based on characteristics visible under high magnification.

Although the structures are difficult to identify, the specific terms for these structures are found in many reference materials on tree diseases and so are included here (Figure 7.1). A **pycnidium** (pycnidia) is a small, flask-shaped fruiting structure, usually with a single porelike opening, that contains conidia. A fruiting structure that is similar in shape to a pycnidium but that contains sexual spores is called a **perithecium** (perithecia). A **cleistothecium** (cleistothecia) is a round structure without a pore or opening, often with distinct hyphal appendages, that contains the sexual spores of powdery mildew fungi. An **acervulus** (acervuli) is a saucer-shaped fruiting structure containing conidia that develops under, then breaks through, the host plant's epidermal cells. An **apothecium** (apothecia) is similar in shape to an acervulus but contains sexual spores. Some plant-pathogenic fungi, such as the imperfect stage of powdery mildews, can produce conidia directly from hyphae on the plant surface. This gives leaves infected by these fungi their characteristic powdery appearance.

Spores are the main means by which fungi spread to new hosts, and the type of fruiting structure has an influence on how spores will be disseminated. Spores borne on hyphae without any specialized fruiting structure are easily detached and moved by air currents. Dry spores from mushrooms and conks are picked up by air currents as they are released from the lower surface of these fruiting structures. Moisture is important for the dissemination of spores from the other structures. Spores ooze out of the porelike openings of pycnidia and perithecia under moist conditions and are moved to new hosts by the impact of rain droplets. Spores can be transported long distances when rain droplets are picked up by wind during storms. Activities such as pruning during wet weather can also move spores that have been released from fruiting structures by moisture. A few plant pathogenic fungi have spores that are disseminated by specific insects.

Once a fungal spore contacts a plant surface, it lies dormant until conditions are suitable. Then it germinates, producing a specialized hypha called a germ tube. Moisture is required for this germination process. The germ tube then invades susceptible host plant tissues either by direct penetration of intact plant cells or through wounds or natural openings such as stomata.

Figure 7.1 ▪ *Microscopic fungal spore-bearing structures. a) Conidia produced without a fruiting structure. b) Acervulus with conidia. c) Pycnidium containing conidia. d) Perithecium containing sexual spores called ascospores. e) Apothecia, cuplike fruiting structures. f) Cleistothecium, an enclosed fruiting structure that contains sexual spores.*

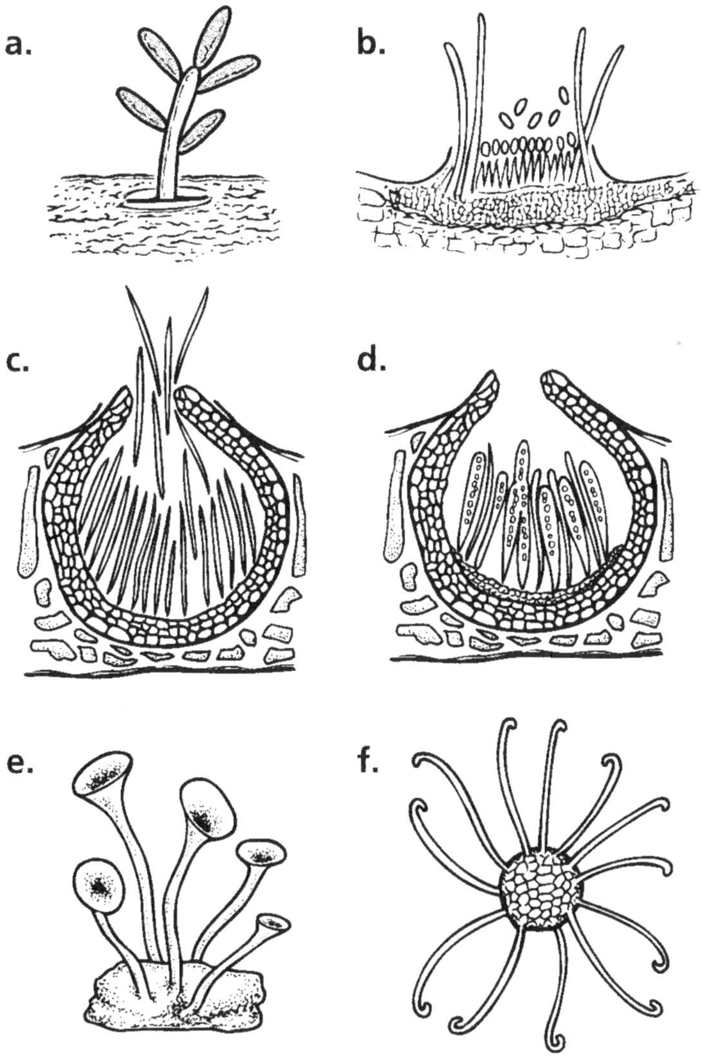

Drawings adapted from *Principles of Phytopathology* by C.B. Kenaga, Balt Publishers, Lafayette, IN.

The germ tube continues to grow, sending hyphal branches into and between host cells.

Some fungal pathogens are restricted in the amount of host tissue they colonize, whereas others invade a large portion of the host plant. For example, a single leaf spot caused by a fungus is usually quite small, whereas a wood-rotting root pathogen can invade and colonize an entire tree root system from a single root infection. Powdery mildews are primarily surface colonizers and form specialized absorbing structures that penetrate the host epidermis and obtain nutrients for the fungus. The vascular wilt fungi, however, enter the xylem of a tree through a wound and then colonize a large portion of the vascular system without emerging on the plant surface.

Fungi use enzymes and toxins as they grow through host tissues to break down plant cells and absorb nutrients. Symptoms are induced directly by these chemical weapons or indirectly as the invaded plant loses nutrients and water.

Many plant pathogenic fungi can survive in the soil or on plant debris as well as on their living host plant. The ability to use nonliving organic matter as a food source enables these fungi to survive in an area for some time in the absence of a susceptible host. In contrast, some pathogenic fungi grow and survive only in living host tissue and will not continue to grow once the infected tissue has died. These fungi survive from year to year as resistant spore-bearing fruiting structures or in infected plants in warm climates where susceptible host tissue is actively growing year-round. In the spring, spores produced by these fungi in southern climates can be blown northward to cause infections.

Bacteria

Bacteria are single-celled microorganisms found in virtually every environment on earth. Like fungi, most bacteria obtain their food from nonliving organic matter. Only a small group of bacteria are able to invade living plants and cause disease. Plant pathogenic bacteria are mostly rod-shaped microorganisms with rigid cell walls and often have one or more **flagella** (whiplike tails) that enable them to move through films of water. Bacterial cells are surrounded by a coating of polysaccharide, called a **slime layer,** which gives some protection from adverse environmental conditions. When large numbers of bacteria are present in plant tissue, the cells and polysaccharide slime form an ooze that can be seen on the surface of the infected tissue.

Bacteria reproduce primarily by simple cell division and do not form any visible fruiting structures on infected plants. Cell division can occur at a very rapid rate (bacterial cells can divide every twenty minutes when conditions are favorable), so bacterial populations can become quite high in a relatively short period of time. Symptoms develop when the number of bacterial cells in the plant tissue reach a certain threshold. For example, for most bacterial leaf spot diseases, bacterial population must reach about 1 million cells before a lesion is visible. Moderate to warm temperatures are favorable for development of some bacterial diseases, whereas others are more prevalent under cool conditions. Free moisture from rainfall, irrigation, or heavy dew is critical to the development of virtually all plant diseases caused by bacteria.

Unlike fungi, bacteria do not have the ability to invade intact plant tissue. They must enter plants through natural openings, such as stomata or wounds. Because bacteria are so small, wounds from windblown soil particles are large enough for entrance into a host plant. From these entry points, bacteria move through and multiply in the spaces between cells, producing toxins or enzymes that break down cell walls.

Most plant pathogenic bacteria survive over winter in infected plant debris; most do not have the ability to survive in the soil. Bacteria spread from plant to plant by splashing water (rainfall or irrigation), insects, or cultural practices that result in bacterial contamination of tools.

Phytoplasmas, or Mycoplasmalike Organisms (MLOs)

Phytoplasmas are closely related to bacteria but do not have the rigid cell wall typical of bacteria. They are amoebalike in shape and colonize only the phloem tissues of infected plants. Little is known about this group of plant pathogens. Phytoplasmas are spread by the feeding activity of certain species of phloem-feeding insects, such as leafhoppers, and apparently overwinter in infected perennial plant hosts.

Diseases caused by phytoplasmas are called **yellows** diseases. Symptoms of yellows include witches' brooming, chlorosis, and decline. Elm yellows and ash yellows are two important diseases of woody plants caused by phytoplasmas.

Viruses

Viruses are among the smallest plant pathogens and can be seen only with the aid of an electron microscope. Viruses are particles of nucleic acid surrounded by a protein coat and have no cellular structure. Viruses replicate inside plant cells, using plant cell contents to form more virus particles. It is not fully understood how viruses induce symptoms in host plants, but many symptoms are quite striking and unique to virus diseases. Leaf mosaic, distortion, and **ringspots** are common virus symptoms. Trees and shrubs infected with viruses rarely die but may show some decline over several years. Viruses must enter plants through wounds. Insects—particularly those that feed by piercing cells and removing cell contents (aphids, for example)—spread many viruses during their feeding activities. In addition, viruses can be spread by propagation of virus-infected stock plants. In a few cases, viruses can be spread from plant to plant by nematodes or by movement of infected pollen. Viruses overwinter in infected perennial plant hosts.

Nematodes

Nematodes are microscopic wormlike animals. Most live freely in fresh or salt water or in the soil, but some are parasitic to animals or plants. Most plant pathogenic nematodes feed on the roots of plants, but an important exception to this rule is the pine wood nematode, which colonizes the wood (xylem) of affected pines. A single nematode does not cause significant injury to a woody plant; nematode damage becomes noticeable when nematode populations are high. Above-ground symptoms of plants suffering from root nematode injury include stunting, chlorosis, and wilting. These symptoms are similar to those caused by other factors that inhibit root function, such as root rot, poor drainage, soil compaction, and construction injury. Root symptoms of nematode injury include galls, lesions, excessive root branching, injured root tips, and root rot when affected roots are invaded by secondary microorganisms.

Development of Infectious Disease

The four elements necessary for the development of plant disease are:

- *Susceptible host.* All plants are not susceptible to all pathogens. For disease to occur in a given plant, that plant must be able to be infected by a particular pathogen.
- *Plant pathogen.* A microorganism capable of causing disease is a vital component of disease. Most plant pathogens are host-specific and will cause disease in only a few host plants.

- *Favorable environment.* Plant pathogens have certain temperature and moisture requirements for growth and entry into plants. For example, environmental factors can influence the production of spores in fungi. Without a favorable infection environment, a plant pathogen will not be able to cause disease even when present on a susceptible host.

- *Time.* The interaction of host, pathogen, and environment occurs over the course of some period of time (usually hours) before infection takes place. Time also influences the growth stage of the host and the development of symptoms on an infected plant. Symptoms often change considerably over the course of weeks or months.

When all four of these elements are present, disease is the result. The process can be inhibited or reduced when one or more of these elements is deleted or altered.

These elements are often illustrated together in a pyramid configuration, called the disease pyramid (Figure 7.2). The disease pyramid is useful to remember when exploring methods of disease management.

Principles of Disease Management

Several principles of disease management take advantage of different aspects of the disease pyramid. Each of these principles can be used to manage a wide variety of plant diseases.

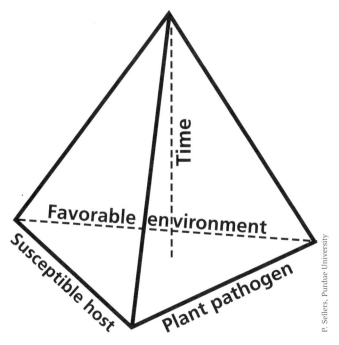

Figure 7.2 ▪ *The disease pyramid*

P. Sellers, Purdue University

Host Resistance

Resistance refers to use of nonsusceptible or less susceptible species. Because most diseases have a restricted host range, many disease problems can be avoided by using nonsusceptible species in the landscape. Plant breeders have identified certain cultivars (varieties) of some susceptible species that are less susceptible, or resistant, to common diseases that normally affect that plant species. For example, numerous cultivars of flowering crabapple are resistant to apple scab, fire blight, and rust, which are common diseases of crabapples.

Eradication

Eradication refers to the removal of diseased plants or plant parts, which will help in the management of several infectious diseases by reducing the amount of pathogen present in the location. Although some plant pathogenic fungi can move long distances through air currents, in most cases plant pathogens are spread most efficiently over short distances, such as within a plant canopy or from one plant to an adjacent one. Destruction of infected plants or infected branches on an otherwise healthy plant will reduce the spread of a disease to other susceptible hosts in the area.

Tools used to remove diseased plant parts should be cleaned in a household disinfectant or alcohol between cuts to avoid spreading plant pathogens on the tool surface. Many pathogens overwinter on fallen infected plant debris. Removal of this debris, such as raking fallen leaves infected with fungal leaf spot diseases, will reduce the amount of pathogen surviving in that landscape over the winter.

Avoidance

Avoidance is one of the best ways to deal with plant disease. The introduction of plant diseases can be avoided by selecting disease-free planting material when constructing new landscapes. Inspect nursery stock for signs or symptoms of infectious disease prior to installation to avoid future disease problems. Diseases can also be avoided by proper plant selection. This is particularly important when planting in wet or shady sites, which favor the development of root rots and foliage diseases, respectively.

Cultural Practices

Some cultural practices create a favorable environment for disease to occur, and altering these practices will reduce disease development. For example, overhead irrigation creates a favorable climate for foliar infection by fungi and bacteria because these pathogens need a film of water to invade leaves and are spread from plant to plant by splashing water. Changing irrigation practices to reduce leaf wetness will reduce the amount of disease. Soaker hoses eliminate wet foliage during irrigation, and pruning limbs to promote air circulation helps foliage dry quickly. Because many diseases of woody plants are more severe under adverse environmental conditions, maintaining plant health by proper watering and fertilizing will reduce the occurrence of these stress-related diseases.

Chemical Applications

When cultural methods are not adequate to reduce infectious diseases to acceptable levels, chemical applications may be needed. **Fungicides** are the primary chemical group applied for disease management in woody plants. Most fungicides are protectants, but some can provide a certain amount of curative action in the early stages of disease development. Some fungicides can be injected into infected trees as a therapeutic treatment. With some diseases, a specific growth stage of the host can be targeted for protection by fungicide application. Chemical control will not be successful if disease pressure is high due to a favorable environment, highly susceptible host, or excessive amount of pathogen **inoculum** (spores or diseased plant material). Because different fungicides have different modes of action and are effective against different fungi, it is important to match the fungicide to the specific disease you wish to control.

Two types of chemicals—**antibiotics** and **copper compounds**—have been used to manage bacterial diseases. They have been primarily used in nursery and fruit production industries, and their use is rarely warranted in the landscape. Currently there are no effective chemical control measures for virus or nematode diseases in landscape plantings.

> There are several factors to consider when deciding about fungicide use on landscape plants. These factors are summarized by John Hartman of the University of Kentucky as follows:
> * Is the host plant valuable?
> * Is the disease properly identified?
> * Is the disease life- or health-threatening?
> * Does this plant have a history of this disease?
> * Are effective, legal treatments available?
> * Will one or two applications suffice?
> * Have cultural control practices been used?
>
> If you answer "no" to any of the above inquiries, you should question the use of a fungicide.

Specific Diseases

Foliar Diseases

The following diseases of conifers and broadleaf plants are grouped together because the foliage is the primary tissue infected. Some diseases, such as apple scab and powdery mildew, may also affect fruit. Nevertheless, foliage is the major target of infection and the primary area of symptom expression.

Some of these diseases (leaf blisters, powdery mildew, black spot) are readily identified by symptoms and signs visible to the unaided eye. In other cases, it may be necessary to use a hand lens or microscope to examine fruiting structures of fungal pathogens before a disease can be confirmed (Rhizosphaera needle cast, brown spot, downy mildew). Needle blights and needle casts of evergreens usually cannot be distinguished unless fruiting bodies are present. Such fruiting structures can occur within lesions on one or both sides of the leaves, but their presence depends on the time of year and age of infected needles. Because fruiting structures are often present only in humid conditions, it may be necessary to place symptomatic foliage in a moist chamber for twenty-four to forty-eight hours to induce sporulation and gain a positive identification of disease. A plastic bag containing the sample and moist toweling, sealed to hold in moisture, will work well.

Needle casts—conifers ▪ This group of diseases is caused by fungi that infect new growth but do not cause the loss of needles until the following winter or spring. The characteristic loss of infected needles gives this group of diseases the name "needle cast."

Cyclaneusma needle cast
Causal agent: *Cyclaneusma minus* (syn. *Naemacyclus minor*).

Hosts: Many two-needled pines are susceptible, but it is primarily a problem of Scots pine.

Symptoms: Second- or third-year needles develop small, light-green spots in summer or fall. Needles continue to fade until they become yellow with distinct brown bars or dashes across the needle. Off-white to yellow, waxy apothecia appear within a month of symptom expression. These may not be noticed with the unaided eye but are easily seen with a hand lens or microscope (Figure 7.3, color plate section). Overall symptoms of this disease resemble extensive fall needle drop (Figure 7.4, color plate section).

Disease cycle: The fungus overwinters in needles on the ground or infected needles remaining on trees. Spore release from fruiting structures occurs when windy weather follows rain. Needles are susceptible to infection throughout the growing season.

Management: This needle disease is not a major problem in the midwestern landscape but has the potential to cause economic damage to Christmas-tree plantings. Cultural practices that increase air movement between trees will reduce the amount of infection. Resistant Scots pines are not yet available, but considerable variation in susceptibility among Scots pines exists. Protective fungicide applications reduce the spread of this disease, but the expense of repeated applications (four sprays are usually needed) may preclude their use on landscape trees unless disease incidence is severe.

Lophodermium needle cast

Causal agent: *Lophodermium seditiosum.*

Hosts: Many pines can be infected, but the disease is most problematic on Austrian, red, and Scots pines.

Symptoms: Most damage is seen in nursery and plantation settings. One-year-old needles develop brown spots with yellow margins, which eventually turn reddish brown in late winter or early spring. Discolored needles fall from the tree by early summer. Black football-shaped apothecia of the fungus may be visible on cast needles just below the needle surface (Figure 7.5, color plate section). The resulting bulge and longitudinal splitting of the needle surface is typical of this disease. Branches close to the ground are most severely infected and may have only tufts of green growth at the tips of branches (Figure 7.6, color plate section).

Disease cycle: Moist weather from midsummer to early fall causes spore release from cast needles. Spores are windblown or rain-splashed to current-year needles, where the fungus develops and overwinters. The first symptoms do not occur until the following spring.

Management: Because this fungus requires a cool, moist environment to infect, irrigate nursery stock early in the day to encourage rapid drying. Good weed control around trees also aids rapid drying. Diseased needles on trees in windbreaks serve as a source of inoculum, so plant nonhost species in windbreaks around nurseries or plantations. Fungicides can be used as protectant sprays. Spray applications must be initiated in July when spores are first released and must be repeated three times at two- to three-week intervals.

Rhabdocline needle cast

Causal agent: *Rhabdocline pseudotsugae* and *R. weirii.*

Host: Douglasfir.

Symptoms: One-year-old needles develop yellow spots in late winter or early spring. Spots turn reddish brown and appear as bands or cause entire needles to discolor (Figure 7.7, color plate section). Brown to reddish orange apothecia develop in the spots, causing the needle epidermis to split. Infected needles turn brown and drop by early summer while current-season needles remain green (Figure 7.8, color plate section). The disease is most severe on lower branches and on trees in areas with poor air movement. Infected trees show suppressed growth and vigor.

Disease cycle: The fungus overwinters in infected needles on trees. Spore release and needle infection occur any time from May through July, but only young needles are infected, and cool, wet weather is required. Symptoms on newly infected needles appear in late winter. Apothecia develop the following spring, and defoliation occurs in the summer—one year after infection.

Management: This disease is primarily a problem in Christmas tree plantations and nurseries but occasionally causes damage in landscape plantings as well. Shear or prune healthy trees before infected ones to minimize disease spread. Control weeds, allow adequate spacing between trees, and otherwise promote good air flow to prevent wet conditions conducive to infection. The fungus will not sporulate on fallen needles, so disease control in an urban environment is reasonable through weed control, removing infected branches, and other cultural practices mentioned. Inspect older needles in early spring. If fruiting bodies are present, commercial growers may consider fungicide applications at budbreak and again every seven to ten days until new growth is fully elongated. Resistant varieties are not available; susceptibility varies, however, with origin of the Douglasfir seed.

Rhizosphaera needle cast

Causal agent: *Rhizosphaera kalkhoffii.*

Hosts: The disease commonly occurs on Colorado blue spruce. Other spruce and pine species can be infected, but damage is usually not severe in landscape plantings. Norway spruce is resistant to the pathogen.

Symptoms: Initial symptoms occur in late summer as yellowing of first-year needles. These rapidly turn brown or purple-brown but do not fall from the tree until the following summer or autumn, twelve to eighteen months after the initial infection (Figure 7.9, color plate section). The fungus produces pycnidia in the needles, which appear as black pinhead-sized bodies that occur in rows down the needles (Figure 7.10, color plate section). These will extend above the surface of the needle when moist and can be seen with a hand lens. If not visible on dry needles, they will develop in twenty-four to forty-eight hours when infected needles are kept in a bag with a moist paper towel. The discoloration and defoliation generally occur on lower branches first and move up the tree, but can also appear scattered throughout the tree. Severely infected trees will have healthy needles only at the tips of branches.

Disease cycle: The fungus overwinters in fruiting structures on infected needles. Spores are released from spring until autumn. They readily infect young needles but can also infect older growth on trees under stressful growing conditions. Infection will occur more rapidly under warm, wet conditions.

Management: Cultural practices that will help reduce this disease include the use of healthy planting material and the continual inspection of trees for signs of the disease. Premature needle drop is a symptom that warrants follow-up inspection. In commercial production areas, the infected trees should be sheared after working with healthy trees. Disinfect shearing tools before working with the next tree. Good air circulation will help prevent infection. Maintain adequate spacing between trees, and keep surrounding vegetation mown and pruned. Resistant cultivars do not appear to be a choice at this time. Chemical controls are effective if the disease is not too severe. Such controls are preventive and applied when needles are half elongated and again when fully elongated. Because this fungus requires twelve to eighteen months for symptom expression, at least two years of fungicide sprays are usually required.

Needle blights—conifers ▪ Needle blights are very similar to needle casts and are caused by fungal pathogens. Lesions caused by needle blight pathogens often encompass more than half of a needle, and infected needles often remain on the tree, giving it a blighted appearance. Fruiting structures within these lesions are used for positive disease diagnosis.

Brown spot needle blight

Causal agent: *Mycosphaerella dearnessii* (syn. *Scirrhia acicola*).

Hosts: Primarily Scots pine in the Midwest, but other pines are also susceptible.

Symptoms: Yellow spotting of current-year needles occurs in July, and a small drop of resin often will be found in association with each spot. Spots turn brown in August and develop into bands, often with a chlorotic halo (Figure 7.11, color plate section). Needles die from the tip toward the base, and infected needles drop in the fall and the following spring. Infection is heaviest at the base of the tree, on the north side, or where moisture persists. Defoliation gives the trees a bare appearance (Figure 7.12, color plate section). In less severe cases, the disease will accelerate the loss of second- and third-year needles.

Disease cycle: Fruiting bodies (blackened **stromata** on which conidia are produced) form in the needles by August and overwinter there. Spores are released and infection occurs in late spring and early summer when susceptible developing needles are present in a moist environment. Older needles are resistant to infection. New fruiting structures form in infected needles by August, and the cycle continues.

Management: Do not shear trees or work among trees when the foliage is wet. Sterilize tools before moving from an infected to a healthy tree. Practices to improve air movement between trees will discourage infection. If symptoms and fruiting bodies are identified in the fall, consider fungicide application the next spring when needles are half grown and again thirty days later. You may need to shorten intervals between sprays in wet weather. In new plantings, look for resistance found in some of the long-needled Scots pine varieties from Central Europe. Do not plant seedlings near established pine windbreaks.

Dothistroma blight

Causal agent: *Dothistroma septospora* (perfect stage: *Scirrhia pini*).

Hosts: Many pines are susceptible, but Austrian and ponderosa pines are most commonly infected. In most cases, Scots and red pines are resistant to this disease.

Symptoms: Symptoms first occur in early fall as yellow to tan needle spots and dark-green bands on needles (Figure 7.13, color plate section) that quickly turn brown to red. Needle tips die, leaving the needle base green (Figure 7.14, color plate section). Fruiting structures develop in the dead tips in the fall and appear as black pinhead-sized spots. Look for infection in the lower part of the tree first. Early needle drop is common, but infected needles remaining on the tree are more important than fallen needles as a source of inoculum.

Disease cycle: The fungus overwinters on infected needles. Spores are released in wet weather and spread by wind and water. Generally, fungal fruiting bodies appear in the fall and release spores the following spring and summer. Infection occurs from May to October, but symptoms do not appear until early fall.

Management: Cultural measures such as weed control and proper plant spacing help reduce disease incidence and spread by promoting rapid drying of needles. In Christmas tree plantations, shearing of wet trees can spread spores of this fungus. Registered fungicides can be used on a preventive basis, and usual recommendations suggest two sprays, once in mid-May and again when new needles are expanded. Resistance within Austrian and ponderosa pine species is now in development.

Foliar diseases—broadleaf trees and shrubs ▪ Most deciduous trees can sustain a significant amount of foliar disease before growth is adversely affected. Spring infection of new growth has the potential to be more damaging than summer infections because new leaves are more susceptible to infection and because spores produced from these early infections can infect additional leaves in several secondary disease cycles before cold weather arrives. For these reasons, disease severity is often determined by early spring weather conditions that influence primary infection.

To the tree-care specialist and to the owner, aesthetic injury is often just as important as damage to health and **vitality**. Although foliar diseases have little impact on the health of a tree unless they recur for several years, one year's damage may be aesthetically unacceptable in some landscape situations. Unfortunately, by the time symptoms are seen, it is often too late to use any effective management practice that will help the current year's growth. Control measures for most foliar diseases of broadleaf woody plants focus on preventing the recurrence of disease in the future.

Apple scab

Causal agent: *Venturia inaequalis.*

Hosts: Crabapple, apple, pear, mountain ash, pyracantha, and many other members of the rose family.

Symptoms: Leaf spots appear in spring as small olive-green spots on either leaf surface. As spores form, lesions develop a velvety appearance (Figure 7.15, color plate section). Within a few weeks, the lesions turn brown. Later lesions are more elongate and often follow veins, but the same velvety look is present. As leaves age, they turn yellow (except for the scab lesions) and fall from the tree. In severe years, susceptible crabapples may be defoliated by late June. Flower parts, fruit, and succulent twigs can also be infected. Tissues may become curled or puckered, and fruit and twig lesions may be somewhat raised.

Disease cycle: The fungus overwinters in fallen infected leaves. Spores are released in wet spring weather. Infection occurs under a wide range of temperatures, but wet plant surfaces are necessary. The severity of the primary infection increases with the duration of wetting. The disease is capable of causing severe damage in wet springs. Secondary cycles of infection occur primarily by conidia that move with water splash or run along leaf surfaces. For this reason, secondary infections are more elongate and follow veins.

Management: This disease is so common in areas with wet spring weather that it is expected annually; the question is only how severe the infection will become. For new plantings, there are many choices of desirable resistant varieties. Resistance is by far the preferred means of management. Sanitation and removal of foliage may help decrease the primary inoculum levels, but the fungus is so common and spores so readily dispersed that infection is still likely to occur. Fungicides can be used to control this disease but require multiple applications on a preventive basis, beginning when buds break and repeating until two weeks after petal fall.

Black spot of rose

Causal agent: *Diplocarpon rosae.*

Hosts: Rose species and cultivars vary from highly susceptible to highly resistant.

Symptoms: Black spots with fringed margins appear on either leaf surface but predominantly the upper surface of leaves (Figure 7.16, color plate section). Infected leaves turn yellow, except for the black spots, and drop from the plant. Similar symptoms occur on petioles and fruit. Flower petals develop red spots and some distortion. Canes may become infected during the first year of development. Lesions are purplish red, then black, and slightly raised. Black spot causes plant disfigurement and weak growth, predisposing the plant to other infectious and noninfectious problems.

Disease cycle: The fungus overwinters on rose canes and fallen leaves. Primary infection occurs when spores are splashed to new leaves in the spring. Many secondary cycles follow, with a peak in late summer. Environmental conditions that promote infection are wet leaf surfaces, high humidity, and warm temperatures.

Management: Resistance to this disease is available in various rose cultivars. In large rose plantings where susceptible varieties must be grown, it helps to plant a mix of susceptible and resistant cultivars. Measures to increase air flow reduce disease severity by promoting rapid drying of foliage. Because the fungus survives in fallen leaves and infected canes, these must be removed in the fall. Protectant fungicides are commonly used. Begin application as new leaves appear, and apply weekly well into the fall on highly susceptible varieties.

Coccomyces leaf spot

Causal agent: *Coccomyces* spp. (syn. *Blumeriella jaapii*).

Hosts: Cherry, almond, chokecherry, and plum.

Symptoms: Leaf spots appear as soon as leaves reach full size. New spots may continue to develop until late summer. Spots are initially dark purple, becoming reddish brown (Figure 7.17, color plate section). Spots are only about 3 millimeters across but can coalesce to cause large areas of the leaf to turn brown. The leaf turns yellow and drops from the tree, or the spots drop out of the leaf, causing a shot-hole appearance. Severe infection on cherry can cause defoliation, loss of yield, and loss of vitality.

Disease cycle: The fungus overwinters in dead leaves on the ground. In the spring, spores are released and blown to new leaves, causing initial infection. Secondary cycles occur by conidia produced on the underside of lesions in wet weather.

Management: Remove fallen leaves in autumn. Prune trees so as to increase space between branches to promote air movement through the planting. Fungicides can be used on bearing fruit trees but are not usually recommended on ornamental species.

Cristulariella leaf spots

Causal agent: *Cristulariella depraedens* and *C. moricola*.

Hosts: Maple, pecan, black walnut, butternut, magnolia, sassafras, ash, and many other woody plants.

Symptoms: Spots on maple are initially greenish gray and water soaked, becoming grayish brown with dark borders and as much as 3 centimeters in diameter (Figure 7.18, color plate section). In cool, moist conditions the lesions coalesce to produce a scalded leaf appearance. Dead tissues may fall out of the leaves. On other hosts, spots range from pinpoints to target-shaped or irregular gray-green blotches. White crystalline deposits appear on the lesions, often in rings. In severe cases and under cool, wet summer conditions, extensive defoliation is possible.

Disease cycle: The fungus presumably overwinters on infected plant debris, but detailed information is lacking. Spores form at the edge of lesions on the lower leaf surface and are dispersed by splashing water. Infection occurs under cool, wet conditions.

Management: Remove leaves and dead plant material in the fall to reduce the amount of inoculum for infection the following spring. This disease has little impact on tree health; fungicides usually are not warranted in landscape plantings.

Downy mildew

Causal agent: *Peronospora sparsa* (rose), *Plasmopara cercidis* (redbud), *P. ribicola* (currant), *P. viburni* (viburnum), and *Pseudoperonospora celtidis* (hackberry and sugarberry).

Hosts: Rose, redbud, currant, viburnum, hackberry, and sugarberry. Rose is the host most seriously affected, and the disease is more often seen in commercial production than in landscape plantings.

Symptoms: Light-green or otherwise off-color spots appear on the upper leaf surface of infected plants. The lesions darken to reddish brown or brown (Figure 7.19, color plate section). The underside of these lesions is covered with a fine, grayish white downy mass of spore-bearing hyphae. The tufts may be missed with the unaided eye but can be seen with a hand lens. Any succulent aerial part of the plant may be infected. In severe cases or when plant parts are infected before maturity, tissue distortion may occur. **Necrosis** and early defoliation follow (Figure 7.20, color plate section).

Disease cycle: This group of fungi overwinters as resistant, thick-walled structures called **oospores** that form in infected, dead plant material. The oospores survive in the soil and are splashed to lower leaves in the spring, serving as the source of primary infection during extended wet periods. The fungus develops within the leaves and produces a second type of spore structure that emerges through lower stomata. In highly humid conditions, spores are formed and are distributed by wind and water, causing repeating cycles of disease spread.

Management: Downy mildew requires moist conditions, but the temperature range is broad (cool or warm, but not hot). The disease can be suppressed by proper plant spacing, placement in sites of good air flow, or other measures to promote rapid drying of foliage. Valuable specimens or shrubs can be sprayed with fungicides for disease protection in wet, damp weather. Start when disease first appears, and continue at weekly intervals as long as moderate, wet conditions persist.

Hawthorn leaf spot

Causal agent: *Entomosporium mespili* (perfect stage: *Diplocarpon mespili*).

Hosts: More than sixty species of plants, all in the Pomoideae group of the rose family. This disease commonly occurs on several varieties of ornamental hawthorn, especially English hawthorn and Paul's scarlet hawthorn.

Symptoms: In spring and early summer, minute reddish spots appear on the leaves (Figure 7.21, color plate section). Spots are angular and sometimes surrounded by a yellow halo. Affected areas increase in size and run together as the foliage grows. Eventually acervuli of the fungus develop within the lesion, and the spore mass appears gray to white. The disease may cause extensive premature defoliation, sometimes before midsummer.

Disease cycle: The fungus overwinters as spores on fallen leaves or as mycelia in plant tissues. Splashing rain and wind move spores to young, susceptible foliage in the spring. Thereafter, many secondary cycles of infection occur, especially in wet weather.

Management: Remove and dispose of fallen leaves to decrease fungal inoculum. Avoid overhead irrigation, which promotes disease spread. Increase air flow around plants by pruning out lower branches, properly spacing plants, and properly placing surrounding plants and ground covers. Succulent growth is most susceptible, so do not prune plants in the summer because this practice will promote new succulent tissues. Resistant varieties are an option. Washington hawthorn has shown only light infection levels even under high disease pressure, whereas 'Paulii' English hawthorns in the same location were defoliated. Cockspur hawthorn is resistant. Preventive fungicide applications can be used beginning in early June and repeated at seven- to ten-day intervals for three or four applications.

Leaf blotch of horsechestnut

Causal agent: *Guignardia aesculi.*

Hosts: California, Ohio, yellow, and red buckeye; and common, Japanese, and red horsechestnuts.

Symptoms: Leaf spots begin as discolored, water-soaked areas that may be small or large enough to cover the entire leaf, giving it a scorched appearance. Spotting appears in late June or early July. Lesions turn light reddish brown, often with a yellow margin (Figure 7.22, color plate section). Leaflets may become distorted, curled, and brittle. Black pycnidia form within the lesion on the upper leaf surface and are easily seen with a hand lens. Most disease development occurs after the tree has finished its annual growth, so tree vitality is rarely affected. The disease is a problem in nurseries because of early defoliation.

Disease cycle: The fungus overwinters in the perfect stage in fallen foliage. The spores from these structures are the primary inoculum released in moist spring weather. Leaf spots form within ten to twenty days following infection, and the imperfect stage (pycnidia) develops within the lesions. In wet conditions, secondary disease cycles are initiated throughout the summer.

Management: Remove fallen leaves around infected trees to reduce the primary inoculum available in the spring. Space trees in the landscape to allow air flow between trees. This disease does not usually warrant chemical control in landscape situations. If repeated serious infections have occurred on high-value specimen trees, fungicide sprays may be used. Begin spray applications at budbreak, and repeat at ten- to fourteen-day intervals as long as wet weather persists. Application of a fungicide such as lime sulfur when trees are dormant will also reduce the incidence of disease.

Leaf curl and leaf blister

Causal agent: Several *Taphrina* species cause blisterlike foliage distortion. A few of the more common diseases are peach leaf curl caused by *T. deformans,* oak leaf blister caused by *T. caerulescens,* plum pockets caused by *T. communis* and *T. pruni,* and yellow blisters on poplar by *T. populina.*

Hosts: Common hosts in the Midwest include peach, plum, oak, and poplar.

Symptoms: The fungus infects the leaves, causing thickened areas that become puckered, wrinkled, and cupped as the fungus and leaf both develop in spring and early summer. Leaf curling and deformity of leaves, buds, and stems are not unusual. Some species infect only flowers and fruit. A common symptom is blisterlike growths on leaves. These blisters are initially light green on the top of the leaf, and gray or whitish on the underside of the leaf. As they age, blistered areas can become red or brown (Figures 7.23 and 7.24, color plate section). Premature leaf drop may occur in early autumn. Repeated early defoliation can weaken trees and predispose them to other problems. Generally, however, this disease is not considered to be a significant landscape problem.

Disease cycle: *Taphrina* spp. overwinter as spores on buds and twigs. Spores germinate and infect leaves and flowers as they break bud, especially in cool, wet weather. A single layer of spore-producing tissue develops on the infected plant part, giving the blistered area a white or translucent appearance when fresh. Spores are released from this tissue from late spring to midsummer, and will remain in buds or on twigs until the following spring.

Management: Promote tree vitality through pruning, fertilization, and watering. Fungicides are rarely needed but will provide some control if applied once as a dormant spray to buds and twigs.

Phyllosticta leaf spot

Causal agent: *Phyllosticta* spp.

Hosts: Maple (especially amur, Japanese, silver, sugar, and red maples), witch hazel, rose, mountain ash, filbert, magnolia, linden, dogwood, and sycamore.

Symptoms: Small, circular, brown leaf spots appear in spring or early summer (Figure 7.25, color plate section). On some hosts, lesions are more irregular in shape, bleached, and almost translucent.

As lesions age, they turn pale, often with a distinct purple border. In cool, wet weather, lesions coalesce to cover much of the leaf surface. In such conditions, defoliation may occur. Small fruiting bodies of the fungus (pycnidia) can be seen as black pinpoint-sized dots in the lesion (Figure 7.26, color plate section). The pycnidia often occur in a circular pattern. In most cases, the disease does not affect tree health.

Disease cycle: The fungus is thought to overwinter in fallen infected leaves. Spores cause primary infection in cool, wet weather. After leaf lesions develop, further cycles of infection occur by spores produced within the initial lesions. In years when spring weather is cool and wet for an extended time, infection by Phyllosticta may cause defoliation by mid-June.

Management: In most cases, there is no need to manage for this disease. Remove fallen leaves and prune to promote quicker drying of foliage. In rare cases, fungicides would be recommended. Fungicides must be applied three or four times, at ten-day intervals, starting as buds begin to open.

Powdery mildew

Causal agent: There are probably more than three hundred species of fungi known to cause powdery mildew on various host plants. The imperfect genus involved is *Oidium.* Six closely related genera cover most of the perfect stages of powdery mildew fungi on woody plants. These include *Erysiphe, Microsphaera, Phyllactinia, Podosphaera, Sphaerotheca,* and *Uncinula.*

Hosts: Most species of woody shrubs and trees can be infected. Some species of powdery mildew fungi infect only a few closely related hosts, whereas others have a broad host range.

Symptoms: Powdery mildews are first visible on leaves as white or dusty gray patches (Figures 7.27 and 7.28, color plate section). Flowers and fruit may also be infected. Symptoms appear about midsummer and progress to cover entire leaves by fall. In some cases the growth is superficial (lilac), and in other cases leaves become distorted, dwarfed, and discolored (oak). Early defoliation may occur. Black pinpoint-sized fruiting structures (cleistothecia) form in the white mycelium in the fall. These serve as resting or overwintering structures. The severity of symptoms depends on the host species, the age of tissue infected, environmental conditions, and the fungus involved.

Disease cycle: Powdery mildew fungi survive the winter on plant tissue and dormant buds as mycelium or cleistothecia. Spores are released from the cleistothecia in wet spring weather and move to uninfected tissue in water or wind. Mycelium growing on the surface of leaves form white conidia, giving the foliage a white, powdery look. As wind and rain disperse these conidia, secondary infections are initiated. Cycles continue as long as days are warm and dry followed by cooler, damp nights. Cool temperatures or hot, dry summer conditions usually cause formation of cleistothecia.

Management: Most powdery mildews on trees do not have a significant impact on tree health. There are times, however, when management is needed, especially when plants have suffered repeated infections for several years. In many of these cases, cultural practices will control the disease. Place plants in sunny locations with good air movement. Dense, shady, or damp areas favor disease development. Remove dead foliage around the plants in the fall to decrease the level of primary inoculum the next spring. Avoid excessive fertilization and watering as these practices encourage succulent new growth, which is more susceptible to powdery mildew. Resistant varieties continue to offer the best source of disease control. Fungicides can be used to prevent infection, but treatment must be started as soon as the first symptoms are seen. Once the disease becomes widespread, it cannot be controlled in that year.

Septoria leaf spot

Causal agent: *Septoria* spp.

Hosts: Azalea, cottonwood, and dogwood.

Symptoms: Leaf spots vary from small flecks, to white or silvery spots, to brown circular spots (Figure 7.29, color plate section), to larger irregular spots with tan centers. Rings or zones can occur within the larger spots, giving them a target appearance. Tiny black fruiting bodies (pycnidia) form within the lesion. Usually the rest of the leaf stays green. If lesions are numerous, however, the foliage turns yellow and drops prematurely. In most cases, the disease has little impact on overall tree health.

Disease cycle: The fungus overwinters in dead leaves and stems from the previous year's infection. Primary infection occurs by spores released in the spring that infect the lower leaves of the tree.

Secondary disease cycles occur when conidia are produced in leaf lesions during wet weather.

Management: Sanitation (removing fallen leaves and dead plant material in the fall) may help reduce inoculum for primary infection the following spring. Fungicides are available but not usually recommended.

Shoot and Twig Blights

The shoot and twig blights encompass diseases that show symptoms and signs on foliage and stems. Although cankers may be involved in the disease expression, cankers are not the primary symptom.

Shoot and twig blights—conifers ▪ Conifers will develop brown needles from these diseases, but growth does not usually wilt. Because new growth is often affected, the diseases can be confused with root problems or environmental stress.

Phomopsis blight and Kabatina blight

Causal agent: *Phomopsis juniperovora* causes Phomopsis blight, and *Kabatina juniperi* causes Kabatina blight.

Hosts: Phomopsis blight can occur on many species of the cypress family, but natural stands usually do not show much damage. The major problem is in nursery and landscape settings. Species most often affected are eastern red cedar and creeping, Rocky Mountain, and savin junipers. Arborvitae, white cedar, cypress, Douglasfir, fir, juniper, yew, and larch can also become infected. There are many resistant cultivars available in the landscape and nursery industry. Kabatina blight affects many of the same juniper, arborvitae, and cypress hosts as Phomopsis blight.

Symptoms: Phomopsis blight causes a tip blight of branches. Only the newest growth is affected, leaving mature leaves unaffected (Figure 7.30, color plate section). Initial infection occurs as yellow spots on leaves. These progress into the shoots, causing tips to turn light green and then reddish brown. At the base of the dead tip, a gray band of tissue marks the margin of infected tissue. Black fruiting structures (pycnidia) form within this band in mid-June; they are pinpoint-sized and gray to black. The dead stem tips remain on the branches for several months, eventually turning gray.

Kabatina blight causes symptoms similar to Phomopsis blight but shows on one-year-old twigs. In the spring, before new growth is initiated, fruiting structures (acervuli) can be seen on twig tips that were infected the previous year (Figure 7.31, color plate section).

Disease cycle: Infection by the Phomopsis blight fungus can occur any time that succulent new tissue is present along with a wet period. Long wet periods promote a more severe disease situation. Conidia are blown or splashed from pycnidia on twigs infected the previous year. Repeated cycles of infection occur as long as succulent tissue is present. Mature tissues are unaffected. Pycnidia appear on new growth by early summer.

Kabatina blight requires wounding for infection. Winter injury and insect activity are common sources of wounding. Fruiting structures of Kabatina will be evident in the spring on one-year-old twigs infected the previous season. The fruiting structures of *Phomopsis juniperovora* and *Kabatina juniperi* appear very similar with a hand lens but can be distinguished with the aid of a microscope.

Management: Promote air circulation and quicker foliar drying by proper plant spacing, pruning of surrounding plant material, and watering early in the day. Resistant varieties remain the most effective control. Fungicides can be used to prevent infection by these fungi. Repeat applications are necessary for Phomopsis blight for as long as succulent growth is present in conjunction with wet weather. Kabatina blight is difficult to control with fungicides.

Sphaeropsis (Diplodia) blight

Causal agent: *Sphaeropsis sapinea* (syn. *Diplodia pinea*).

Hosts: Many pines can be infected, but Austrian, Scots, mugo, and ponderosa are the most commonly affected species in the Midwest. The disease can be seen occasionally on red, Swiss stone, and eastern white pines; Douglasfir; and blue, Norway, and white spruce. It is more likely if trees are stressed and near infected susceptible species.

Symptoms: Injury to pine may be very severe in landscape plantings. Rarely is the disease a problem in forested areas or sites with trees that are within their natural range. The disease first appears as browning of needles at the tips of shoots (Figure 7.32, color plate section). Needles may be shorter than normal, and sometimes resin droplets exude from infected needles. Small black pycnidia of the fungus can be seen with the unaided eye at the base of needles, just under the fascicle, or sheath tissue (Figure 7.33, color plate section). Pycnidia also form on scales of two-year-old seed cones and on bark of infected shoots. Often the damage appears in the lower part of the tree, but shoots throughout the tree may show symptoms with time. Repeated infection of branch tips results in deformed tree growth and loss of vitality. The fungus can also cause cankers with excessive and obvious sap exudate. Branches that become girdled will die. Sapwood may be discolored with a gray to black stain.

Disease cycle: The fungus overwinters in infected cones, shoots, and needles. Spores are released in the spring during rainy periods, but high relative humidity is required for infection to occur. Therefore, the disease is usually more severe in wet springs. The new shoots are susceptible to infection from two weeks after budbreak until about mid-June. The fungus penetrates the needles and quickly causes necrosis. Second-year seed cones are infected in late May or early June and serve as a reservoir of future inoculum.

Management: The causal fungus infects needles directly but can also infect wounded tissue. Therefore, it is best to avoid pruning (and wounding) trees when they are most susceptible from late spring to early summer. Do not plant susceptible trees near mature, infected pines. If infected trees are found, remove any dead or cankered wood and cones, if possible. Removal of cones may not be practical on large trees. Fungicides may be necessary, but chemical control of this disease is difficult unless strict sanitation measures are also followed. Fungicide applications must include three treatments. The first occurs when buds begin to open, the second when candles are half grown, and the third when candles are fully expanded. Consider avoiding the use of the most susceptible pines in landscape plantings.

Shoot and twig blights—broadleaf trees and shrubs
▪ The shoot blight phase of these diseases appears as a sudden, brown wilt of new growth.

Anthracnose

Causal agent: Many genera of fungi cause anthracnose on various hosts. The genera usually involved with tree anthracnose diseases in the Midwest include *Discula, Glomerella, Gnomonia, Kabatiella, Marssoniella, Marssonina,* and *Monostichella*.

Hosts: The trees usually associated with the above anthracnose fungi are ash, birch, dogwood, filbert, maple, oak, redbud, sycamore, and walnut.

Symptoms: Spots or irregular necrotic areas appear on the leaves and twigs of infected trees in late spring and early summer (Figures 7.34 and 7.35, color plate section). On some species, the necrosis follows along veins (Figure 7.36, color plate section). In wet weather, the new growth becomes infected and may develop curled or distorted leaves. Symptoms can look similar to frost injury, which often occurs at the same time. With some hosts (such as sycamore), anthracnose fungi cause branch cankers. Girdled stems die, producing a disfigured tree. In very wet years, premature defoliation is common.

Disease cycle: Anthracnose fungi that infect only leaves overwinter on dead foliage on the ground. Cool, wet spring weather favors spore production and spread by wind and water to succulent new growth. Leaf lesions form, and spore production soon follows. Secondary cycles continue with cool, wet conditions. In a year with a cool, wet spring and early summer, infected trees often exhibit defoliation in June or early July. Anthracnose fungi that infect both stems and leaves overwinter in buds and bark and on cankers. Spores produced in the spring are splashed or blown to nearby leaves. The fungus can then grow into the petiole and eventually into the stem to form a stem canker. Secondary cycles of infection occur. Sycamore, oak, and dogwood have anthracnose diseases that infect leaves and stems.

Management: Anthracnose diseases rarely cause tree death but may cause early defoliation. A healthy tree will recover and refoliate with little permanent damage, so management practices are targeted at promoting tree vigor. An exception to this occurs with dogwood anthracnose, where stem cankers can girdle trunks and kill trees. If this disease is confirmed on a dogwood tree, removal of all infected plant parts, as well as application of protectant fungicides, is necessary. On most species, the removal and destruction of fallen leaves and major stem cankers reduce the potential for infection, but with oak and sycamore the cankers are so small and numerous that pruning is not possible. Fungicides are available to prevent anthracnose but are rarely recommended—except with dogwood anthracnose—because of the cost of treating mature trees and because the disease is seldom fatal. If fungicides are used, they must be initiated just before buds open. Repeat applications must be made when leaves are half grown and ten to fourteen days later.

Brown rot of stone fruits

Causal agent: *Monilinia fructicola* or *M. laxa.*

Hosts: Stone fruit trees, including both ornamental and wild trees in the genus *Prunus*: almond, apricot, sweet and sour cherries, nectarine, peach, plum, and prune.

Symptoms: First indication of this disease is collapse and browning of flowers. Infection can be limited to flowers or may progress into the shoots. In most cases, the canker and dieback phase of this disease does not usually cause serious damage. Infection is usually limited to blossom infection and some shoot dieback. Small cankers form on the twigs, causing a dark discoloration and sap exudate. Infected fruit is quickly covered with powdery gray tufts of spores (Figure 7.37, color plate section). As the fruit decays, it shrivels and forms a "mummy."

Disease cycle: The fungus overwinters on mummies either on the tree or on the ground around the tree. Fruiting bodies (apothecia) of the perfect stage of the fungus form in the mummies, and spores are released in warm, moist conditions when the host is in bloom. Flowers or new shoots become infected. Blossom and peduncle infections serve as sources of conidial development. These conidia infect other blossoms and fruit under moist conditions. Spores are carried by wind and rain, infecting directly or at wound sites.

Management: Select a sunny, open site for stone fruit trees; be certain that there are no wild fruit trees nearby. Trees should be kept pruned to encourage air movement and drying within the canopy. Infected trees can be helped by removing mummies and cankered tissue on infected trees to decrease the inoculum level. Fungicide applications are important for protecting fruit-bearing trees, but are usually not warranted for ornamental *Prunus* species. Fungicide application is important, especially for commercial growers. Control targets the protection of flowers so that spores are not present to infect fruit later. Sprays must be initiated when pistil tips extend above the flowers. Repeat applications continue until just after petal drop and are reinitiated about three weeks before harvest.

Phomopsis canker of Russian olive

Causal agent: *Phomopsis arnoldiae* (syn. *P. elaeagni*).

Hosts: Russian olive.

Symptoms: Shriveled, gray foliage that remains attached to trees is the first symptom of this disease. A definite canker can usually be seen at the base of the wilted branches (Figure 7.38, color plate section). The bark is reddish brown to black, whereas the sapwood is reddish brown. The cankered area oozes an amber-colored gum, and the face of the canker becomes sunken, black, and cracked with age. The disease can be a problem in the nursery as well as in landscapes. Seedlings and saplings exhibit wilting and death with no apparent canker formation. This also occurs with small branches on mature trees.

Disease cycle: Little is known about the spread of this fungus in nature. Pycnidia form in stromata in the face of the canker and have been reported in roots of seedlings. Stromata remain prominent in the cankers for at least one year. It is thought that infection occurs with wind and rain movement of spores to wounds and possibly to wet plant surfaces. New growth is more susceptible than older tissues.

Management: As with other canker diseases, practices to promote tree vitality are important, along with the close inspection of new trees for any cankers and dieback symptoms. Do not purchase or plant infected trees because it is likely that the canker will continue to be a problem to tree growth. Established infected trees should be pruned to remove cankered wood well below the canker during dry weather. Disinfect tools between cuts. Check for newly developed resistant varieties of Russian olive before planting this species.

Black knot

Causal agent: *Apiosporina morbosa* (syn. *Dibotryon morbosum*).

Hosts: Many *Prunus* species, both edible and ornamental, are susceptible. Included are flowering almond, apricot, blackthorn, cherries (bird, bitter, black, mahaleb, Nanking, pin, sand, western sand, sour, and sweet), chokecherry, peach, and plum (American, beach, Canada, common, damson, Japanese, myrobalan, and Sierra).

Symptoms: The first symptom, which often goes unnoticed, is a swelling of the twigs of the current year's growth. Knots or galls develop from swellings on branches and trunks of infected trees. Bark on the galls splits, and galls appear corky and green. By the following spring, the galls are hard and black (Figure 7.39, color plate section). They are obvious on branches in association with bent or curved twigs. Galls can be one foot or longer. Girdled branches usually die.

Disease cycle: This fungus overwinters as fruiting structures on the surface of knots. The spores are released in wet spring weather, and infection follows on succulent shoots or wound sites. Swelling does not appear until the fall after infection. Cankers continue perennial development on the stem, and two years after initial infection the knot has its first fruiting structures at the edges of the swellings. Spores are released and initiate new infections. In some cases, fruiting structures form in as little as one year after infection.

Management: Wild plums and cherries are very prone to infection by black knot. Symptoms on wild *Prunus* may not always be obvious, so these species need to be carefully observed for knots. Infected wild trees should be removed. Remove galls on established trees during the dormant season, when galls are fully developed for the year. To be certain that all of the gall is removed, cut several inches below the knot. Fungicides can be used to help control the disease once sources of disease have been removed, but they will not be effective as the only treatment. Fungicides are applied from green tip to shuck fall. Shuck fall is about three weeks after petal fall.

Bacterial blight of lilac

Causal agent: *Pseudomonas syringae* pv. *syringae.*

Hosts: Discussed here on lilac, although this pathogen can cause problems on many plants, including stone fruits, peach, forsythia, mock orange, and pear. On lilac, the Chinese, Japanese, Persian, and common lilacs (especially whites) are most susceptible.

Symptoms: Leaves develop brown spots or blotches, often with yellow halos, which run together and quickly involve the entire leaf. Young shoots may have black stripes or a one-sided effect because only part of the shoot is infected. Young leaves turn black and die quickly, giving the plant the appearance of a fire blight infection (Figure 7.40, color plate section). Flowers turn brown and limp, whereas flower buds turn black. Stems may become infected through the leaves or directly through the bark. Black lesions result on infected stems.

Disease cycle: As with most bacterial diseases, this one is prevalent in rainy seasons or with frequent overhead irrigation while tissues are succulent. The bacteria overwinter in infected host tissue. Bacteria invade succulent tissues or wounds any time cool, wet conditions prevail.

Management: Remove infected shoots several inches below visible cankers. Prune when dry, and disinfect pruners between cuts. Prune lilacs and surrounding plants to allow good air flow within and around the plants. Rapid drying of the plants will discourage infection. Avoid overhead irrigation, especially in spring. Because succulent tissue is more susceptible to infection, use balanced but not excessive rates of fertilizer, especially nitrogen. This will reduce the amount of succulent tissue. Copper fungicides may provide some benefit in disease prevention if used two or three times, starting when new growth appears. Spray every seven to ten days when conditions are favorable for infection.

Fire blight

Causal agent: *Erwinia amylovora.*

Hosts: The most significantly damaged plants include apple, crabapple, pear, cotoneaster, hawthorn, quince, firethorn, and mountain ash. Other species of plants may be infected, but all are within the rose family.

Symptoms: Flowers and new leaves appear water-soaked, quickly wilt, and turn brown to black (Figure 7.41, color plate section). Leaves remain attached to the stems. Stem tips curl over with a "shepherd's crook" appearance typical of this disease. Symptoms appear quickly, as though the host had been scorched with fire. The bacteria move down to the shoot base, causing a limb or trunk canker (Figure 7.42, color plate section). Cankers are dark-colored, and wood in the cankered area becomes sunken as surrounding wood continues to grow. Cankers can girdle and kill entire trees.

Disease cycle: The causal bacterium overwinters in wood at the edge of cankers. New infections each spring usually begin in the flowers. In the spring when conditions are warm and wet, the bacteria multiply on the surface of flowers and other plant tissues and may appear as amber-colored droplets (ooze) on the surface of cankers. Bacteria are moved by wind, water, insects, people, pruning, or many other vectors to young, succulent plant parts. Natural openings or wounds make suitable infection sites; for example, rain can wash bacteria from the petals to the nectaries (natural openings) at the base of the flowers. Repeated infections can occur from inoculum developed in primary infections during the growing season if wet conditions and succulent tissues are present.

Management: When establishing new plantings of rosaceous plants, look for resistance to fire blight as the most effective disease-control practice. In an infected planting, and while trees are dormant, remove all cankered wood, pruning a few inches below the last visible sign of the canker. Canker removal will eliminate a large part of the primary inoculum for the following year. Pruners do not need to be disinfected between cuts unless pruning is done during the growing season. If pruning is done during the growing season, six to twelve inches of healthy tissue should be removed along with the cankered areas. Because young, succulent shoots are very susceptible to infection, avoid using high rates of nitrogen fertilizer, which promotes rapid shoot elongation. It is best to use a balanced fertilizer and to consider split applications of nitrogen (half before growth starts and half after petal fall). Copper compounds and antibiotics are available to help manage this disease in commercial settings such as nurseries and orchards. Spray applications are timed to protect flowers because flowers are usually the first site of infection each year.

Stem Diseases

The following diseases all result in death of localized areas on stems (cankers). Cankers are often sunken but can be raised or merely discolored. The tissues under the bark of a canker are usually discolored and dead. Leaves and stems beyond the canker will die, resulting in significant branch dieback. Cankers are common in trees stressed by environmental or site problems. In most cases, management strategies are targeted at alleviating stress and improving tree health.

Stem diseases—conifers ▪ Infectious stem diseases are relatively uncommon on conifers. The exception is Cytospora canker of spruce. Sphaeropsis of pine (discussed in shoot and twig blights) can cause stem cankers as well as shoot blight.

Cytospora canker of spruce

Causal agent: *Cytospora kunzei* (syn. *Leucocytospora kunzei*). Perfect stage: *Leucostoma kunzei* (syn. *Valsa kunzei*).

Hosts: Most common in Colorado blue spruce. Also susceptible: black, Oriental, white, Norway, and Engelmann spruces. Douglasfir, balsam fir, eastern hemlock, larch, and red and Eastern white pines may also serve as hosts.

Symptoms: Lower branches show symptoms first, with a progression of symptomatic branches moving up the tree (Figure 7.43, color plate section). Needles turn purplish brown on entire branches rather than branch tips. White or light-blue resin can be found on older infected branches (Figure 7.44, color plate section). The resin becomes more noticeable as needles drop. A canker is present and can be found by exposing the discolored inner bark, which will be brown. Small, black, pinhead-sized pycnidia of the fungus form within the cankered bark. Cankered branches die. It is common to see infected spruces lose lower branches over a period of years until the tree is unsightly.

Disease cycle: The fungus overwinters as pycnidia, perithecia, and mycelium in cankered bark. Spores are released during the growing season and infect branches of the same or nearby trees at wound sites. Spores of the fungus are moved by wind, rain, and vectors of the fungus—including insects, birds, and humans. The fungus grows in the inner bark, girdling and killing branches. This disease commonly affects stressed spruce. Drought-stressed trees are particularly susceptible. The fungus usually attacks trees that are at least fifteen years old.

Management: Manage spruce trees for optimum vitality to help avoid infection. If Cytospora has been a problem in the area, consider planting something other than blue spruce, which is very susceptible to this disease. It is best to avoid wounding trees, but when cankers appear, they must be removed. Remove diseased branches, preferably in late winter or in dry weather. Disinfect pruners between cuts. Do not shear trees in wet weather. There are currently no effective chemical control measures for this disease.

Stem diseases—broadleaf trees and shrubs ▪ The pathogens causing stem diseases are often called "opportunistic pathogens" because they are most common on trees and shrubs under stress. These diseases tend to develop slowly over months or years and become more noticeable when stems become girdled and dieback is evident.

Botryosphaeria cankers
Causal agents: This group of canker diseases is caused by *Botryosphaeria dothidea, B. obtusa, B. quercuum,* and *B. rhodina.* The conidial forms can appear as *Botryodiplodia, Diplodia, Dothiorella, Lasiodiplodia,* and *Sphaeropsis.*

Hosts: The host list for Botryosphaeria canker could fill this page. *Botryosphaeria dothidea* infects a wide range of ornamental and fruit trees, especially sweet gum, rhododendron, dogwood, elm, linden, redbud, and sycamore. *B. obtusa* is also a problem on fruit trees and many ornamental trees. Of these, crabapple and oak seem most affected. *B. quercuum* is a problem on oaks and has been found regularly in the Midwest causing stem cankers. *B. rhodina* attacks hundreds of genera but is common on Russian olive, sycamore, and peach.

Symptoms: Dieback symptoms are typical of Botryosphaeria infections. Annual or perennial cankers occur in trees stressed by flooding, drought, winter injury, nutrient imbalance, poor soils, and so forth. Canker type will vary with the fungal species and host infected. Cankers can be small spots that have been limited by callus formation, or they can become large, girdling cankers with or without callus tissue. Leaf and twig death is common (Figure 7.45, color plate section), and infected trees often lack vitality.

Disease cycle: The fungus produces pycnidia, perithecia, or both in the face of the canker. Fruiting structures are evident in old cankers as they rupture the bark surface. When wet, fruiting bodies exude spores that can be splashed, washed, blown, or moved by insects to new infection sites. This can occur at any time when conditions permit but is most common in late spring or early summer.

Management: Canker prevention is in part dependent on the avoidance of environmental stress. Proper plant selection for the site goes a long way toward avoiding infection. Promote tree health through proper fertilization and watering to minimize infection. Prune and destroy cankered branches. Fungicides are of no practical benefit.

Cryptodiaporthe canker of poplar
Causal agent: *Cryptodiaporthe populae.*

Hosts: Many species of poplar are infected, especially those in the Tacamahaca and Aegieros groups. In Midwest landscapes, Lombardy poplar is particularly susceptible. Some aspens are also infected, including both bigtooth and quaking.

Symptoms: Death of small, scattered twigs begins the disease progression. Leaves turn yellow and drop early. Cankers appear throughout the tree, especially in branch axils. The bark over cankers is not usually discolored, but the tissues beneath the bark become brown to black. Scattered black pycnidia form in the canker face, giving it a pimpled appearance. In wet weather, these sporulate and produce greenish to amber spore tendrils. As the cankers age, the bark splits and exposes the wood. Callus formation is common. If cankers girdle twigs, dieback results (Figure 7.46, color plate section). The fungus can grow into larger stems and cause perennial cankers. This disease has been commonly reported on trees weakened by transplanting, drought, wounding, or other stresses.

Disease cycle: The fungus overwinters as pycnidia and mycelium in the bark. In the spring, the pycnidia rupture the bark and conidia are dispersed by rain, insects, or birds. Pycnidia may be produced throughout the growing season, so repeated cycles of infection are possible.

Management: Use only disease-free material when planting poplar or aspen, and avoid susceptible cultivars. Proper site selection for the species will greatly aid in disease prevention by reducing stress. Avoid pruning or otherwise wounding trees. Chemical control measures are not effective.

Thyronectria canker of honey locust

Causal agent: *Thyronectria austro-americana.*

Hosts: Honey locust, including thornless and podless cultivars, and Oriental honey locust.

Symptoms: This canker disease is first evident as yellow and wilted foliage. Close examination shows elongated cankers in wood of all ages (Figure 7.47, color plate section). As cankers girdle stems, dieback occurs. Cankers can be annual or perennial but are usually associated with wounds or pruning sites. The face of the canker may be slightly depressed to sunken and cracked with a yellow-orange color, especially where bark is thin. On thick bark areas of the tree, the canker is difficult to see. The sapwood under the canker is discolored a reddish brown. Signs of the fungus can appear as clusters of pycnidia that emerge through the face of the canker (Figure 7.48, color plate section). At first the structures will be pink, but they darken to black with age. This disease is believed to be a problem of stressed trees, especially those in urban sites. It can be fatal if cankers occur at the base of the tree.

Disease cycle: The fungus overwinters on infected trees. Warm, humid conditions are necessary for infection. Sites of infection include pruning wounds, natural openings, sunburned bark, and other wounds. The fungus grows in the cambium and outer xylem, and cankers form. Fruiting structures form in the canker within a month.

Management: This disease is common on stressed honey locust. Management includes proper placement of trees, adequate watering to avoid drought, avoidance of wounding or physical damage, and pruning only in cool, dry weather when inoculum levels are lowest. Chemical control options are not available.

Leucostoma and Valsa cankers

Causal agents: Species of two genera of fungi can cause cankers on a variety of hosts. The perfect stages involved are *Leucostoma* and *Valsa.* Their imperfect stages are *Leucocytospora* and *Cytospora,* respectively.

Hosts: Apple, apricot, ash, birch, cherry, chokecherry, elder, maple, mountain ash, Russian olive, peach, pear, plum, poplar, prune, serviceberry, and willow have been reported as hosts. The disease also occurs on conifers as discussed previously.

Symptoms: The fungi involved are stress pathogens often found on dead branches. Symptoms include dead buds, twigs, and branches, with cankers occurring throughout the tree. Often cankers can be seen at the base of dead branches. Canker color and type will vary with the host. Cankers are discolored and sunken, but on hosts such as cherry the canker may be hidden by the bark (Figure 7.49, color plate section). Cherry and peach may exude gum at the canker site, giving the name "gummosis" to the disease. Fruiting bodies (conidial stroma and perithecia) form just beneath the bark surface and appear as bumps on the canker until moisture is available. In wet weather, yellow to orange masses of spore tendrils are present on the canker face.

Disease cycle: The pathogens overwinter in cankers. Moisture is necessary for spore release from fruiting structures. Rain serves as the means of spore dispersal to new wound sites. Infection occurs on weakened plant tissue, but healthy tissue may also be infected. Cankers are most commonly initiated from fall to spring, though infection can occur any time weather conditions permit. Growth of the fungus is most active when the host is dormant.

Management: To avoid this disease, plant trees that are well adapted to the site and weather conditions of the area. Stressed trees are more susceptible than healthy trees. Avoid wounding, and use management practices that will promote tree health. Prune cankered branches well below the margin of the diseased tissue. Chemical controls are not effective.

Nectria canker

Causal agent: *Nectria galligena.*

Hosts: Many woody plants are susceptible and include alder, apple, ash, aspen, birch, cherry, dogwood, elm, filbert, hawthorn, hickory, holly, hornbeam and hophornbeam, horse chestnut, linden, magnolia, maple, mountain ash, mulberry, oak, pear, pecan, poplar, quince, redbud, sassafras, serviceberry, sourwood, sumac, sweet gum, tupelo, walnut and butternut, and willow.

Symptoms: Cankers begin as small, dark areas on young twigs, often centered on old branch stubs or wounds. The canker grows slowly and may girdle small stems but rarely large limbs. Cankers are perennial. The fungus develops and the canker enlarges when the tree is dormant. During the following growing season, callus tissue forms at the edge of the canker. The fungus invades the callus tissue during the next dormant season, followed by another year of callus formation. This process continues, giving the cankers a target appearance (Figure 7.50, color plate section). The fruiting structures of this fungus appear from fall to spring as reddish spore masses on the bark in and around the canker.

Disease cycle: The fungus invades at wound sites. This may include natural wounds such as leaf scars or branch stubs. It may also include weather-related injury sites or mechanical wounds. Spore discharge occurs in spring and fall, when conditions are wet. The fungus grows through the wound site and into the cambium, killing bark, cambium, and outer sapwood. Fungal development occurs while the host is dormant. The host is able to produce callus around the canker during the growing season. If the fungus survives, it will again grow through the cork layer of the callus and cause canker enlargement the next dormant season.

Management: There is little that can be done to effectively manage this disease. Because the fungus is more common on stressed trees, increasing tree vitality will reduce infection as well as help the tree continue to produce callus tissue. Avoid wounding, and remove badly cankered wood only in dry weather. There are no effective chemical control measures for this disease.

Crown gall

Causal agent: *Agrobacterium tumefaciens.*

Hosts: Many woody and herbaceous plant species are susceptible. Common hosts include rose, euonymus, willow, grape, apple, crabapple, and walnut. Conifers are resistant.

Symptoms: Stem galls caused by this bacterial pathogen begin as small swellings that appear individually or in clumps on the lower stem near the soil line (this area is often called the crown of the plant, hence the name for the disease). Galls continue to enlarge and on some hosts can initially appear white in color, then become dark brown with age (Figure 7.51, color plate section). Cracking bark over the gall surface gives a rough appearance to affected tissues. Galls may also develop higher on the stem and branches. Affected plants may be stunted. Galls caused by insects or from abnormal plant growth (burls) can be mistaken for crown gall disease. Insect galls do not normally occur at the soil line, however, and will usually contain holes caused by the inhabiting insect. The bark on noninfectious burls usually remains intact, unlike the bark of crown galls.

Disease cycle: Unlike most bacterial plant pathogens, *Agrobacterium tumefaciens* can survive for several years in soil without the presence of a susceptible host. The pathogen must enter plants through wounds to cause disease. Crown gall is a unique disease in that genetic material from the bacterium becomes incorporated into the host plant's genetic code during the infection process. The bacterial genes cause uncontrolled cell division in host tissue, resulting in gall formation. Bacteria from developing galls are released back into the soil.

Management: Prevention is the best method of managing crown gall. Avoid unnecessary injuries. Inspect all nursery stock for the presence of galls prior to planting. Removal of galls from an infected plant does not always cure the plant because the symptoms are due to a genetic change that may occur throughout the host. If a plant with galls appears stunted, remove the infected plant. Large trees with crown gall often show no adverse effects, so removal is not necessary. If you know that the causal bacterium is present in the soil, choose resistant plants for that site. Table 7.1 shows which species are resistant and which are susceptible to crown gall.

Vascular Diseases

The pathogens that cause vascular diseases invade and colonize the water-conducting tissues of infected plants. These pathogens may enter the plant through the roots or through the above-ground parts of the plant, but a large portion of the xylem or phloem is eventually colonized. When the pathogen colonizes the xylem of infected plants, wilting, leaf scorch, and death can result in large part because water conduction within the stem has been blocked. When the pathogen invades primarily phloem tissues, chlorosis, stunting, and witches' brooming are common symptoms. Vascular diseases are virtually impossible to eradicate once a tree is infected. Some of these diseases, such as Dutch elm disease, will result in the rapid death of large trees, whereas others cause dieback that progresses relatively slowly. Confirmation of vascular diseases requires laboratory analysis of recently infected branches or stems.

Vascular disease—conifers ▪ There is only one vascular disease of conifers that causes a problem in the Midwest—pine wilt.

Table 7.1 ▪ *Resistance of selected woody ornamentals to crown gall*

Resistant	*Susceptible*
Bald cypress (*Taxodium distichum*)	Apple (*Malus*)
Barberry (*Berberis*)	Birch (*Betula*)
Beech (*Fagus*)	Crabapple (*Malus*)
Boxwood (*Buxus*)	Dogwood (*Cornus*)
Deutzia (*Deutzia*)	Elm (*Ulmus*)
Ginkgo (*Ginkgo biloba*)	Euonymus (except *E. alatus*)
Golden-rain tree (*Koelreuteria paniculata*)	Honeysuckle (*Lonicera*)
Holly (*Ilex*)	Lilac (*Syringa*)
Hornbeam (*Carpinus*)	Plum, peach, cherry (*Prunus*)
Larch (*Larix*)	Rose (*Rosa*)
Linden, littleleaf (*Tilia cordata*)	Walnut (*Juglans nigra*)
Magnolia (*Magnolia*)	Willow (*Salix*)
Pine (*Pinus*)	
Serviceberry (*Amelanchier*)	
Spruce (*Picea*)	
Tuliptree (*Liriodendron tulipifera*)	
Yellowwood (*Cladrastis lutea*)	
Yew, Japanese (*Taxus cuspidata*)	
Zelkova (*Zelkova*)	

Pine wilt

Causal agent: The pine wood nematode, *Bursaphelenchus xylophilus.*

Hosts: Several species of pine are known hosts. Pines most commonly affected include Scots, Austrian, and Japanese black pines.

Symptoms: Gray-green discoloration of the foliage is usually the first symptom observed in infected pines. The discoloration progresses to yellow, then brown (Figure 7.52, color plate section). This symptom can occur any time midsummer to late fall or late winter to spring. Trees infected in the fall do not break bud the following spring. Prior to foliar symptoms, the resin content of the wood decreases significantly, but this symptom may go unnoticed unless the tree is pruned. Pines declining from environmental stress or transplant shock will develop symptoms similar to pine wilt. A laboratory test is necessary to confirm this disease.

Disease cycle: The pine wood nematode is vectored by certain species of cerambycid beetles. *Monochaemus carolinensis* appears to be the primary vector in the United States. Adult beetles infested with the nematode emerge from dead pines in the spring and begin feeding on young pine shoots. During this feeding, immature nematodes move from the insects into the feeding wounds and enter the resin canal system of the tree, where they mature, mate, and reproduce. Nematode populations build up to extremely high numbers by the time foliar symptoms are first observed (as early as four to eight weeks after infection). Cerambycid beetles are attracted to dying trees and deposit eggs in them. The emerging adult beetles become infested with the nematode, completing the cycle. *Monochaemus* spp. have also been found to transmit pine wood nematode when depositing eggs, thereby introducing the nematode to trees dying from other causes.

Management: Although control measures are not recommended for infected trees in forest situations, removal of infected trees in landscapes or Christmas-tree plantations is recommended. Infected trees must be destroyed (burned or buried) to eliminate the breeding sites for the beetle vector. Maintaining the health of landscape pines through good cultural practices will reduce the number of stressed and dying trees available to attract the insect vector, thereby reducing spread of the nematode through oviposition.

Vascular diseases—broadleaf trees and shrubs ▪ These diseases can kill mature shade trees and cause great aesthetic as well as monetary loss. Disease identification is crucial in preventing spread to other trees.

Dutch elm disease (DED)

Causal agent: *Ophiostoma ulmi* (formerly *Ceratocystis ulmi*).

Hosts: Members of the elm family. Elm species vary in susceptibility. American elm is highly susceptible. Siberian elm is considered to be tolerant to this disease. Chinese elm is highly resistant or immune.

Symptoms: The first symptom observed in American elm is yellow foliage on one or more branches, from late spring to midsummer. The affected foliage soon becomes wilted and brown; this symptom is called "flagging." Although an entire tree may wilt in one growing season (Figure 7.53, color plate section), in most cases symptom progression occurs over a few years. As with other vascular diseases, brown discoloration of the outer sapwood may be visible on recently wilted branches (Figure 7.54, color plate section).

Disease cycle: The causal fungus is spread by the feeding activities of two species of bark beetle, the native elm bark beetle (*Hylurgopinus rufipes*) and the lesser European bark beetle (*Scolytus multistriatus*). These insects breed under the bark of dead elms and accumulate spores of the fungus as emerging adults. The insects feed on twigs of healthy elm trees and deposit spores of the pathogen in feeding wounds. The fungus colonizes the water-conducting tissue (xylem) of the twigs and moves throughout the tree. Affected trees die as the xylem becomes blocked. Because dying or dead trees are preferred breeding sites for the insect vectors, the disease cycle is efficient in maintaining a supply of contaminated insects. The disease also spreads from an infected elm to adjacent elms through root grafts.

Management: Management of DED depends mainly on eliminating bark beetle breeding sites. Prompt removal of dead and dying elm trees and proper sanitation (chipping or debarking) of elm wood are initial steps of effective management. Root grafts between infected trees and adjacent elms should be severed by trenching with a vibratory plow to a depth of three to four feet. Trenching should be done prior to removal of infected trees. Because the fungus is introduced to twigs rather than through roots, removal of infected branches as soon as flagging is observed may stop the spread of the fungus within the tree, although the fungus often moves too quickly for this method to be effective. Fungicide injection treatments have met with some success, but this is an expensive procedure and should be regarded as a temporary measure for highly valuable trees. If an infected tree is standing on nearby property, fungicide injection may provide added protection for the valuable specimen until the nearby threat can be removed. Without community-wide sanitation, Dutch elm disease is almost impossible to control.

Oak wilt

Causal agent: *Ceratocystis fagacearum*.

Hosts: Most oak species. The red oak group (red, black, pin, shingle, and others) is highly susceptible, whereas the white oak group (white, bur) is more resistant.

Symptoms:

Red oak group: Wilting and tan or bronze foliar discoloration over the entire tree canopy can occur throughout the growing season. The discoloration begins at the leaf margins and progresses toward the midvein (Figure 7.55, color plate section). Defoliation of symptomatic and green leaves occurs soon after symptom development (Figure 7.56, color plate section). Brown to black streaks may be visible in the sapwood of affected branches. Death of infected red oaks usually occurs within several weeks after symptoms are first observed. After a tree has died of oak wilt, fungal growths called **mycelial mats,** or **pressure pads,** form under the bark on the trunk, causing the bark to crack (Figure 7.57, color plate section). The mycelial mats are gray to black and can vary in length from one to several inches.

White oak group: Symptoms progress more slowly in infected white oaks. Wilting of individual branches is the first symptom observed. Foliage can develop marginal discoloration, but this is not as extensive as in infected red oaks, and symptomatic leaves usually remain attached to branches. Dieback occurs over a period of several years. Mycelial mats rarely form on infected trees of the white oak group.

Disease cycle: The causal fungus survives in the trunk and roots of infected trees up to four years after the tree has died. Sap-feeding beetles are attracted to the mycelial mats that form under the bark of recently killed trees and carry spores from these mats to other oak trees. The insects feed on sap exuding from fresh wounds and introduce the spores to the wounded tissue. The fungus enters the water-conducting tissue of the tree (the xylem) through these wounds and grows in vessels. Plugging of the vessels results in restriction of water movement. Trees infected with the oak wilt fungus die basically from lack of water. The pathogen can also move through trees via root grafts—the primary means of spread in groves of oak trees. Root-graft transmission occurs both in the white oak and red oak groups.

Management: Because there is no cure for trees infected with the oak wilt fungus, management of this disease must focus on preventing infection. Avoid trimming or wounding oaks during spring and early summer, when sap oozing from wounds attracts the sap-feeding beetles that spread the fungus. If pruning during this time is unavoidable (to repair storm damage or construction injury), applications of wound paints have been reported to reduce sap flow and therefore reduce chances of infection via beetles. Most transmission of oak wilt occurs through root grafts, however, so disruption of root grafts is critical to disease management. Root grafts can be severed by digging a trench three to four feet deep and several inches wide around an infected tree prior to tree removal. To prevent the formation of mycelial mats and subsequent spread of the fungus by insects, infected oak trees must be cut down and destroyed by chipping, debarking, or burying.

Verticillium wilt

Causal agent: *Verticillium dahliae, V. albo-atrum.*

Hosts: More than 300 species of plants. In the landscape, the disease is most frequent on maple, redbud, ash, catalpa, and tuliptree.

Symptoms: Like most vascular wilt diseases, symptoms in plants infected by Verticillium develop in response to water stress. Symptoms range from sudden wilt of individual branches (Figure 7.58, color plate section) to leaf scorch, stunted leaves, and branch dieback that occurs sporadically over several years. In many instances, symptoms de-velop on only one side of an infected tree. Larger infected branches, and occasionally small ones, exhibit brown, black, or greenish streaks in the sapwood (Figure 7.59, color plate section).

Disease cycle: The fungus is an excellent soil inhabitant and can survive in the soil for many years. The fungus enters plants through the root system and colonizes the water-conducting tissue (xylem) of susceptible hosts. Water transport becomes blocked by both fungal growth and gums and other substances that are part of the host defense system. Highly susceptible trees might die within one season, but in most cases dieback occurs over a few to several years. The fungus will remain in the soil even if infected trees are removed.

Management: There is no cure for trees affected by Verticillium wilt. Symptom progression may be slowed by maintaining tree vigor through proper pruning, watering, and fertilization. In some cases, these procedures can delay the death of infected trees for several years. If Verticillium has been diagnosed as the cause of death of a tree in a landscape site, replant the area with resistant tree species. Table 7.2 contains a list of susceptible and resistant woody plant species.

Wetwood and slime flux

Causal agent: *Enterobacter cloacae* (formerly *Erwinia nimipressuralis*) and other bacteria.

Hosts: Common in elm, oak, and mulberry. Infrequent on maple, paper birch, butternut, redbud, sycamore, and walnut.

Symptoms: The most common symptom of this condition is oozing sap, called **slime flux,** which flows from bark cracks or other wounds in the trunk or limbs. Sap runs down the trunk, causing dark streaks that become gray or white when dry (Figure 7.60, color plate section). Slime flux develops foul odors as secondary microorganisms colonize the oozing liquid. When affected trees are cut, wetwood is visible as water-soaked, discolored regions of the wood. These wet regions are not decayed, however, because decay fungi do not grow well in water-soaked wood. Wetwood can contribute to dieback in affected branches, and dripping slime flux can retard callus production and wound closure.

Disease cycle: The bacteria associated with wetwood are common soil and water inhabitants that enter trees through wounds. Trees may be infected for several years before symptoms develop.

Table 7.2 ▪ *Resistance of selected woody ornamentals to Verticillium wilt*

Resistant	Susceptible
Apple (*Malus*)	Ash (*Fraxinus*)
Beech (*Fagus*)	Barberry (*Berberis*)
Birch (*Betula*)	Black locust (*Robinia pseudoacacia*)
Boxwood (*Buxus*)	Box elder (*Acer negundo*)
Crabapple (*Malus*)	Currant (*Ribes*)
Dogwood (*Cornus*)	Maple (*Acer*)
Fir (*Abies*)	Redbud (*Cercis canadensis*)
Firethorn (*Pyracantha*)	Russian olive (*Elaeagnus angustifolia*)
Ginkgo (*Ginkgo biloba*)	Viburnum (*Virbunum*)
Hawthorn (*Crataegus*)	Yellowwood (*Cladrastis lutea*)
Honey locust (*Gleditsia triacanthos*)	
Hornbeam (*Carpinus*)	
Juniper (*Juniperus*)	
Katsura tree (*Cerdiciphyllum japonicum*)	
Larch (*Larix*)	
Linden (*Tilia*)	
Oak (*Quercus*)	
Pear (*Pyrus*)	
Pine (*Pinus*)	
Spruce (*Picea*)	
Sweet gum (*Liquidambar*)	
Sycamore (*Platanus*)	
Willow (*Salix*)	
Yew (*Taxus*)	

Note: This list is meant to be a general guideline. Some genera contain both resistant and susceptible species. There are far more susceptible plants than listed here. These seem to be particularly susceptible.

Liquid eventually oozes from wounds in infected trees as gases produced by the bacteria cause an increase in internal sap pressure.

Management: No measures will cure trees of slime flux. In the past, recommendations were to install drain tubes in affected trees to relieve pressure and direct the flow of sap away from the trunk surface. This procedure is no longer recommended because any drilling of holes in a tree breaks the natural barriers formed in response to the initial wound, and formerly water-soaked wood might be subject to decay by fungi. Thus, this procedure could allow spread of decay fungi throughout the trunk. Proper branch-pruning techniques reduce the incidence of wetwood by promoting rapid closure of pruning wounds. Cul-

tural practices that prevent wounding of trunks and roots will reduce infection by the bacteria responsible for wetwood. Fertilization helps to invigorate affected trees. If the affected tree is in severe decline, removal is recommended.

Bacterial leaf scorch

Causal agent: *Xyllela fastidiosa*.

Hosts: Elm, oaks, sycamore, mulberry, sweet gum, sugar maple, and red maple. This pathogen also causes Pierce's disease of grape. Bacterial leaf scorch is primarily a disease of landscape trees rather than trees in forested areas.

Symptoms: Browning of leaf margins (leaf scorch) occurs in mid- to late summer. In elm, some oaks, and mulberry, a yellow margin sometimes develops between scorched leaf margins and healthy green inner leaf tissue (Figure 7.61, color plate section). In sycamore and oak, the interior edge of symptomatic leaf tissue often is red-brown. Severely scorched oak and mulberry leaves drop earlier than healthy leaves. In sycamore, symptomatic leaves curl upward but remain attached. Initially a single branch develops leaf scorch symptoms. Symptoms recur each year, with an increase in the number of branches affected. Growth reduction and dieback of affected branches occurs in severely affected trees. No discoloration is visible in the wood of symptomatic branches, in contrast to fungal vascular wilt diseases such as oak wilt or Dutch elm disease. Symptoms of bacterial leaf scorch may resemble those caused by noninfectious disorders such as drought stress or wind desiccation. Confirmation of bacterial leaf scorch involves a serological test performed on petioles of scorched leaves.

Disease cycle: The bacterium has been found in a large number of herbaceous and woody plant hosts, but many infected plants show few, if any, symptoms. Xylem-feeding sharpshooter leafhoppers and spittlebugs are known to spread *X. fastidiosa* in grape and peach and are believed to be the vectors in landscape trees as well. The pathogen can also be spread through root grafts.

Management: Currently, cultural practices to alleviate root stress in infected trees are the only means of extending the life of an infected tree. Control of insect vectors is not practical, and there are no chemical treatments to prevent infection or to use as therapy on infected trees. If an infected tree shows extensive dieback and leaf scorch, it should be removed.

Elm yellows (elm phloem necrosis)

Causal agent: Elm yellows phytoplasma (formerly elm yellows mycoplasmalike organism).

Hosts: Elm species, including American, slippery, winged, and some hybrids. Siberian elm appears to be immune.

Symptoms: Foliar symptoms can occur any time during the summer. Initial symptoms include yellowing and drooping of foliage (Figure 7.62, color plate section). Symptomatic leaves drop, and twigs and symptoms develop first on one or a few branches. An entire tree might develop symptoms in just a few weeks. Discoloration of the inner bark (phloem) tissues of infected trees occurs as foliar symptoms develop. The brown discolored tissue is most easily observed in the trunk (upper branches usually do not show this symptom) by cutting away the outer bark. When exposed to air, the inner bark of infected trees develops a dark brown color more rapidly than the inner bark of uninfected trees. The discolored inner bark of infected trees often emits a wintergreen odor due to the production of methyl salicylate (oil of wintergreen). This odor is easily detected by enclosing a portion of moist, fresh inner bark tissue in a jar for a few minutes. The characteristic odor is not present in dead trees. Although some infected elms survive for several years, most die within one to two years after foliar symptoms first appear. Phytoplasmas cannot be cultured onto agar media to confirm their presence. Confirmation of elm yellows is accomplished by examining suspect living phloem tissues under an electron microscope or under a light microscope using special stains. A presumptive diagnosis can be made using foliar symptoms, the presence of discolored phloem tissue, and the presence of wintergreen odor in the infected inner bark.

Disease cycle: Phloem-feeding insects are believed to spread the elm yellows phytoplasma. The pathogen overwinters in infected hosts and is believed to be transmitted primarily during the late summer and fall.

Management: No control measures are available for this disease. Use of resistant Asiatic or European elms will reduce losses due to elm yellows. Removal of infected trees is advised.

Ash yellows

Causal agent: Ash yellows phytoplasma (formerly ash yellows mycoplasmalike organism).

Hosts: Ash species, primarily white ash and green ash in both landscapes and forest stands. Ten other ash species are also reported hosts. The same pathogen also causes lilac witches' brooming, a decline disease of several species of lilac.

Symptoms: Reduced radial and branch growth, loss of apical dominance in branches (a condition called *deliquescent branching*), and progressive decline are typical symptoms of ash yellows. Shortened twig growth is common, resulting in tufted foliage. Leaves of infected trees are often smaller than normal and light green in color, and they may develop early fall coloration. Eventually a progressive dieback of branches begins (Figure 7.63, color plate section), and witches' brooms may develop. Witches' brooms occur most frequently on trees with severe dieback and on stumps of diseased trees. They commonly develop at the base of trunks (Figure 7.64, color plate section) but occasionally can be found several feet above ground. Vertical cracks often occur on the lower trunk. Symptom progression is slower and the disease less severe in green ash than in white ash. Although witches' brooms are diagnostic for ash yellows, only a small percentage of infected trees display this symptom. Laboratory confirmation of ash yellows is based on a staining technique using a fluorescence microscope.

Disease cycle: The ash yellows pathogen is presumed to be spread by phloem-feeding insects such as leafhoppers. Little is known about other hosts for this phytoplasma, but research is ongoing.

Management: There are currently no measures to control this disease. Trees with severe dieback should be removed. Species diversity in landscapes and forest stands will reduce the overall impact of tree loss due to ash yellows. Cultural practices to reduce tree stress might help to slow the progression of symptoms.

Root Diseases

The primary site of infection for the following diseases is the root system. Some root pathogens attack fine roots only, whereas others can cause rot of large, woody roots as well. Trees with root disease develop symptoms after a significant portion of the root system has been affected. Poor growth, wilting, and leaf scorch are typical symptoms for any root problem, including infectious root disease. It is important to note that root diseases caused by wood-rotting fungi may result in a weakened tree that could become a hazard to nearby people or property.

Phytophthora root and crown rot

Causal agent: Several *Phytophthora* species.

Hosts: Wide range of broadleaf and conifer trees and shrubs. Causes crown or collar rot on apple, dogwood, rhododendron, cherry, yew, hemlock, pine, and fir. Causes bleeding canker on beech, birch, maple, dogwood, and sweet gum. Many other shade and ornamental plants are also susceptible.

Symptoms: Stunting, poor growth, early fall coloration, dieback, wilt and eventual death are associated with Phytophthora (Figure 7.65, color plate section). Discoloration of the inner bark and wood at the base of the infected plant is usually present and visible if the outer bark is scraped away (Figure 7.66, color plate section). There is a distinct margin between healthy and diseased crown tissues. Reddish-brown liquid may exude from the cankered area (hence, the name "bleeding canker"). Laboratory diagnosis is necessary to confirm the presence of Phytophthora because other root problems mimic the above-ground symptoms of this disease.

Disease cycle: Phytophthora is a soil-inhabiting fungus that requires high moisture to complete its life cycle. Therefore, the disease is most common under conditions of saturated soils. The fungus might initially invade small roots as well as crown tissue. The pathogen is spread by movement of contaminated soil or diseased plants or by splashing water. This disease is a common problem in nurseries and may be introduced into a landscape on contaminated nursery stock.

Management: Improving drainage will help to avoid the conditions optimum for this disease. Although excision of basal cankers has been performed in the past, this practice is not recommended due to the extensive injury caused by the excision process and the necessity to excavate soil to reach infected plant roots and crown tissue under the soil. Diseased plants should be removed. Soil applications of fungicides provide effective control of Phytophthora in nurseries and can provide some control in landscape situations, especially if drainage patterns are altered to reduce soil flooding.

Thielaviopsis root rot (black root rot)

Causal agent: *Chalara elegans* (syn. *Thielaviopsis basicola*).

Hosts: Wide host range of primarily herbaceous plants. Hollies—especially Japanese, blue, and inkberry—are the primary woody plants affected.

Symptoms: Poor twig growth, chlorosis, sparse foliage, and dieback are above-ground symptoms of Thielaviopsis root rot (Figure 7.67, color plate section). Infected fine roots show dark-brown or black lesions that can coalesce, turning much of the fine-root system black in severely affected plants (Figure 7.68, color plate section).

Disease cycle: The causal fungus survives over winter as dark, thick-walled spores in roots and soil. Infection occurs in young fine roots only; woody roots are not affected. Above-ground symptoms develop as fine roots die. This is often a problem in nursery production and can be carried to the landscape on infected nursery stock. Thielaviopsis root rot of Japanese holly is most common in the southern United States.

Management: Inspect nursery stock for blackened roots before planting. Although fungicide drenches are used in nurseries for management of this disease, they are usually not effective in landscapes. Remove symptomatic plants, and replace with a nonhost species. If a susceptible host must be used for replacement, remove the diseased plant and as much soil as possible from the plant's root zone to reduce the amount of inoculum in the planting area.

Armillaria root rot

Causal agent: *Armillaria mellea.*

Hosts: Wide range of broadleaf and conifer trees and shrubs. Plants commonly affected include apple, oak, and cherry.

Symptoms: As with most root diseases, above-ground symptoms include poor growth, premature fall coloration, dieback, and death. Armillaria also causes wood decay. Signs of the causal fungus are usually visible as white or tan mycelial growth, called **mycelial fans,** present between the bark and wood tissues in the lower trunk or large roots. The fungus also produces dark-brown to black shoestringlike structures called **rhizomorphs,** which can be found under loose bark, in the soil, or on the surface of the roots or lower trunk (Figure 7.69, color plate section). The fruiting body of Armillaria is a tan- to honey-colored mushroom, which may be present in small or large clusters at the base of living or dead host trees (Figure 7.70, color plate section). The mushrooms develop in late summer or fall. Presence of these signs of the causal fungus is diagnostic for the disease.

Disease cycle: Armillaria is a common soil-inhabiting, **saprophytic** fungus that spreads primarily through growth of vegetative mycelium. The mycelium can directly penetrate bark of the roots or lower trunk, causing cankers in these tissues. The fungus can remain suppressed in healthy trees but will actively invade trees stressed by adverse environmental conditions, construction injury, or severe insect infestations. When the lower trunk is girdled by the fungus, the tree dies and the fungus further colonizes the dead wood. The fungus can then move to adjacent trees via growth of rhizomorphs from the colonized tree or root contact between colonized tree and nearby trees. Young trees planted into a site where older, Armillaria-infected trees were present can be killed as well.

Management: Maintain the health and vitality of landscape plants to prevent infection by Armillaria and to help infected trees survive with little damage. Evaluate infected trees for hazard potential because the fungus will decay wood and weaken the structural integrity of the tree. Remove stumps and roots of dead trees to reduce the chances of infection for adjacent living trees, although this will not eradicate the fungus from the area. There are no chemical control measures effective against Armillaria.

Ganoderma root and butt rot

Causal agent: *Ganoderma* spp., especially *G. lucidum* and *G. applanatum.*

Hosts: Wide range of broadleaf trees. Plants commonly affected include honey locust, maple, oak, ash, willow.

Symptoms: Above-ground symptoms include poor growth, premature fall coloration, dieback, and death of affected trees. Ganoderma also causes wood decay; **wind-throw** or trunk breakage is common in infected trees. Fruiting structures (conks) of the fungus are often present at the base of infected trees (Figures 7.71 and 7.72, color plate section). The conks of *G. lucidum* are annual and can appear singly or in clusters. The structures are reddish brown and shiny on the upper surface and white or tan on the lower surface. The conks of *G. applanatum* survive for several years and become hard and woody with concentric ridges. They are brown on the upper surface and interior, and white on the lower surface. Presence of these signs of the causal fungus are diagnostic for the disease.

Disease cycle: Little is known about the disease cycle of Ganoderma diseases. *G. lucidum* commonly attacks trees in landscape situations. *G. applanatum*, on the other hand, is a common forest pathogen. The fungus apparently enters trees through wounds (such as lawn-mower injuries) in trunk bases or large roots and is presumed to be spread by spores released from fruiting structures. There is no evidence of tree-to-tree spread of these wood-rotting fungi. Environmental stress appears to increase susceptibility of landscape trees to *G. lucidum.*

Management: Maintaining the health and vigor of landscape plants will help the plants resist infection by Ganoderma. Because these fungi can cause significant wood decay, infected trees should be evaluated for hazard potential. The presence of conks at the base of a tree is a sign that extensive wood decay is present. Removal of these fruiting bodies does not affect the progression of the disease because these structures represent only a small portion of the total fungal mass. There are no chemical control measures effective against these pathogens.

Nematode root diseases

Causal agent: Several species of plant-parasitic nematodes.

Hosts: Wide range of broadleaf and conifer trees and shrubs. Many other shade and ornamental plants are also susceptible. Nematode problems are most often found in nurseries but occasionally damage landscape plantings.

Symptoms: Symptoms of plants parasitized by nematodes are similar to those caused by other root problems. Stunting, poor growth, and small foliage occur on plants affected by root nematodes. Symptoms on roots include swelling of root tips; root proliferation; lesions on fine roots; or shortened, stubby root systems (Figure 7.73, color plate section). Since above-ground symptoms of nematode problems are not distinctive, analysis of root tissue and the soil in the root zone for plant-parasitic nematodes is necessary to confirm nematode diseases.

Disease cycle: Plant-parasitic nematodes are microscopic roundworms. They attack plant roots by piercing root cells with a specialized structure called a stylet. Nematodes reproduce by means of eggs. A single nematode does not have a significant impact on tree health; damage to root systems occurs when populations are high. Some nematodes, such as root knot nematodes, penetrate roots and feed in a sedentary manner, resulting in swelling of the root around the nematode. Others remain outside of the root tissue and feed by piercing cells of fine roots.

Management: In nurseries, nematode diseases are managed by crop rotation with a nonhost species and by preplant fumigation of soil in nursery beds. In the landscape, no treatments are available to cure a plant affected by root nematodes. Reduce other root stress factors by providing adequate moisture and avoiding root disturbance to lessen the detrimental effects of nematode feeding. If a nematode problem is confirmed by soil analysis, use resistant hosts as replacement plants. Spot fumigation of a planting site might help reduce nematode populations if a susceptible host must be replanted in the site.

Rust Diseases

Rust diseases are caused by an unusual group of fungi. Most of the rust pathogens affecting trees and shrubs will infect two different hosts (called alternate hosts) to complete the fungal life cycle, and will produce more than one spore stage on each host. The term *rust* comes from the rusty orange-red color of one of the spore stages. Rust fungi can attack foliage, stems, or fruit and can cause bizarre growths on infected plants.

Western gall rust and pine-oak gall rust

Causal agent: *Endocronartium harknessii* causes western gall rust; *Cronartium quercuum* causes pine-oak rust.

Hosts: Scots, mugo, jack, ponderosa, and lodgepole pines.

Symptoms: These rust fungi cause round galls to form on branches and main stems of pines (Figure 7.74, color plate section). In the spring, the gall surface cracks open, revealing orange-yellow spores. Witches' brooming sometimes develops on a heavily infected tree.

Disease cycle: Unlike most rust fungi, the western gall rust fungus does not require two different host species to complete its life cycle. Spores are released from galls in late spring and early summer and infect current-year shoots. Small galls develop one year after infection, and spores are released from the galls two years after initial infection. These spores then infect other pine shoots. Galls can continue to produce spores for several years. After several years, individual trees can develop hundreds of galls.

For pine-oak gall rust, spores produced on pine infect oaks, primarily in the red oak group. Inconspicuous threadlike projections of the rust fungus on oak leaves provide spores for infection of nearby pines. There is little damage to oaks.

Management: Sanitation is the primary means of managing this disease. Remove heavily galled trees, or prune out individual branches with galls. Sanitation should be performed in early spring before spores are released from the galls.

Gymnosporangium rust diseases

Causal agent: Three species of the rust fungus *Gymnosporangium. G. juniperi-virginianae* causes cedar-apple rust. Cedar-quince rust is caused by *G. clavipes,* and cedar-hawthorn rust is caused by *G. globosum.*

Hosts: Juniper, apple, crabapple, quince, and hawthorn. Each of these fungi requires two host species to complete its life cycle.

Symptoms: On juniper and red cedar, **telial galls** form on infected twigs. The galls are round and dark brown, and range in size from $^1/_4$ inch to $1^1/_2$ inches in diameter for cedar-apple rust. Galls formed by cedar-hawthorn rust are smaller and more irregular in shape. In spring, orange to yellow gelatinous tendrils emerge from the galls (Figure 7.75, color plate section). Distinct galls do not form on junipers infected by cedar-quince rust; instead, juniper twigs are swollen and the bark cracks. An orange gelatinous substance oozes from the bark cracks on infected twigs in the spring. These diseases usually do not have a significant impact on the health of the juniper host, though twig dieback may occur with cedar quince rust. Leaf spots develop on broadleaf hosts of both cedar-apple and cedar-hawthorn rusts. The spots first appear as small yellow dots on the upper leaf surface, then rapidly enlarge and develop a bright red-orange color. Small cuplike structures with protrusions of fungal tissue, called **aecia,** are visible on the undersides of mature leaf lesions (Figure 7.76, color plate section). Defoliation occurs when leaves are heavily infected. Leaf spots are rare on broadleaf hosts of cedar-quince rust. Rather, distortion or enlargement of infected twigs, buds, and fruit occur on broadleaf hosts. Pink tubelike aecia develop on infected twigs and fruits (Figure 7.77, color plate section). Dieback of infected hawthorn twigs is common.

Disease cycle: Each of these rust fungi requires two host species to complete its life cycle—one a juniper or red cedar and the other apple, crabapple, quince, or hawthorn. Spores are released during wet weather in April or May from galls or infected twigs on junipers. These spores are blown by air currents to the broadleaf host, where infection of the leaves (or twigs and fruit in the case of cedar-quince rust) occurs. Spores from lesions on infected leaves or fruits of broadleaf hosts are windblown to junipers in late summer. The fungi overwinter on the juniper host.

Management: While separation of the alternate hosts is often recommended, spores from juniper galls can move a quarter of a mile or more to infect the broadleaf host, so separation is not always possible. If juniper infection is light and there are few junipers in the area, physical removal of the galls might help reduce infection of nearby broadleaf hosts. Resistant cultivars of apple and crabapple are available. Protection of the broadleaf host with fungicide sprays is warranted if these diseases are chronic problems on high-value trees. Fungicides are applied several times during the spring to protect emerging leaves, growing twigs, and developing fruit.

Ash rust

Causal agent: *Puccinia peridermiospora.*

Hosts: Several species of ash, including white, green, and black ash. Cordgrass (*Spartina*) is the alternate host.

Symptoms: Yellow spots develop on infected ash leaves (Figure 7.78, color plate section), petioles, and twigs in late spring and early summer. Infected tissues become swollen, resulting in distortion of leaves and twigs (Figure 7.79, color plate section), and produce orange powdery spores. Infected leaves drop, and severely affected trees may be defoliated by midsummer.

Disease cycle: The pathogen overwinters as spores on the alternate host—cordgrass. In spring, these spores germinate to produce another spore type

that is carried by air currents to ash leaves, petioles, and young shoots. Infection of these tissues occurs, resulting in spots. These tissues become swollen and produce orange cuplike aecia. Spores from these structures are windblown and infect cordgrass, causing blisterlike spots.

Management: Under most circumstances, this disease does not have a serious impact on the health of infected trees. However, repeated defoliation can occur on trees near wetlands where large populations of the alternate host occur. Under these conditions, high-value trees can be protected by weekly fungicide applications during the spring when foliage is expanding. Avoid planting ash trees in areas where cordgrass is common.

Viral Diseases

Viruses can cause diseases in woody plants, but they are rarely damaging to plant health. Viral diseases are usually of concern to nursery propagators and not usually encountered by arborists.

Causal agent: Several different plant pathogenic viruses.

Hosts: Wide range of broadleaf trees and shrubs. Common hosts include roses and ash. Conifers are rarely affected.

Symptoms: Symptoms are often quite striking. Yellow mottling (called mosaic) and yellow or white ringspots and line patterns are typical virus disease symptoms (Figures 7.80 and 7.81, color plate section). In some cases, these symptoms are diagnostic for virus diseases. Other viruses induce mild symptoms such as poor vigor, stunting, and reduced leaf size. Latent infections of some viruses produce few or no symptoms. Serological testing is necessary to confirm the presence of viruses.

Disease cycle: Viruses are transmitted in woody plants by propagation (cuttings from infected plants), insects such as aphids and leafhoppers, and certain species of root-feeding nematodes. Virus particles move throughout the infected host, resulting in a systemic infection. The rate of virus spread in landscapes appears to be very small in most cases.

Management: In nurseries, plant only certified virus-free stock, fumigate soil to reduce nematode populations, and rogue out symptomatic plants. There are no treatments that will cure plants of virus infection. In the landscape, virus-infected plants are usually no more than a curiosity, however. Removal of roses with virus symptoms may be warranted in large plantings.

Disease Complexes

Tree decline

Causal agent: Several noninfectious stress factors in combination with secondary fungal pathogens and insect pests.

Hosts: Any tree species can be affected. Trees in urban areas are especially prone to decline.

Symptoms: Small leaf size, chlorosis, early fall coloration, and poor annual twig growth are initial symptoms of decline. Dieback of twigs and branches occurs as decline progresses (Figure 7.82, color plate section). Symptom development usually occurs over the course of several years. Trees may eventually die as insects, especially borers, invade the trunks of declining trees.

Disease cycle: Defoliation by diseases or leaf-feeding insects, or environmental stress from such factors as drought, excess water, or cold injury to bark tissues can weaken trees and begin the decline process. Root injury from construction activities, soil compaction, changes in drainage patterns, or addition of soil over established roots can also initiate decline. Insect borers are attracted to stressed trees and cause further damage by their feeding or breeding activities in inner-bark tissues. Environmental stress also predisposes trees to infection by several canker fungi, which accelerate the development of dead twigs and branches.

Management: Prevention is the key to managing tree decline. If tree species are suited to site conditions, they are less likely to suffer from site-related stress (see Chapter 4). Large trees with large root systems eventually outgrow restricted planting sites, such as the area between a sidewalk and street. Some tree species do not tolerate wet sites or high-pH soils and decline when installed in sites with those conditions. Proper plant choice helps to avoid these problems. Maintaining tree health after planting is also very important to reduce the occurrence of decline. Water trees during dry periods. This irrigation should be applied in one or two extended irrigation events rather than several brief watering periods in which water does not penetrate deeply into the soil. Application of moderate amounts of fertilizer every two to three years can help maintain the vitality of healthy trees. Changes in the growing site after a tree has been established could cause tree decline. Avoid any root injury or soil compaction from construction equipment. If possible, identify the specific stress factors contributing to the decline, and take appropriate steps to reduce the stress. Remove dead wood. Vertical mulching may help trees in areas with severe soil compaction. If the tree has been attacked by borers, take appropriate control measures. Keep in mind that trees in serious decline will seldom regain their full health or ornamental value, even with the cultural practices mentioned above. Removal is recommended for trees with severe dieback symptoms.

Karen Rane
Plant Disease Diagnostician
Department of Botany and Plant Pathology
Purdue University

Nancy Pataky
Extension Specialist, Plant Pathology
Department of Crop Sciences
University of Illinois

Acknowledgments

The authors are grateful to Cynthia Ash, University of Minnesota, John R. Hartman, University of Kentucky, and Jill Pokorny, USDA Forest Service, St. Paul, Minnesota, for their excellent comments on this manuscript. The authors also acknowledge the contribution of photographic images from several colleagues, including Ralph Green, Peggy Sellers, Mark Gleason, Melodie Putnam, Robert Wick, Jill Pokorny, Gail Ruhl, Donald White, and Emily Hoover.

Selected References

Dreistadt, S.H., J.K. Clark, and M.L. Flint. 1994. *Pests of Landscape Trees and Shrubs: An Integrated Pest Management Guide.* Publication 3359. University of California Division of Agriculture and Natural Resources.

Pirone, P.P. 1978. *Diseases and Pests of Ornamental Plants.* New York: John Wiley and Sons.

Riffle, J.W., and G.W. Peterson. 1986. *Diseases of Trees in the Great Plains.* USDA Forest Service General Technical Report RM-129. Fort Collins, Colorado: USDA Forest Service.

Sinclair, W.A., H.H. Lyon, and W.T. Johnson. 1987. *Diseases of Trees and Shrubs.* Ithaca, New York: Cornell University Press.

Tattar, T.A. 1989. *Diseases of Shade Trees.* San Diego: Academic Press.

Color Plate Section

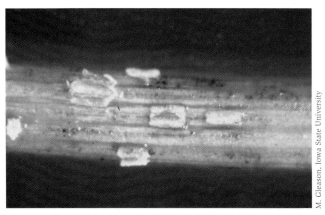

Figure 7.3 ▪ *Cyclaneusma needle cast, showing apothecia*

Figure 7.4 ▪ *Cyclaneusma needle cast on Scots pine*

M. Gleason, Iowa State University

U.S. Forest Service North Central Forest Experiment Station Collection

Figure 7.5 ▪ *Lophodermium needle cast on white pine, showing apothecia*

Figure 7.6 ▪ *Lophodermium needle cast on Scots pine*

University of Illinois Department of Crop Sciences Collection

University of Illinois Department of Crop Sciences Collection

Figure 7.7 ▪ *Rhabdocline needle cast on Douglasfir*

R. Wick, University of Massachusetts

K. Rane, Purdue University

C. Ash, University of Minnesota

Figure 7.8 ▪ *Rhabdocline needle cast on Douglasfir*

Figure 7.9 ▪ *Rhizosphaera needle cast on blue spruce*

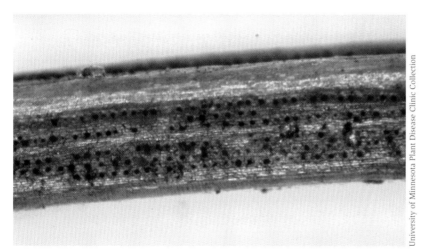

University of Minnesota Plant Disease Clinic Collection

Figure 7.10 ▪ *Rhizosphaera needle cast on blue spruce, showing pycnidia*

U.S. Forest Service North Central Forest Experiment Station Collection

Figure 7.12 ▪ *Brown spot on Scots pine*

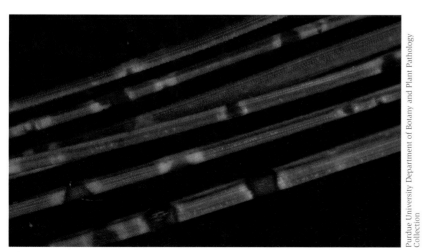

Purdue University Department of Botany and Plant Pathology Collection

Figure 7.11 ▪ *Brown spot needle blight on Scots pine*

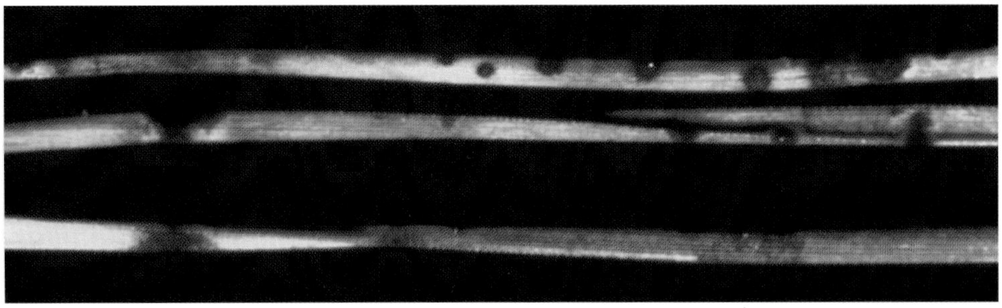

Figure 7.13 ▪ *Dothistroma needle blight on Austrian pine*

Figure 7.14 ▪ *Dothistroma needle blight on Austrian pine*

Figure 7.15 ▪ *Apple scab on flowering crabapple*

Figure 7.16 ▪ *Black spot on rose*

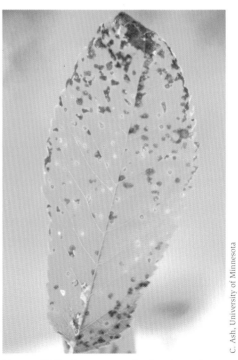

Figure 7.17 ▪ *Coccomyces leaf spot on cherry*

R. Wick, University of Massachusetts

Figure 7.18 ▪ *Cristulariella leaf spot on maple*

R. Wick, University of Massachusetts

Figure 7.19 ▪ *Downy mildew on rose*

C. Ash, University of Minnesota

Figure 7.20 ▪ *Downy mildew on viburnum*

University of Illinois Department of Crop Sciences Collection

Figure 7.21 ▪ *Hawthorn leaf spot*

R. Wick, University of Massachusetts

Figure 7.22 ▪ *Horsechestnut leaf blotch*

D. White, University of Illinois

Figure 7.23 ▪ *Oak leaf blister*

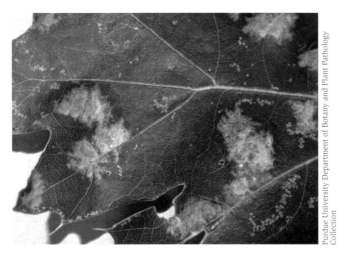

Purdue University Department of Botany and Plant Pathology Collection

Figure 7.24 ▪ *Oak leaf blister, showing brown coloration*

University of Minnesota Plant Disease Clinic Collection

Figure 7.25 ▪ *Phyllosticta leaf spot on maple*

University of Minnesota Plant Disease Clinic Collection

Figure 7.26 ▪ *Phyllosticta leaf spot on maple, showing pycnidia*

R. Wick, University of Massachusetts

Figure 7.27 ▪ *Powdery mildew on azalea*

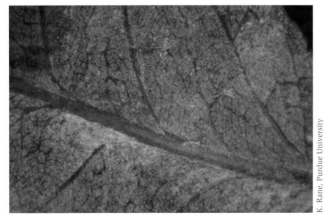

K. Rane, Purdue University

Figure 7.28 ▪ *Powdery mildew on rose*

G. Ruhl, Purdue University

Figure 7.29 ▪ *Septoria leaf spot on redtwig dogwood*

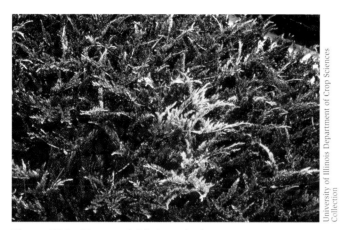

Figure 7.30 ▪ *Phomopsis blight on juniper*

University of Illinois Department of Crop Sciences
Collection

Figure 7.31 ▪ *Kabatina blight on juniper,
showing acervuli*

K. Rane, Purdue University

Figure 7.32 ▪ *Sphaeropsis blight on Scots pine*

M. Putnam, Oregon State University

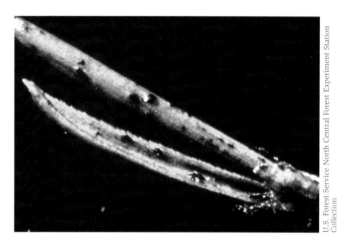

Figure 7.33 ▪ *Sphaeropsis blight on Scots pine, showing
pycnidia*

U.S. Forest Service North Central Forest Experiment Station
Collection

Figure 7.34 ▪ *Anthracnose on dogwood*

K. Rane, Purdue University

Figure 7.35 ▪ *Anthracnose on white oak*

Figure 7.36 ▪ *Anthracnose on sycamore*

Figure 7.37 ▪ *Brown rot on cherry*

Figure 7.38 ▪ *Phomopsis canker on Russian olive*

Figure 7.39 ▪ *Black knot on plum*

M. Gleason, Iowa State University

Figure 7.40 ▪ *Bacterial blight on lilac*

M. Gleason, Iowa State University

Figure 7.41 ▪ *Fire blight on apple*

Purdue University Department of Botany and Plant Pathology Collection

Figure 7.42 ▪ *Fire blight on apple, showing sunken canker*

University of Illinois Department of Crop Sciences Collection

University of Minnesota Plant Disease Clinic Collection

Figure 7.43 ▪ *Cytospora canker on spruce*

Figure 7.44 ▪ *Cytospora canker on spruce, showing resin exuding from canker*

Figure 7.45 ▪ *Botryosphaeria canker on mountain ash*

Figure 7.46 ▪ *Cryptodiaporthe canker on Lombardy poplar*

Figure 7.47 ▪ *Thyronectria canker on honey locust*

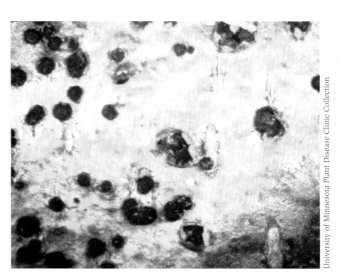

Figure 7.48 ▪ *Thyronectria canker on honey locust, showing pycnidia*

Figure 7.49 ▪ *Valsa canker on cherry, cut to show discolored inner bark*

D. White, University of Illinois

Figure 7.50 ▪ *Nectria (target) canker*

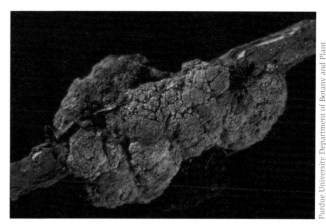

Purdue University Department of Botany and Plant Pathology Collection

Figure 7.51 ▪ *Crown gall on euonymus*

University of Illinois Department of Crop Sciences Collection

Figure 7.52 ▪ *Pine wilt on Scots pine*

University of Illinois Department of Crop Sciences Collection

Figure 7.53 ▪ *Dutch elm disease on American elm*

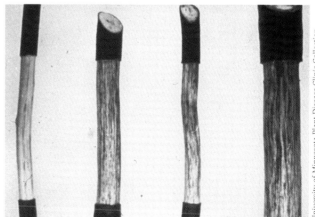

University of Minnesota Plant Disease Clinic Collection

Figure 7.54 ▪ *Dutch elm disease, showing streaking in wood*

University of Minnesota Plant Disease Clinic Collection

Figure 7.55 ▪ *Oak wilt on red oak*

R. Green, Purdue University

Figure 7.56 ▪ *Oak wilt on red oak, showing defoliation*

University of Minnesota Plant Disease Clinic Collection

Figure 7.57 ▪ *Oak wilt on red oak, showing pressure pad*

University of Illinois Department of Crop Sciences Collection

Figure 7.58 ▪ *Verticillium wilt on maple*

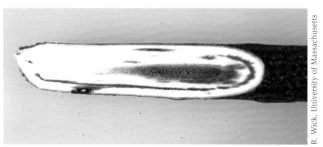

R. Wick, University of Massachusetts

Figure 7.59 ▪ *Discoloration in redbud sapwood due to Verticillium wilt*

M. Putnam, Oregon State University

University of Illinois Department of Crop Sciences Collection

Figure 7.60 ▪ *Slime flux on elm*

Figure 7.61 ▪ *Bacterial leaf scorch on mulberry*

R. Green, Purdue University

C. Ash, University of Minnesota

Figure 7.63 ▪ *Ash yellows*

Figure 7.62 ▪ *Elm yellows (elm phloem necrosis)*

C. Ash, University of Minnesota

Figure 7.64 ▪ *Ash yellows, showing witches' brooming*

University of Illinois Department of Crop Sciences Collection

Figure 7.65 ▪ *Phytophthora root rot on rhododendron*

R. Wick, University of Massachusetts

Figure 7.66 ▪ *Phytophthora root rot on rhododendron, showing discoloration of inner bark and wood*

R. Wick, University of Massachusetts

Figure 7.67 ▪ *Thielaviopsis root rot on Japanese holly, causing branch dieback and yellowing of foliage*

R. Wick, University of Massachusetts

Figure 7.68 ▪ *Thielaviopsis root rot on Japanese holly, showing root lesions*

University of Illinois Department of Crop Sciences Collection

Figure 7.69 ▪ *Armillaria root rot, showing rhizomorphs*

C. Ash, University of Minnesota

Figure 7.70 ▪ *Mushrooms of Armillaria mellea*

University of Illinois Department of Crop Sciences Collection

Figure 7.71 ▪ *Ganoderma root rot on honey locust, showing fruiting structures*

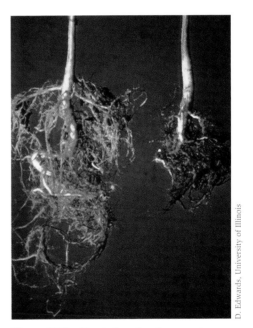

D. Edwards, University of Illinois

Figure 7.73 ▪ *Stunted root system on cherry due to nematodes (*Pratylenchus *sp.)*

University of Illinois Department of Crop Sciences Collection

Figure 7.72 ▪ *Ganoderma fruiting structures*

Figure 7.74 ▪ *Western gall rust on Scots pine*

Figure 7.75 ▪ *Telial galls of cedar-apple rust*

Figure 7.76 ▪ *Cedar-hawthorn rust, showing aecial stage on hawthorn leaves*

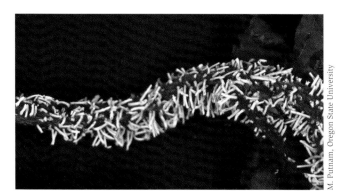

Figure 7.77 ▪ *Cedar-quince rust, showing aecia on hawthorn twig*

Figure 7.78 ▪ *Ash rust*

Figure 7.79 ▪ Ash rust, showing distortion of petioles

M. Gleason, Iowa State University

Figure 7.80 ▪ Virus ringspots on ash

University of Illinois Department of Crop Sciences Collection

Figure 7.81 ▪ Virus symptoms on rose

R. Wick, University of Massachusetts

Figure 7.82 ▪ Tree decline

R. Green, Purdue University.

Figure 8.9 ▪ *Leaf injury caused by potato leafhopper on 'October glory' red maple. Note stunting of leaves, short internode, and marginal browning.*

Figure 8.10 ▪ *(a) Leaf discoloration caused by honeylocust plant bug. (b) Heavily infested thornless honey locust. Very few leaves have expanded fully. Most are heavily distorted.*

Figure 8.11 ▪ *(a) Stippling caused by lace bug feeding on sycamore. (b) Spiny black lace bug nymphs are visible along veins on the leaf undersides. Black tar spots of excrement are present between veins.*

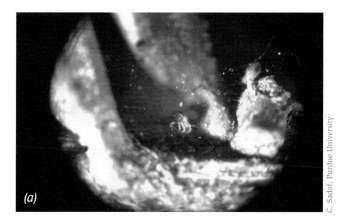

Figure 8.12 ▪ *(a) Spruce spider mite walking on webs at the base of a spruce needle. (b) Leaves of burning bush with white stippling caused by twospotted spider mite. Note that when needles of conifers become stippled, the foliage gets a bronzed appearance.*

Figure 8.13 ▪ *Hemlock rust mite on eastern hemlock. Mites look like flecks of brown dust along the tops and edges of the needle surface.*

Figure 8.14 ▪ *Sooty mold growing on honeydew excrement produced by tuliptree scale on magnolia. Note orange color of tuliptree scales. The stem can be sticky to the touch.*

Figure 8.15 ▪ *Euonymus scale on twig of winter creeper euonymus. Plant tissue is intact beneath the scale that has been flipped over. Female scales are covered by a waxy brown shell. Males of this species are covered by white waxy shell.*

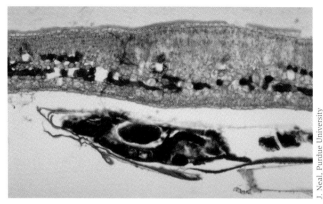

J. Neal, Purdue University

Figure 8.16 ▪ *Cross-section of a euonymus leaf and a male scale on the leaf underside. Red lines through leaf are the stained tracks left by the scale as it fed. Note that unlike soft scales and honeydew producers, the scale bypassed the vascular bundles and is feeding on cell fluids.*

C. Sadof, Purdue University

Figure 8.17 ▪ *Cottony maple scale on twigs of red maple. From a distance, white egg sacks resemble popped corn.*

C. Sadof, Purdue University

Figure 8.18 ▪ *(a) Two-circuli mealybug in twig crotch of hawthorn. (b) Lady beetle larva extracted from cottony maple scale egg mass.*

C. Sadof, Purdue University

Figure 8.19 ▪ *Mugo pine covered with pine needle scale.*

C. Sadof, Purdue University

Figure 8.20 ▪ *Leaf curl on hedge of burning bush caused by the black bean aphid.*

Figure 8.22 ▪ *Wooly elm aphid curling leaves of red elm. Note waxy coating on aphids.*

Figure 8.21 ▪ *Apple aphid on cotoneaster. Note large number of aphids present but no leaf curl.*

Figure 8.23 ▪ *Honeysuckle witches' broom aphid on honeysuckle. Note stunting of new growth and death of leaf tissue.*

Figure 8.24 ▪ *White, waxy flecks of pine bark adelgid on the trunk of white pine*

Figure 8.25 ▪ *Pine spittle bug on Scots pine. Nymphs and adults can be found inside the globs of spit.*

C. Sadof, Purdue University

C. Sadof, Purdue University

C. Sadof, Purdue University

Figure 8.26 ▪ *Red bumps produced by maple bladder gall on silver maple*

Figure 8.27 ▪ *(a) Young galls produced by Cooley spruce gall adelgid on tips of spruce shoots. (b) Young galls produced by eastern spruce gall adelgid at base of new shoot growth. (c) Leaf distortion caused by feeding on Douglasfir. Adelgid nymphs produce the white waxy tufts on the needles.*

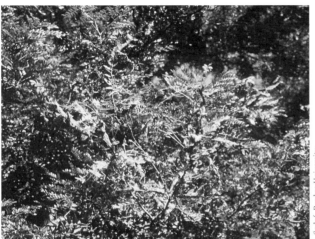

C. Sadof, Purdue University

Figure 8.29 ▪ *Position of webs produced by three web-making defoliators. (a) Mimosa webworm ties together leaves of honey locust. (b) Fall webworm produces large webs on ends of branches. (c) Eastern tent caterpillar produces webs in the crotches of tree branches.*

C. Sadof, Purdue University

C. Sadof, Purdue University

Figure 8.30 ▪ *(a) Adult fall webworm and egg mass on the underside of a crabapple leaf in June. (b) Recently hatched egg mass of eastern tent caterpillar wrapped around the twig in early spring.*

Figure 8.31 ▪ *Bagworm larval cases on arborvitae*

Figure 8.32 ▪ *Late instar gypsy moth larvae. Note the red and green spots on its back.*

Figure 8.33 ▪ *(a) Removal of last year's needles by European pine sawfly on Scots pine gives branches superficial resemblance to a mule's tail. (b) Early signs of injury by European pine sawfly larvae. Young green larvae with black heads are present above the thumb. The vertically oriented needle has been partially defoliated by larvae. The remaining shred of needle will turn a straw color.*

C. Sadof, Purdue University

Figure 8.34 ▪ *Slime-covered pear sawfly on leaves of cotoneaster. Leaves are skeletonized when upper surface of leaf tissue is removed.*

C. Sadof, Purdue University

Figure 8.35 ▪ *Skeletonization caused by adult Japanese beetles feeding on leaves. Note the coppery color of the beetle elytra and the white-fringed tufts just below the wings on the abdomen.*

C. Sadof, Purdue University

Figure 8.36 ▪ *Skeletonization on leaves of Zelkova caused by elm leaf beetle grubs*

(a)

C. Sadof, Purdue University

(b)

C. Sadof, Purdue University

Figure 8.37 ▪ *Distinctive leaf notching most likely caused by black vine weevil on (a) wintercreeper euonymus, and (b) yew. Most notching of yew is found in the center of the shrub.*

(a)

C. Sadof, Purdue University

Figure 8.38 ▪ *Circular notches cut by the leafcutter bee on eastern redbud. This bee is not a pest and is an important pollinator in the urban landscape.*

C. Sadof, Purdue University

(b)

C. Sadof, Purdue University

Figure 8.39 ▪ *(a) Birch leafminer injury on birch. (b) When leaf is held into the light, small circular halos are present where adult wasp has laid eggs. The leafminer and its frass are also visible in the blotch-type leaf mine.*

J. Obermeyer, Purdue University

Figure 8.40 ▪ *Oviposition injury on oak caused by emergence of the periodical cicada*

C. Sadof, Purdue University

Figure 8.41 ▪ *Twig dieback on white pine caused by either northern pine or Pales weevil chewing on twigs in the spring*

C. Sadof, Purdue University

Figure 8.42 ▪ *Shepherd's crook on white pine caused by white pine weevil*

C. Sadof, Purdue University

Figure 8.44 ▪ *Flowering dogwood heavily infested with dogwood borer. Note death of limbs.*

C. Sadof, Purdue University

Figure 8.43 ▪ *Death of the top whorl of a Scots pine caused by Zimmerman pine moth larval feeding at the top whorl*

C. Sadof, Purdue University

Figure 8.45 ▪ *Strawlike pupae of a clearwing moth (the dogwood borer) emerging from a trunk*

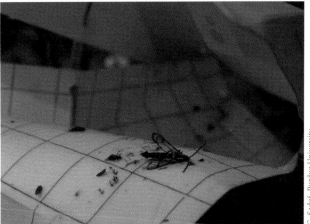

C. Sadof, Purdue University

Figure 8.46 ▪ *A male peach tree borer caught in a sex pheromone trap. Note the clear wings and wasplike shape.*

C. Sadof, Purdue University

Figure 8.47 ▪ *Larva of a round-headed borer (pine sawyer beetle) feeding in bark of a Scots pine. Note abundance of sawdust and flaking bark.*

(a)

C. Sadof, Purdue University

(b)

C. Sadof, Purdue University

Figure 8.48 ▪ *(a) Raised bark surface of birch trees infested with bronze birch borer. (b) Packed excrement revealing the zig-zag tunnelling by a bronze birch borer larvae beneath the tree bark.*

C. Sadof, Purdue University

Figure 8.49 ▪ *Tunnelling by a European elm bark beetle just beneath the bark of an elm. Note that the "spine" of the gallery is parallel to the grain of the wood.*

P. Nixon, University of Illinois

Figure 9.1 ▪ *Voles are compact rodents with stocky bodies and short legs and tails*

P. Nixon, University of Illinois

Figure 9.3 ▪ *Voles girdle trunks and roots, killing or damaging the tree or shrub*

P. Nixon, University of Illinois

Figure 9.4 ▪ *Look for vole runways leading from dense areas and cutting through turf*

Figure 9.14 ▪ *Contact repellents are applied directly to the plant*

Figure 9.15 ▪ *Repellent containers are hung on or near the vegetation to be protected*

Figure 9.16 ▪ *Sapsuckers sit vertically on a trunk or along the long axis of a limb, drilling holes between branches*

G. Czapar, University of Illinois

Figure 10.1 ▪ *Poison ivy*

University of Illinois Department of Crop Sciences Collection

Figure 10.2 ▪ *Yellow nutsedge*

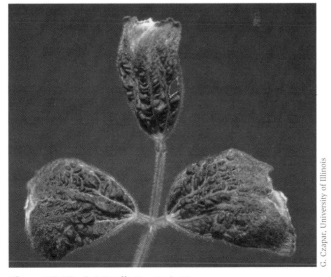

G. Czapar, University of Illinois

Figure 10.10 ▪ *2,4-D effects on plant*

CHAPTER 8

Managing Insects and Mites on Woody Plants

Cliff Sadof

This chapter discusses insect and mite pests of woody plants in the Midwest. It begins by covering the basic biology of these pests and the types of **damage** they can cause. It then reviews life cycles and control strategies for common types of pests in the urban landscape. In the process, specific information on the more important pests is provided.

What Are Insects and Mites?

Insects and mites belong to a group of animals called **arthropods** because their bodies share some common structures. The name *arthropod*, which means "jointed foot," was given to this group because the legs of all of its species are jointed. Unlike people, who support their limbs with an internal skeleton, arthropods have an exterior support structure called an **exoskeleton** that also serves as their skin. Arthropods are direct descendants of earthwormlike ancestors and include the vast majority of species in the animal kingdom. These include lobsters, shrimp, crabs, pillbugs, millipedes, centipedes, scorpions, spiders, mites, and insects.

Insect Structure

Insects are segmented and have three basic body regions: **head**, **thorax**, and **abdomen** (Figure 8.1). The head bears the eyes, antennae (feelers), and mouthparts; it also contains the brain. The thorax is directly

behind the head. It has three segments that are usually firmly joined together, and each of these segments usually has one pair of jointed walking legs. The wings, if present, are on the second and third thoracic segments. The **pronotum** is a distinctive piece of exoskeleton that lies between the head and the attachment of the first pair of wings on the first segment of the thorax. In some insect groups, such as with grasshoppers, the pronotum can be greatly enlarged to cover wing attachments on the second and third thoracic segments. The abdomen is usually as long as, or longer than, the head and thorax combined. It has a variable number of distinct segments that contain the gut and reproductive organs. Externally, it is usually softer than the head and thorax because it needs to be flexible enough to hold food, water, air, fat reserves, and eggs.

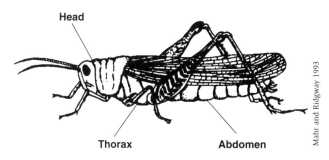

Figure 8.1 ▪ *All insects have three body regions: head, thorax, and abdomen. Note that the hind legs are jointed and modified for jumping.*

The head of **adult** insects has a variety of mouthpart types (Figure 8.2). Beetles, bees, ants, grasshoppers, lacewings, and dragonflies have **chewing** mouthparts. Insects with piercing and **sucking** mouthparts have a sharp, hollow, beaklike structure used to penetrate plant or animal tissue and suck up fluid. These are found in aphids, scale insects, leafhoppers, plant bugs, mosquitoes, and all of the predatory true bugs. Lapping and sponging mouthparts are primarily found in some flies, including house flies. The mouths of butterflies and moths are coiled into a long tube used to siphon liquids such as nectar from flowers. Some adult insects, such as mayflies or adult male scale insects, do not feed at all and have nonfunctional mouthparts. Like those of adults, the mouthparts of immature insects can be shaped to chew or to suck fluids.

Insects have three pairs of **true legs,** one on each segment of the thorax. These legs are jointed and can be modified for particular functions. For example, the hind legs of grasshoppers (Figure 8.1) are modified for jumping, and the front legs of Japanese beetles are modified for digging into the soil. Immature stages of some larval insects, especially **caterpillars** and sawflies, can also walk with fleshy, unjointed legs called **prolegs**. These appendages are not jointed and are attached to segments of the abdomen.

Most species of insects have two pairs of wings as adults. These wings can be clear or can be covered with fine scales, as in the case of moths and butterflies. Some insect groups, such as grasshoppers and beetles, have a thickened front pair of wings. These protect the abdomen when the insect is not flying. Flies have only one pair of fully developed wings. The hind pair of wings is greatly reduced. All in all, the number of wings present in insects can be quite variable.

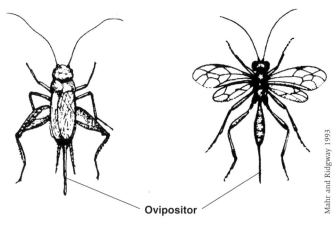

Mahr and Ridgway 1993

Figure 8.3 ▪ *A cricket (left) and an insect-parasitic wasp (right), each with an obvious ovipositor. The cricket inserts its eggs in the soil and the parasitic wasp "stings" its host insect, laying its egg inside the host.*

Insect Growth and Development

Most insects start life in an egg stage. The process of egg laying is called **oviposition**. Adult females of many species lay their eggs in the area where their young feed. For example, elm leaf beetle adults lay eggs on the leaves where young beetle **grubs** will feed. Lesser peach tree borer moths lay eggs on the bark of flowering cherry, where caterpillars can bore into the trunk. Insects use specialized organs called **ovipositors** to place their eggs in the correct location (Figure 8.3). Some ovipositors are internal except during oviposition (as with most flies); others are external and very obvious (as with crickets, cicadas, and sawflies). A few insects, such as aphids, give birth to live young.

The two ways that insects grow from egg to adult are called simple and complete metamorphosis. **Simple metamorphosis** occurs with insects whose young look very similar to the adults except that wings are not present and they are not reproductively mature. In the immature stage, these insects are called **nymphs** (Figure 8.4). Insects with simple metamorphosis that attack woody plants include aphids, cicadas, plant bugs, leafhoppers, planthoppers, treehoppers, mealybugs, scales, thrips, crickets, and katydids.

Insects with **complete metamorphosis** have a wormlike, maggotlike, or grublike immature stage (Figure 8.5). These types of immature stages are called **larvae.** At one extreme, the body plan of larval insects can be clearly recognizable, as in the case of caterpillars and sawflies (Figure 8.6). In this case, jointed walking legs are clearly visible on the thorax, and fleshy unjointed walking appendages, called prolegs, are easily distinguished on the abdomen. At the other extreme, the body plan of larval insects can be hard to distinguish,

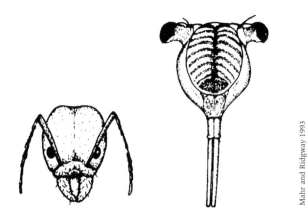

Mahr and Ridgway 1993

Figure 8.2 ▪ *Chewing mouthparts of an ant (left) and sucking mouthpart of a cicada (right).*

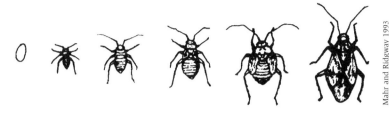

Figure 8.4 ▪ *A plant bug is an example of an insect with simple metamorphosis. After hatching from the egg, the nymph grows, occasionally shedding its skin, until it reaches the adult winged and reproductive stage, after which it no longer grows.*

as in the case of **maggots** (Figure 8.7). Larvae change into an intermediate form called **pupae** before they become winged adults (Figure 8.5). Pupae do not feed and are inactive. They are usually found in a protected location, such as within a cocoon, under tree bark, or within the soil. Insects with complete metamorphosis include all beetles, butterflies, moths, bees, wasps, ants, flies, and lacewings. Important woody-plant insect pests with complete metamorphosis include eastern tent caterpillars, Japanese beetles, and European pine sawflies.

As both nymphs and larvae grow, they must shed their skins, or exoskeletons, through a process called **molting.** Most species of insects molt a set number of times before they become adults. The distinct immature stages between successive molts are called **instars.** For example, elm leaf beetles have three instars, and hawthorn lace bugs have five instars. The first instar is the form of the insect that hatches from the egg. The second instar is the form the insect takes after the first instar molts, and so on. Many insects are **susceptible** to management activities at certain instars. For example, applications of certain insecticides, such as *Bacillus thuringiensis,* are most effective against early instars of pests. Also, many natural enemies, especially parasitic wasps and flies, attack only certain pest instars.

Adult insects are characterized by having wings and by being reproductively mature. (With insects, it seems that there are exceptions to every rule; many adult aphids and all adult fleas are wingless.) Once an insect reaches an adult stage, it never grows any further and

never molts again. Therefore, small beetles do not grow into large beetles, and small flies do not grow into large flies (Figure 8.8).

The rate of insect growth and development largely depends on temperature and the genetic traits of the species. Within limits, warmer temperatures speed development and shorten generation time. Time required for an insect to complete one generation varies considerably with the type of insect, the availability of food, and to some degree the geographical location, climate, and site conditions. Tuliptree aphids can complete a generation in about ten days under ideal conditions, and they have many generations a year on tuliptrees. In comparison, the eastern tent caterpillar has only one generation per year. Euonymus scales have only two generations per year in Indiana and three generations per year in Louisiana. In years with an abnormally mild fall, the scale can have a third generation in the Midwest. In summer, warm-season spider mite populations on honey locust or burning bush increase more rapidly in warm sites with a southern exposure than in cooler sites with a northern exposure.

In temperate climates with cold winters, insects either die or go into an overwintering protective state of arrested development called **diapause.** A given insect species diapauses in a specific state of development. For example, eastern tent caterpillars spend the winter as eggs, Zimmerman pine moths as larvae, and elm leaf beetles as adults.

Importance of Growth and Development to Pest Management

For the most part, immatures and adults with simple metamorphosis feed on and injure the same parts of a woody plant. These pests should be monitored by examining susceptible parts of the plant for the presence of pests and their natural enemies. Likewise, applications of insecticides can be effective against adults and larvae feeding on these plant parts. For example, both adult and immature lacebugs feed on leaves, where insecticide applications can kill adults and immatures.

Figure 8.5 ▪ *The imported cabbageworm is an example of an insect with complete metamorphosis. After hatching from the egg, the larvae grows, occasionally shedding its skin, until it is fully grown. The larva then molts one more time and transforms into the pupa. The pupa in turn molts and transforms into the adult winged and reproductive stage, after which it no longer grows.*

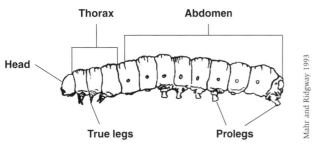

Figure 8.6 ▪ *This caterpillar shows the basic body form of a larval insect. Certain groups of larvae, especially caterpillars and sawfly larvae, have auxiliary legs, called prolegs, on the abdomen.*

Larvae and adults of most species with complete metamorphosis will often use different foods. In many cases, only the larvae injure the plant when they feed. For example, adult moths, flies, and wasps of most woody-plant pests feed on nectar and pollen, whereas their immatures feed on plants. Applications of pesticides usually will kill only immature stages, not adults or pupae. These pests should be monitored by examining their feeding sites for eggs and early signs of damage by the immatures. In some cases, specialized traps have been developed to monitor the flight of adults to help target damaging immature stages.

As a group, beetles are a notable exception, with both adults and immatures injuring plants. Still, pupae do not feed. In some cases, these beetles feed on the same part of the plant—as with elm leaf beetles, whose adults and grubs feed on leaves. In other cases, adults feed on different parts of the plant. The **skeletonization** of leaves by adult Japanese beetles and the feeding on roots by immature grubs are notable examples. Monitoring and management activities need to be directed at the susceptible part of the plant at the proper time of year.

A Note About Mites

Mites are not insects but are classified with insects and several other groups in the phylum Arthropoda. Arthropods are characterized by their hard exoskeleton, or skin, and by their jointed appendages. Mites are in the class Arachnida, which also includes spiders and scorpions and the order Acari. Mites have two body regions and usually four pairs of legs. They lack wings. In contrast, most adult insects have wings, three body regions, and usually three pairs of legs. Mites grow and develop by simple metamorphosis, and most are very small.

Mites that are important pests of woody plants are about ¹⁄₂ millimeter (¹⁄₅₀ inch) or smaller when fully grown. Spider mites, in the family Tetranychidae, are important pests of spruce, honey locust, oak, maple, and crabapple. These mites discolor leaves by extracting leaf fluids. Other mites, in a group of closely related families, are called the **eriophyoid mites.** These mites are characterized by a cigar-shaped body and four visible legs. Some species, such as the hemlock rust mite, discolor leaves in the same way as spider mites. Other species cause the plant to produce **galls,** such as the ash flower gall. Not all mites are harmful to woody plants. Small, fast-moving, translucent, teardrop-shaped mites in the family Phytoseiidae regularly feed on spider mites in the landscape.

How Do Insects and Mites Injure Woody Plants?

Most insects and mites injure woody plants when they feed on them. Insects with chewing mouthparts injure plants by cutting into or removing whole parts of plant tissue. Examples include defoliation by eastern tent caterpillar, skeletonization of leaves by Japanese beetle, **boring** into a tree trunk by bronze birch borer, and boring into a leaf by birch leafminer. Insects with sucking mouthparts injure plants when they pierce plant tissue and suck out its contents. Examples of **injury** symptoms include the white spots on the surface of a cotoneaster, where lace bugs have extracted the green contents of leaf cells. Alternatively, insects such as the honeylocust plant bug can distort leaves by killing parts of the leaf as it unfolds from the leaf bud. Similarly, leaves and stems might be curled when insects such as aphids pierce plant stems and suck fluids from developing leaves and shoots. In many cases, however, the damage is caused by the accumulation of **honeydew** and unsightly black **sooty mold.**

Insects can also injure plants when they lay eggs, or oviposit, into plant tissue. For example, when a cicada lays an egg into the stem of an oak tree, it can kill the shoot that lies beyond the egg-laying site. **Gall making**

Figure 8.7 ▪ *The three standard insect body regions may be difficult to distinguish in the larvae of some insects, such as this onion maggot. In these highly modified insects, structures such as legs and mouthparts may be reduced or absent.*

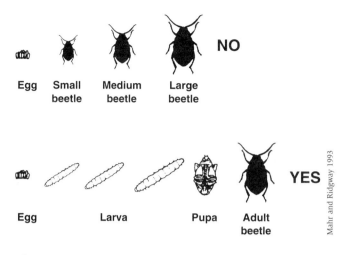

Egg · Small beetle · Medium beetle · Large beetle · **NO**

Egg · Larva · Pupa · Adult beetle · **YES**

Mahr and Ridgway 1993

Figure 8.8 ▪ *The upper life cycle shows the common misconception that little insects are smaller versions of adult insects. The lower life cycle illustrates the correct growth pattern of a beetle, one of many insects with complete metamorphosis. In many cases, when adult insects look similar but differ substantially in size, they are likely to be different species with different habits.*

is another form of injury that occurs when plant tissue swells around the site where an insect is feeding. An example of this is when the horned oak gall maker lays an egg in the twig of a pin oak and a gall forms around the developing larva.

At what point, then, does injury become damage? When insects and mites feed on plants, they injure them. When this injury harms plant health or makes a client dissatisfied with plant appearance, the plant is damaged. Understanding the needs and expectations of each client is critical to the successful management of client properties.

Detection of a single insect does not by itself justify treatment because it is not likely to cause enough injury to damage the tree. For example, consider a 30-foot-tall oak tree with approximately 100,000 leaves. Loss of ten leaves to a single caterpillar is not likely to harm plant health. More important, your client is not likely to notice it. Studies conducted with potential clients show that approximately 10 percent—in this case, 10,000 leaves—must be missing before the tree's appearance becomes unacceptable to the majority of clients. At this level, plant health is not likely to be affected.

Other factors, such as whether the caterpillars are dropping their excrement on your client's picnic table, should also be part of the assessment process (see Chapter 1).

Common Pests of Trees in the Midwest

To help you recognize them in the field, we have grouped these pests by the types of injury you will see. Life cycles of representative pests are included in each of the following groups. *Please note that the time of insect activity will vary depending on temperature and location.* Times given in this chapter are most applicable to Indiana. Insect activity could occur several weeks later in more northern states and several weeks earlier in more southern states. Damage associated with each type of pest is described to help you assess the impact on both tree health and client satisfaction.

The groups of pest that will be described are
- agents of leaf distortion and discoloration
- producers of honeydew, spittle, unsightly wax, or insect remains
- producers of bumps or swellings on leaves and twigs
- defoliators
- leafminers
- twig, leader, limb, and trunk feeders
- agents of **disease** transmission and rapid decline

Agents of Leaf Distortion and Discoloration

This group of insects and mites injures plants by piercing leaves and ingesting leaf juices, causing the leaves to **curl** or discolor. Pests in this category can be distinguished by how they distort leaves, the kind of excrement they leave on a plant, and whether they produce **webs.**

Leafhoppers can speckle the leaf surface with white flecks, or they can cause leaves to **yellow,** curl, or **stunt.** They feed on fluids in the **vascular system** of the plant. White flecks are caused by removal of green pigments from feeding on leaves. Yellowing, curling, or stunting is caused when damage associated with insect feeding reduces the flow of nutrients and water in and out of leaves. Because their food is liquid plant sap, the excrement of these pests is a sugary liquid called honeydew. Problems caused by pests that produce large amounts of honeydew are discussed in the section titled "Producers of Honeydew, Spittle, Unsightly Wax, or Insect Remains."

When plant bugs suck juices from expanding young leaves, they can kill portions of actively growing tissue and distort leaves. On expanded leaves, plant bugs remove the green chlorophyll from leaves, causing them to appear stippled with white spots—from the plant bug having removed sap from green leaf tissue that contains **chlorophyll**. Some species kill portions of leaf tissue as they feed and leave behind circular areas of brown dead tissue. The liquid excrement of most plant bugs is deposited as a black **tar spot** that is diagnostic for many pest species.

Spider mites and some eriophyoid mites can cause leaves to become stippled or **bronzed** when their stylet mouthparts pierce leaf tissue. Neither of these mites leaves behind honeydew or tar spots. Most spider mites spin fine webs on the leaf surface, where they lay their eggs. The eriophyoid mites that bronze or distort leaf tissue do not leave webs. The eriophyoid mites that produce galls will be discussed in another section.

Related Pests

Aphids can curl leaves, distort plant growth, or even kill plants. Because they also produce honeydew, they are discussed in the section on honeydew producers. Leafminers will produce brown areas but are discussed separately because of their unique way of feeding. Leaf folders and leafrollers, which curl leaves as they feed, are discussed with the concealed caterpillars.

Leafhoppers

Although many leafhoppers feed on woody plants, the potato leafhopper causes the most damage in the Midwest.

Potato leafhopper: Empoasca fabae (Harris)

Order and family: Homoptera: Cicadellidae.

Hosts: Many. Primarily a problem on maples. Red maples are most susceptible. Silver, sugar, and Norway maples are less susceptible.

Resistant varieties: 'Autumn Blaze', a hybrid of silver and red maple.

Damage and diagnosis: Shoots of trees become stunted, bearing leaves that are curled and brown at the margin (Figure 8.9, color plate section). Small, wedge-shaped, pale-green adults with white eyes or spiny, yellow-eyed immature stages can be found on leaf undersides.

Biology: This pest winters along the Gulf of Mexico and is blown north to the Midwest sometime between late April and early June. They colonize crops with green foliage. Typically they settle in alfalfa fields during the early spring migration. They often move to maples and other deciduous trees just after the first cutting of alfalfa, when drying hay is left in the field.

Control: The key to control is applying a broad-spectrum pesticide before leaves start to curl. Pyrethroid insecticides are particularly effective. Monitor maples for the presence of these lime-green leafhoppers on leaves, and spray an insecticide when you see an average of three hoppers (adult or nymph) per shoot on a tree. Determine the density of hoppers by inspecting one shoot on four sides of each tree. Examine the last three leaf pairs of each shoot by slowly turning leaves and looking for hoppers. Although there are many natural enemies of the potato leafhopper, including parasitic wasps and fungal diseases, their use has not been explored for controlling this pest on deciduous trees.

Honeylocust leafhopper: Macropsis fumipennis (Gillette and Baker)

Order and family: Homoptera: Cicadellidae.

Host: Honey locust.

Damage and diagnosis: Small areas of fine, white speckles are present on leaflets of infested trees. This injury is typical of the many less harmful leafhoppers that feed on woody plants. These pests rarely cause problems for clients. They are often found on trees infested with a more serious pest—the honeylocust plant bug. Although both pests are lime-green, the wings of the honeylocust leafhopper are held rooflike over the body, and it has a head as broad as the first segment of the thorax. Nymphs are not spined.

Biology: Wintering as eggs laid in honey locust twigs, this pest has at least two generations per year. Nymphs hatch from eggs in the spring when leaves break bud. Nymphs and adults feed on leaflets, leaflet stalks, petioles, and **rachises**. Some aspects of the biology, such as the host of the second generation of this pest, are poorly understood.

Control: Not needed. Compare with honeylocust plant bug.

Plant Bugs

Plant bugs feed by piercing leaf tissue and flushing in enzymes to digest cell walls and other plant parts. They feed on this partially digested slime by sucking up the fluid with their tube-shaped mouths. Leaves damaged by plant bug feeding can be covered with numerous white spots called **stipples**. Leaf injury can also appear as round holes. Leaves can become severely distorted when plant bugs feed on them as the leaves are unfolding in the spring.

Although many natural enemies of plant bugs are known, their use has not been explored for controlling this pest on deciduous trees. Pesticide applications should target nymphs because eggs are not affected. Determine this stage by looking for spiny nymphs near egg masses on leaf undersides and monitoring to determine egg hatch. Short residual materials, such as soaps, oils, or pyrethrins, can be effective on nymphs if coverage is adequate. Broad-spectrum materials can also provide effective control.

Honeylocust plant bug: Diaphnicoris chlorionis (Say)

Order and family: Homoptera: Miridae.

Host: Honey locust.

Damage and diagnosis: Leaves of infested trees become distorted or covered with brown **necrotic** spots as insects feed on emerging leaflets (Figure 8.10, color plate section). Adults have a green body with wings held flat over the body, with a head narrower than the first segment of the thorax. Nymphs are spiny. Extensive injury to trees in May or June can cause leaves to drop and can result in the production of a second flush of leaves in June. This puts tremendous stress on these trees, making them more susceptible to honeylocust borer and Thyronectria canker.

Biology: With only one generation per year, the honeylocust plant bug spends the winter as an egg on plant twigs. When the weather warms, eggs hatch to produce nymphs that feed on plants. Nymphs can be found feeding on green buds before leaves have unfolded. Most of the injury is caused by developing nymphs that turn into adults by early to mid-June. Adults lay eggs in June.

Control: It is important to recognize that use of broad-spectrum insecticides on honey locust can kill spider mite predators and promote defoliation by honeylocust spider mites later in the year. To prevent these outbreaks, delay applications of pesticides until you are certain that honeylocust plant bug threatens plant appearance. Although no formal studies have been conducted, field observations show extensive injury occurs when more than one bug is present per compound leaf when leaves are less than 4 inches long in the spring. When you must use an insecticide, use one with a short residual activity.

Eastern ash plant bug: Tropidosteptes amoenus (Rueter)

Order and family: Hemiptera: Miridae.

Host: Green ash.

Damage and diagnosis: Leaves attacked by this pest appear to be bleached white. Small tar spots of excrement are also present under leaves. Extensive feeding distorts leaves and can be confused with herbicide injury. Confirm the presence of this pest by looking up through leaves into the sunlight. This highlights the black fecal spots as well as the small reddish nymphs and red-brown adults feeding on leaf undersides.

Biology: Eggs spend the winter under loose bark and hatch in spring near the time when plant leaves begin to appear (late April to early May). Nymphs feed for about three weeks before they become adults. Adults lay eggs that hatch into nymphs in late July and August. Eggs from this generation are present through the winter.

Control: Use broad-spectrum insecticides to control nymphs of this pest. **Horticultural oils** and insecticidal soaps can burn young leaves.

Lace Bugs

Lace bugs are a distinctive group of plant bugs known for their lacy wings held flat over their bodies.

Lace bugs: Coenothus, Corythuca, Stephanitis *spp.*

Order and family: Hemiptera: Tingidae.

Hosts: *Trees*: Linden, sycamore, hackberry, hickory, oak, cherry, walnut, buckeye, willow, hawthorn, and basswood. *Shrubs*: Cotoneaster, pyracantha, rhododendron, azalea, and serviceberry.

Damage and diagnosis: Leaves are stippled and bleached white where lace bugs have been feeding (Figure 8.11, color plate section). During heavy infestations, leaves can drop. When this occurs on tall trees, lace bugs can create an added nuisance by falling on and biting people below. Tar spots of excrement are also present under leaves. Adults have clear, lacy, flat wings shaped like an angel's lyre. Nymphs are black and spiny. Black wine-flask–shaped eggs are laid into leaf tissue. Although damage might superficially resemble spider mites, no webs are present on leaf undersides.

Biology: Many lace-bug species are restricted to a single kind of plant. They have one to three generations a year, depending on species and temperature. Adults winter in bark crevices and other sheltered areas. They emerge in spring soon after leaves break bud. Nymphs take about thirty days to become adults.

  Control: Look for spiny nymphs by finding egg masses on leaf undersides when monitoring to determine egg hatch. Natural enemies, including some predaceous plant bugs and parasitic wasps, can help keep these pests under control. Follow general recommendations for plant bug control. Be advised that on prostrate shrubs, such as cotoneaster, it can be difficult to get effective coverage and control with insecticidal soap.

Spider Mites

Spider mites feed on plant leaves by piercing leaf tissues and sucking the green liquid that oozes out. Leaves appear bronzed after the green color is lost from many tiny feeding spots. Heavy infestations can **defoliate** trees and cover leaves with fine webbing. The best way to confirm a spider mite infestation is to hold a sheet of white paper under a branch and then tap the branch sharply. If present, mites will fall off and be seen as tiny specks crawling over the paper. The ability to crawl clearly distinguishes mites from the grit that can be knocked off a plant. Leaves infested with spider mites will usually have fine webbing and eggs on the leaf undersides. Although spider mite injury is superficially similar to that of lace bugs, spider mite injury can be distinguished by the presence of webs, egg shells on the midvein, and lack of tar spots on the leaf surface (Figure 8.12, color plate section).

  Spider mites are tiny eight-legged insects that are closely related to spiders. Several kinds are important pests of ornamental trees, shrubs, and bedding plants. Under favorable conditions, spider mites can build up rapidly and seriously threaten plant health. Some mite species are active during the cool season, others during the warm season. Some mites winter in the leaf litter, others on the trunk of the plant.

Managing mites ▪ *Decision making:* If you are monitoring every two weeks, consider applying a pesticide when an average of two dozen mites fall from a branch each time you strike it over an $8\frac{1}{2}$ x 11 inch sheet of paper. Try to monitor once each week in problem areas when conditions are favorable for mites. For example, keep a close watch for warm-season spider mites on plants with a southern exposure in the middle of the summer. Chemical controls are usually not needed in the fall on plants that normally drop their leaves.

  Cultural control: Spider mites thrive on plants that are suffering from water or nutrient stress. Be sure to keep plants well watered, and give them adequate light. Do not overfertilize or underfertilize.

  Biological and natural control: When the weather is wet, many kinds of spider mites are attacked by a **fungus**. In some cases, this is enough to keep mites from becoming a problem. Heavy rain can also reduce spider mite numbers by knocking them off the trees.

  Small lady beetles, lacewings, minute pirate bugs, and predatory mites are among the many arthropods that feed on spider mites. Increase the numbers of these helpful bugs in the landscape by avoiding pesticide use when possible. Apply pesticides only when spider mites or other pests threaten plant health or appearance. When pests other than mites are a problem, choose a pesticide least harmful to mite predators or one with a short residual activity. Examples of these are microbial insecticides for caterpillars (for example, *Bacillus thuringiensis*) or insecticidal soaps, horticultural oils, and pyrethrin.

  Natural enemies can be purchased and released for the control of spider mites. Successful use of imported natural enemies depends on many factors, including the initial numbers of mites and other natural enemies present, weather, handling of natural enemies, and time of year. Effective release rates for natural enemies in the landscape are not yet known.

  Dormant-season chemical control: If chemical control is necessary, a **dormant**-season treatment might help. Horticultural oil at the 3 percent to 4 percent rate can help reduce spider mite problems by smothering the mites that winter on woody parts of the plant. Thorough coverage is essential. Injury to plants can be avoided by following label guidelines. See special notes about the sensitivities of some junipers to injury. *Spraying blue-needled conifers with oil will turn them green and is not advised.* Dormant treatments are not effective for twospotted spider mites because they do not winter on twigs.

  Growing-season chemical control. Chemical control during the growing season is an entirely different matter. There are a wide range of miticides that kill mites in different ways. Those that kill only eggs and immatures—for example, Hexygon (hexythiazox)—can be useful at the start of a mite season because the remaining stages of mites provide food for the beneficials that contribute to season-long control. Similarly, insecticidal soap and horticultural oil have a low impact on natural enemies because of their short residual activity. The remaining miticides have longer activities and should be used to rescue plants from spider mites when the potential for biological control is low. Many of these materials need to be reapplied to kill eggs that have hatched since the last spraying. Morestan is an exception to the rule because it kills eggs and adults. Because resistance to these broad-spectrum materials can be a problem, be sure to change the class of pesticide once every three weeks.

Cool-season spider mites ▪ Cool-season spider mites are most troublesome during spring and fall when evening temperatures are less than 60°F. Controls are less likely to be needed in hot summer months.

Spruce spider mite: Oligonychus ununguis (Jacobi)
Order and family: Acari: Tetranychidae.

Hosts: Spruce, arborvitae, hemlock, juniper, some pines.

Damage and diagnosis: Injured needles appear brownish. Adults are oval-shaped ($1/60$ inch) and black or tan (Figure 8.12, color plate section). (Also see "hemlock rust mite.") Young are light grayish green. The round and brownish eggs of this spider mite are often found at the base of needles.

Biology: Eggs remain on the plant in the winter and hatch early in spring, with outbreaks occurring in April and May. Most severe damage occurs during September and October.

Control: See earlier discussion on control of spider mites. Note that oils and soaps turn blue-needled conifers green and can injure some junipers.

Southern red mite: Oligonychus illicis (McGregor)
Order and family: Acari: Tetranychidae.

Hosts: Broadleaf evergreen plants, especially Japanese hollies and azalea.

Damage and diagnosis: This small red mite feeds almost exclusively on the tops of leaves. Feeding on mature leaves causes them to appear bronzed. In April and May, leaves can become distorted when mites feed on leaves as they unfold. Red eggs, laid mostly on upper surfaces, are easily visible with a hand lens.

Biology: Eggs remain on the plant in the winter and hatch early in spring, with outbreaks occurring in April and May. After a summer **dormancy**, activity resumes in the fall.

Control: See earlier discussion on controls for spider mites.

Warm-season spider mites ▪ These mites thrive in the warm summer months. When the daily high–low temperature range is 95° to 75°F, the number of spider mites on a plant can double in half the time it takes when the high-low is 75° to 55°F. Large numbers of mites can build when plants are sheltered and have a southern exposure because they are warmer and drier. Controls are more likely to be needed when infestations are found at the beginning of the hot season than during the early spring or mid-autumn.

Twospotted spider mite: Tetranychus urticae (Koch)
Order and family: Acari: Tetranychidae.

Hosts: More than 150 plants, including bedding plants, weeds, trees, and shrubs, especially burning bush and potentilla (Figure 8.12, color plate section).

Damage and diagnosis: On woody plants, this mite prefers young foliage. In heavy infestations, it covers foliage with fine webbing and causes leaves to drop. During the warm months, adult mites ($1/60$ inch) are a whitish green with a dark-colored area on each side. In the spring and fall, they tend to become rusty orange. Eggs are round and pale white.

Biology: The twospotted spider mite spends the winter in protected places, such as beneath the loose bark of trees or in grass and weeds. They *do not* overwinter on woody plants.

Control: Dormant-season oil treatments are not effective because these mites do not winter on twigs or branches. Follow other control guidelines for mites.

European red mite: Panonychus ulmi (Koch)
Order and family: Acari: Tetranychidae.

Hosts: Flowering fruit trees and deciduous trees and shrubs in the rose family.

Damage and diagnosis: Causes leaves to bronze in the heat of the summer. This brownish red, elliptical mite is about $1/32$ inch long, with four rows of spines that run down its back. Eggs are bright red to orange and have a stalk that resembles a miniature onion set with the sprout attached. In the summer, most of the eggs are laid on plant leaves.

Biology: In the fall, eggs are laid in a cluster on twigs and branches of small trees, often in such great numbers that twig crevices and scars seem to be covered with brick-red dust. The European red mite spends the winter in the egg stage.

Control: See earlier discussion on control of spider mites.

Honeylocust spider mite: Platytechtranychus multidigtali (Ewing)
Order and family: Acari: Tetranychidae.

Host: Honey locust.

Damage and diagnosis: This small round mite feeds on leaf surfaces, causing them to turn bronze by

July. Adults are greenish in summer and turn reddish in fall. They are a common problem in continuous plantings of honey locust and can cause premature leaf drop in the fall. Webs produced by this spider mite are often less prominent than other species of spider mites.

Biology: These mites spend the winter as brick-red adults under bud scales. Eggs are laid in midspring.

Control: When possible, avoid continuous plantings of honey locust. See earlier discussion on control of spider mites.

Oak red mite: Oligonychus bicolor (Banks)

Hosts: Oak, birch, beech, chestnut, elm, maple, and hickory.

Damage and diagnosis: This small red mite infests the upper leaf surfaces of oak trees and is most predominant on the lower branches. Feeding damage is usually concentrated around the leaf midrib. Do not confuse natural pubescence on midveins of some oaks with webs associated with spider mite injury. In the summer, red barrel-shaped eggs are laid on the tops of leaves. In the fall, eggs are laid in the crevices and around axils of small twigs, where they remain dormant until spring.

Biology: These mites overwinter in bark crevices and on twigs as eggs.

Control: See earlier discussion on control of spider mites.

Eriophyoid Mite

Hemlock rust mite (eriophyoid mite): Nalepella tsugifoliae (Keifer)

Order and family: Acari: Nalepellidae.

Hosts: Hemlock, fir, spruce, and yew.

Damage and diagnosis: Heavily infested plants will turn a bluish color, then yellow, before leaves drop. Adults are cigar-shaped mites, barely visible and resemble tiny light-colored maggots when viewed in the field with a 10X hand lens. No webs are present (Figure 8.13, color plate section).

Biology: Wintering as an inactive adult, this mite is more of a problem in the early spring. Populations drop off during midsummer.

Control: See controls for spider mites. Repeated applications of pesticide are less likely to be required for eriophyoid mites than for spider mites.

Producers of Honeydew, Spittle, Unsightly Wax, or Insect Remains

Pests in this group produce substances that clients will readily see in the landscape. Generally speaking, however, only heavy infestations of these pests threaten plant health. They feed on fluids in the vascular system of plants. Because their food is liquid plant sap, their excrement is a sugary liquid called honeydew. Honeydew can be a problem when large amounts fall from trees down to cars, walks, or picnic areas. Areas below trees become sticky, attracting stinging wasps and ants that feed on the sweet honeydew. In time, honeydew will become food for a sooty mold fungus (Figure 8.14, color plate section). This can make the surfaces of leaves, stems, and trunks appear as if they have been covered with soot. Plants in this condition grow more slowly because the mold shades leaves, reducing their ability to capture light used for **photosynthesis**.

Insects such as armored scales, soft scales, mealybugs, and adelgids produce waxes that are easily visible to clients and are unsightly. Some aphids, such as the leaf curl ash aphid, can produce waxes in addition to honeydew. In many species, the majority of the wax is produced during egg laying. Spittlebugs are more notable for the frothy "spittle" that they leave on tips when they feed on plant tissue rather than honeydew production. Honeydew is used as food by many natural enemies of pests. This, combined with the tendency of many of these pests to stay in the same place for long times, increases the likelihood of effective control by these natural enemies. Tips for conserving natural enemies are discussed for each group.

Related pests not already mentioned include the two-marked treehopper, *Enchenopa binotata* (Say), which coats twigs with **conspicuous white wax** after laying an egg in the tissue. It is commonly found on redbud and viburnum and is not considered a major pest.

Scales and Their Relatives

Honeydew-producing scale insects [Order: Homoptera; families: Coccidae (soft or Lecanium scales), Kermesidae (oak kermes), Erioccocidae (bark scales), Pseudococcidae (mealybugs)] are common pests of shade trees and shrubs. These insects uncoil a long, fine tubelike mouth to feed directly on plant parts that transport fluid and nutrients. Distinguish these scales from galls by using your thumbnail to flip over suspicious-looking bumps on honeydew-covered twigs and branches. The bark will rip if you break off a gall. It will be intact beneath a scale or mealybug (Figure 8.15, color plate section). Live scales will burst and bleed when squashed.

Armored scales (family: Diaspididae) and pit scales (family: Asterolecaniidae) are not producers of honeydew. Armored scales do not produce honeydew because they feed on plants in a slightly different way than soft scales and their relatives. They burst and destroy the plant cells on which they feed and will often bypass plant vascular bundles that carry nutrients through the plant (Figure 8.16, color plate section). Honeydew producers will feed on fluid that moves through the vascular system. As with the honeydew-producing scales, check to see if bumps on twigs and branches are part of the plant or a scale insect. Live scales or eggs beneath the waxy armor will burst and bleed when crushed.

Managing scales and their relatives ▪ The following are general guidelines. *Cultural control:* Scales and mealybugs thrive on trees that are under stress. Plant trees that are correctly suited to the landscape site. Slow-growing plants with variegated leaves can require more care. Keep them watered and properly fertilized. If a plant is normally a rapid grower—such as willow, lilac, or yellow-twig dogwood—cut out heavily infested branches with pruning shears to physically remove scales from the tree.

Biological control: Conserving natural enemies is the best way to control scales and mealybugs. The stationary life of scales and mealybugs makes them an easy target for many natural enemies, including lady beetles and parasitic wasps. These beneficial insects can keep the numbers of scales quite low in a natural woodland setting. Avoid use of broad-spectrum pesticides on these trees. Water the area to reduce dust that can kill fragile natural enemies. Be on the lookout for small holes in scales that show where parasitic wasps might have emerged. Also look for the larvae and adults of lady beetles that feed on scales.

Chemical control: Chemical control should be used only as the tool of last resort to save plants with dead limbs and heavy scale populations. Always look for signs of natural-enemy activity before deciding to treat with a pesticide. Most pesticides cannot penetrate scales or mealybugs. Although pesticides can kill **crawlers**, it is difficult to coat the entire plant for total control. The scales that remain can multiply rapidly because females produce large numbers of young that survive in the absence of natural enemies. Most natural enemies of scales are more susceptible to pesticides than the scales themselves. Horticultural oil, insecticidal soap, and insect growth regulators are less harmful to beneficial insects.

Dormant-season oil treatments are most effective for scales and mealybugs that winter as immatures or as females that have not produced eggs. Impact on natural enemies is minimal. Summer oil treatment will smother actively crawling and recently settled crawlers. Look for crawlers by either examining twigs with a hand lens or by tapping a branch over a white sheet of paper. Crawlers vary in color depending on species. They are usually the size of a spider mite. Treat when you have a live scale population. Apply at the end of the crawler activity stage when scale covers are still clear. (See Table 8.1 for a list of common Midwest scales and their relatives, along with corresponding crawler and winter stages.)

A broad-spectrum insecticide treatment is the treatment of last resort. It should be used to rescue severely injured trees, especially those with branches that have recently been killed by scales. Application of these materials early in the crawler period will kill crawlers and natural enemies for several weeks. Pesticides with systemic activity are effective against honeydew-producing scales and their relatives because they feed on liquids moving through the plant vascular system. In contrast, systemic materials tend to be less effective against armored scales because they do not feed exclusively on these plant liquids.

Foliar-applied systemic pesticides are effective when soft scales or mealybugs are feeding on leaves in summer. Acephate (Orthene), a popular foliar-applied systemic insecticide, might burn the leaves of some soft maples and hawthorn. Soil-applied systemic insecticides such as imidacloprid (Merit) can be quite effective against overwintering soft scales and mealybugs that feed in the spring. Applications should be made at least four weeks before eggs are produced, or perhaps during the previous fall.

Soft or Lecanium scales (Coccidae) ▪ Soft scales are not covered by a waxy shell and are fairly transparent when they begin feeding. They spend most of their lives feeding on the plant vascular tissue on the same spot of a plant, unable to walk. After eggs hatch beneath females or in cottony egg cases, young scales and mealybugs are called crawlers because of their tendency to walk. Crawlers are small (less than $1/32$ inch) and flattened, looking like dust on the plant surface as they take up to 72 hours to settle on a feeding site. Soon after they initiate feeding, they become almost transparent. Scale infestations spread via the movement of nursery stock plants or when crawlers walk or are blown by the wind to nearby plants or plant parts.

Table 8.1 ▪ *Common Midwest scales and their relatives*

Kind and description of scale	Plants most seriously affected	Approximate crawler activity	Winter stage[1]
SCALES THAT DO NOT PRODUCE HONEYDEW			
ARMORED SCALES WITH DARK COVERS			
Hemlock scale			
Abragallaspis ithacae (Ferris) Small (¹/₁₆") elongate to oval gray scales on leaves or needles. Can discolor leaves and cause premature leaf drop.	hemlock, fir, spruce, pine	June & August–September	second instar nymph
Obscure scale			
Melanaspis obscura (Comstock) Small (¹/₁₆"), round gray scales. Twigs appear covered with silver shells when rubbed. Black central nipple.	pin oak and red oak, esp. in urban areas	July	second instar nymph
Oystershell scale			
Lepidosaphes ulmi (L.) Small (¹/₈") gray or brown scales shaped like oyster shells. May completely encrust branches.	lilac, birch, dogwood, ash, elm, poplar, soft maple, privet, willow, walnut, hemlock	May & July	eggs under scale cover
San Jose scale			
Quadraspidiatus perniciousus (Comstock) Tiny gray circular scales about the size of a pinhead and having a yellow central nipple.	flowering ornamental fruit trees, rose, quince, mountain ash, pyracantha, and others	mid-June–mid-July	second instar nymph
Winged euonymus scale			
Lepidosaphes yanangicola Small oystershell-shaped (¹/₁₆") covers found along ridges of winged euonymus branches (burning bush). Much thinner than oystershell scale.	burning bush	May, July & September	eggs under scale cover
ARMORED SCALES WITH WHITE COVERS			
Euonymus scale			
Unaspis euonymi Elongated (¹/₁₆") white ridged scale covers of males on leaves. Females on stems resemble oystershell scales but are more flattened.	euonymus, pachysandra, bittersweet	late May–early June, late July–August	mated adult female
Pine needle scale			
Chionaspis pinifoliae (Fitch) and *Chionaspis heterophyllae* (Cooley) Small elongated (¹/₈") white scales attached to needles of evergreens. *C. heterophyllae* is usually found on pines only. *C. pinifolae* is found on other hosts. Individuals of both species winter as eggs or mated adult females.	pine, fir, spruce	May & July June	eggs under scale mated adult female

Kind and description of scale	Plants most seriously affected	Approximate crawler activity	Winter stage[1]
Scurfy scale			
Chionaspis furfura (Fitch) Small elongate ($^1/_{10}$"), dirty white, pear-shaped scales. Lie flat on bark. Purplish-red crawlers.	young elms, apple, willow, dogwood	May & July	eggs under scale
Juniper scale			
Carulaspis juniperi (Bouche) Tiny ($^1/_{16}$") circular grayish-white scales with a yellow center. Packed between leaf scales of juniper and arborvitae.	juniper, arborvitae	early May & late June	mated adult female
Pit scale (pit-shaped bumps on twigs)			
Golden oak scale *Asterolecanium variolosum* (Ratzeburg) This scale makes a circular pit ($^1/_{16}$") around its gold-colored body. Edge of body is surrounded by a waxy fringe.	oak, esp. pyramidal English oak	June	mated adult female

SCALES THAT PRODUCE HONEYDEW

Cottony maple scale (soft scale)			
Pulvinaria innumerabilis (Rathvon) Oval ($^1/_4$") green to brown scales attached to undersides of branches. In spring, when depositing eggs, scales resemble strings of popcorn. Crawlers are found on the undersides of leaves.	soft maple, boxelder, linden, honey locust	June	mated adult female
European elm scale (bark scale)			
Gossyparia spuria (Modeer) Oval-shaped ($^1/_4$"), reddish-brown scales surrounded by a white waxy fringe. Found on bark, often in the crotch of small branches.	elms of all ages	mid-May– mid-June	second instar nymph
Fletcher's scale (soft scale)			
Parthenolecanium fletcheri (Cockerell) Round ($^1/_4$"), deep brown scales found on yews deep in plant.	arborvitae, baldcyprus, false cypress, juniper, hemlock, yew	mid-June– mid-July	second instar nymph
Magnolia scale (soft scale)			
Neolecanium cornuparvum (Thro) Large female up to $^1/_2$" long. Skin is covered with white waxy powder.	magnolia only	September	crawlers (become active again at budbreak)

continued

Kind and description of scale	Plants most seriously affected	Approximate crawler activity	Winter stage[1]
Pine tortoise scale (soft scale)			
Toumeyella parvicornus (Cockerell) Round (¼"), reddish-brown scale with black to dark brown stripes, or spots in a pattern that gives them a turtlelike appearance. Infestations mixed with **striped pine scale** (*T. pini* [King]) can be difficult to control because its life cycle is poorly understood. This scale has a white or cream-colored stripe on its back and is found toward branch ends.	pine only	mid-June–mid-July	mated adult female
Tuliptree scale (soft scale)			
Toumeyella liriodendrii (Gmelin) Females up to ½" long, with orange ridges on a brown body. Black crawlers.	tuliptree, magnolia, walnut, linden	September	crawlers (become active again at budbreak)
MEALYBUGS			
Two-circuli mealybug			
Phenacoccus dearnessi (King) Tiny white nymphs that winter on twigs and trunks line ridges that appear covered with frost. Adults move to twigs and branches, swell with eggs (⅛") and are covered with white wax.	hawthorn	September	crawlers (become active again at budbreak)

[1]Dormant applied oil sprays are not effective against scales that winter in the egg stage under scales.

Cottony maple scale: Pulvinaria innumerabilis (Rathvon)

Hosts: Soft maples, boxelder, linden, hawthorn, and honey locust.

Damage and diagnosis: Look for ¼-inch–long, oval, green to brown scales, attached to undersides of branches. In spring, they deposit long (½ inch) white sacks of eggs. During outbreak years, streets lined with infested trees appear as if they were strung with popcorn (Figure 8.17, color plate section). Honeydew production occurs during the entire growing season but peaks in spring prior to egg sack production and in late summer. Crawlers are found on the undersides of leaves until late summer, when they migrate to twigs.

Biology: Winters as clear, green, mated adult females that turn brown by early May, when they begin producing white cottony egg masses containing up to a thousand eggs. In June, eggs hatch to crawlers that walk to leaf undersides, where they spend the summer as first instars. Scales crawl back to twigs in late summer, where they mature into adults. Winged adult males mate with wingless females in the early autumn.

Control: These scales are rarely a problem. Outbreaks are infrequent and typically last two or three years. Indiscriminant use of broad-spectrum pesticides can induce or prolong outbreaks. In the Midwest, where many streets are lined with silver and red maples, outbreaks of this pest will literally cover streets with a fine layer of honeydew and sooty mold. Clients might become concerned about the paint on their cars, the sticky sidewalk, and the abundance of stinging wasps attracted by the honeydew. Although soil-applied systemic insecticides can kill the scales on a tree and stop the rain of honeydew, they ultimately destroy the natural enemies that normally keep the pest from becoming a problem.

Showing your client some evidence of natural-enemy activity might allow you to steer away from the pesticide option and use dormant applied oil instead. As discussed earlier, look for the small holes produced by wasp parasitoids. Dissect egg masses and look for lady beetle larvae with white waxy coats that make them resemble mealybugs (Figure 8.18, color plate section). The black mouthparts used to tear apart scales are visible with a 10X hand lens when you turn a larva over on its back. You might give the client some twigs in a jar to grow some red-spotted black lady beetle adults and wasp parasites, so that the client may see these beneficial insects firsthand.

Tuliptree scale: Toumeyella liriodendrii *(Gmelin)*

Hosts: Tuliptree, magnolia, walnut, and linden.

Damage and diagnosis: With orange-brown females up to $^1/_2$ inch in diameter, this is one of the largest species of scale in North America (Figure 8.14, color plate section). When females on twigs are swollen with eggs, these orange-ridged scales are about the size of a plump currant. Branches of heavily infested trees are coated black with sooty mold. Honeydew begins to accumulate significantly after females mate with males in mid-June.

Biology: One of the largest soft scales in North America, this scale winters as second instars on twigs and resumes feeding when the plant comes out of dormancy in the spring. Females produce up to 3,000 eggs that hatch into black crawlers in late August and September. Crawlers migrate to stem.

Control: Many natural enemies present.

Mealybugs ▪ These insects are covered with powdery wax soon after eggs hatch into crawlers. Males stop crawling just before they change into winged adults. Females continue to crawl on the plant, feeding on leaves, shoots, and branches until they produce a cottony mass with up to a thousand eggs, called an egg carton.

Two-circuli mealybug: Phenacoccus dearnessi *(King)*

Host: Hawthorn.

Damage and diagnosis: Tiny white nymphs line ridges in bark and twigs during fall, making them appear as if covered with frost. Adults move to twigs and branches. Females swell with eggs ($^1/_8$ inch) and are covered with white wax (Figure 8.18, color plate section).

Biology: Winters as second-instar nymphs on bark and twigs. They resume feeding when plant breaks dormancy in the spring. After eggs are produced, nymphs spend the summer feeding on leaves. Nymphs migrate to bark and twigs in fall.

Control: Many natural enemies, including a lady beetle whose larvae superficially resemble mealybugs.

Armored scales ▪ These insects have a life cycle similar to that of soft scales, and they too have an abundance of natural enemies in the landscape. Unlike soft scales, armored scales are coated with a waxy armor and do not produce honeydew. You can separate this waxy cover from the body of an armored scale to see the fleshy body beneath. Winged males crawl out from the waxy cover and mate with covered females who produce up to a hundred eggs. Eggs crawl out from beneath the covers.

Euonymus scale: Unaspis euonymi

Hosts: Euonymus, pachysandra, and bittersweet.

Damage and diagnosis: Leaves of heavily infested plants are covered with the white flecks of elongated ($^1/_{16}$ inch) male scale covers (Figure 8.15, color plate section). Females on stems resemble oystershell scales but are half the size and more flattened. Females on leaves are surrounded by halos of yellow in spring.

Biology: Winters as a mated female on stems. Egg laying begins in late May and lasts through early June. Males produce white covers and tend to be more common on leaves than on stems. Females tend to be more common on stems than on leaves. A second generation of crawlers is produced from late July to early August. Partial third generations occur in some years.

Control: Variegated varieties of euonymus are more susceptible than green varieties. Dormant-season oil sprays are quite effective if you can achieve adequate coverage.

Oystershell scale: Lepidosaphes ulmi *(L.)*

Hosts: Lilac, birch, dogwood, ash, elm, poplar, soft maple, privet, willow, walnut, and hemlock.

Damage and diagnosis: Small ($^1/_8$ inch long) gray or brown scales shaped like oyster shells are present on branches and twigs. Branches and twigs that are encrusted with scales will readily die.

Biology: Winters as an egg beneath the scale cover of a female. Eggs hatch into crawlers in May and July.

Control: Dormant-period oil sprays are not effective. Summer oil sprays are a better option for this scale.

Pine needle scales: Chionaspis pinifoliae *(Fitch) and* Chionaspis heterophyllae *(Cooley)*

Hosts: *C. heterophyllae* is found on pine only. *C. pinifoliae* is found on pine, fir, and spruce.

Damage and diagnosis: Needles of heavily infested plants are flecked white with scale covers (Figure 8.19, color plate section). These two species of closely related scales are difficult to distinguish in the field. Both species are small, elongated (¹/₈ inch) white scales attached to needles of evergreens. Scales beneath cover are purplish.

Biology: Individuals of both species winter as either eggs or mated adult females. Those that winter as eggs under scales produce crawlers in May and July. Those that winter as mated females produce crawlers in June only. Wintering females are less coldhardy than eggs. As a result, few survive to produce crawlers in the northern part of the region or after a cold, snowless winter.

Control: Several treatments might be needed to control this scale. Dormant oils are only partially effective because many scales winter as mated adult females. To time summer oil sprays, inspect branches to determine when crawler period is ending.

Aphids

Aphids are generally pear-shaped with two visible bumps, known as **cornicles**, on the hind end. Wings, when present, are clear and rooflike over the body when at rest. Most species are **polymorphic,** meaning that they can assume a different form at different times of year or when feeding on different plants. Two of the more common polymorphisms are winged or wingless adults, and reproduction with or without mating. When many species of aphids find themselves feeding on high-quality shoots, they produce wingless daughters that can produce daughters without mating. This allows them to rapidly increase their numbers without mating or producing wings. As food quality deteriorates, winged offspring are produced that can fly to better feeding sites. As a group, aphids feed on a wide range of woody plants and have a wide range of life cycles.

Aphids damage plants when they suck plant fluids, injure plant tissues, and curl leaves (Figure 8.20, color plate section). Most aphids cause only minor damage to the health of the tree and pose more of a nuisance from honeydew secretion (Figure 8.14, color plate section). Some aphids, such as woolly elm aphid (Figure 8.22, color plate section), cause extensive curling early in the year. Other aphid species, such as honeysuckle witches' broom aphid (Figure 8.23, color plate section), can distort shoot growth and kill branches (see description below). Deposition of honeydew is more of a nuisance over cars and high-traffic areas because of the honeydew's tendency to attract stinging wasps and to coat surfaces with unsightly sooty mold.

Management strategies ▪ *Cultural control:* Trees such as crabapple and tuliptree are susceptible to aphids for most of the year. In terms of cultural control, such trees should be planted only where honeydew is not likely to be noticed or cause a problem. Avoid planting these trees near picnic and parking areas. Keep plants well watered and properly fertilized. Overfertilization can prolong aphid infestation by stimulating shoot growth. Use resistant varieties when possible.

Biological control: Natural enemies of aphids are abundant in Midwestern landscapes. These include predaceous insects such as lady beetles, flower flies, lacewings, small parasitic wasps, and several fungal diseases. Note that parasitized aphids are brownish and appear swollen, much like a kernel of puffed grain. Conserve natural enemies by avoiding or delaying pesticide applications when possible to allow the number of beneficial insects on plants to increase. When insecticides are needed, avoid using long-lasting, broad-spectrum materials when natural enemies have been detected. Application of insecticidal soaps or summer oils can kill large numbers of aphids while allowing natural enemies to recolonize aphid infestations after these materials have dried.

Chemical control: If chemical control is needed, dormant applications of oils can kill aphids that winter as eggs on trees. Applications of soaps and oils can also be effective in the summer months. Broad-spectrum contact insecticides can kill more aphids than soaps or oils but might foster outbreaks of spider mites later in the season. Applications of pesticides are most effective before significant leaf distortion has taken place. Foliar-applied systemic insecticides (for example, acephate) are required after this time to allow the pesticide to reach and kill aphids hidden beneath curled foliage. Soil-applied systemic insecticides such as imidacloprid (Merit) can be quite effective against early season leaf distorters. Imidacloprid requires applications at least four weeks before eggs hatch or perhaps during the previous fall. Persistence of up to a year make it an ideal candidate for controlling honeysuckle witches' broom aphid.

Apple aphid: **Aphis pomi** *(De Geer)*

Order and family: Homoptera: Aphididae.

Hosts: Apple, crabapple, cotoneaster, hawthorn, mountain ash, pear, and quince.

Damage and diagnosis: Curls actively growing shoots and creates a honeydew nuisance. Continues through late July, when leaf growth stops. Winged females have a black head and thorax and a green body. Males are wingless. All wingless forms are light green (Figure 8.21, color plate section).

Biology: Wintering as an egg on twigs, this aphid hatches into inconspicuous nymphs that become noticeable in late May. Aphids remain on the same host until populations build. Winged females will fly to find new woody hosts.

Tuliptree aphid: **Macrosiphum liriodendri** *(Monell)*

Order and family: Homoptera: Aphididae.

Host: Tuliptree.

Damage and diagnosis: Yellows leaves in summer and fall, causing premature leaf drop and honeydew nuisance. Feeds only on tuliptree. Light-green aphids and pink aphids are found on leaf undersides. Pink forms tend to be wingless.

Biology: Overwinters as eggs in bark crevices of tuliptree. Eggs hatch into inconspicuous first instars in spring. Winged and wingless forms start to appear in late June. Aphids are present through October.

Green peach aphid: **Myzus persicae** *(Sulzer)*

Order and family: Homoptera: Aphididae.

Hosts: *Spring:* Peach, almond, cherry, and plum. *Summer:* More than 200 species of herbaceous plants, including many vegetables and bedding plants.

Damage and diagnosis: Extensive curling of leaves on shoot tips during heavy infestations can make trees appear as if they delayed leafing out. Winged adults are light green with black-tipped legs. Wingless forms of adults and nymphs are pear-shaped and straw-colored to light green, with a dark stripe along each side and down the back of the abdomen.

Biology: Eggs that winter on the woody host plant hatch into females that produce male and female offspring. Aphids remain on trees for two to three generations until they fly to a herbaceous plant host, where they have multiple generations during the summer. In the fall when the weather starts to cool, males and females fly to woody plant hosts. After mating, females lay overwintering eggs on twigs.

Woolly elm aphid: **Eriosoma americanum** *(Riley)*

Order and family: Homoptera: Aphididae.

Hosts: American elm, red elm, and serviceberry.

Damage and diagnosis: Leaves of infested trees appear tightly curled and contain waxy adelgids. Adults are somewhat purplish when wax is removed. On serviceberry, woolly aphids are found on stems in midsummer (Figure 8.22, color plate section).

Biology: This aphid is representative of those causing early season shoot distortion. This species overwinters as an egg on elm bark, then hatches into a female that produces up to two hundred young females without mating. The females and their young produce a second generation that curls leaves and produces young that cause elm leaves to curl. Winged forms produced in this and the following generation during early summer will fly to serviceberry, where they lay eggs that hatch into nymphs that crawl down to feed on tree roots. After several summer generations, a winged generation returns to feed on elms.

Related pest species: Several species of woolly aphids in the **genus** *Eriosoma* use elm as their overwintering host. Most notable are the woolly apple aphid (*Eriosoma lanigerum* [Harris]), which feeds on the roots of apples, crabapples, and mountain ash, and the leaf curl ash aphid (*Prociphilus fraxinifolii* [Riley]), which feeds on ash.

Honeysuckle witches' broom aphid: **Hyadaphis tartaricae** *(Aizenberg)*

Order and family: Homoptera: Aphididae.

Host: Honeysuckle.

Damage and diagnosis: New growth of plants is stunted (Figure 8.23, color plate section), and twigs become branched into clusters called **witches' brooms.** These brooms are easily detected in winter or summer. Cream-colored aphids are found between folded leaves in summer. Affected branches die in winter. Heavy infestations can kill plants. The spring generation is winged. The summer generation has winged and wingless forms.

Biology: This aphid is representative of those causing severe distortion and **dieback.** Eggs that winter on branch tips hatch into wingless females in early May, just before leaves unfurl. Once leaves are out, aphids start feeding on leaves. Females from overwintering eggs produce males and females that have multiple generations throughout the summer.

Resistant host varieties: 'Arnold's Red', 'Clavey's Dwarf', and 'Emerald Mound'.

Adelgids

Most of the insect species in this group will produce a white wax at some point in their lives. Some species attack conifers, and others attack deciduous trees. Some species will produce galls (see "Producers of Bumps or Swellings on Leaves and Twigs"). The biology of adelgids and the general control strategy are similar to that described for aphids. As with aphids, the principal control strategy for this pest is the conservation of the many natural enemies in the landscape. For the purposes of identification, it is important to note that, unlike aphids, adelgids lack cornicles on their hind end. Many adelgids have complicated life cycles that require several different host species.

Pine bark adelgid: Pineus strobi (Hartig)
Order and family: Homoptera: Adelgidae.

Hosts: Primarily white pine and, to a lesser extent, Austrian and Scots pine.

Damage and diagnosis: White, cottony masses are present on the trunk and under main branches of infested trees (Figure 8.24, color plate section). Does not cause significant harm to tree health but is unsightly.

Biology: This insect has three to four generations per year on white pine. It winters as an immature under white, cottony mass. Eggs are laid in early spring and hatch in late April. Some confusion exists about the biology of this pest. There have been reports that this species requires spruce as an alternate host.

Control: Because of the many natural enemies of this pest and its inability to greatly harm tree health, it is best to rely on methods that conserve natural enemies. These include using insecticidal soaps or oil, as well as knocking off the adelgids with a high-pressure jet of water. Broad-spectrum materials are effective against adults and nymphs but not eggs.

Spittlebugs

Spittlebugs are closely related to the planthoppers discussed previously. As such, they have sucking mouthparts that allow them to penetrate plant tissue and feed on plant **phloem**. They are easily detected by the frothy spittle produced by nymphs (Figure 8.25, color plate section). Spittle keeps nymphs in a moist environment and hides them from some natural enemies. Infested shoots appear as if someone had spit on a branch. Some spittlebugs, such as the Saratoga spittlebug, *Aphrophora saratogensis* (Say), are important pests for Christmas-tree producers but are not likely to be encountered in the ornamental landscape. For arborists, spittlebugs are a nuisance because spittle is usually noticed by clients well before enough spittlebugs are present to affect tree health. Treatments are often applied to trees whose owners are repulsed by the appearance of "spit" on their trees.

Pine spittlebug: Aphrophora parallela (Say)
Order and family: Homoptera: Cercopidae.

Hosts: Pines, spruce, balsam fir, and hemlock.

Damage and diagnosis: White globs of spittle hiding black-headed nymphs on twigs in spring (Figure 8.25, color plate section). Honeydew and presence of adult hoppers in summer. Twig and branch dieback can occur when high densities of this pest are present.

Biology: This pest spends the winter as an egg deposited in branches and twigs. In spring, eggs hatch into nymphs that begin feeding on shoots. Only adults are present in midsummer.

Control: This pest has a wide variety of natural enemies, including several parasitic wasps and some fungal diseases. It is important to conserve natural enemies when selecting a control option. Use of insecticidal soap or horticultural oil can be effective if coverage is thorough. Use of broad-spectrum insecticides can also control this problem.

Producers of Bumps or Swellings on Leaves and Twigs

This group of insects and mites can cause plants to produce bumps on a tree. Gall makers cause leaves, stems, or twigs to swell into characteristic structures called galls. You can distinguish between galls and scales on a plant surface by trying to flip over the bump with your thumbnail. When you flip over scales, the plant tissue is undisturbed (Figure 8.15, color plate section). In contrast, flipping over a gall will rip plant tissue. **Pit scales** (see Table 8.1) differ from other scales in that they actually cause plant tissues to swell around the settled scale.

Gall Makers

Galls are abnormal growths on plants caused by living organisms, including **bacteria**, fungi, **nematodes**, mites, and insects. There are hundreds of kinds of galls, each characteristic of the organism that stimulates its growth. These organisms use the galls for food and protection. Plants produce galls to restrict injury caused by the pest, placing a barrier between the pest and the rest of the plant. Because galls stay put, they are highly visible to other organisms. Some insects colonize galls to share the home made by the gall maker. Other insects penetrate galls to feed on the gall maker itself.

Management considerations ▪ Galls located on aboveground parts of a tree seldom, if ever, kill the tree. They are nevertheless unsightly and can distort plant growth. Two exceptions are the horned and gouty oak galls (described below), which can cause considerable damage to shade trees. Conservation of natural enemies and a little bit of patience are the most reliable options for long-term management.

Cultural control: No one can reliably predict the time it will take natural enemies of a gall to bring it under control. Physical removal of galls by pruning does get the gall problem out of the trees and may console a client who is having a hard time waiting for the problem to take care of itself. Pruning, however, can be impractical on heavily infested trees. Removal of galls that fall to the ground and those that are in the trees at the right time of year offers the additional advantage of lowering the numbers of pests in the area that are capable of producing galls.

Chemical control: Insects and mites that cause galls are well protected beneath the swollen plant tissue for most of their lives. Because of this, it is very difficult to time insecticide applications to coincide with the brief periods when they are effective against these pests. Solving the problem is further complicated by difficulties in achieving adequate coverage for tall trees. This is especially true when applying dormant oil to kill gall-forming insects that overwinter outside of their protective galls on twigs and branches. For most galls, except Cooley and eastern spruce gall, chemical control is ineffective.

Biological control: When removing galls from infested trees, it is good to remember that many of their natural enemies live in the galls. Physically removing every last gall from trees will also remove natural enemies. Leaving a few galls in the area might actually increase the long-term stability of a gall-management program. This is especially true for some leaf-gall formers that winter as adults on twigs. Removal of fallen leaves with old galls can simply reduce numbers of natural enemies present without reducing numbers of gall-forming insects that can attack the tree. For some galls (for example, ash flower gall), insecticide use has been shown to prolong the gall problem.

Maple bladder gall: Vasates quadripedes *(Riley)*

Order and family: Acari: Eriophyidae.

Hosts: Silver maple and red maple.

Damage and diagnosis: Small, wartlike growths on the foliage are red in spring, then turn green and finally black in summer (Figure 8.26, color plate section). They occur singly or in clusters and can be so abundant that the leaves become crinkled and deformed and drop early. These galls never cause permanent injury and actually have little effect on tree health and vigor. They do, however, detract from the normal beauty of the foliage.

Biology: Mites that cause maple bladder gall overwinter in cracks and crevices of the bark as inactive adults. As the buds swell in the early spring, the mites migrate out to the bud scales. When the buds open, mite feeding causes the newly developing leaves to form galls. Mites live, feed, and mate inside galls all summer. In the fall, mites move back to the bark before leaves drop.

Control: Because this gall maker spends the winter as an adult on the tree, keeping some old galls around will not contribute to future gall problems and might conserve natural enemies.

Ash flower gall: Eriophyes fraxiniflora *(Felt)*

Order and family: Acari: Eriophyidae.

Host: Ash.

Damage and diagnosis: Groups of brown, dried galls are seen on trees in summer and winter. Galls deform male flowers, which become surrounded by a fringe of disfigured green leaves in spring and early summer.

Biology: Green ash is commonly attacked by this small mite that spends the winter as an inactive adult in the bud scales. Adult mites feed on flower buds when they begin to emerge in spring. This feeding causes the formation of groups of galls surrounded by a fringe of disfigured flowers. As galls dry, they migrate to new flower buds.

Control: Adult mites are most susceptible to dormant applications of oil when they become active in spring prior to budbreak. Control is only marginally effective, and some broad-spectrum insecticides have actually worsened the problem.

Horned oak gall: Callirhytis cornigera *(Osten Sacken)*

Order and family: Hymenoptera: Cynipidae.

Hosts: Oak, especially pin oak.

Damage and diagnosis: This wasp can cause trees to produce large numbers of horned galls up to 2 inches long around stems. This, in turn, **girdles** stems and can cause significant branch dieback.

Biology: Female wasps emerge from galls on stems in late spring (May). Eggs laid in oak leaves hatch into larvae that produce a blisterlike gall along the leaf vein. In midsummer (July), adults fly from leaf galls and lay eggs in twigs. Galls begin forming on twigs that summer as larvae develop. Larvae remain in twigs for two or more years until adults emerge to attack leaves.

Control: Due to the severe injury that can be caused by this gall maker, remove twig galls during the first winter they are visible. This and other available control options are not very satisfactory.

Related species: Gouty oak gall, *Callirhytis quercuspunctata* (Bassett), has a similar life cycle but lacks horns.

Cooley spruce gall adelgid: Adelges cooleyi (Gillette)

Order and family: Homoptera: Adelgidae.

Host (with galls produced): Spruce.

Alternate host (with no galls produced): Douglasfir.

Damage and diagnosis: This conelike gall is produced on the tips of new growth of Colorado blue, Sitka, and Engelmann spruces. The gall is green or purplish, 1 to 2 inches long, $^1/_2$ to $^3/_4$ inches in diameter, and resembles a small pineapple in an early stage of development. Galls turn brown and are easily visible in winter. On Douglasfir, needles become twisted and yellowed (Figure 8.27, color plate section).

Biology: This insect takes two years to complete its life cycle on Douglasfir and spruce. Winged adults fly from Douglasfir to spruce in late July. Adults lay eggs, and the eggs hatch into nymphs that spend the winter on spruce twigs. Nymphs become active on spruce in early spring just before the buds break. They develop into adults in May that lay eggs on twigs. When these eggs hatch, nymphs crawl to the base of spruce needles and cause them to produce the characteristic galls. In midsummer, galls on spruce open to release winged adults that fly to Douglasfir to lay eggs. These eggs hatch into nymphs that overwinter on Douglasfir. After budbreak, nymphs become active and start to distort leaves. They develop into wingless adults in May. These adults produce offspring that become winged and wingless adults in July. Wingless adults remain on Douglasfir, and winged adults fly to spruce to complete the cycle.

Control on spruce: The presence of old galls on spruce in the winter suggests that infested Douglasfir are near enough for adelgids to have laid eggs on spruce the previous summer. Scout spruce to target trees that need treatment. Apply broad-spectrum insecticides to the tree just prior to budbreak to kill nymphs that wintered on the tree as eggs. By killing these nymphs, you prevent adults from laying the new generation of eggs on young needles, where galls are formed in late May. Pruning out old galls makes the plant look nice but does not control the problem.

Control on Douglasfir: Look for signs and symptoms that nymphs are present on twigs. Early signs include the production of waxy fibers by young nymphs. Later in spring, needles begin to twist and yellow. Applications of insecticidal soap or oil can effectively control the nymphs and prevent further twisting. Broad-spectrum insecticides are also effective.

General control: Do not interplant spruce and Douglasfir because they are alternate hosts of the Cooley spruce gall adelgid.

Eastern spruce gall adelgid: Adelges abietus (Linnaeus)

Order and family: Homoptera: Adelgidae.

Hosts: Norway, white, black, and red spruce.

Damage and diagnosis: A pineapple-shaped gall ($^1/_2$ to 1 inch long) is produced at the base of the new shoot growth (Figure 8.27, color plate section). Heavy infestations can distort shoot appearance.

Biology: Like Cooley spruce galls, these also open in midsummer to release the adelgids inside. However, the adelgids *remain* on the spruce. Greenish immature females overwinter in cracks and crevices at the base of the buds. In the spring, the eastern spruce gall adelgids mature and deposit eggs under a mass of cottony threads. These eggs hatch about when the buds open and the new needles are exposed. When the spring generation of nymphs begins feeding, plants produce bulbous galls containing many cells filled with the immature adelgids.

Control: Scout for last year's galls in the dormant season to target plants that need treatment in the spring. Apply broad-spectrum insecticides to plants just after budbreak to kill nymphs that hatch from cottony egg masses at the base of needles. Late-September application of material directed at immature females may provide some additional control. Some spruce are resistant to this problem.

Defoliators

Insects in this group consume entire leaves or leaf parts. Patterns of defoliation can help to identify the pest. Some insects, such as eastern tent caterpillar, gypsy moth or yellownecked caterpillar, consume the entire leaf with the possible exception of the midrib (Figure 8.29, color plate section). Others skeletonize leaves by feeding only on tissues between leaf veins (Figures 8.34, 8.35, and 8.36, color plate section). This is characteristic of insects with small mouthparts, including many young caterpillars, sawflies, and beetles that feed on older leaves where eggs have hatched. Black vine weevil adults and their relatives leave angular **notches** on the leaf margin (Figure 8.37, color plate section). **Circular scars** are cut along leaf edges by leafcutter bees (Figure 8.38, color plate section).

In addition to the pattern of defoliation, the presence and location of webs are useful diagnostic tools to use in distinguishing some caterpillar defoliators (Figure 8.29, color plate section). For example, eastern tent caterpillar produces webs in tree crotches, whereas fall webworm produces large, loose webs on the ends of branches. In contrast, webs produced on the ends of honey locust branches by the mimosa webworm fold leaves together. The bagworm caterpillar simply covers itself with a small silken web and cut leaves.

Management Considerations

In addition to the effects of defoliation on plant appearance, clients are often concerned about the effects of defoliation on plant health. Complete defoliation during a single season is not likely to kill a tree unless it was severely weakened by some other set of factors prior to defoliation. Many trees defoliated by early season pests (before July 1) will produce a new set of leaves. In the process, trees consume an enormous amount of energy that they would normally store in stems and roots for later use. After defoliation, trees are usually less vigorous and more susceptible to diseases and boring insects that thrive on weakened trees. Repeated and consecutive defoliation further weakens trees, killing them outright or causing them to be too weak to withstand attack by other insects and diseases.

As with most insect pests, insecticides are more effective against defoliators when the insects are immature and small. This is even more important for insects whose webs can hide them from pesticide sprays. The following section starts with a discussion of two kinds of defoliators—exposed and concealed caterpillars. The concealed type requires a different management strategy than the exposed type.

Caterpillars

These are the wormlike immature stages of butterflies and moths. This is the stage of moth that will defoliate trees, mine leaves (see "Leafminers"), or bore beneath tree bark (see "Twig, Leader, Limb, and Trunk Feeders"). Caterpillars are more susceptible to control with foliar insecticides than adult moths that simply feed on flower nectar.

From a control perspective, it is important to be sure that the wormlike specimen is a caterpillar and not a sawfly. Some pesticides, such as *Bacillus thuringiensis* 'Kurstaki', is effective against most caterpillars but not against sawflies. Caterpillars are distinguished from sawflies by having two to five pairs of prolegs capped with small barbs called **crochets** (Figures 8.6 and 8.28). Sawflies have six or more pairs of prolegs and lack crochets.

Concealed caterpillars ▪ Many moth caterpillars attempt to hide from bird predators and other natural enemies by covering themselves with a combination of webbing, excrement, and leaves. This covering can simplify mechanical control of this pest. When isolated webs or overwintering forms of these defoliators are detected, you can prune them out of the tree and reduce the need for spraying insecticides. Unfortunately, these webs can greatly complicate control of these pests with pesticides. If you choose to control the young caterpillars with *Bacillus thuringiensis* 'Kurstaki', you must apply materials before they are deeply embedded in their web and leaf covering. As caterpillars become more embedded in their webs, many of the broad-spectrum insecticides become more effective than al-

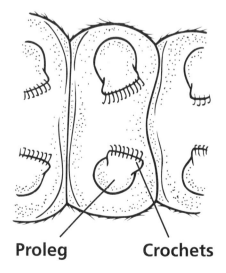

Figure 8.28 ▪ *Underside of a caterpillar showing the location of prolegs and crochets.*

ternative materials. Pyrethroids, in particular, are quite effective because of their high activity at low doses.

Mimosa webworm: Homadaula anisocentra (Meyrik)

Order and family: Lepidoptera: Plutellidae.

Hosts: Honey locust, mimosa.

Damage and diagnosis: Leaves on ends of branches become webbed together and turn brown as lime-green caterpillars skeletonize leaf tissue (Figure 8.29, color plate section). Heavily infested trees appear frosted brown. Larvae drop from the trees to the ground on silken strands just prior to pupation and can annoy pedestrians. Each silk-covered pupa superficially resembles a kernel of puffed rice. Masses of pupae can be found in bark crevices as well as glued onto structures under shingles, windows, and door frames from October through May.

Biology: Pupae winter in sheltered areas. In early June, adults emerge and lay eggs on trees. First webs can be seen on ends of branches in mid-June. Larvae take three weeks to turn into pupae. The second-generation adults fly and lay eggs starting in late July. Caterpillars are out in early August and start dropping from trees as pupae at the end of the month.

Control: The main goal is to control the problem without killing the predators of honeylocust spider mite, which can cause a different problem. Target the first generation of caterpillars to prevent serious defoliation by the second generation. Second-generation caterpillars are more numerous and hatch over a longer period of time than the first generation. This makes it more difficult to effectively time pesticide applications. Look for early signs of webbing before leaves turn brown. These webs are first found in tree tops. Take advantage of urban structures such as parking garages to get a good look at the tops of these trees when you scout. Apply insecticide on young larvae. When possible, use pesticides that kill only caterpillars, such as *Bacillus thuringiensis* 'Kurstaki'. See other comments for concealed caterpillars.

Fall webworm: Hyphantria cunea (Drury)

Order and family: Lepidoptera: Arctiidae.

Hosts: Most deciduous trees.

Damage and diagnosis: Large webs are found at the edge of the canopy (Figure 8.29, color plate section). Heavily infested trees can be completely covered by the webs produced by caterpillars of the fall generation. Webbing is more massive than mimosa webworm. Caterpillars are yellowish green with black spots and long white hairs and grow up to 1½ inches long. Young larvae skeletonize leaves, and older larvae consume them.

Biology: Brown pupae spend the winter in leaf litter in a loosely webbed cocoon. In June, adults fly and lay large white egg masses (more than two hundred eggs per mass) under leaves (Figure 8.30, color plate section). Eggs hatch into larvae that feed for four to six weeks. A second generation occurs in late summer.

Control: Focus control on the first generation with the same strategies described for mimosa webworm. Although the second generation is unsightly, it is less likely to harm tree health because it occurs only a few weeks before leaves will normally fall from trees.

Eastern tent caterpillar: Malacosoma americanum (Fabricius)

Order and family: Lepidoptera: Lasiocampidae.

Hosts: Flowering fruit trees.

Damage and diagnosis: Caterpillars form webs, or nests, in crotches of trees (Figure 8.29, color plate section). Caterpillars are dark in color with a white stripe on their backs. They defoliate trees in April and May. This early season defoliation is not likely to kill the tree. In early May, large caterpillars (up to 2 inches) wander from trees to look for a site to pupate. The sight of caterpillars roaming across pavement, patios, or backyard lawns can upset clients. Egg masses wrapped around twigs (Figure 8.30, color plate section) are easily found in winter, when leaves are not on trees.

Biology: Egg masses winter on twigs. Eggs hatch when cherry leaves unfold. Caterpillars crawl to a tree crotch and start to form webs. Caterpillars remain in webs during the day to avoid predation from birds. At night, caterpillars crawl from the mass of webs to feed on leaves.

Control: When possible, mechanical control is preferred. Look for egg masses in the winter, and remove them. You can easily remove the infestation with a gloved hand because these caterpillars stay in relatively small nests during the day. Kill caterpillars by crushing them or dropping them in a bucket of soapy water. When many nests are present or the nests are hard to reach, an insecticide will give better control. Apply materials to leaves as described for mimosa webworm. Do not burn nests. This will cause serious harm to the tree.

Bagworm: Thyridopteryx ephemeraeformis (Haworth)

Order and family: Lepidoptera: Psychidae.

Hosts: Many evergreen and deciduous trees. Commonly arborvitae, juniper, false cypress, spruce, fir, and pine. Occasionally honey locust and Japanese maple.

Damage and diagnosis: Caterpillars live in silken "bags" covered with leaves of the host plant (Figure 8.31, color plate section). Young caterpillars (¼ inch) are difficult to see because the leaves that cover them are fresh and resemble the rest of the foliage. In early stages of infestations, leaves appear to be walking. As the infestation progresses, defoliation becomes more apparent. Entire trees can be stripped of foliage. Large bags (up to 2½ inches) are easily visible in winter and superficially resemble Douglasfir cones. Check for live bagworms in early spring by slicing several females and looking for eggs. In June, using this technique to look for small green caterpillars can help determine when eggs are hatching in the overwintering bags. This pest is more of a problem south of the Great Lakes.

Biology: Winters in bags as eggs in the body of mated adult females. Eggs start to hatch in early June and can continue until early July. Driving rains can kill newly emerging caterpillars by washing them off the foliage. Young caterpillars immediately cover themselves with leaves as they feed. In August, the winged adult male flies out of his bag to one containing a wingless female. After mating, the female stays in the bag and produces up to a thousand eggs.

Control: Look for overwintering bags on plants. Physically remove them before egg hatch to prevent damage. When too many bags are present (more than ten per tree), an insecticidal control is preferred. Insecticidal control is most effective during the growing season on small bags (less than 1 inch long). *Bacillus thuringiensis* is quite effective on bagworms at this stage. In the future, entomophagous nematodes might be a useful tool against this pest because it spends its life in a moist, humid bag. Cool weather in late May and June can stretch out the period of egg hatch to a month or more. Be sure to check infested sites for bagworms again in July when this weather pattern is present.

Fruittree leafroller: Archips agyrospila (Walker)

Order and family: Lepidoptera: Tortricidae.

Hosts: Many deciduous species, including flowering fruit trees.

Damage and diagnosis: Individual leaves are rolled by lime-green caterpillars with black heads. Caterpillars hold the roll together with webbing, feed on the interior of the roll, and skeletonize the leaf. Individual caterpillars can fold many leaves. Commonly a spring pest.

Biology: Spending the winter as an egg mass on a twig, eggs hatch soon after leaf buds have opened. Caterpillars feed on flower buds and move to leaves, where they begin folding and feeding. Individual caterpillars can fold many leaves until they pupate in late May.

Control: As with other concealed caterpillars, control is easiest in the early season with broad-spectrum pesticides or *Bacillus thuringiensis* prior to extensive leaf folding.

Related pests: More than 200 species of insects will damage ornamental plants by rolling, folding, or tying leaves as they feed. Some, such as the leaf crumpler, *Acrobasis indigenella* (Zeller), which feeds on cotoneaster and crabapple, lay eggs in the summer that hatch into caterpillars that winter in the larval stage. These can be controlled by pruning or with an early season insecticide spray that kills larvae when they resume feeding.

Exposed caterpillars ▪ Exposed caterpillars feed on leaves and are not hidden from view by webs or by plant tissue such as leaves. As such, they are more easily killed with insecticide sprays.

Gypsy moth: Lymantria dispar (Linneaus)

Order and family: Lepidoptera: Lymantriidae.

Hosts: Many trees and shrubs, especially oak, apple, birch, mountain ash, willow, and quaking aspen. Lists of resistant species are available.

Damage and diagnosis: Infested trees can be completely defoliated by hairy caterpillars growing up to 2 inches long. Although many deciduous tree species will leaf out again, complete defoliation two to three years in a row can kill a tree. During heavy infestations, the accumulation of caterpillar excrement below trees can become a nuisance.

Young caterpillars present in early May are dark and lack spots. Mature caterpillars present in June are dark with six pairs of red and five pairs of blue spots along their backs. Occasionally, outbreaks of gypsy moth can coincide with infestations of forest or eastern tent caterpillars. Forest tent caterpillars can be easily distinguished by white "keyhole" markings along the top of their backs. Eastern tent caterpillars have a white stripe along the top of their backs. Proper identification of gypsy moth is critical for planning management strategies. Gypsy moth pupae can be found on trunks or on other structures in late June to July. White adult females can be found laying light-brown egg masses from mid- to late July through early August.

Biology: Egg masses containing from fifty to 1,500 eggs can be found on tree trunks and nearby sheltered areas, including door jams, picnic benches, firewood, vehicles (underneath), and nursery containers (at the bottom). Eggs hatch in late April into black caterpillars that climb to the top of a tree or structure so they can be blown by the wind to a new tree. When the caterpillars land on a tree, they begin feeding on leaves. As caterpillars become large, they feed only at night. When full grown in late June, caterpillars will wander to sheltered areas to construct cocoons. In mid-July, white female and brown male moths emerge. Female gypsy moths do not fly. They sit on trees and release a scent that attracts males. After mating, females will walk to find a sheltered place to lay eggs.

Control: Applications of *Bacillus thuringiensis* are quite effective on this moth through the third-instar caterpillars. Diflubenzuron (for example, Dimilin) and insect growth regulators can also provide effective control. Most other broad-spectrum insecticides can readily kill caterpillars while they are feeding. Gypsy moth can often be an emotional issue for a community. Be sure to consult your local Extension educator to see how you as an individual arborist can fit into the local gypsy-moth management plan.

Special considerations: Gypsy moth is the most serious forest defoliator in the northeastern states. Currently Ohio and Michigan are the two midwestern states with established populations. If you find this pest in an area where it has not been established, be sure to notify your state department of agriculture.

Yellownecked caterpillar: Datana ministra (Drury)
Order and family: Lepidoptera: Notodontidae.
Hosts: Most deciduous trees.
Damage and diagnosis: White egg masses, each with up to a hundred eggs, are easily visible on leaf undersides. Young caterpillars will first skeletonize leaves and then strip them of foliage as they

mature. Younger larvae are brick-brown with yellow stripes along the body. Older larvae are black with yellow stripes and are up to 2 inches long. Late-season defoliation does not significantly harm tree health but can be unsightly.

Biology: After spending the winter as pupae, adults emerge in June and July to lay egg masses on leaf undersides. Eggs hatch in late July into caterpillars that feed in groups through August. Large caterpillars pupate in the soil, where they spend the winter.

Control: Look for young caterpillars in July, and treat before caterpillars become large and cause major damage. Broad-spectrum insecticides are more effective against larger caterpillars than *Bacillus thuringiensis* 'Kurstaki'. Although late-season defoliation is unsightly, it does minimal harm to tree health because it occurs close to the time of normal leaf drop.

Sawflies

Sawflies are thick-waisted wasps. They are called sawflies because adults have a sawlike ovipositor that they use to insert eggs into plant tissue. Their immatures are wormlike and resemble caterpillars. They have six or more pairs of prolegs that lack crochets (Figures 8.6 and 8.28). On some sawflies, such as pear sawfly (described below), the prolegs might be difficult to distinguish.

Some sawflies, such as European pine sawfly and mountain-ash sawflies, will feed in groups that can be particularly destructive. These have the distinctive behavior of arching their backs and regurgitating when a branch is disturbed. *Bacillus thuringiensis* does *not* kill sawfly larvae because they are not caterpillars.

European pine sawfly: Neodiprion sertifer (Geoffrey)
Order and family: Hymenoptera: Diprionidae.
Hosts: Scots, Austrian, and mugo pine.
Damage and diagnosis: Damaged branches have old needles removed. New growth on old branches resembles a mule's tale (Figure 8.33, color plate section). Early in the season, look for yellow scars where eggs are laid on needles. Young larvae are dark green and difficult to see. Needles consumed by young larvae resemble slender brown straw. As damage accumulates, more straws become visible on branches. Late-instar larvae grow to 1 inch and are dark green with a black head and black longitudinal stripes.

Biology: After larvae become about 1 inch long, larvae pupate in brown, leathery cocoons ($\frac{1}{2}$ inch long) that can be found along the trunk or on the ground. Adults emerge in the fall. Chewed needles are first visible in mid- to late April.

Control: Sawfly larvae are easily killed by most broad-spectrum insecticides, insect growth regulators, botanicals, or insecticidal soap or oil. Most effective control is achieved when pesticide is applied early in the season, when sawflies are young. After sawflies are an inch long, they stop feeding and construct cocoons. Application of insecticide at this time is no longer needed.

Sawflies regularly suffer from a lethal viruslike disease that greatly reduces their numbers. If you notice larvae that are hanging limp from pine needles, there is no need to apply an insecticide. This viruslike disease is not likely to be commercially available in the near future.

Pear sawfly: Caliroa cerasi *(L.)*

Order and family: Hymenoptera: Tenthredinidae.

Hosts: Flowering fruit trees and cotoneaster.

Damage and diagnosis: Black, slime-colored larvae scrape away the leaf surface (Figure 8.34, color plate section). Eventually the scraped area turns brown. Most injury occurs during the midsummer generation.

Biology: Adults fly in late spring to lay eggs that hatch in May. Larvae skeletonize leaf surfaces. A second generation occurs in midsummer. Pear sawfly winters as a late-instar larva in the soil and pupates in early spring.

Control: See controls for European pine sawfly. Homeowners can control this problem on shrubs by applying wood ash to larvae. Control of first generation can help to reduce the problems with the second generation.

Beetles

Beetles are a diverse group of insects that have hard or leathery forewings. These forewings, known as **elytra,** can be brightly colored or plain. Although lady beetles eat insects and not plants, their orange or red spotted forewings are a good example of brightly colored elytra. Immature beetles are called grubs. They lack prolegs and do not resemble caterpillars or sawflies. The larvae of some beetles (for example, black vine weevils) are legless. Unlike caterpillars and sawflies, both adults and immatures can feed on plants.

Beetles can skeletonize leaves or consume entire leaf portions (Figures 8.35 and 8.36, color plate section).

Leaf notching is a distinctive type of defoliation caused by black vine weevils and their relatives (Figure 8.37, color plate section). These beetles remove tissue from the leaf edge and leave a characteristic notch. Controls for beetles can be directed against adults or larvae.

Japanese beetle: Popillia japonica *(Newman)*

Order and family: Coleoptera: Scarabeidae.

Hosts: Many deciduous trees and shrubs, especially linden, sassafras, sycamore, Norway maple, birch, elm, and flowering fruit trees.

Damage and diagnosis: Leaves become skeletonized, with *all* tissue removed between leaf veins (Figure 8.35, color plate section). Adults have copper-colored wings and a green pronotum. Can be found during the day feeding in large groups on leaves or fruit. This introduced pest is present only from Michigan and eastern Illinois east to the Atlantic states and south to North Carolina and Kentucky.

Biology: Winters as late-instar grubs in soil, where they feed on plant roots. This stage is more commonly known as one of the many white grubs that attack turf. Adults pupate in late May or early June. Adults emerge to feed on trees in late June, with peak densities occurring around July 1. Adults can be seen flying until early August. Eggs, laid underground, hatch into the larval stage during the first week of August. Grubs feed on roots until weather cools in October, when they move down into the soil.

Control: Apply a broad-spectrum insecticide, such as carbaryl, to leaves when beetles are seen feeding on trees. These beetles will be present for about six weeks. Most materials will kill beetles only for four to five days. Repeat insecticide applications when necessary to reduce further injury. Do not use Japanese beetle traps to control these beetles. This will bring more beetles and damage to the area.

Elm leaf beetle: Xanthogaleruca luteola *(Muller)*

Order and family: Coleoptera: Chrysomelidae.

Hosts: Elm and zelkova.

Damage and diagnosis: Elongate green grubs (up to $\frac{3}{8}$ inch) with two black stripes along their sides skeletonize leaves by scraping leaf tissue between veins. Tissue remaining between veins turns brown. Yellowish green adults with black stripes along their elytra ($\frac{1}{4}$ inch) chew holes in leaves (Figure 8.36, color plate section). Grubs feeding on leaves are the major source of damage. Adults can be a nuisance in the spring and fall because they often seek shelter from the winter inside homes and other structures.

Biology: Adults winter in sheltered areas. Yellow-orange eggs are laid in rows on leaf undersides from late April to early May. Eggs hatch into larvae that skeletonize leaves for about three weeks. Late-instar larvae crawl down bark to find a pupation site. In two weeks, the pupae become adults whose grubs can cause extensive injury in July. Adults of this generation emerge in August and seek shelter when the weather cools.

Control: Target young grubs to achieve best control. Look for eggs on trees, and apply materials after all eggs have hatched. Broad-spectrum insecticides applied to leaves will kill larvae and adults. Systemic insecticides applied to the soil can also control beetles. *Bacillus thuringiensis* 'tenebrionis' ('San Diego') will kill young larvae only. The broad emergence period of the second generation of beetle grubs will limit the effectiveness of this material. Neem (for example, Bioneem), a botanical extract of a tropical tree, is reportedly a more effective control when applied to young larvae.

If you are managing all the elms and zelkovas in an area, you can reduce injury from the second generation by targeting the first generation of beetles. Monitor the first generation, and apply pesticides on young larvae, or spray the trunk of trees with a long-lasting insecticide to kill late-instar grubs as they migrate down the trunk to pupate in late May or early June.

Black vine weevil: Otiorhyncus sulcatus *(Fabricius)*

Order and family: Coleoptera: Curculionidae.

Hosts: Many trees and shrubs, especially yew, azalea, rhododendron, English ivy, and euonymus.

Damage and diagnosis: Adults chew distinctive notches into the margins of leaves (Figure 8.37, color plate section). Note that these notches are distinct from those caused by leafcutter bees (Figure 8.38, color plate section). Legless grubs feed on roots and can girdle the plant in the spring by feeding on the root crown.

Biology: Early and late-stage grubs winter in soil and resume feeding in spring. In mid-June, adults begin to emerge from the soil and continue to emerge for several weeks. After two or three weeks of feeding, adults begin to lay eggs on the soil surface. Adults lay up to 500 eggs over the course of a month. They winter in all but the egg stage.

Control: Foliar insecticides applied in mid-July will kill beetles before they lay the bulk of their eggs. Soil drenches of insecticide in late August will kill grubs before they feed. Entomophagous nematodes can readily kill pupae and larvae in the soil. Nematodes must be kept moist to be effective. Applying them at night and irrigating are necessary. Because the nematodes are not effective against eggs, apply them during the spring and fall when larvae and pupae are present. Effective strains of *Steinernema carposcapsae* are commercially available. Look for new and more effective strains to be available in the future.

Related pests: Several other closely related root weevils cause very similar injury to trees and shrubs. Control methods are similar. Note that leafcutter bees, *Megachile* spp., will also cut notches in leaf margins (Figure 8.38, color plate section). These notches are circular, however, and quite distinct from the irregular notches of the weevils. Leafcutter bees are considered beneficial because they pollinate plants and will not harm tree health.

Leafminers

Insects in this group feed between the upper and lower surface of a leaf as immature larvae. This process, known as **leaf mining,** discolors leaves in a characteristic pattern that falls into one of two categories: **serpentine** or **blotch mines**.

Serpentine leaf mines are shaped like a snake. Blotch mines form an irregular blotch with no particular shape at all. Mines can be caused by the immatures of beetles, flies, wasps, and butterflies. Mines can be distinguished from **leaf scorch** by holding a leaf up to the light and looking for the silhouette of the larva and the black excrement (Figure 8.39, color plate section).

Like the galls and scales already described, insects that cause mines are easily found by natural enemies that feed on them. For a variety of reasons—including weather, host plant variety, and pesticide use—leafminers often outstrip the potential of natural enemies to keep them under control.

Adult leafminers lay their eggs on or in the leaf. The key to leafminer control is to apply an insecticide that will be on or in leaf tissue during egg hatch or when adults are laying eggs. Young mines can be found by holding a leaf up to the light. You can see a halo of discoloration near where eggs were laid or where young mines are formed.

Learn the life cycle of the leafminer that you want to control so you can time insecticide applications. Controls for some leafminers, such as those attacking birch and hawthorn, are effective only if directed against the first generation of insect mines in the spring. Clients seeking to control these leafminers must be informed that late-season applications will not solve the problem. Advise the clients that treatment can begin the following spring.

Systemic insecticides—such as imidacloprid (Merit), acephate (Orthene), avermectin (Avid), or chlorpyrifos (Dursban)—are especially effective in small mines when larvae are small and before mined leaf tissues become brown. Success with some of the soil-applied systemic insecticides, such imidacloprid, requires applications at least four weeks before adults lay eggs, or perhaps a fall application. Entomopathogenic fungi and nematodes are likely to be important controls in the near future.

Birch leafminer: Fenusa pusilla (Lepeletier)
Order and family: Hymenoptera: Tenthredinidae.

Hosts: Birches, especially gray (*Betula populafolia*), paper (*B. papyrifera),* and European white (*Betula pendula).*

Damage and diagnosis: This pest is representative of many leafminers. Infested leaves have one or more brown, irregularly shaped blotch mines (Figure 8.39, color plate section). Heavily infested trees appear scorched brown. Young mines produce circular halos of discoloration that are especially visible when leaves are held up to the light. Larvae are orange. Egg laying produces smaller but still visible halos when leaves are viewed in the light. Adults are small (¼ inch) black sawflies.

Biology: Pupae spend the winter in soil at the base of infested trees. Adult sawflies fly to leaves in early May, about one week after leaves unfold. Eggs are laid into young leaves. Larvae mine leaves for two to three weeks until they chew a hole in the leaf and drop to the ground to pupate. There are three to four generations per year.

Control: See general notes on leafminers. Note location of heavy infestations. Target controls for the first generation in the spring of the following year. Look for adult activity and egg-laying scars on trees soon after leaves have unfolded.

Other leafminers: Common leafminers not mentioned include hawthorn leafminer, native holly leafminer, locust leafminer, elm leafminer, and boxwood leafminer. Each miner feeds on plants associated with its name.

Twig, Leader, Limb, and Trunk Feeders

Pests in this category injure twigs, leaders, limbs, and trunks, causing small portions or entire trees to turn brown and die. Insects that are responsible for this injury fall into two categories: oviposition injurers and chewing injurers.

Oviposition Injurers

When insects lay their eggs inside the stems of trees, they girdle twigs and effectively cut them off from the tree's water and nutrient supply. This causes twigs to wither, turn brown, and drop. Because there is little that can be done to effectively manage these pests, it is important to learn their life cycles so you can effectively explain these problems to clients.

Annual and periodical cicadas: Tibicen spp. and Magicada spp.
Order and family: Homoptera: Cicadidae.

Hosts: Many deciduous trees.

Damage and diagnosis: When adults lay enough eggs in twigs, they can kill them. This is primarily a problem on new nursery stock and when large numbers of periodical cicadas emerge. Damaged twigs and branches have a series of slits where females have laid their eggs. Damage from the periodical cicada is most severe near mature stands of trees where cicadas can complete their long life cycle (Figure 8.40, color plate section). Adult periodical cicadas have orange wings with black bodies and red legs. Damage from the annual or dog-day cicada is minimal.

Biology: Nymphs of all cicadas feed on roots of trees. Nymphs of annual cicadas feed on roots for two to five years, and those of periodical cicadas feed on roots for thirteen or seventeen years before they become adults. Adult annual cicadas are present from mid-July to late summer. After adult periodical cicadas emerge in late May or early June, they fly for six weeks. Male cicadas produce a shrill call that is quite distinctive. When they emerge by the thousands, the call of the males to their mates is both distinctive and overwhelming. During the adult flight period, adults mate and then females lay eggs in twigs. Several weeks after eggs are laid, nymphs hatch, feed, and drop to the ground to dig for tree roots, where they suck on plant sap. Damage associated with root feeding has not been measured and is assumed to be minimal.

Control: Field trials with applications of broad-spectrum insecticides show that none can effectively reduce injury from the periodical cicada. Contact your local Extension Service office to find out when and if the periodical cicada is expected in your area. Discussing the issue with your clients in early spring, before cicadas emerge, will help you better manage the situation.

Chewing Injurers

All pests in this category spend some time feeding somewhere beneath the bark of a tree as larvae. Although there is some overlap, these pests are divided into four categories based on how they feed as an adult or on which part of the tree they feed. Twig chewers scar or girdle a twig when adults feed on the twig surface (Figure 8.41, color plate section). Twig or leader borers kill twigs and leaders when adults feed or when eggs laid on this part of the tree hatch into larvae that bore into the stem until they develop into adults (Figure 8.42, color plate section). Large-limb and trunk borers lay eggs on the limb or in crevices of the trunk surface that hatch into larvae that feed beneath the bark surface until they develop into adults (Figures 8.43 and 8.44, color plate section). Bark beetles (see "Agents of Disease Transmission and Rapid Decline") mate at or near the bark surface, and adults lay eggs in tunnels beneath the bark (Figure 8.49, color plate section). For good photos and descriptions of all borers damaging deciduous trees in the United States, obtain a copy of *A Guide to Insect Borers in North American Broadleaf Trees and Shrubs,* USDA Forest Service Agricultural Handbook AH-706.

Management considerations ▪ *Cultural control:* When these insects chew on or inside twigs, trunks, and limbs, they separate all or part of infested trees from their supply of water and nutrients, killing all or part of these plants. Pests in this group thrive when the tree is under stress. Proper watering, fertilization, and mulching are critical to a good control program. Some pests in this group breed on dead or dying trees. For these pests, **sanitation,** or the destruction of dead and dying trees and limbs, is an important tactic for killing borers and reducing the number of available breeding sites.

Chemical control: Applying insecticide to the bark and twigs of trees is an effective way to kill insects that must chew through the bark. Timing is critical to successful chemical control. You must know when an insect is chewing through the bark surface to get the insecticide to kill the pest. Some pests, such as the twig chewers that feed on the outside of twigs for ex-

tended periods, are susceptible to chemical control for a relatively long period. Insects that bore into twigs, limbs, and bark are controlled by insecticides over a much shorter period of time. These insects are killed only when larvae attempt to enter a limb or twig, or as adults and larvae chew their way out of these areas. Traps are available to help monitor the life cycle of many of these pests and improve timing of pesticide applications.

Biological control: Some pests in this group have been successfully controlled with entomophagous nematodes. Unlike chemical control, these materials kill larvae after they have hatched and they are beneath the bark surface. Trunks and limbs must be drenched with a nematode **solution** to allow the nematode to swim through borer holes to the pest below. This method has been most effective against clearwing borers and root collar weevils, whose immatures attack live trees. It is likely to be effective against other pests in this group because they all feed in the moist environment beneath plant bark. New developments, such as the availability of pelletized and emulsion formulations, and more aggressive nematode strains, will speed the adoption of this technique.

Twig chewers ▪ These insects scar or girdle a twig when adults feed on twig surfaces. On conifers, twigs will turn brown several weeks after adults have fed (Figure 8.41, color plate section). On deciduous trees, symptoms appear sooner. Eventually injured twigs fall and clients become concerned. For the most part, this injury is unsightly and does not harm tree health. Injury is more damaging to newly planted trees or when the leader is attacked. Sanitation or coating twigs with insecticide when insects are feeding will prevent damage.

Pales weevil: Hylobius pales *(Herbst)*
Order and family: Coleoptera: Curculionidae.
Hosts: Pine, spruce, fir, hemlock, larch, and cedar.
Damage and diagnosis: Adults chew the twig surface in the fall and spring, causing twigs to ooze sap and turn brown in early summer. Adults are black snout-weevils; larvae are white and legless. Can be a problem in sites where pines line a drive and some trees have been removed and stumps remain. Severe problems occur at Christmas-tree plantations and tree nurseries, where young pines are planted next to tree stumps.
Biology: Adults are attracted to cut pine and mate on pine stumps when the weather warms in spring. Females burrow into roots of cut stumps to lay eggs. Larvae feed on these roots until they

pupate in chip-bark cocoons and emerge as adults in September. During the summer, adults spend days in leaf litter and nights feeding on the twigs. Adults live for two years and lay eggs during both summers.

Control: Removal of breeding sites (stumps of host plants) or spraying with residual insecticide can reduce the chances for tree injury. Improve timing of sprays by monitoring for the emergence of adults in spring. Place freshly cut disks of pine (2 inches thick) on the soil surface in a discrete area near an infested site, and check upper and lower surfaces for adults. When adults are found, apply a broad-spectrum insecticide to conifer stumps to kill mating weevils. Repeat on live trees to kill adults attempting to feed on twigs in the fall.

Related pest: The northern pine weevil, *Pissodes approximatus* (Hopkins), causes similar injury and has a similar life cycle and control. It is smaller than the Pales weevil and has two white marks on its elytra.

Twig girdler: Oncideres cingulata *(Say)*

Order and family: Coleoptera: Cerambycidae.

Hosts: Many deciduous trees, but not maple. Particularly a problem on oak and hickory in the Midwest.

Damage and diagnosis: The adult female **girdler** chews a ring around the outside of a twig. Leaves on the twig **wilt** and turn brown after an adult female has girdled it. Twigs dry and fall to ground in late summer. You should break open the end of a fallen twig to look for larva.

Biology: Larvae winter in twigs that have fallen to the ground. In the spring and summer larvae develop to pupae that emerge as adults in late summer. The mated adult female lays an egg on the part of twig beyond the ring that she has girdled. The twig that dries and falls to the ground contains the larva inside, which develops into an adult.

Control: Collect and destroy branches that have fallen to the ground. Removing and destroying shoots on the tree is not likely to be an effective control because adults can continue to lay eggs until the weather cools. No insecticides are labeled for this pest.

Other twig girdlers: Other girdlers common on oaks in the Midwest include several *Agrilus* spp. whose larvae mine around the twig just beneath the bark surface. Adults of these beetles are metallic wood-boring beetles (family: Buprestidae) and are related to bronze birch borer.

Related pest: In contrast to girdlers, twig **pruners** sever the twig when tunneling larvae chew from the twig center. Symptoms, host range, and controls of twig pruners are similar to girdlers. The end of a pruned twig will be stuffed with excelsior-like shavings and excrement. It is important to note that the biology of pruners (family: Cerambycidae; genus: *Elaphidionoides*) is not clear, but adults are believed to be active in the spring. Squirrels will also cut twigs and cause them to drop. Cut ends of these twigs will look more ragged than they would from pruner or girdler damage. (See Chapter 9.)

Twig or leader borers ▪ These insects kill twigs and leaders when adults feed or when eggs laid on this part of the tree hatch into larvae that bore into the stem until they develop into adults.

European pine shoot moth: Rhyacionia buoliana (Denis and Schiffermüller)

Order and family: Lepidoptera: Tortricidae.

Hosts: Pines, especially Austrian and mugo.

Damage and diagnosis: Look for dead and U-shaped terminals present from previous year's feeding, or hardened globs of pitch at the base of a large bud. After budbreak, look for fresh sawdustlike excrement in infested shoots. Infested shoots should fail to elongate and have short needles (compare with Diplodia tip blight, Chapter 7). In late summer, you should see a few red needles mixed with green needles on a terminal.

Biology: Caterpillars winter in needles near shoot tips that have been mined during the previous summer. In April, caterpillars crawl to shoots and bore through the base of buds into shoots before budbreak. There, caterpillars continue to feed and develop into pupae. Adults emerge in late May, and eggs hatch on needles in early June.

Control: Small infestations can be controlled by pruning out shoots. A **sex pheromone** trap is available to time the flight of adult moths. Target caterpillars entering shoots in May or eggs hatching in early June. *Bacillus thuringiensis* can be effective if timed correctly. Longer lasting broad-spectrum materials can also be effective. Systemic broad-spectrum insecticides applied to control caterpillars chewing in needles can also be effective.

Related pests: Nantucket pine tip moth, eastern pine shoot borer, and white pine weevil (see below) all cause similar injury to pine twigs and leaders.

Nantucket pine tip moth: **Rhyacionia frustrana (Comstock)**

This pest causes the same kind of injury as the closely related European pine shoot moth. One generation per year occurs in the northern part of its range and four generations per year in the south. A sex pheromone trap is available to help time insecticide sprays. This pest is not common north of Columbus, Ohio; Indianapolis, Indiana; and Springfield, Illinois.

Eastern pine shoot borer: **Eucosma gloriola (Heinrich)**

This pest has a similar host plant range, but caterpillars hollow out shoots 6 to 8 inches from the tip and leave a diagnostic oval hole from where larvae exit and fall to the ground in July. They pupate in the soil and winter in the ground. Adults fly in early May, laying eggs on the current year's growth. Eggs hatch and chemical control is best in mid-May, about a month earlier than the European pine shoot moth. No sex pheromone is available to time adult flight. Pruning and destruction of infested shoots in June can provide some control in the landscape.

White pine weevil: **Pissodes strobi (Peck)**

Order and family: Coleoptera: Curculionidae.

Hosts: Pines, especially white pine, Norway, and Colorado blue spruce.

Damage and diagnosis: The leader on infested trees is curled into a shape that resembles a shepherd's crook (Figure 8.42, color plate section). Lateral branches from the infested tree's first **whorl** might also be curled. The top two to three years of growth can be affected. In early summer, legless, ¼-inch–long, white, C-shaped grubs can be found in stems or beneath the bark surface. In late summer, chip-bark cocoons are formed by larvae at the base of injured stems.

Biology: Adults winter in leaf litter and fly to treetops to mate when the weather warms in the spring. Females lay many eggs in terminals that hatch into grubs that bore into shoots. Legless larvae continue to feed until July, when they pupate in chip-bark cocoons. Adults emerge in August and chew on twigs.

Control: Prune and destroy damaged leaders that contain larvae or chip-bark cocoons before adults emerge. Applications of broad-spectrum insecticide to treetops should be timed to kill adults gathering on twigs in early spring (April) or adults feeding on twigs in August. Mixed-species plantings of pines are less likely to build damaging numbers of this pest than pure stands of susceptible species.

Large-limb and trunk borers ▪ These insects lay eggs on the limb or in crevices of the trunk surface that hatch into larvae that feed beneath the bark surface until they develop into adults.

Zimmerman pine moth: **Dioryctria zimmermani (Grote)**

Order and family: Lepidoptera: Pyralidae.

Hosts: Pine, primarily Austrian and Scots, and occasionally Douglasfir.

Damage and diagnosis: In the spring, leaders of infested trees wilt and curve downward to resemble a shepherd's crook or fishhook, much like the white pine weevil (Figure 8.42, color plate section). At the base of the leader, however, you might find a greasy-looking grayish caterpillar feeding in the whorl. No oval hole is present in the shoot, as with the eastern pine shoot borer. In older trees, wounds caused by these caterpillars are found along the trunk at branch whorls. Wounds are gummy and can be covered with white crumbs of caterpillar excrement. Growth above infested terminals is often poor in comparison to healthy trees. Branches joined to the main trunk at infested whorls or treetops can be girdled and killed (Figure 8.43, color plate section).

Biology: First-instar caterpillars winter in shallow pits that they dug in the bark the previous fall. When the weather warms in early April, the caterpillars crawl out of their resting places along the exposed bark surface to bore into branches where they join the central trunk. They produce gummy wounds, sometimes **girdling** and killing limbs or treetops. Once in the tree, caterpillars feed until they pupate in July. In August, moths emerge and lay eggs on the tree trunk near the branch whorl. Young caterpillars chew bits of bark to make a shallow pit, called a **hibernaculum**, near to where they hatched from eggs. Here they spend the winter covered with bits of silk, excrement, and pine resin.

Control: Sanitation or the removal of heavily infested trees can greatly improve your ability to manage this pest. Adult moths will often lay eggs on old wound sites or on nearby trees. Reducing tree stress will also help trees resist attack. Chemical controls with a long-lasting, broad-spectrum insecticide are most successful when applied in early April before the weather warms. This kills young caterpillars as they crawl from overwintering sites to bore beneath the bark. August sprays that target egg hatch can also be effective.

Clearwing borers ▪ Clearwing borers are a group of closely related moths that superficially resemble wasps and bore into trees or stems. Key aspects of their biology are summarized in Table 8.2.

Clearwing borers (in general)

Order and family: Lepidoptera: Sessiidae.

Hosts: The common name of pests in this group usually includes the name of the host plant that these borers attack.

Damage and diagnosis: Trunks or branches injured by this pest have loose or peeling bark (Figure 8.44, color plate section). Sawdustlike excrement can be seen coming from borers that attack aboveground portions of the tree. Caterpillars beneath the bark are usually creamy white. When adults emerge, a straw-colored pupal skin is left hanging out of the trunk or branch (Figure 8.45, color plate section). Borers that attack at the tree base or just below the soil line might have excrement pellets and pupal skins hidden from view. Infested trees have dead limbs or twigs.

The clear wings, slender bodies, and flight habits of adult moths in this group cause them to superficially resemble wasps (Figure 8.46, color plate section). Unlike wasps, however, adult moths lack chewing mouthparts and have bodies covered with scales. Adult moths have strawlike mouthparts used for sucking nectar. For good color images of all clearwing borers that damage trees in the eastern and north-central United States, obtain a copy of *A Guide to Clearwing Borers of the North Central United States,* NCR Publication No. 394, from your local Extension office.

Biology: Late-instar caterpillars spend the winter beneath the bark of infested trees. Larvae turn into pupae in the tree bark. Just prior to emergence, the pupa pushes its way out of the bark. When the adult emerges from the pupa, it leaves the pupal skin in the branch or trunk. Soon after females emerge, they crawl a short distance on the bark, arch their abdomens, and release a scent into the wind. This scent, called a sex pheromone, helps females find a mate by attracting males who are downwind. After mating, eggs are laid on the bark. Eggs hatch into caterpillars that chew a hole in the bark. Depending on the species, moths can

have one to two generations per year. Oak borers take two years to develop into adults.

Control: *Chemical:* Use traps baited with the sex pheromone of the clearwing moth to time the application of a long-lasting, broad-spectrum insecticide on the trunk and limbs of infested trees. Apply the insecticide fourteen days after the first male is found in a trap. This coincides with the beginning of the time when most eggs will be hatching. Traps and baits are commercially available and usually come with picture identification sheets.

Biological: When using entomophagous nematodes, be sure to apply them with plenty of water when the insect is in the caterpillar stage and the temperature is between 55° and 85° F. In a given generation, most individual clearwing moths should be caterpillars from the last week of August through the first week of May. Moths with a May flight period should be caterpillars only through the first week of April. Moths with two generations per year should be in the caterpillar stage three weeks after the peak of the pheromone trap catch.

Cultural: Improper use of plastic trunk wraps can make trees more susceptible to clearwing borers that attack tree trunks. Tightly coiled wraps keep bark moist and can protect borers from parasitic wasps that normally attack them through the bark surface. Loosely coiled plastic wraps with at least $^{1}/_{4}$ inch of air space do not cause this problem. Adults are attracted to recently pruned wood. Avoid pruning during flight season.

American plum borer: **Euzophera semifuneralis (Walker)**

Order and family: Lepidoptera: Pyralidae.

Hosts: Ornamental plum and other flowering fruit trees, London plane tree, hickory, linden, poplar, sweet gum, and ginkgo.

Diagnosis: Flaking bark and sawdustlike excrement are most often found on the lower 3 feet of trunk or near soil line but can attack higher on tree. Wet spots or **ooze** is visible on infested trees. Tunnels are filled with excrement. White cocoons are visible beneath the bark.

Biology: Winters as a larva in a thin white cocoon called a hibernaculum. Adults emerge in May, mate, and lay eggs on the bark surface. These hatch into caterpillars that crawl until they find a crack where they chew into the tree. The second generation, which produces the overwintering caterpillars, flies in late July and August.

Table 8.2 ▪ *Common clearwing borers*

Name	Months when males fly (approximate)	Plants attacked	Habits	Identification	Lure type
Lilac borer *Podesia syringae* (Harris)	May–late July	ash, lilac, privet, fringe tree	Usually attacks near base of canes. Feeds beneath bark and in wood.	Brown slender moths resembling paper wasp. Brown wings.	clearwing borer
Branded ash clearwing *Podesia aureocinta* (Purrington & Nielson)	late July–September	ash	Attacks trunks and limbs.	Similar to lilac borer, except for a narrow band on abdomen.	clearwing borer
Peach tree borer *Synanthedon exitiosa* (Say)	mid-June–August	peach, cherry, *Prunus*	Attacks at or below soil level, and lower 3' of trunk.	Blue-black, with slender body. Wings have amber sheen.	clearwing borer
Dogwood borer *Synanthedon scitula* (Harris)	probably June (literature is not clear)	dogwood, apple, pear	Attacks trunk and limbs.	Blue-black, ½" long, with two narrow yellow bands on abdomen.	dogwood borer
Oak borer *Paranthrene simulans* (Grote)	May–June	oak	Attacks branches and trunk. Bores several inches into wood. Takes two years to mature.	Resembles large yellowjacket wasps.	clearwing borer
Lesser peach tree borer *Synanthedon pictipes* (G. & R.)	May–July & July–September	cherry, plum, *Prunus*	Attacks branches or scaffold limbs of trees.	Resembles a peach tree borer, only smaller and without amber wings.	lesser peach tree borer
Viburnum borer *Synanthedon viburni* (Englehardt)	July	viburnum	Usually attacks near base of canes. Feeds beneath bark and in wood.	Similar to lesser peach tree borer in size and color. Has white scales on face.	lesser peach tree borer
No common name *Synanthedon fatifera* (Hodges)	July	viburnum	Usually attacks near base of canes. Feeds beneath bark and in wood.	Similar to lesser peach tree borer in size and color. Has black scales on face.	clearwing borer

Control: This insect thrives on street trees that have been mechanically injured. Proper care of trees is critical for managing this pest. Sex pheromone traps can be used to time chemical controls. Apply insecticide fourteen days after the first male is found in a trap. This coincides with the beginning of the time when most eggs will be hatching. Entomophagous nematodes can be effective when caterpillars are in the larval stage before they have covered themselves with the white cocoon. This should occur about three weeks after the peak of the sex pheromone trap catch, or early June and late August.

Round-headed borers ▪ Borers in this group are beetles whose round-headed larvae produce round tunnels as they feed in the wood (Figure 8.47, color plate section). Adults also have long antennae and are commonly called long-horned beetles.

Locust borer: Megacyllene robiniae *(Forst.)*
Order and family: Coleoptera: Cerambycidae.

Host: Black locust.

Damage and diagnosis: Infested trees have flaking bark and produce sawdustlike excrement (Figure 8.47, color plate section). Larvae of these insects often make tunnels in the heartwood as well as beneath the bark of the tree. Holes seen in the side of the tree where adults emerge are round. Adults are black and yellow, superficially resembling yellowjacket wasps because of their coloration, cylindrical body, and long antennae. Adults commonly emerge from piles of firewood.

Biology: Larvae spend the winter in tree trunks and resume feeding when leaf buds swell in the spring. Infested trees ooze sap and sawdustlike excrement from round holes. Larvae keep tunnels clean by constantly kicking out the excrement. They dig under the bark and deep into the wood. Pupae form by the end of July. Adults chew their way out of the trunk and emerge in late August and September. They often fly to goldenrod, where large numbers can be found feeding on pollen. After mating, the female places smooth white eggs ($1/2$ inch long) in V-shaped cracks in the bark or in old borer holes. Eggs hatch into larvae that chew into bark, where they spend the winter.

Control: Apply a long-lasting, residual insecticide in late August to kill new adults as they chew out of the tree and to kill larvae as they chew into the tree. Spring is a good time to try killing larvae with entomopathogenic nematodes.

Related pests: The family Cerambycidae contains many wood-boring insects that attack a wide range of woody plants.

Flat-headed borers ▪ The greatly expanded second thoracic segment of these larvae make them appear as if they have a flattened head. These borers produce an oval tunnel when they dig into the wood. Unlike the larvae of clearwing borers and round-headed borers, these insects pack their excrement in the borer hole. Adults are a metallic color and are called metallic wood-boring beetles.

Bronze birch borer: Agrilus anxius *(Gory)*
Order and family: Coleoptera: Buprestidae.

Hosts: *Frequent:* European white birch. *Less often:* Gray birch, paper birch, and yellow birch. *Rarely, if ever:* River birch, including 'Heritage'.

Damage and diagnosis: Infested trees have the general symptoms of borer injury, dead limbs, yellowed branches, and eventual tree death. Infested trees have a ridged bark where borers have made their zigzag pattern under the surface (Figure 8.48, color plate section). Holes from where adults emerged are D-shaped. Adults are coppery brown with a keel-shaped abdomen, and are one of the many species of metallic wood-boring beetles.

Biology: Wintering as a late-instar larva in the tree trunk, adults emerge from late May to early June from exit holes and have only one generation per year. Adults fly to the tree canopy and chew small notches on leaves as they feed. Eggs are laid in cracks and crevices, under loose bark on the sunny side of trees, or on areas where a tree has been mechanically injured. Adults' flight lasts about six weeks. Two weeks after eggs are laid, they hatch into larvae that chew into the wood. When you peel off the bark of an infested tree, you can easily see the dark-brown mounds that zigzag along the wood where larvae have been boring.

Control: Like most other borers, these insects thrive on stressed trees. Healthy trees are less susceptible to borers. Mulch trees to prevent mower injury and to moderate soil temperatures and soil moisture. Infested trees should be treated with a long-lasting residual insecticide when adults begin to fly. Coat the leaves to kill the adults that feed on them. Coat the bark to kill larvae that hatch from eggs. Entomophagous nematodes might be useful against this pest in the future.

Flatheaded appletree borer: Chrysobothris femorata (Olivier)

Order and family: Coleoptera: Buprestidae.

Hosts: Most deciduous trees, notably maple, flowering fruit trees, poplar, and linden.

Damage and diagnosis: A common problem for trees subject to the stress of transplanting. Infested trees can be killed outright by the girdling larvae or can be snapped in half during in a wind storm. Mature white larvae are up to 1 inch long. Adults emerging from D-shaped exit holes are ½ inch long and metallic colored.

Biology: Wintering as a pupa or late-stage larva, most adults emerge in June. Adult females lay single eggs on the bark surface in cracks and crevices that hatch into larvae that bore beneath the bark to feed on the vascular tissue in the typical zig-zag pattern. Just prior to pupation, the larva bores toward the center of the trunk to pupate. Adults usually take one year to complete their life cycle.

Control: Minimize plant stress during the first three years after transplanting. In addition to the measures described for bronze birch borer, it is important to wrap the trees to prevent **frost cracking**. Applications of residual contact insecticides in late May or early June can also be helpful.

Agents of Disease Transmission and Rapid Decline

Many insects move between plants and pass on disease. A good example of this is fire blight, a bacterial disease that rapidly kills branches of plants in the rose family. It is passed on by bees as they move between flowers in trees. Because there are many good reasons not to kill bees, this disease is managed by planting resistant varieties of plants, pruning, and in some cases applying antibiotics. Sucking insects such as some aphids, leafhoppers, and whiteflies, or rasping insects such as western flower thrips, pass on diseases that cause tremendous problems for greenhouse growers and vegetable producers. These insects do not yet pass on many diseases that midwestern arborists are likely to encounter.

In contrast, some boring insects that pass on disease are a serious concern for arborists because they thrive on diseased and declining trees. When these insects spread the disease to healthy trees, trees decline and provide more high-quality food for these insects. This increases the number of insects feeding on diseased trees that can spread even more disease to healthy trees. Managing these insects requires breaking the cycle of **positive feedback** between the insect and the disease. The relationship between Dutch elm disease and elm bark beetles provides a good example of how this cycle can be broken. Similar disease-insect relationships that arborists are likely to encounter are listed in Table 8.3.

Elm Bark Beetles and Dutch Elm Disease

Smaller European elm bark beetle: Scolytis multistriatus (Marsham); native elm bark beetle: Hylurgopinus rufipes (Eichoff)

Order and family: Coleoptera: Scolytidae.

Hosts: Elm.

Damage and diagnosis: These bark beetles are important because they carry and spread Dutch elm disease, a lethal disease of American elm. Beetles infested with the fungus *Ceratocystus ulmi* pass on the disease when they feed on the twigs and shoots in the canopy of elm trees. Infested branches have twigs with yellow leaves. The disease spreads rapidly down the branch, eventually killing the tree. Spines of native elm bark beetle galleries go across the grain, and those of smaller European elm bark beetles go with the grain (Figure 8.49, color plate section).

Biology: Breeding in the trunks and limbs of dead and dying elms, this beetle winters as a late-instar larva beneath the bark. In the spring, adults are attracted to the scent of recently pruned trees. They fly to the shoots of healthy elms and feed on the crotches of twigs and young bark. Dutch elm disease is spread to these limbs by adults carrying spores of *Ceratocystus ulmi* from diseased

Table 8.3 ▪ Disease-insect relationships

Insect	Host	Disease
Pine sawyer beetle (*Monochamous* spp.)	Scots pine	pine wilt (nematode) (*Bursaphelenchus xylophilus*)
Sap beetles (Nitidulidae)	oak	oak wilt (fungus) (*Ceratocystus fagacearum*)
Engraver beetles (*Ips* spp.)	pine	blue stain fungus
Elm bark beetle	elm	Dutch elm disease

logs and trees. When there is an epidemic of Dutch elm disease, most of the beetles are breeding in diseased wood and carrying the spores. After feeding on shoots, adults fly to a dying elm to mate and breed in a limb or trunk. After the first beetles come to the breeding site, beetles of either sex emit a scent that attracts large groups of beetles to attack the tree. This mass attack helps to weaken the tree and makes it more susceptible to the bark beetle grubs. These attractive scents are common among species of bark beetles and are called **aggregation pheromones.**

The smaller European elm bark beetle (SEEB) has two generations per year, and the native elm bark beetle (NEB) has only one generation per year.

Control: Controlling these pests is most effective when elms in a community are managed in a co-ordinated plan that includes inspecting for trees with yellowing branches and for dead and dying trees. Beetles are controlled by managing the places where they breed. Trees recently killed or dying (greater than 30 percent yellowed canopy) from Dutch elm disease must be removed and destroyed by chipping or burning prior to April 15. This kills beetles developing in breeding logs before they fly to spread the disease.

Systemic insecticide injections are not likely to reduce the spread of the disease because the beetles must chew into the twigs or bark to reach the part of the tree that has the insecticide. In the process, infested beetles can transmit disease. Good sanitation, particularly the quick removal of dead limbs or dying trees, is much more effective than insecticidal applications. To prevent spread of the disease by beetles, avoid routine pruning during the summer months. Healthy elms that are pruned during the flight season attract both species of bark beetles.

Cliff Sadof
Associate Professor
Department of Entomology
Purdue University

Acknowledgments

I would like to thank Whitney Cranshaw of Colorado State University, Mark Harrell of the University of Nebraska, and David Smitley of Michigan State University for their critical review of earlier versions of this manuscript. I would also like to thank Daniel L. Mahr of the University of Wisconsin–Madison for allowing the use of a previously published summary of insect biology for the introductory section. This material was modified from the publication *Biological Control of Insects and Mites: An Introduction to Beneficial Natural Enemies and Their Use in Pest Management,* by D. Mahr and N. Ridgway, 1993, North Central Regional Publication 481. Figures 8.1 through 8.8 are also from the above publication and were developed by J. Myer-Lynch of the Cooperative Extension Publications Unit, University of Wisconsin Extension.

Selected References

Cranshaw W.S., D. Leatherman, and B. Kondratieff. 1993. *Insects That Feed on Colorado Trees and Shrubs.* Bulletin 506A. Fort Collins: Colorado State University Cooperative Extension Service.

Dreistadt, S.H., J.K. Clark, and M.L. Flint. 1994. *Pests of Landscape Trees and Shrubs: An Integrated Pest Management Guide.* Publication 3359. Oakland: University of California Division of Agriculture and Natural Resources.

Gaugler, R., and H.K. Kaya. 1990. *Entomopathogenic Nematodes in Biological Control.* Boca Raton, Florida: CRC Press, Inc.

Jeppson, L.R., H.K. Keifer, and E.W. Baker. 1975. *Mites Injurious to Economic Plants.* Berkeley: University of California Press.

Johnson, W.T., and H.H. Lyons. 1994. *Insects That Feed on Trees and Shrubs.* 3d ed. Ithaca, New York: Cornell University Press.

Mahr, D., and N. Ridgway. 1993. *Biological Control of Insects and Mites: An Introduction to Beneficial Natural Enemies and Their Use in Pest Management.* North Central Regional Publication 481. Madison: University of Wisconsin-Extension.

CHAPTER 9

Vertebrate Pests and Their Management

Robert Corrigan and Philip Nixon

This chapter concerns **vertebrate** pests of ornamental and nursery environments. Many Plant Health Care professionals refer to vertebrate pests as animal pests, nuisance wildlife, or simply "critters." Regardless of the name used to describe them, in some situations vertebrate pests can be more damaging and cause more concern than insect pests.

The goal of this chapter is to explain the biology, behavior, and management of important vertebrate pests of ornamental and nursery environments, including **voles,** moles, beavers, tree squirrels, rabbits, deer, and certain birds.

Voles

Voles are important **rodent** pests in nursery and ornamental areas. People often refer to voles as meadow mice or field mice. There are nineteen species of voles in North America, but the three species of greatest pest significance in turf and landscaped areas are

- Meadow vole, *Microtus pennsylvanicus*
- Prairie vole, *Microtus ochrogaster*
- Pine vole, *Microtus pinetorum*

Voles are a problem because they gnaw on the trunks and roots of various fruit trees and ornamental plants. Although they also can be involved in disease transmission, voles for the most part are not important health pests.

Identification

In general, voles are compact rodents with stocky bodies and short legs and tails (Figure 9.1, color plate section). Their eyes are small and their ears partially hidden. (Pine voles have small eyes and ears that are hidden by their fur.) The **underfur** is generally dense and covered with thicker, longer **guard hairs.** Voles usually are brown or gray, although many color variations exist. The adult vole weighs from 1 to 2.5 ounces.

The small mammal most often confused with voles in yards is the **shrew** (Figure 9.2). Shrews are not rodents and are related to moles. (Rodents are of the or-

University of Nebraska Cooperative Extension

Figure 9.2 ▪ *The shrew is a small, mouse-sized mammal with an elongated snout, a dense fur of uniform color, small eyes, and five clawed toes on each foot*

der Rodentia, which is a group of herbivorous animals distinguished by a single pair of **incisors** with a chisel-shaped edge in the upper jaw. Shrews, on the other hand, belong to the order Insectivora and are insect feeders.) Although shrews are common in and around turf and landscaped areas, they do not cause damage in yards or gardens and are of no pest significance. In fact, shrews are beneficial in that they consume insects, slugs, snails, and other invertebrates that might be pests of ornamentals.

General Biology and Behavior

Understanding the behavior of voles is important for identifying vole activity and damage. The specific biology and behavior vary according to species, but most voles have a similar generalized biology, which is presented here.

Voles are prolific small mammals. They can produce from five to ten litters per year, with an average of five young per litter. **Gestation** is about twenty-one days, and females can mate again the day that the young are born. Young voles grow quickly, are weaned at two or three weeks of age, and are sexually mature in a month or two.

When conditions are favorable, voles are perhaps the most prolific breeders of all rodents. There are cases of meadow voles producing up to seventeen consecutive litters in one year, resulting in an amazing eighty-three offspring. The high reproduction is offset by relatively high mortality rates. The vole is the most common food source for predatory birds and is a significant component of the diet of coyotes, foxes, snakes, skunks, and other animals. Most voles do not live for more than a few months. If they are lucky and are not killed by a predator, voles can potentially live up to two years.

Voles are **herbivores.** The stems and leaves of various grasses constitute the majority of their diet, but they will also consume other green vegetation and fruits. Voles do not **hibernate** and are active throughout the year. During severe winters and snow cover, when green vegetation is scarce, voles **girdle** trunks and roots, killing or damaging the tree or shrub (Figure 9.3, color plate section). Voles might be active day or night, but most activity occurs at dawn and dusk. Their activity includes short, quick visits from the **burrow** through their **runways** and back. They typically will make fifteen to twenty forays from the nest, each foray lasting only about ten minutes. Thus, the vole itself is rarely seen. Most people realize they have voles only from the damage that is visible.

The meadow vole constructs well-defined, visible surface runways through turf areas. The runways measure about 1.5 to 2 inches (4 to 5 centimeters) in width. It is the sight of these paths that causes homeowners to call pest-management professionals.

Vole runways in turf are formed by a combination of the vole eating the grass blades and the constant traveling over the runway. The voles also spread excavated dirt from the burrow system in the runway, resulting in a bare path in some areas.

The nests of voles might be constructed on the surface, in underground burrows, or beneath the protection of some object lying on the ground. Burrows might be located beneath protective cover such as vegetation, shrubbery, rocks, raised gardens, and planter boxes.

Occasionally nests are located in the open spaces in yards. In areas containing fruit trees, burrows are commonly established beneath the tree out to the dropline of the fruit. Burrow entrances measure about 1 to 1.5 inches (2.5 to 4 centimeters) in diameter. When clients call to ask about mysterious holes and pathways in their yards and gardens, and they give these measurements, it is usually a good indication of a vole infestation.

The home range of the vole varies. In general, most voles prefer to stay close to the burrow once they have located good food and cover. When food is not abundant, the home range might extend to half an acre or more.

Identifying Vole Activity and Damage

One of the keys to managing voles is to realize that in many cases voles are associated with dense cover. Inspections should begin along building exteriors. First, inspect the immediate landscaping outside of the building, looking for runways leading from any dense areas cutting through turf (Figure 9.4, color plate section). Residences with low-lying landscaping—such as arborvitae, creeping yews, junipers, and similar species—are good candidates for vole activity.

Runways that are broadest and appear especially well worn are usually high-activity areas. These areas become marked by vole urine and **feces,** and accumulations of droppings often will be found. As populations build, many of the individuals within the vole colony use the same major runways. Time spent inspecting to identify locations where runways lead to burrows beneath cover will pay off in proper trap or bait placement and will facilitate effective control.

When a vole burrows into the root system of ornamental plants, the result might be leaning young trees and dieback on shrubs and young trees. The opening of the burrow is usually near the base of the plant and is easily seen. Bark feeding at the base of trees and shrubs during the winter can also cause dieback the following summer. Close examination of affected plants will show extensive bark removal. Keep in mind that damage is likely to be more severe during extended cold spells with deep snow cover. In some cases, management might only be needed in the form of fencing or **repellents** during those times.

The amount of damage that can be tolerated depends on the location of impacted plants as well as the species of plants involved. Damage in more conspicuous parts of the landscape, such as near main walks and entrances, is more critical than in obscure landscape areas. Damaged specimen shrubs are more of a problem than are a few shrubs in a mass planting. If you notice vole activity while working in the plantings during the summer and fall, be ready to use management practices during the winter before severe damage occurs.

Management

The most effective methods of managing voles is via cultural practices, the use of traps (for minor infestations), and the use of **rodenticides.**

Cultural and habitat modification ▪ As mentioned earlier, voles are most prolific when they have access to abundant amounts of vegetation and cover. Eliminating weeds and dense ground cover around lawns reduces the capacity of these areas to support voles. Lawns and other turf should be mowed regularly. Mulch should be cleared 3 feet (1 meter) or more from the bases of trees in areas of vole activity.

Trapping ▪ Mouse "snap traps" can be used to control a small population of voles. Place the trap perpendicular to the runway with the trigger end in the runway. A peanut butter–oatmeal mixture or apple slices make good baits. Fall and late winter are periods when many vole species are easiest to trap. Trapping is not effective in controlling large vole populations because time and labor costs are prohibitive. Traps should be placed as near to the nest zones as possible and beneath cover. To avoid injuring other wildlife and pets, place the traps beneath boxes, or protect them by some other means. Placing two or three traps 6 inches apart will facilitate quicker results.

Rodenticides (poison baits) ▪ Zinc phosphide is the most commonly used **toxicant** for vole control. It is a single-dose toxicant available in pelleted and grain bait formulations. Zinc-phosphide baits generally are placed by hand in runways and burrow openings.

Although **prebaiting** (applying similar nontreated bait prior to applying toxic bait) is not usually needed to obtain good control, it might be required in some situations, such as when a population has been baited several times and developed "bait shyness." Zinc-phosphide baits are potentially hazardous to ground-feeding birds, especially **waterfowl.** Placing bait into burrow openings will reduce this hazard.

The **anticoagulant** baits used against house mice and rats are also effective in controlling voles. Anticoagulants are slow-acting toxicants requiring five to fifteen days to take effect. Multiple feedings are needed for most anticoagulants to be effective.

One or more anticoagulant baits are registered for controlling voles in many states, but the state regulations must be consulted prior to use.

In addition to hand placement, baits also can be placed in various types of bait containers that will protect bait from moisture and reduce the likelihood of nontarget animals and children having access to the bait. PVC pipe or water-repellent paper tubes with a bait glued to the inside surface provide effective bait containers. Research has shown tube sizes of about 5 inches (12 centimeters) long by 1.5 inches (4 centimeters) wide to be effective and practical.

Other methods ▪ Methods other than habitat modification, trapping, and use of baits are not effective against voles. Ultrasonics or any other electronic devices are of no value. **Fumigants** usually are not effective because the complexity and shallowness of vole burrow systems allow the fumigants to escape. Shooting is not practical or effective. Repellents containing thiram (also a **fungicide**) or capsaicin (the hot component of chili peppers) as an active ingredient are registered for meadow voles to protect the bases and trunks of trees.

These products (or repellents using other ingredients and registered for other garden and turf pests, such as rabbits and chipmunks) might afford very short-term protection, but thus far the use of repellents is generally not recommended due to low efficacy. Finally, no types of frightening agents are effective against voles, and no plant exists which, when planted, will repel or scare voles away from an area.

Moles

Moles belong to the mammalian order Insectivora, which also includes shrews. Seven species of moles exist in the United States, but only a few are of pest significance. The eastern mole, or common mole (*Scalopus aquaticus*), is the most numerous and has the widest range of all North American moles. The most distinguishing features of the mole are its fleshy, pointed snout, greatly enlarged rounded front feet with stout claws, and short, nearly naked tail. The eastern mole is about 6 to 8 inches long with short, velvety gray fur. This mole is responsible for most of the complaints concerning mole damage.[1]

Moles feed primarily on earthworms, beetle grubs, ants, and various other animals found in the soil. A smaller portion of their diet consists of various seed and vegetable matter. But they usually do not eat bulbs or the roots of trees, shrubs, or other plants.

Moles can be destructive pests in lawns, gardens, nurseries, parks, golf courses, and cemeteries. During their burrowing activities, they produce mounds and ridges that disfigure lawns and sometimes dislodge plants or injure roots (Figure 9.5). Although tunnels under trees and shrubs can injure roots and expose them to drying air, causing those roots to die, too few roots are affected to impact the health of the trees or shrubs—even in heavy infestations. Thus, moles do not warrant control except for aesthetic effects on turfgrass.

Keep in mind that although moles can be significant pests, they are also beneficial mammals. They make soils healthier because their tunnels permit air and water to penetrate deeper soil levels. They feed voraciously on all types of insects found in the soil, some of which are pests of lawns, gardens, and horticultural plants. They also provide food for hawks, owls, snakes, and other animals. Therefore, moles should be controlled only when they are causing significant damage.

Beavers

Beavers are well known as industrious builders of dams and for having fine fur coats. Although the public usually associates beavers with wild, natural areas in the western United States, the beaver (*Castor canadensis*) has regained much of its original range through reintroduction and wildlife protection programs. The beaver occurs throughout North America with the exception of Mexico, parts of the desert southwestern United States, and the northernmost areas of Canada and Alaska.

Their dams cause flooding of landscaped areas, roads, and otherwise dry areas. They fell small trees and girdle large ones.

Identification

Beavers are stocky aquatic rodents about 3 feet long and weighing 35 to 50 pounds. They usually have reddish brown fur, though lighter and darker shades—from yellowish brown to black—can occur. They have a large, broad, hairless tail that is used as a prop when sitting upright and as an aid in swimming and communication while in the water.

General Biology and Behavior

Beavers are primarily nocturnal rodents, active about twelve hours each night except during the coldest weather. They are occasionally active during the day, and daytime sightings are common.

They have a 128-day gestation period, with three or four kittens born in burrows or lodges between March and June. **Weaning** occurs after six to twelve weeks, and they become sexually mature in one and one-half years.

Young beavers leave their colony when they are about two years old. These young beavers are likely to colonize previously unoccupied ponds and other aquatic areas or to build a dam and flood new areas. Young beavers are eaten by mink, and adults sometimes fall prey to coyotes and bobcats.

They feed on a wide variety of plants, including duckweed, water-lily roots, other aquatic plants, grasses, and field crops such as corn and soybeans. They feed extensively on the leaves and bark of young twigs, on the cambium of larger branches, and on the trunks of trees and woody shrubs.

University of Nebraska Cooperative Extension

Figure 9.5 ▪ *Moles "swim" through soil, often near the ground surface*

[1]Parts of this discussion were adapted from Miller and Yarrow 1994.

University of Nebraska Cooperative Extension

Figure 9.6 ▪ *Beavers gnaw and girdle trees for food and construction*

Identifying Beaver Activity and Damage

Beavers construct dens in pond banks, earthen dams, and road embankments. Occasionally they build large lodges along shorelines or in the middle of ponds. The lodges are several feet high, several feet wide, and constructed of mud and sticks. Both lodges and shoreline dens have underwater entrances.

Beavers construct dams made of mud and sticks to impound water in which to build their lodges or dens. These dams might be small or large, depending on the need. They can range from 3 to 10 feet high and from 50 feet to a quarter mile long. In ponds, roadside ditches, and other locations where the water level is steady and banks are available for burrowing, resident beavers might not build any dams or lodges.

Beavers gnaw off small trees to use for food and construction. Remaining stumps are several inches to a foot or more high and tapered, with obvious large tooth marks (Figure 9.6). They prefer aspen, cottonwood, willow, sweet gum, and buttonbush, but they will feed on most woody plants. Severed trunks range from 1 inch to 6 feet diameter at breast height (dbh). Beavers frequently fell trees up to 10 inches dbh and girdle larger trees. They particularly prefer to girdle large pines and sweet gum, apparently to feed upon the sweet gum or resin that these trees possess.

Legal Status

Beavers can be taken in many states during the furbearer hunting season. In some states, nuisance bea-

ver can be removed or killed year-round, though you might need to document extensive damage before removal will be allowed. In general, the beaver is considered to be useful for its fur and for its water conservation through dam building. Check with your state natural resources or conservation agency for specific information.

Management

Beaver management in residential areas by the landscaper is aimed primarily at protection of valuable trees from attack. Because a colony of beavers can affect a fairly large area that usually includes several owners as well as roads and other public areas, decisions to remove animals are usually made by a community or homeowners' group. In the past, live-trapped beavers could be easily relocated to more natural areas, where their presence would be appreciated. In recent years, however, the successful comeback of this mammal has made it difficult to find areas where it is desired and lacking in numbers.

Exclusion ▪ Exclusion usually takes the form of fencing placed around valuable trees, which sometimes can prevent serious damage. Beavers are extremely strong, however, and can tear out essentially any protection. With that in mind, trees growing on the banks of ponds and other aquatic areas inhabited by beavers probably cannot be saved from attack. Trees growing farther from the water's edge are less likely to be attacked.

When protecting trees, realize that trees and shrubs represent the beaver's winter food supply, so it is unrealistic to expect to protect all of the trees and shrubs near an area where beavers live. Select a few trees to protect that are vital to the landscape and allow the others to be attacked and destroyed. Ideally you should choose to protect trees that are less preferred by beavers—such as oaks, hickories, or maples.

Protect individual trees or groups of trees with strong fencing such as chain-link fence or solid barriers such as heavy steel plate. **Hardware cloth,** wood fencing, and even sheet metal are easily destroyed by beavers. Barriers should be anchored to heavy posts, preferably set in concrete—another testament to the strength of beavers.

The distance that beavers will travel from water depends on the availability of nearby food and the relative abundance of predators. A beaver will travel fairly long distances through drainage ditches, streams, and other water courses to gather branches and bring them back to the pond. The best guide is to observe the range of their branch-gathering activities and protect valuable trees accordingly.

Providing alternative food ▪ Providing woody plant material as food for beavers to help avoid continued damage to landscape plantings has shown to be at least moderately useful. Pruned branches and small trees cut in other areas and left near a beaver pond will be removed and used by the resident beavers. This can result in fewer standing trees being felled by the beavers.

Planting fast-growing trees that are favored species—such as alders, cottonwood, and willows—near the beaver pond also can reduce damage to valuable trees. Unfortunately these new plantings require protective fencing for a couple of years to prevent the beavers from harvesting them when they are still very small. In at least one instance, this type of planting that was opened to the beavers when the trees had achieved some size appeared to be useful in reducing attack on other trees.

Preferred trees such as alders, cottonwood, and willows usually sprout readily from the stumps left by the beavers. If these stumps are allowed to remain and perhaps be protected for a year or two to nourish the root system, these trunk sprouts can grow to several feet and provide additional alternative food for the beavers.

With any of these alternative food methods, keep in mind that standing trees will probably still continue to be felled and used, so valuable trees must be protected to make it more likely that they will continue to survive. Trees of less preferred species will still be taken if they are the only source of food.

Trapping ▪ If legal, beavers can easily be trapped out of an area with only a moderate amount of knowledge and effort. One of the most common and effective traps is a Conibear 330. This spring trap kills the beaver almost instantly and is placed across runs or upstream of broken dams where the beaver will enter it (Figure 9.7).

Runs are visible as elongated, smooth trenches in the bottom of ponds, streams, and ditches that the beavers use to swim from one area to another. A properly placed Conibear trap staked across a run usually traps a beaver within a couple of days.

These traps are also effective when placed 12 to 18 inches upstream of a break created in the beaver dam. A break created in the morning with the trap set in the afternoon will usually trap a beaver by nightfall.

Tree Squirrels

Tree squirrels are well known to most people (Figure 9.8). Their agile antics of jumping and scampering through trees provide amusement to many. They seem to have a zest for life. However, these antics commonly take the form of damage-causing activities that are hard to relate to the squirrels' need for food, water, or shelter.

Identification

Tree squirrels, like rats, mice, woodchucks, and chipmunks, belong to the rodent family. The gray squirrels (*Sciurus* spp.) are probably the most common tree squirrel pest, but in some locales, the pine (or red) squirrel (*Tamiasciurus hudsonicus*) and the fox squirrel (*Sciurus niger*) are also important.

Gray and fox squirrels vary in color. Both species might be entirely black in some areas. In the Midwest, fox squirrels are typically grizzled brown on their backs with an orange underside, causing some people to call the fox squirrel a "red squirrel."

The pine squirrel is reddish brown on its back with white underparts. It has small ear tufts and often a black stripe separating the dark back from the lighter belly.

General Biology and Behavior

Tree squirrels generally inhabit wooded areas. The nests are built in tree cavities and forks, in leaf nests, or inside buildings, garages, and sheds. The leaf nests are easily identified, especially when constructed in deciduous trees, because they can be readily spotted during the winter months. Leaf nests are constructed with a frame of sticks filled with dry leaves and lined with leaves, strips of bark, and other dry vegetative materials.

Most mature tree squirrels have two litters of young each year (early spring and late summer), although the younger squirrels produce only one litter. The number of young varies between three and five squirrels.

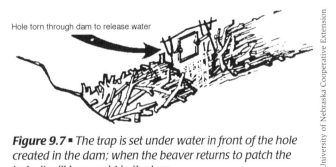

Hole torn through dam to release water

Figure 9.7 ▪ *The trap is set under water in front of the hole created in the dam; when the beaver returns to patch the hole, it will be caught in the trap*

University of Nebraska Cooperative Extension

University of Nebraska Cooperative Extension

Figure 9.8 ▪ *Squirrels are major pests of ornamental plants– gnawing stems, consuming buds, and stripping bark*

The gestation period is forty-two to forty-five days. Young squirrels are sexually mature when they are one year old.

The home range of tree squirrels varies significantly depending on the season and availability of food. Under average conditions, most tree squirrels remain within one acre of their tree nest. Tree squirrels are most active in early morning and late afternoon. They feed on nuts, seeds, buds, leaves, bulbs, bark, insects, and fruit.

Damage

Squirrels can be serious pests of ornamental plantings because they regularly gnaw and clip stems and branches, consume buds, and strip bark from various trees. Damage to ornamental plants in important locations of the landscape, such as near building entrances, needs to be controlled. In urban areas, an individual squirrel is frequently guilty of the majority of damage that occurs. The removal or exclusion of that individual usually solves the problem.

The most common landscape damage consists of the ground being littered with large numbers of twigs nipped off of the trees. When this occurs, more than one individual squirrel is usually responsible, but the damage is usually short enough in duration that little long-term damage is caused to the trees. Raking up the twigs usually solves the problem for the client without any action being taken against the squirrels.

Legal Status

Fox and gray squirrels are classified as game animals in most states. Consult local or state authorities to determine legal status.

Management

Depending on the location of the area receiving damage, it might be very difficult to control squirrel damage because squirrel populations can be extremely large. New squirrels often replace those removed or killed via traps or shooting.

Exclusion ▪ Squirrels can be denied from some types of trees by encircling the trees with a 2-foot-wide collar of metal located 6 feet off the ground. The metal can be attached using encircling wires held together with springs to allow for tree growth.

Repellents ▪ The taste repellents Ro-pel®, thiram, and capsaicin can be applied to trees and shrubs, providing some protection. However, the effectiveness of repellents depends on many factors (refer to discussion on deer management later in this chapter).

Trapping ▪ For small squirrel infestations, live trapping is a cost-effective approach to controlling damage. Because tree squirrels are classified as game species in most states, trapping permits might be required from the state wildlife agency. Any of the various nutmeats, sunflower seeds, fresh orange slices, sweet corn, and oatmeal are attractive baits for tree squirrels.

Some tree squirrels become trap-shy if they nudge and prematurely set off a trap or if they escape from a trap before the trap door completely closes. Thus, it might be more time efficient to prebait traps by placing all traps unset with the doors locked open until the squirrels become accustomed to them. Baits placed in and around the traps will attract the squirrels and reduce their cautious behavior.

Good locations to place **live traps** for tree squirrels include the bases of trees frequently used by the squirrels, sides of buildings (sometimes tree squirrels climb directly up the side of brick buildings or use ivy-covered chimneys to gain access to structures), roof areas, or immediately inside or outside the opening of the attic or area in which the squirrels are gaining entry.

All traps should be checked at least once, and preferably twice, per day to remove live-trapped animals as soon as possible after their capture. This will help reduce the possibility of the animals injuring themselves in the trap. Additionally, by placing a blanket or similar cover over the trapped animal, the squirrel will remain relatively calm. Live-trapped squirrels can be humanely destroyed (if legal) or taken at least 5 miles from the trap site and released in an area where they will not cause a problem for someone else. Some wildlife experts, however, discourage this practice because of the stress placed on the transported and resident squirrrels and concerns regarding the transmission of diseases. Live-trapped squirrels should never be handled because they are vicious biters and possess extremely sharp teeth and powerful claws.

Shooting ▪ Where firearms are permitted, shooting is an effective method of immediately eliminating a squirrel problem. A shotgun with No. 6 shot or a 22-caliber rifle is suitable. Consult your local wildlife agency prior to initiating any shooting program.

Cottontail Rabbits

Rabbits are enjoyed by many people. Children and adults alike enjoy seeing rabbits around their homes. Unfortunately, rabbits are among the most serious vertebrate pests around ornamental plantings.[2]

Identification

The eastern cottontail rabbit (*Sylvilagus floridanus*) is approximately 15 to 19 inches (37 to 48 centimeters) in length and weighs 2 to 4 pounds (0.9 to 1.8 kilograms). Males and females are basically the same size and color. Cottontails appear gray or brownish gray in the field. Rabbits molt twice each year but remain the same general color. They have large ears, although smaller than those of jackrabbits, and the hind feet are much larger than the forefeet. The tail is short and white on the undersurface, and its similarity to a cotton ball led to the rabbit's common name.

General Biology and Behavior

In the Midwest, rabbits begin mating in late winter or early spring, with the first litters born in March and April. The gestation period is twenty-eight to thirty-two days, and the average litter size is five to six young. If conditions are good, as many as six litters can be produced in a year, but two to three litters are more typical. Young cottontails are born nearly furless, with their eyes closed. Their eyes open in seven to eight days, and they leave the nest in two to three weeks.

Most rabbits live only twelve to fifteen months. Weather, disease, predators, encounters with cars and hunters, and other mortality factors combine to keep a lid on the rabbit population. Rabbits eat a wide variety of plants, including grasses, grains, alfalfa, vegetables, fruit trees, vines, and many ornamentals. In the spring,

they are often pests of a homeowner's flower and vegetable gardens. In fall and winter, they damage and kill valuable woody plants.

Cottontails construct **forms,** or nests, on the ground. Forms are usually established in areas of good cover so the animal is protected from predators. During warm weather, however, forms are sometimes located in areas that are quite open, such as a simple depression in a lawn. Rabbits take quick advantage of habitats created by humans, such as junk piles, old cars, weedy fencerows, and stacks of lumber, and they use these areas as daily hiding and resting places.

Rabbit activity varies considerably. Rabbits tend to be most active in the early morning and at night. During the early spring, it is common to see rabbits in the middle of the day. The home range varies from 1 to 5 acres in good habitat but can be considerably larger when resources are scarce. Rabbits do not migrate, but those in more open areas might move considerable distances during the winter to wooded areas, vegetated ditches, or other areas with heavier cover.

Damage

In fall and winter, rabbits damage and kill valuable woody plants by gnawing bark or clipping off branches, stems, and buds. In winter in northern states, when the ground is covered with snow for long periods, rabbits often severely damage expensive home landscape plants, orchards, forest plantations, and park trees and shrubs. Some young plants are clipped off at snow height, and large trees and shrubs might be completely girdled. When the latter happens, only sprouting from beneath the damage or a delicate bridge graft around the damage will save the plant. Entire hedges can be girdled during particularly cold periods with heavy snow cover in areas with dense rabbit populations. Even light damage might not be tolerable on young, expensive plants in heavily traveled and easily noticed areas.

Among shade and ornamental trees, the hardest hit are mountain ash, basswood, red maple, sugar maple, honey locust, ironwood, red and white oak, and willow. Sumac, rose, Japanese barberry, dogwood, and some woody members of the pea family are among shrubs commonly damaged. Evergreens seem to be more susceptible to rabbit damage in some areas than in others. Young trees might be clipped off, and older trees might be deformed or killed.

The character of the bark on woody plants also influences rabbit browsing. Most young trees have smooth, thin bark with green food material just beneath it. Such bark provides an easily accessible food

---

[2]Parts of this discussion were adapted from Craven 1994.

source for rabbits. The thick, rough bark of older trees often discourages gnawing. Even on the same plant, rabbits avoid the rough bark but girdle the young sprouts that have smooth bark.

Rabbit damage can be identified by the characteristic appearance of gnawing on older woody growth and the clean-cut, angled clipping of young stems (Figure 9.9). Distinctive round pellets of feces in the immediate area are also a good sign of rabbit activity.

Legal Status

In most states, rabbits are classified as game animals and are protected as such at all times except during the legal hunting season. Some state regulations might grant exceptions to property owners, allowing them to trap or shoot rabbits outside the normal hunting season on their own property.

Management

Controlling nuisance rabbits around ornamental plantings is best accomplished via an IPM approach involving exclusion, habitat removal, use of chemical and physical repellents, or by live trapping and removal of problem rabbits.

Because of the cottontail's reproductive potential, no lethal control is effective for more than a limited period. Control measures are most effective when used against the breeding population during the winter. Habitat modification and exclusion techniques provide the best long-term, nonlethal control. No toxic baits are available for controlling rabbits.

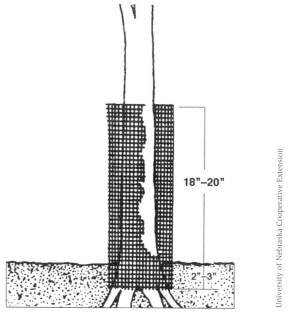

Figure 9.10 ▪ *A cylinder of hardware cloth or other wire mesh can protect trees from rabbit damage*

Habitat modification ▪ One form of natural control is manipulation of the rabbits' habitat. Although frequently overlooked, removing brush piles, weed patches, dumps, stone piles, and other debris where rabbits live and hide provides excellent and long-term rabbit management. It is especially effective in suburban areas, where fewer suitable habitats are likely to be available.

Exclusion ▪ One of the best ways to protect plants is to put up a fence. For temporary exclusion, the fence does not have to be tall or especially sturdy. A fence of 2-foot (60-centimeter) **chicken wire** with the bottom tight to the ground or buried a few inches is sufficient. The mesh should be 1 inch (2.5 centimeters) or smaller so that young rabbits will not be able to go through it.

A more substantial fence of welded wire, chain link, or hog wire might be more costly, but with proper care it will last many years and provide relief from the constant aggravation of rabbit damage. Keep in mind that inexpensive chicken-wire fences need be replaced every few years.

Cylinders of ¼-inch (0.6-centimeter) wire hardware cloth will protect valuable young orchard trees or landscape plants. The cylinders should extend higher than a rabbit's reach while standing on the expected snow depth and should stand 1 to 2 inches (2.5 to 5 centimeters) out from the green trunk. Larger mesh sizes of ½ to ¾ inch (1.2 to 1.8 centimeters) can be used to reduce cost, but the cylinder must stand far enough away

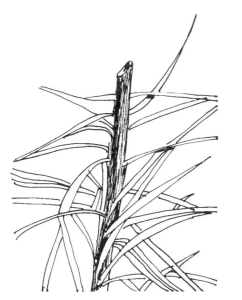

Figure 9.9 ▪ *Rabbits damage woody plants by gnawing on bark and clipping off branches.*

from the tree trunk to ensure that rabbits cannot eat through the holes (Figure 9.10).

Commercial tree guards or tree wrap is another alternative. Several types of paper wrap are available, but they are designed for protection from sun or other damage. When rabbits are abundant and food is in short supply, only hardware cloth will guarantee protection. Small-mesh (¼-inch, 0.6-centimeter) hardware cloth also protects against mouse damage.

Repellents ▪ Most of the repellents used against deer are also used for controlling rabbit browsing (see discussion on deer). For best results, use repellents and other damage-control methods at the first sign of damage.

Most repellents can be applied, like paint, with a brush or sprayer. Many commercially available repellents contain the fungicide thiram and can be purchased in a ready-to-use form.

Taste repellents are usually more effective than odor repellents against rabbits. The degree of efficacy, however, is highly variable, depending on the behavior and number of rabbits and alternative foods available. It is usually a mistake to rely on repellents alone to protect valuable plants. When rabbits are abundant and hungry, use other control techniques along with chemical repellents.

Trapping ▪ Providing that the population is not too dense, trapping is an excellent approach to long-term management of rabbits—especially if the rabbits are trapped and removed during the late autumn. Several excellent styles of commercial live traps are available from pest-control supply distributors, hardware stores, and various catalogs. Most commercial traps are wire and last indefinitely with proper care. Average cost is about $20 to $30.

Traps should be placed in areas where rabbits have been seen or near suspected nesting areas. Traps located near cover will increase success because the rabbits won't have to cross large open areas to get to them. In winter, the traps should be faced away from prevailing winds to keep snow and dry leaves from plugging the entrance or interfering with the door. All traps should be checked daily to replenish bait or remove the catch; daily checks are essential for effective control and for humane treatment of the animals. If traps fail to make a catch within a week, they should be moved.

Trapping rabbits is easier during the winter than in the warmer months, when many food sources exist. Baits such as cob corn (dry ear corn) or dried apples are excellent. Position the bait at the rear of the trap.

When using cob corn, use half a cob and push a nail into the pith of the cob; this keeps the cob off the floor and visible from the open door. Dried leafy alfalfa and clover are also good cold-weather baits. During the summer, apples, carrots, cabbage, and other fresh green vegetables are good baits. These soft baits become mushy and ineffective once frozen.

Commercial wire traps can be made more effective (especially in winter) by covering them with canvas or some other dark material. Be sure the cover does not interfere with the trap's mechanism.

Release rabbits in rural areas several miles from where they have been trapped if local regulations allow **relocation.** Do not release them where they will create a problem for someone else.

Shooting ▪ Shooting is a quick, easy, and effective method of controlling rabbits, providing it is permitted by local firearms laws and done safely. In some states, the owner or occupant of a parcel of land may hunt rabbits all year on that land, except for a short time before the firearm deer season. Check with your state wildlife agency for regulations. Because of the abundance of rabbits in favorable habitats, it might be too time consuming to attempt to shoot all of the rabbits. Besides, removing rabbits one year never guarantees that the rabbit population will be low the next year (this is also true for trapping).

White-Tailed Deer

Deer are probably the most widely distributed and best-recognized large mammals in North America. The white-tailed deer (*Odocoileus virginianus*) is found throughout the eastern half of the United States. Deer are important game animals. With the additional aesthetic value of deer to landowners and vacationers, importance of deer as a wildlife resource cannot be disputed.[3]

Unfortunately, over the past decade deer have become significant pests. They damage a variety of trees and ornamental plantings. Unlike moles, rats, and other species implicated in damage, deer cannot be casually eliminated when causing a problem.

These factors often make deer damage control a difficult social and political problem as well as a biological and logistical one. Control methods are built around effective herd management. Thus, the various state

---

[3]Parts of this discussion were adapted from Craven and Hygnstrom 1994.

wildlife agencies are often indirectly or directly involved through subsidy of control techniques, direct-damage compensation payments, or technical advice.

Scare devices and repellents have a place in deer damage control. Effective control for parks, estates, and other large areas, however, usually depends on excluding the deer with one of several types of fences. Toxicants, fumigants, and trapping are not used in deer control.

Identification and Biology

Deer are familiar to nearly everyone. They are even-toed **ungulates** of the family Cervidae. Adult animals weigh 50 to 400 pounds (23 to 180 kilograms), depending on species and location. At birth, **fawns** are rust-colored with white spots. Their spotted coats are shed in three to four months and are replaced by a grayish brown fall and winter coat. The summer coat of adult animals is reddish brown. Underparts of the tail, belly, chin, and throat are white during all seasons.

Antlers grow on males (bucks) from April to August. Antler development is nourished by a layer of soft, vascularized "velvet" on the antlers. The dried velvet layer is rubbed off and the antlers polished during the fall **rut,** or breeding season. Antler size depends on nutrition, age, and genetics. The tines of the white-tailed deer antlers arise from a central beam. The antlers are **deciduous** and are shed in midwinter. Deer lack upper incisors, which is why deer-feeding damage on twigs and plantings results in the characteristic uneven and ragged-edged branches.

Most breeding occurs from October to January, but peak activity is in November. Most does breed during their second fall, though on good range some doe fawns (6 months old) will breed. Gestation is about 202 days. The peak of fawn drop is in May or June. Most reproducing fawns give birth to a single fawn, but adult does typically bear twin fawns.

Deer are most active in early morning and evening. They have a home range of several hundred acres, but this varies with season, sex, and habitat quality. In northern areas, deer gather, or **yard,** in dense cover for the winter. They can move long distances from summer range to a winter yard. Life expectancy is dependent on hunting pressure and regulations. Records show whitetails living up to 20 years.

Deer are creatures of the forest edge rather than the dense, old-growth forest. They thrive in agricultural and urban areas interspersed with woodlots and wooded streambanks. They favor early successional stages that keep brush and sapling **browse** within reach. Dense cover is used for winter shelter and escape.

Food Habits

For the most part, deer are browsing animals that consume the leaves, stems, and buds of various woody plants. The plant species vary considerably in quality and regional availability. When available, forbs are eaten in spring and summer. Fruits and nuts, especially acorns, are seasonally important. Grasses are relatively unimportant. Agricultural crops—including corn, soybeans, small grains, alfalfa, vegetables, and fruit trees—are readily eaten when available.

Damage

Ornamental trees or nursery stock can be permanently disfigured by deer browsing. Regeneration of some forest species might be impaired. Young trees and shrubs are also damaged when deer rub their antlers on trunks and limbs. Whether damage-reduction efforts are warranted depends on the extent and location of damage. A few twigs nibbled off of a tree or shrub during the winter will likely result in little more than a bushier plant due to multiple lateral bud growth, and control is probably not warranted. However, severely browsed shrubs and trees might be greatly disfigured or killed. Replanting with less-attractive species might prove effective, but in many areas with large deer populations, other methods must be used to reduce damage to an acceptable level.

Identifying the feeding damage of deer is not difficult. Because deer lack upper incisors, browsing usually leaves a jagged or torn surface on twigs or stems (Figure 9.11), whereas rabbit or rodent damage is

Figure 9.11 ▪ *Deer feeding results in a jagged or torn surface on twigs or stems.*

University of Nebraska Cooperative Extension

identified with a sharp 45° cut. The height of damage from the ground often rules out any mammal other than deer.

Deer tracks and pellets are also a helpful confirmation of deer damage because they are usually visible in the area of damage. The hoofprints of deer are about 2 to 3 inches long, split, pointed at the front, and more rounded at the rear.

Legal Status

Deer are protected during all times of the year except hunting seasons. In cases of severe or persistent damage, some states might issue special permits to shoot deer at times other than the legal hunting seasons. Regulations vary on the necessary permits and on disposal of dead animals. No lethal deer control should be initiated before consulting with the appropriate state wildlife agency. Some states provide technical assistance or direct compensation for deer damage.

Management

For commercial operations, the two most practical approaches for controlling deer damage are exclusion and repellents. In areas of high deer pressure, fencing—though initially expensive—is the most cost-effective approach. A cost-benefit analysis should be conducted, taking into account the potential life of the fence.

Exclusion ▪ Deer fence technology has dramatically reduced the cost of protecting ornamental plantings from deer herds. New electric-fence configurations are effective, durable, and less expensive than some traditional designs.

A wire-mesh fence is effective if it is solidly constructed and at least 8 feet high. Deer can jump over a 6- to 8-foot fence with little difficulty. The fence should be close to the ground because deer will also slink under a fence. An effective fence can be made from two 4-foot widths of hog-wire fencing joining one on top of the other and attached to well-supported 12-foot posts.

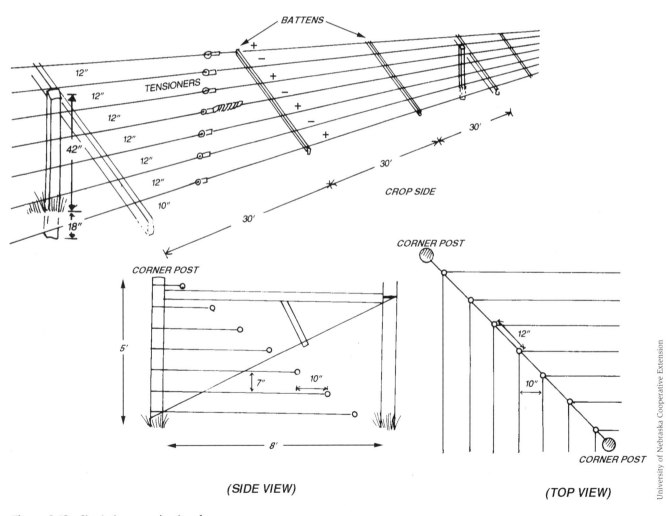

Figure 9.12 ▪ *Slanted seven-wire deer fence*

University of Nebraska Cooperative Extension

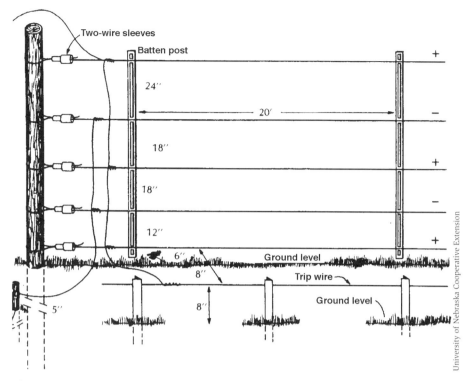

Figure 9.13 ▪ *The Penn State electric fence*

Two basic designs have been used—one permanent for areas needing constant protection, the other temporary for intermittent protection (Figure 9.13). With both, it is best to use a hot wire on an outrigger so that deer encounter the wire before the fence. It is also advisable to use a tandem-charger arrangement to ensure a constant power source if the primary charger malfunctions. New fence designs offer other alternatives and might eventually replace older designs. All are presented as alternatives to fit various price ranges, topographies, and damage situations.

Because there are now several different models and arrangements for electric deer fences, consult your state conservation agency for suppliers of deer fencing, materials, and instructions.

Costs can be prorated over the life of the fence, which is about twenty years.

To save materials, construct a fence that slants away from the area to be protected. This fence requires only one width of fencing plus wire-strand **outriggers.** Attach the angled posts at a 45° angle so that the high ends are at least 6 feet from the ground (Figure 9.12). Deer will walk under the overhang and be unable to jump over the wire strands. Keep plants mowed under the overhang. Plant growth might prevent deer from going under the fence far enough, and they might jump over it. An electrified version of this fence tested at the Cary Arboretum in New York has proven very effective.

Chicken wire, though inexpensive, is weak and does not last long. Snow fence has been reported to work well for small areas (up to 40 by 60 feet). Deer can easily jump over a snow fence placed around a larger area. Snow fencing is less expensive than wire and will last many seasons.

Electric fences ▪ Electric fences are less expensive to build than mesh fences, but they require more maintenance and might be totally ineffective when not electrified. Deep snow, broken insulators, and plants all can short the electric current. Deer will learn to avoid an electric fence. If the fence is high enough or has enough wires, it will provide the same deterrence as a conventional fence.

Scare devices ▪ If action is taken early and properly, deer can be frightened away from certain areas. Thus, steps should be taken as soon as possible if deer are seen investigating ornamental plantings. It is difficult to break patterns of behavior or movement once deer have been established.

A dog on a long run can keep deer out of a limited area, but care and feeding of the dog can be time consuming. Free-running dogs are not advisable unless they are kept in an enclosed area.

Repellents ▪ Repellents are the most common damage-control measure used for deer, especially on woody plants in small areas. High cost, limitations on use, and variable effectiveness make most repellents impractical for large areas. Also keep in mind that success with repellents is measured in the reduction, not total elimination, of damage. Therefore, for expensive plantings in areas of deer activity, excluding the deer is the only way to prevent damage.

For large acreages and in commercial operations, machine spray methods are the most economically efficient. The cost of these applications often can be further reduced by including compatible repellents in regularly scheduled pesticide applications. (Check the label for compatibility information.)

The effectiveness of repellents depends on several factors. Rainfall will dissipate some repellents, so re-application is necessary after a rain. But some repellents do not weather well, even in the absence of rainfall. Deer's hunger and the availability of other, more palatable food will have a great effect on success. In times of food stress, deer are likely to ignore either taste or scent repellents. When using a commercial preparation, follow the manufacturer's instructions.

Repellents are generally of two types: those that produce an offensive taste while material is being consumed by deer (**contact repellents**) and those that produce an odor obnoxious to deer (**area repellents**). When using these products, it is important to consider the amount of plant material deer must consume before taste aversion is effective, as well as the sphere of influence of an odor-based material.

Contact repellents are applied directly to the plants (Figure 9.14, color plate section). They are most effective when trees and shrubs are **dormant**. New growth that appears after treatment is unprotected. Area repellents are applied near the plants to be protected and repel deer by smell alone. They are usually less effective than contact repellents but can work in some situations where contact repellents cannot be used.

During the winter or dormant season, contact repellents should be applied on a dry day when temperatures are above freezing. Young trees should be treated completely, but it will be more economical to treat only the terminal growth of older trees. Treatments must consider maximum snow depth—generally up to heights of 6 feet (1.8 meters). During the growing season, contact repellents can be applied at about half the concentration recommended for winter use.

The following discussion of common repellents provides only a representative sample of the wide range of repellent formulations available.

- *Human hair.* Reports are mixed on the effectiveness of human hair. Some claim success in small areas with specimen trees, whereas others claim that an empty bag blowing in the breeze is just as effective as one filled with hair. Therefore, in cases of expensive stock, this repellent is risky. The hair is usually placed in a nylon stocking, onion bag, or other small-mesh bag and hung on the plant to be protected. Several bags can be hung from a fence or string around the perimeter of the area to be protected. You can obtain hair readily and inexpensively at barber shops. Hair should be replaced several times during the growing season.

- *Bone tar oil (Magic Circle®).* This repellent is applied as an area repellent by hanging soaked rags, saturated cord, or other such devices around the area to be protected. A saturated cord is probably easiest to use. Bone tar oil does not weather well under some conditions.

- *Paradichlorobenzene or naphthalene:* Mothballs or flakes can be used as an area repellent, hung in mesh bags or scattered on the ground. These repellents have to be replaced because they evaporate.

- *Hot pepper sauce (Hot Sauce Animal Repellent®).* A formulation of 2 tablespoons (30 milliliters) of hot pepper sauce in 12½ gallons (47.5 liters) of water containing an additive that promotes retention, such as Wilt-Pruf® or Vapor-Gard®, has been reported to repel deer when sprayed on Christmas trees. This is a good example of using some imagination in making vegetation distasteful.

- *Blood meal.* Blood meal is hung in bags, spread on the ground, or mixed in water and used as a spray. Blood meal does not weather well. Blood is common in nature, so the effectiveness of blood meal is questionable.

- *Tankage.* Tankage, or putrefied meat scraps, is a slaughterhouse byproduct. Tankage is placed in open sandwich bags, mesh bags, or metal cans. The containers are hung on or near the vegetation to be protected (Figure 9.15, color plate section). If cans are used, aluminum cans are best because they will not rust. The tops from the cans should be removed and the sides punctured to permit precipitation to drain. You might have to replace the containers periodically because fox or other animals sometimes pull them down. Tankage repels by smell, as will be readily apparent. A byproduct of the poultry industry called feathermeal (ground chicken feathers) can be used in the same way.

- *Thiram.* The taste of this fungicide repels deer (and rabbits). A number of ready-to-use commercial formulations contain thiram. These include Hopkins Thiram 42-S®, Chaperone®, Science Deer and Rabbit Repellent®, Bonide Rabbit-Deer Repellent®, Nott Chew-Not®, and Gustafson 42-S®. Thiram-based repellents are most effective when applied to dormant trees or shrubs. A common mix for paint or spray is 2 quarts (1.96 liters) of 42-S (42 percent active ingredient), 1 gallon (3.8 liters) of water, and 2 quarts (1.96 liters) of Rhoplex AC-33 or a similar adhesive. The 42-S is mixed in the water before adding the adhesive.

- *Cat feces.* The manure and urine of tigers, lions, cougars, or other large cats is reported to act as an area repellent. The manure can be obtained from most zoos, but its weathering properties are poor.

- *Fermented egg solids (Deer-Away®, MGK BGR®).* Putrescent egg solids are the main ingredient in a relatively new commercial formulation developed for use on conifer plantations. It presumably acts by odor, and reports indicate it is effective. Label directions are explicit. Available in both liquid and powder formulations, it can be used in a wide variety of damage situations.

- *Hinder®.* This is an odor repellent, in a commercial formulation of ammonium soaps of higher **fatty acids**. It can be used on fruit trees, ornamentals, and food crops. Hinder® can be applied in conjunction with pesticide sprays.

Toxicants ▪ No toxicants are registered for deer control. Poisoning deer with any product for any reason is illegal and unlikely to be tolerated by the public.

Birds: Sapsuckers and Woodpeckers

The holes caused by **sapsuckers** and woodpeckers are often blamed on insect borers. Although much woodpecker damage results from the birds chiseling out borer larvae, sapsuckers commonly attack trees without borer problems. The rows of holes caused by sapsuckers are easily identified.[4]

Identification and Damage

All woodpeckers, flickers, and sapsuckers belong to the family Picidae. These birds have short legs with two backward-pointing and two forward-pointing sharp-clawed toes and short, stiff tail feathers. These characteristics enable them to cling to tree trunks and branches as they use their stout, sharply pointed beaks to dig out insects and excavate nesting cavities.

Yellow-bellied sapsuckers are found in the Midwest and are almost 8 inches long with black-and-white backs and off-white breasts. The yellow belly is evident only on some birds in just the right lighting situation. Males have red on the throat and top of the head. Females have little or no red coloration.

These woodpeckers live during the summer in the northern United States and southern Canada and mi-

grate south through the lower Midwest between mid-September and mid-October. They overwinter in the southern United States and migrate north through the lower Midwest between late March and mid-May. These are the only times that trees are damaged in the lower Midwest, although the same bird apparently visits the same tree year after year.

Sapsucker damage is found on many ornamental and fruit trees, commonly pines, birches, maples, and apple. They drill a series of holes in either horizontal or vertical rows in tree trunks or large limbs. Because sapsuckers sit vertically on the trunk or along the long axis of the limb, these holes are located between branches (Figure 9.16, color plate section). As sap flows into the holes, the sapsucker uses its brushlike tongue to draw the sap up along with any insects that were attracted to the sap. Sapsuckers will also periodically enlarge the holes and eat portions of the cambium, inner bark, and fresh sap.

Trees that are attacked year after year might suffer from reduced vitality and be susceptible to further injury from insects and disease. In areas where the sapsuckers migrate, such as the lower Midwest, damage is rarely extensive enough to warrant control actions. Trees in areas where the damage is very visible, such as near building entrances, might warrant control to reduce aesthetic damage. Where the birds spend the summer or winter, they can feed heavily enough on trees to kill them. Individual branches or the central leader of the tree can be girdled and might die as a result of severe sapsucker damage.

Legal Status

Woodpeckers are classified under the Migratory Bird Treaty Act as migratory insectivorous birds and are protected by both state and federal law. As a result, certain activities affecting them are subject to legal restriction. It is illegal for any person to kill, take, possess, transport, sell, or purchase them or their parts—such as feathers, nest, or eggs—without a permit issued by the appropriate state or federal agency (such as the U.S. Fish and Wildlife Service). However, a state or federal permit is not required to scare or harass a woodpecker that is causing damage.

Management

Scaring devices and techniques ▪ Prompt and persistent action is required to deter a woodpecker that is attracted to a particular tree or area. The use of a combination of scaring techniques is more successful than relying on just one technique or device.

---

[4]This section adapted from Marsh 1994.

Strips of aluminum foil 3 to 4 inches wide and 3 to 4 feet long or similarly sized strips of cloth or plastic can be hung in front of the damaged area. Tin-can lids or aluminum pie pans tied to heavy string so they will rattle and flash in the sun can also be used. **Raptor** silhouettes or effigies have been successfully used in some cases.

Banging garbage-can lids, clapping boards together, or almost anything else that will frighten birds can be used to try to drive them away. When using any visual or sound repellent, prompt and persistent action is the key to success.

Sticky and tactile repellents ▪ Repellents such as Tanglefoot®, Bird Stop®, and Roost-No-More® can be applied to tree limbs and trunks to discourage sapsuckers. Or the repellents can first be applied to a thin piece of pressed board, ridged clear-plastic sheets, or other suitable material, which is then fastened to the areas where damage is occurring.

Loosely wrapping sapsucker-damaged limbs in burlap, hardware cloth, or plastic will protect the area from further damage. Remove this wrapping once the birds leave the area. Treating the damaged areas with asphalt-based roofing paint has successfully repelled sapsuckers that were damaging fruit trees. These methods are practical for high-value park and shade trees.

In orchards and forested areas, it might be better to let the birds work on one or two of their favorite trees. Trying to protect the one or two favorite trees might lessen the damage to those particular trees, but could result in more trees damaged throughout the planting.

Miscellaneous methods ▪ People often will attempt to control animal and bird pests around buildings and ornamentals using different home-remedy approaches or techniques based on myths or that were effective for other pests. The following techniques are not effective for sapsuckers and woodpeckers and thus are not worth spending time and money on:

- *Poisons.* There are no toxicants available for controlling woodpeckers.

- *Taste and odor repellents.* Chemicals that have objectionable tastes have not been found effective against sapsuckers. Odorous substances such as mothballs and wood treatments (for example, creosote and pentachlorophenol) are not effective.

- *Ultrasonics.* High-frequency sound is above the normal audible hearing range of humans and, unfortunately, above the range of most birds too.

- *Suet.* Placing **suet** stations near damaged areas, especially in the colder parts of the country, has been recommended to entice woodpeckers away from buildings or damaged areas. Suet offered in the warmer seasons of the year, however, might harm woodpeckers. The suet gets onto the feathers of the head, which could lead to matting and eventual loss of feathers. Some bird-damage experts believe that any feeding of birds contributes to the problem, and they therefore recommend against it.

Robert Corrigan
RMC Pest Management Consulting
Richmond, Indiana

Philip Nixon
Extension Entomologist
Department of Natural Resources and
*   Environmental Sciences*
University of Illinois

Selected References

Bohlen, H.D. 1989. *Birds of Illinois.* Bloomington: Indiana University Press.

Craven, S.R. 1994. Cottontail rabbits. In *Prevention and Control of Wildlife Damage,* by S.E. Hygnstrom, R.M. Timm, and G.E. Larson. Lincoln: University of Nebraska Cooperative Extension Service.

Craven, S.R., and S.E. Hygnstrom. 1994. Deer. In *Prevention and Control of Wildlife Damage,* by S.E. Hygnstrom, R.M. Timm, and G.E. Larson. Lincoln: University of Nebraska Cooperative Extension Service.

Hoffmeister, D.F. 1989. *Mammals of Illinois.* Urbana: University of Illinois Press.

Hygnstrom S.E., R.M. Timm, and G.E. Larson. 1994. *Prevention and Control of Wildlife Damage.* Lincoln: University of Nebraska Cooperative Extension Service.

Jones, J.K, Jr., and E.C. Birney. 1988. *Handbook of Mammals of the North-Central States.* Minneapolis: University of Minnesota Press.

Marsh, R.E. 1994. Woodpeckers. In *Prevention and Control of Wildlife Damage,* by S.E. Hygnstrom, R.M. Timm, and G.E. Larson. Lincoln: University of Nebraska Cooperative Extension Service.

Miller, J.E., and G.K. Yarrow. 1994. Beavers. In *Prevention and Control of Wildlife Damage,* by S.E. Hygnstrom, R.M. Timm, and G.E. Larson. Lincoln: University of Nebraska Cooperative Extension Service.

Pearson, T.G. 1936. *Birds of America.* Garden City, New York: Doubleday & Co.

CHAPTER 10

Managing Weeds and Competing Plants

George Czapar and Harvey Holt

Weeds are unwanted plants growing out of place at a particular time. The same plant species might be considered desirable in one setting but a weed in another setting. Ground ivy, for example, can be a useful ground cover in some areas to reduce soil erosion, but it is considered a weed in many lawns, gardens, and landscapes.

Weeds interfere with plant growth by competing for moisture, nutrients, light, and space. Weeds can provide a habitat for rodents and other pests or serve as alternate hosts for **disease**. Some weeds, such as poison ivy (Figure 10.1, color plate section), may also present a health hazard. Finally, weeds give an unsightly and unmanaged appearance to the landscape and can reduce its aesthetic value. In most situations, some type of weed management is necessary for optimum growth of desirable landscape species.

The level of infestation that is economically or aesthetically damaging differs according to the weed species and depends on its time of emergence, life cycle, and growth habit. Weeds compete at different levels of intensity. Some species thrive under specific moisture, temperature, or light conditions, whereas others are well adapted to a wide range of environmental conditions.

In addition, the level of weed infestation that is aesthetically damaging will vary by location. For example, the acceptable level of **weed control** near the entrance to an office building will be different than in a seldom-used area of a park.

A successful weed management program should combine all available control options rather than relying on a single practice and should minimize labor, cost, and environmental hazards. Site preparation, cultural practices, mechanical controls, and herbicides are part of an integrated approach to managing weeds. Properly identifying weeds and understanding the growth and development of unwanted plants are essential components of integrated pest management (IPM). By regularly monitoring susceptible landscapes, you will be able to identify and control *new* weeds before they become established, and help prevent *existing* weeds from increasing.

Weed Biology

Plant Types

Most plants can be classified as grasses, herbaceous broadleaves (forbs), or woody plants. Other plant groups that account for weed species in the landscape include the sedges (such as purple and yellow nutsedge), ferns (such as bracken fern), and *Equisetum* species (horsetail or jointgrass). Sedges are neither grasses nor broadleaves, but they have characteristics similar to grasses. One way to distinguish the two types of plants is to examine the stems: sedges have a triangular, or three-sided, stem (Figure 10.2, color plate section), whereas most grasses have a round or flat stem.

Grasses ▪ Grass seedlings have only one leaf when they emerge from the ground. The leaves are generally narrow and upright with parallel veins. Most grasses have fibrous root systems (Figure 10.3). The growing point on seedling grasses is sheathed and located below the soil surface. It gradually moves up to the soil surface as the plant grows and matures. Examples include barnyardgrass, bentgrass, Bermudagrass, bluegrass, crabgrass, fescue, giant foxtail, Johnsongrass, quackgrass, Reed canarygrass, and ryegrasses.

Herbaceous broadleaves ▪ These are plants that do not develop persistent woody tissue above ground. The seedlings have two leaves as they emerge from the ground, and the leaves are generally broad with netlike veins. Broadleaves often have a taproot and a relatively coarse root system. They have growing points (buds) at the end of each stem and in each leaf axil (Figure 10.4). Examples include buckhorn plantain, Canada thistle, common ragweed, crimson clover, curly dock, dandelion, field bindweed, purple loosestrife, pigweeds, sweet clover, wild carrot, and wild parsnip.

Woody plants ▪ These plants form wood (Figure 10.5). They include brush, shrubs, and trees. Brush and shrubs are woody plants that have several stems and are less than 10 feet tall. Trees usually have a single stem (trunk)

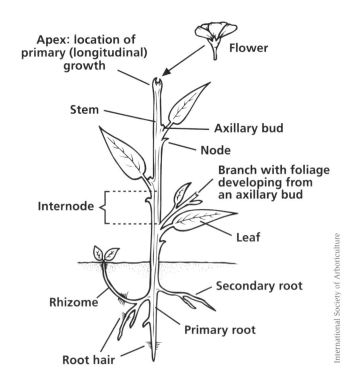

Figure 10.4 ▪ *Parts of a broadleaf plant*

and are over 10 feet tall. Trees consists of two broad groups: hardwoods and conifers. With few exceptions, hardwoods shed their leaves in the fall. Examples include American elm, black cherry, boxelder, cottonwood, flowering dogwood, green ash, silver maple, and sweet gum.

With few exceptions, conifers keep their needles year-round and are therefore known as evergreens. The needles are actually shed after two to three years, depending on species, but there is always outer green foliage. Examples include eastern red cedar, eastern hemlock, juniper, and larch (sheds its needles each fall).

Growth Stages

Plants have four stages of development: seedling, vegetative, reproductive, and maturity (Figure 10.6). In the seedling stage, seed leaves (cotyledons) might be present along with the first true leaves. In the vegetative stage, rapid growth of stems, roots, and foliage occurs. There is also rapid uptake of water and nutrients. Flowering and seed production or fruit-set occurs in the reproductive stage. Growth is limited, and uptake of water and nutrients is slowed. Movement (translocation) of water and plant food (nutrients) is directed to reproductive parts, flowers, fruits, and seeds, whereas movement of plant food to the roots is reduced. In the maturity stage, there is little or no growth and slow movement of water, nutrients, and herbicides in the plant.

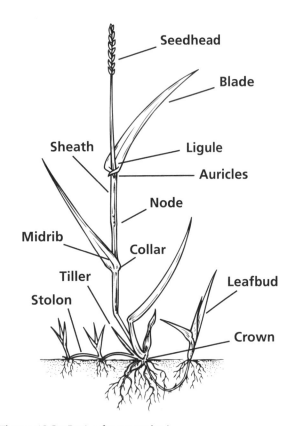

Figure 10.3 ▪ *Parts of a grass plant*

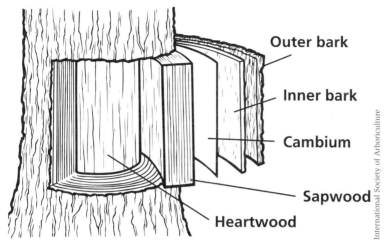

Figure 10.5 ▪ *Generalized structure of a woody stem*

All weeds are most easily controlled at the seedling stage. Compared to a more mature plant, the leaf surface is easily penetrated, surface hairs are fewer and smaller, and the roots are near the soil surface.

Life Cycles

Annuals ▪ Annuals complete all stages of development in less than twelve months. Annuals are frequently classified as winter annuals and summer annuals. Winter annuals germinate in the fall, overwinter, mature, set seed, and die in the spring. Examples include bedstraw, groundsel, pepperweed, common chickweed, henbit, and wild mustard. Summer annuals germinate in the spring, grow, set seed, and die in the fall. Examples include annual morningglory, crabgrass, giant foxtail, giant ragweed, purslane, and sweet clover.

Some weeds are specifically winter or summer annuals, but others can germinate and grow in either fall or spring. Knowing the growth habits of annuals is important in planning how and when to control them. Although spring is a good time to control summer annuals, winter annuals are most effectively controlled in the fall. Because the root systems of annual plants do not persist, controlling top growth can be effective.

Biennials ▪ Biennials complete their life cycle in two years. Biennial plants complete the seedling and vegetative stages of growth the first year. They appear as rosettes, or clumps of leaves, on the soil surface at the end of the first year. Seed production and maturity stages are completed the second year. There are no grasses with a biennial life cycle. Examples of biennials include bull thistle, evening primrose, mullein, musk thistle, teasel, wild carrot, and wild parsnip.

Control should be directed at the first-year plants. After the seedhead has been produced, which is often the most visible part of the plant, the plant begins to die. Fall or early spring is the best time for biennial weed control. Controlling biennial and annual plants with herbicides after flowering and seed production is of questionable benefit. Mechanical control to reduce the height of the flower stalk is often more practical.

Perennials ▪ Perennials might complete all four growth stages in the first year and then repeat the vegetative, reproduction, and maturity stages for several years following, or the reproduction and maturity stages might be delayed for several years. Some perennial plants, such as dandelions, die back to the ground each winter, but the roots persist and produce new plants the next year. Others, such as trees, might lose their leaves but do not die back to the ground. They all reproduce by seed, but many are able to spread and reproduce vegetatively.

Perennials can be divided into general groups based on how they reproduce. Simple perennials spread by seed and cut-root segments. These plants have persistent root systems that do not tend to spread unless broken into parts by mechanical methods. Examples of simple perennials include broomsedge, buckhorn

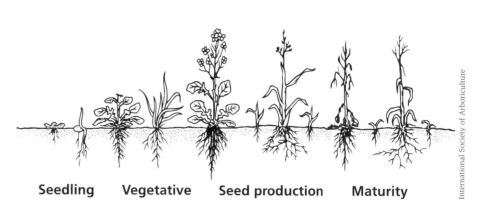

Seedling   Vegetative   Seed production   Maturity

Figure 10.6 ▪ *Growth stages of a weed*

plantain, chicory, curly dock, dandelion, goldenrod, spiderwort, and white heath aster.

Creeping perennials spread vegetatively with stolons—horizontal stems running on the soil surface, usually rooting at the joints (Figure 10.7); by rhizomes—underground horizontal stems modified for food storage and asexual reproduction; or by seed. Creeping perennials exist as a patch that continues to get larger each year. Examples of creeping perennials include Bermudagrass, field bindweed, blackberry, Canada thistle, horsenettle, horsetail, Japanese honeysuckle, Johnsongrass, multiflora rose, poison ivy, purple loosestrife, quackgrass, red sorrel, trumpetcreeper, Virginia creeper, wild grape, and ground ivy (Figure 10.8).

Bulbous perennials reproduce vegetatively from underground bulbs or tubers, and they also produce seed. The bulbs and tubers can be spread in soil disturbance, and they can resprout when the parent plant has been controlled. Examples of bulbous perennials include wild garlic and wild onion.

Perennial plants are also best controlled in the seedling stage. New infestations and small patches can be more effectively managed than established populations. Perennials are difficult to control because of their persistent root systems. If the root system is not controlled, the plant will resprout. As a result, defoliating perennial plants provides only a temporary growth suppression.

Weed Management

Site Preparation

Site preparation and proper landscape design are essential components of a successful weed management

Figure 10.8 ▪ *Creeping root system of Canada thistle*

program. Established weeds should be controlled before planting the site. Although tillage is normally effective for controlling annual weeds, it often has little effect on perennials. Prior to planting, a **translocated herbicide** such as glyphosate (Roundup) may be used to control perennial weeds. After application, allow five to seven days for the herbicide to translocate to perennial root systems before mowing or tillage.

During site preparation, soil fertility levels and **pH** can also be modified. Correct any problems with poor internal drainage. Loosen compacted soils, and properly grade the area so water does not stand. Drip or subsurface irrigation systems may also be installed at this time.

Plant Selection

Select landscape plants that are well adapted to local soils and environmental conditions. Adapted plants will grow more vigorously and will be better able to tolerate stress than species that are not adapted to the area. Group together plants that have similar cultural require-

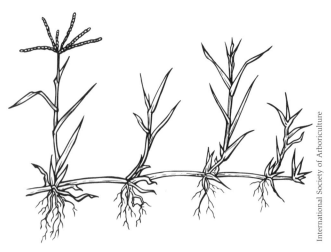

Figure 10.7 ▪ *Vegetative spread by stolons*

ments, such as a specific soil pH. Space plants and use annuals or ground covers to minimize bare soils and widely spaced landscape plantings. Bare soil is inevitably colonized by weeds. Keep in mind that some aggressive ground covers, however, can become weeds by crowding out other landscape species.

Mulching

Mulches are an effective method of preventing **germination** and growth of annual weeds. They prevent light from reaching the soil surface and reduce germination of weed seeds. Mulches also conserve soil moisture and prevent erosion and **soil compaction**. In addition, mulches reduce the risk of root damage from deep cultivation and lessen the chance of mechanical injury from mowers or weed trimmers. Mulching materials can be almost any substance that is thick enough to exclude light, relatively cheap, and easy to work with.

Organic mulches ▪ Many organic mulches are attractive and provide a natural appearance to the landscape. In addition to preventing weed growth, organic mulches improve soil tilth. As mulch decays, it gradually releases minerals and **organic matter**.

Organic mulches should be free of weed seeds and may include bark chips, ground bark, wood chips, composted lawn clippings, leaves, and straw. These mulches are high in **cellulose** and low in nitrogen. As soil microorganisms break down the mulch, they tie up nitrogen from soil reserves. It might be necessary to add nitrogen fertilizer or compost materials before using organic mulches.

Mulch should be applied 3 to 4 inches thick. Keep organic mulches several inches away from the base of trees to avoid crown-rot diseases. Because mulches gradually decompose, it is necessary to periodically add mulch to maintain weed control.

Synthetic mulches ▪ Black or clear plastic has been used as synthetic mulch. Although they are somewhat easier to maintain than organic mulches, synthetic mulches do not improve soil quality and are unattractive unless a top mulch is applied.

Landscape fabrics are another type of synthetic mulch. Unlike plastic mulches, however, fabrics allow air and water penetration to roots. These materials are more durable and effective than plastic sheets, but they are also more expensive.

Stone mulches ▪ Crushed rock, stones, or pebbles can be added as an attractive top mulch for synthetic mulches. Covering synthetic mulches with stone also reduces their breakdown by ultraviolet light. If used alone, however, stone mulches tend to become weed infested. They can also get too hot and are time consuming to remove.

Mechanical Control

Hand weeding, hoeing, and cultivation are widely used to control weeds throughout the growing season. Weeds are much easier to control when they are small. Hand weeding is most effective when the soil is loose or moist and the entire weed root can be removed.

The best time to hoe or cultivate is when the soil is dry. Use shallow hoeing and cultivation to control weeds. In addition to damaging landscape plant roots, deep cultivation can bring up buried weed seeds and also dry out the soil. Mechanical control might not be entirely effective for managing perennial weeds, but if **selective herbicides** are unavailable, it might be the only option.

Mowing

Mowing and weed trimming can be effective weed-control practices and, in most cases, are done as part of routine landscape maintenance. Mowing removes top growth prior to seed formation and can help deplete underground food reserves. Mowing is relatively ineffective, however, on species that grow and produce seed below the normal height of cutting. Further, a plant that has had a single central shoot cut off might send up several new shoots from buds below the cut. Repeated mowing can change an upright, single-stemmed plant to a many-branched prostrate weed that is still able to produce seed.

Although weed trimmers are widely used to cut unwanted vegetation, they can also injure young landscape plants. Trunk damage from weed trimmers can **girdle** and kill young trees. A flexible plastic shield can be placed around trunks of small trees to prevent damage from weed trimmers. As previously noted, mulching can reduce the need to trim around trees.

Preventing New Weed Problems

Preventing new weeds from becoming established in the landscape is an ongoing challenge. Weeds can be carried into an area in several ways—topsoil, **container-grown** plants, mulch, manure, and other material might be contaminated with weed seeds or plant parts. Similarly, mowers and other implements might be contaminated with weed seeds or vegetative parts. Weed seeds also can be carried in irrigation water from rivers, streams, or ponds, or spread by wind and animals.

Herbicides

As previously noted, herbicides are only one part of an integrated weed management program. The need for herbicide use in a well-designed, mature landscape might be minimal. Further, selective herbicides might not be an option in some mixed landscapes that contain turf, annuals, perennials, trees, and shrubs. If herbicides are to be used, it is important to understand how they work.

The proper selection and use of a herbicide depends on the characteristics of the **active ingredient**, including (a) selective or nonselective, (b) translocated or contact, (c) root-absorbed or foliage-absorbed, and (d) persistent or nonpersistent. Effective weed control can be accomplished by combining the desired characteristics of different herbicides, assuming there are no incompatibilities or label restrictions. Premixed and tank-mixed combinations offer convenience and utilize specific characteristics of each component.

Selective

Selective herbicides control only certain types of plants. When applied to mixed vegetation, some plant types (species) will be noticeably unaffected. This selectivity might occur because of the plant's ability to resist the herbicide effect. For example, grasses are naturally resistant to the herbicide 2,4-D, but dandelions and ragweeds are not. Selectivity also occurs by changing the rate applied, applying at a different time, and using a method of application that keeps the herbicide away from desired plants. Examples of herbicides that do not affect most grasses include 2,4-D, dichlorprop (Weedone 2,4-DP), and triclopyr (Garlon). Herbicides affecting only grasses include fluazifop-butyl (Fusilade) and sethoxydim (Poast, Vantage).

Nonselective

Nonselective herbicides will generally control or suppress most weed species. These herbicides are used where complete control or bare ground is desired. Nonselectivity can be rate-related. Herbicides that can be used for nonselective weed control include diquat (Diquat Herbicide-H/A), diuron, glyphosate (Roundup), and glufosinate ammonium (Finale).

Translocated (Systemic)

Translocated, or **systemic**, **herbicides** will move throughout the plant whether they are taken in by the foliage or by the roots. Some herbicides are transported only upward in the plant with the water absorbed by the roots. Because perennial plants will resprout from persistent root systems, translocated herbicides are especially useful for control because they move into the roots (Figure 10.9). Examples of effective translocated herbicides include 2,4-D, dichlorprop (Weedone 2,4-DP), glyphosate (Roundup), sethoxydim (Poast, Vantage), and triclopyr (Garlon).

Contact

A **contact herbicide** does not move within the plant and kills only the green portion of the plants that it touches. As a result, the spray **solution** must cover the plant to be effective. Because annual weeds do not resprout, many can be controlled by contact herbicides. A contact herbicide causes only temporary suppression of perennial weeds. Examples of effective contact herbicides include diquat (Diquat Herbicide-H/A), glufosinate ammonium (Finale), and oxyfluorfen (Goal).

Preemergence (Soil-Applied)

Some herbicides are applied before the weeds are present (**preemergence**). These herbicides must be absorbed (taken up) by plant roots or shoots. If weeds

Figure 10.9 ▪ *Translocated herbicides moving into perennial roots*

International Society of Arboriculture

are already present at the time of application, soil-applied herbicides are often mixed with a herbicide absorbed by the foliage. For example, Roundup may be combined with Surflan to control existing weeds and to control weeds that will germinate later.

Some herbicides are absorbed by both the foliage and the roots or shoots. Herbicide formulation or method of application can determine whether the herbicide is taken up by the foliage or by the germinating seed. Examples of preemergence herbicides include atrazine, prometon (Pramitol), isoxaben (Gallery), pendimethalin (Pendulum), oryzalin (Surflan), DCPA (Dacthal), and bensulide (Betasan).

Postemergence (Foliar-Applied)

Some herbicides are applied after weeds are present (**postemergence**). These herbicides are absorbed by the plant leaves. Examples of postemergence herbicides include 2,4-D, dichlorprop (Weedone 2,4-DP), glyphosate (Roundup), fluazifop-butyl (Fusilade), sethoxydim (Poast, Vantage), and triclopyr (Garlon).

Persistent

Persistent herbicides remain active in the soil environment for an extended period of time. The length of persistence depends on the application rate, the extent of herbicide breakdown, and the amount of leaching in the soil. Soil pH can also affect herbicide availability and the rate of chemical breakdown. Persistence is an important characteristic when long-term (residual) weed control is desired. This might include the control of certain annual weeds among established perennial plantings or total vegetation control. Persistent herbicides should not be considered in areas where they might hinder or delay desirable plant growth, or when there is a risk of water contamination. Examples of persistent herbicides include pendimethaline (Pendulum), prodiamine (Barricade), and oryzaline (Surflan).

Nonpersistent

Nonpersistent chemicals are relatively short-lived in the environment. They are easily broken down by chemical reactions and soil organisms, or they become so tightly bound to soil particles that they are not available for plant uptake. Examples include 2,4-D, glyphosate (Roundup), and glufosinate ammonium (Finale).

Herbicides and Soil Type

The solid portion of soil consists of inorganic minerals and organic materials. The solid, inorganic portion is composed of mineral particles classified as sand, silt, and clay. The varying proportions of these particles determine the **soil texture** (see Chapter 4, Figure 4.3). Soil texture (sand, silt, and clay) and organic matter greatly influence herbicide movement in the soil. Herbicides are more likely to be adsorbed (tied up) in soils high in clay (heavy soils) or organic matter than in sandy or silty soils (light soils). Sand is coarse and has very little ability to hold water or herbicides. Because herbicides can leach readily in sandy soils, herbicide application rates are usually reduced in soils that are high in sand.

Clay soils contain a great amount of small particles, and water tends to move slowly through them. Also, the small size and high number of particles can tie up a sizable amount of herbicide by **adsorption**. Usually, the rate of application of soil-active herbicides increases with higher clay content. Clays vary in their adsorption characteristics. For example, expanding lattice clays are more adsorptive than nonexpanding clays.

Organic-matter content has the most important influence on the adsorptive characteristic of soil. It is better than clay in its ability to tie up most herbicides and is a site where microbial activity often occurs. Soils with high organic-matter content often need higher rates of soil-active herbicides for effective weed control. Label directions will indicate the need for increasing or decreasing chemical application rates in different soils and for different levels of organic matter.

Potential Herbicide Concerns

Although several types of herbicides are used to control weeds in the landscape, only those with the highest potential to cause off-target injury are discussed here. For a more detailed discussion of herbicide options, consult the *Illinois Urban Pest Management Handbook*, available by calling University of Illinois Information Services at (217) 333-2007.

Growth regulators, photosynthetic inhibitors, and plant-enzyme inhibitors are widely used products. Understanding the mode of action, or how these herbicides affect normal weed growth, will help in selecting products and evaluating their effectiveness. It is also important to recognize injury **symptoms** and to distinguish herbicide damage from other problems such as disease or environmental stress.

Growth-Regulator Herbicides

The following are some common characteristics of growth-regulator herbicides such as 2,4-D, dichlorprop (Weedone 2,4-DP), and triclopyr (Garlon):

- These herbicides act as synthetic hormones, interfering with many plant functions and causing a plant to grow out of control. The plant dies, in part because the distorted growth plugs up the vascular system and prevents plant food from reaching the roots.
- Drift to susceptible plants (redbuds, grapes, flowers, and tomatoes) is a concern because these herbicides cause distorted plant growth, even at very low rates. Grasses are usually tolerant to these herbicides at labeled rates.
- These herbicides are available in liquid forms as water-**soluble** salts (amine and mineral salts) and emulsifiable concentrates (ECs). Amine formulations are less volatile than ester formulations. The formulation influences application rate, method and timing of application, and **spray drift** potential.
- Injury symptoms include leaf cupping and twisting, distorted growth, and callus formation (Figure 10.10, color plate section).

Photosynthetic Inhibitors

The following are some common characteristics of photosynthesis-inhibiting herbicides such as atrazine, bromacil (Hyvar), prometon (Pramitol), and simazine (Princep):

- These herbicides prevent normal photosynthesis in susceptible plants by blocking electron transfer. Sunlight is not converted into stored energy, and plant cell membranes are damaged.
- These herbicides have no direct effect on root growth, though root uptake is a common way for the herbicides to enter the plant. They require sunlight to work.
- These herbicides persist in the soil and can be used to provide long-term residual weed control. The length of persistence depends on the herbicide, application rate, climate, and soil.
- Problems can sometimes arise when tree roots spread into untreated areas.
- Injury symptoms include leaf yellowing and interveinal **chlorosis**, and will appear first on older leaves. Damage might become more pronounced when plants are actively transpiring and taking up water.

Plant-Enzyme Inhibitors, Nonpersistent

The following are some characteristics of the herbicide glyphosate (Roundup), which inhibits a specific plant enzyme necessary for making amino acids:

- It is readily translocated in the plant and inhibits EPSP synthase, an enzyme required for the synthesis of amino acids, proteins, and other plant compounds.
- It is generally a broad-spectrum herbicide that must be absorbed by the leaves. Because it is rapidly bound to soil particles, it has essentially no soil activity at normal use rates.
- It requires a week or more to control annual plants, and longer for perennial weeds.
- Plant injury may occur from spot treatment or spray dripping from the application equipment.
- Injury symptoms are slow to develop, even from concentrated sprays. Symptoms include yellowing and browning, especially on new growth.

Individual Tree Control

Controlling individual unwanted trees in a landscape setting requires special planning. Individual stem control is a mechanical or chemical weeding operation that eliminates undesired trees competing for site resources. Injury to desirable plants is a potential problem with chemical methods. However, because herbicides used for control are placed directly on the tree, the potential

Figure 10.11 ▪ *Ax girdling*

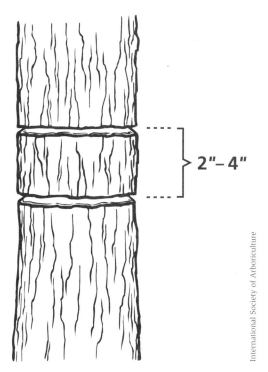

Figure 10.12 ▪ *Chain-saw girdling*

International Society of Arboriculture

Suggested herbicides include glyphosate (Roundup), 2,4-D amine, 2,4-D plus picloram (Tordon RTU), triclopyr (Garlon 3A), and dicamba (Banvel).

Spaced Cuts/Tree Injection

Spaced cuts are made around the stem with an ax, hatchet, or tree injector, and small amounts of herbicide are added to the cuts. This is similar to frilling except that the cuts do not overlap, so labor and herbicide usage are reduced. The cuts, about 1 to 2 inches wide, are spaced around the tree about 1 inch apart, edge to edge. A small amount of herbicide (1 to 2 milliliters) is added to each cut. Specialized equipment is available, but its expense is probably not warranted for small operations. Suggested herbicides include glyphosate (Roundup), 2,4-D amine, 2,4-D plus picloram (Tordon RTU), triclopyr (Garlon 3A), and dicamba (Banvel). The 2,4-D amine is more effective during the growing season than when the trees are **dormant**.

Cut-Stump Herbicides

Cutting down the undesired trees has immediate visual and release effects. Whether done with ax or saw, there is a high probability that the stump will sprout if the cut surface of the stump is not treated with a herbi-

for plant injury results from "backflash" rather than from foliage contact. Backflash refers to herbicide uptake by untreated trees adjacent to the herbicide-treated trees. This uptake can occur through root grafts, herbicide exuding from roots, or herbicide spills.

Girdling

An ax or saw is used to cut through the bark and into the wood around the entire stem of the tree. When done with an ax, this strip is generally 4 inches wide and encircles the stem. The bark in this band is removed from the tree (Figure 10.11). When a chain saw is used, usually two rings 2 to 4 inches apart are cut around the tree (Figure 10.12). This double "chain-saw girdle" is more effective in reducing the likelihood of the **cambium** growing over (bridging) a single narrow kerf of a single girdle.

Frill Treatment

Frill treatment, or frilling, is a variation of girdling. With an ax, hatchet, or similar tool, a series of downward cuts is made around the tree. However, the bark and wood are left as a flap into which a herbicide is added to improve effectiveness (Figure 10.13). Because the cut is very narrow, the addition of herbicides helps prevent the tree from growing over the girdle. It is not uncommon to make the girdle with a chain saw and add the herbicide with a squirt bottle or hand sprayer.

Figure 10.13 ▪ *Herbicide added to frill cut*

cide soon after cutting. Stump sprouts can be important **competition** if allowed to develop too close to landscape trees. The herbicide should be applied immediately after cutting to the cambial area of the stump, where the bark and wood meet. It is not necessary to treat the entire stump. The herbicides effective in frilling are also effective when applied to freshly cut stumps, including glyphosate (Roundup), 2,4-D amine, 2,4-D plus picloram (Tordon RTU), triclopyr (Garlon 3A), and dicamba (Banvel).

Low-Volume Basal Spray

Increasing the **concentration** of herbicide makes it possible to control woody plants while using only one-tenth of the amount of **carrier** (5 gallons of carrier per acre) if a hand sprayer with a very small-diameter spray tip is used. The herbicide mixture contains 20 to 30 percent herbicide in an oil carrier and is applied to the entire lower 12 to 18 inches of the stem in sufficient quantity to wet the surface but not to the point of runoff. Suggested herbicides include triclopyr (Garlon 4), triclopyr plus picloram (Crossbow or Access), and 2,4-D plus dichlorprop (Weedone CB).

Environmental Concerns

Particle Drift

When the wind carries spray droplets beyond the target area, this is called particle drift. Drift occurs at the time of application, and almost any liquid-spray application can result in some drift. Drift can damage other plants in the landscape or contaminate water resources.

You must decide when conditions become too critical to continue spraying. Considerations include characteristics of the product or products being applied, adjacent crops and vegetation, wind speed and direction, and the equipment being used. Controlling drift should be a primary concern when using any herbicide. For a more detailed discussion on reducing pesticide drift, consult the appropriate *Illinois Pesticide Applicator Training Manuals*, available by calling University of Illinois Information Services at (217) 333-2007.

Volatility

Volatilization occurs when the active ingredient changes from a liquid to a vapor during or after application. This phenomenon is important because the herbicide vapor can move a great distance and injure sensitive plants. Volatilization occurs from plant or soil surfaces. The potential increases as air and surface temperatures increase. Vapor losses are reduced when the herbicide becomes attached to plant foliage or bound to soil. Volatility is of concern when ester formulations of herbicides are applied during periods of temperatures greater than 85° to 95° F. Because stone and asphalt surfaces become much hotter than the surrounding air temperature, herbicide applications near these surfaces have higher volatility potential than plant foliage does.

Figure 10.14 ▪ *Effects of herbicide leaching. If a herbicide is leached too deep, weeds can become established at the soil surface, or deep-rooted perennial plants can be injured. The advantage or disadvantage of this occurrence depends on which plant is the weed.*

International Society of Arboriculture

Table 10.1 ▪ *Environmental conditions that affect soil persistence*

Conditions that increase soil persistence	Conditions that decrease soil persistence
Cool temperatures	Warm temperatures
Limited rainfall	Heavy or frequent rainfall
High use rates	Low use rates
Compacted soils	Good soil aeration
Clay soils	Sandy soils

Water Quality

Protecting groundwater and surface water from contamination should be a top priority in both urban and rural areas. Herbicides applied to the landscape should be used carefully to avoid contaminating wells, rivers, streams, and other water resources.

Leaching is the movement of a herbicide with water downward through the soil. Leaching can reduce herbicide effectiveness and also pose a risk to groundwater. The extent of leaching depends on the herbicide, the rate of application, the soil, and the amount of rainfall. Herbicides leach faster in sandy soils than in soils high in clay or organic-matter content.

Because herbicides have different physical and chemical characteristics, the potential for leaching varies considerably. Three characteristics that are often used to estimate pesticide movement in soil are solubility, adsorption, and persistence.

Water solubility ▪ Herbicides with high water solubility tend to leach more readily, whereas insoluble herbicides tend to remain at or near the soil surface. As the herbicide is leached from the soil surface, new weeds might become established above the herbicide (Figure 10.14). Some herbicides with very low water solubility can be used safely around perennial plants because of the deeper perennial root systems.

Adsorption ▪ Adsorption is the degree to which a herbicide binds to soil organic matter and clay. Some herbicides are tightly adsorbed and have little or no soil activity. Although a herbicide might be very water-soluble, it will not leach if it is strongly attracted to soil particles or organic matter.

Persistence ▪ Soil persistence is influenced by many environmental factors, such as those shown in Table 10.1.

Table 10.2 ▪ *Relative persistence of herbicides in warm, moist soil at crop use rates*

Little or no soil activity
    glyphosate (Roundup, Rodeo)

Less than one month
    2,4-D
    dichlorprop (Weedone 2,4-DP)
    fluazifop-butyl (Fusilade)
    sethoxydim (Poast, Vantage)

One to three months
    diuron
    oxyfluorfen (Goal)

Three to six months
    atrazine
    oryzalin (Surflan)
    pendimethalin (Pendulum)
    simazine
    triclopyr (Garlon)

More than six months
    bromacil (Hyvar X)
    picloram (Tordon)
    prometon (Pramitol)

Herbicides vary greatly in their resistance to breakdown in the soil (Table 10.2). Because of the many factors involved, it is not possible to predict the exact time required for a given amount of herbicide degradation to occur. Important environmental factors include soil moisture, rainfall, soil temperature, and soil pH. Soil moisture and temperature are especially important for microbial degradation. Optimal conditions for microbial activity reduce herbicide persistence. Large and frequent rainfalls tend to reduce soil persistence, whereas cold, dry conditions increase soil persistence.

Proper mixing, handling, and disposal of pesticides will reduce the risk of groundwater contamination. Calculate the amount of chemical required for a particular application, and mix only that amount. Always follow the label directions for use, and properly dispose of excess material.

Summary

Successful weed management involves proper site selection and preparation, cultural practices, and mechanical and chemical controls. Regular monitoring of landscapes will help identify and control new weeds before they become established and help prevent existing weeds from increasing. An integrated approach to managing unwanted plants should minimize labor, cost, and environmental hazards.

George Czapar
Extension Educator–IPM
Springfield Extension Center
University of Illinois

Harvey Holt
Professor of Forestry
Department of Forestry
Purdue University

Selected References

Ahrens, W.H. 1994. *Herbicide Handbook*. 6th ed. Champaign, Illinois: Weed Science Society of America.

Dreistadt, S.H. 1994. *Pests of Landscape Trees and Shrubs: An Integrated Pest Management Guide*. Berkeley: University of California, Division of Agriculture and Natural Resources.

Gunsolus, J.L., and W.S. Curran. 1992. *Herbicide Mode of Action and Injury Symptoms*. NCR 377. Urbana: Cooperative Extension Service, University of Illinois.

Montgomery, D., L. Cargill, and J. Barber. 1990. *Roadside Vegetation Management Manual*. E-885. Stillwater: Oklahoma State University Cooperative Extension Service. 34 pp.

Nixon, P., ed. 1996. *Illinois Urban Pest Management Handbook*. Urbana: Cooperative Extension Service, University of Illinois.

North Carolina State University Cooperative Extension Service. 1984. *Herbicide Injury Symptoms and Diagnosis*. Raleigh: North Carolina Agricultural Extension Service, North Carolina State University.

Ross, M.A., and C.A. Lembi. 1985. *Applied Weed Science*. New York: Macmillan Publishing Company.

Stubbendieck, J., G.Y. Friisoe, and M.R. Bolick. 1994. *Weeds of Nebraska and the Great Plains*. Lincoln: Nebraska Department of Agriculture.

University of Illinois Agricultural Experiment Station. 1981. *Weeds of the North Central States*. NCR 281. Urbana: University of Illinois Agricultural Experiment Station.

CHAPTER 11

Cultivating Public Confidence

Jeri Marxman and Rex Bastian

The purpose of this final chapter is to show you how to work with your clientele and with the public at large to communicate the positive effects of Plant Health Care. We will focus on how the PHC approach can improve your knowledge, employee morale, and consumer confidence, as well as expand the services your company offers. We will also discuss how you can work with the public to plan effective control programs that protect—and even enhance—the environment.

With the PHC approach, we tap into a huge reservoir of information to make thoughtful decisions. We involve the client in making decisions about monitoring plant condition and treatment. Rather than simply focusing on the pest, we look at the entire system. The insect, pathogen, tree, soil, water, nutritional status, and root relationships all make up a comprehensive system that must be evaluated. There are many possible courses of action. They may differ in complexity, cost, chances for success, or desirability.

Honesty Is the Best Policy

Let's look at an actual example. I received a frantic call from an existing client who was very concerned about a tree in her back yard. She couldn't remember what kind of tree it was, only that there were "little red things" all over the leaves and she was afraid that it was going to die. I told her that I would stop by and take a look.

When I arrived, she led me to a Redmond linden in the back corner of her yard. The "little red things" turned out to be bladder galls, small bumps on the upper surface of the leaves caused by the activities of tiny mites. After listening to my explanation of what the galls were, she asked if the tree needed spraying. I told her that we could not make the galls "go away" by spraying and that the galls did not threaten the health of her tree. As far as preventing injury, I explained that the tree would need to be treated the following spring as the foliage was emerging. I also explained that, although a treatment might reduce the number of galls, it would not eliminate them. For these reasons, I did not recommend treating the tree.

After listening to my diagnosis, the client was relieved to hear that her tree was not in danger. She agreed with my recommendations and could live with the "bumps," provided they didn't threaten her tree. She was grateful that I was honest with her and did not take advantage of her fears. It was rare for anyone to try to talk her out of spending cash. She told me that she would recommend our company to her friends.

So, what was gained in this exchange? The shallow thinker might say that nothing was gained. In fact, by not spraying the tree, we lost an opportunity to make a few dollars. The tree could have been sprayed right then, and it could have been sprayed once (twice, thrice?!) the following spring.

To me, however, a great deal was gained. We strengthened the feeling of trust between the client and our company. We gained the opportunity for further business through referrals from a pleased client. We eliminated costs associated with chemicals and wasted effort for an unwarranted treatment. Finally, I can feel good about myself by having helped a client save money and by having acted ethically. These long-term benefits far outweigh any short-term gains.

Understanding the big picture leads us to *manage* our landscapes and pests rather than try to *control* and *eradicate* them. Whenever possible, we prescribe management tactics to improve the health and vitality of our landscape materials. The goal of PHC is to prevent pests from getting the upper hand, using management techniques that are environmentally sound. By doing so, we gain a client's confidence and lifelong commitment.

Developing a Client Focus

But why should we worry about what our clients think? There are many reasons. Our services are marketed through meeting the expectations of clients. To sell PHC, it is necessary to build rapport and to explain PHC methods in a way that addresses the concerns of potential clients.

It is evident that we have a way to go to improve our image; arboriculture is changing, and our members are becoming better educated. As leaders in our industry, we have the obligation to provide reason for the public to develop a different image of our industry. By doing so, we all will benefit.

Plant Health Care addresses many consumer concerns. If asked directly, many people will claim to be environmentalists. How much a person is willing to give up to save the environment, however, is highly variable. In our experience, most people will say they would like to see a reduction in pesticide use, which is one of the main goals of PHC practices. PHC requires an understanding of landscape ecology. The interactions between pest and host, as well as soil, water, and environmental conditions, must be considered before logical management options can be developed. If one of our goals is to reduce pesticide use, then we must become more familiar and comfortable with the alternatives to pesticides—biological, cultural, physical, and biorational strategies.

This practice expands our focus beyond traditional tree care. As we learn about trees and natural systems, we will see more opportunities to provide needed services to our clients. Mulching, fertilization, consulting, public speaking, and tree preservation will become more important portions of business.

By supplying these needed services to your clients, your business will grow through referrals. Your clients will generate new business for you. Your clients will be happy to do business with someone who understands the needs and requirements of their trees. Complaints will decline, and the issues associated with dealing with upset clients can be converted into time spent growing the business. Mistakes in tree care will become fewer and fewer, resulting in less risk to the business. Educated and knowledgeable people make fewer mistakes than uneducated people.

Which brings us to the benefits to your work force. By educating your employees as well as yourself, you increase the number of arboricultural ambassadors working with the public. Your clients will continuously meet knowledgeable employees visiting their properties. For many clients, this is a pleasant and unanticipated surprise. Our employees are proud of what they know and are eager to share their knowledge with others. For many employees, this may be the first time they have been offered a chance for career education. The pride they gain from working for a company that invests in their minds instead of their backs will produce gains in safety, quality, productivity, and employee retention. Returns many times the up-front cost of training will be realized.

Understanding Your Clients (and Their Neighbors)

The PHC process begins with people rather than plant diseases or pests. Educating your clients about PHC practice is essential, but the real key is to first understand their expectations and concerns. By listening carefully, your educational effort (and the control system you ultimately recommend) can focus on their objectives.

A 1993 study conducted by Mar-Quest Research examined homeowner perceptions and attitudes. The primary benefits cited for maintaining a healthy lawn included: aesthetics, "curb appeal," resale value, and pride. Less important were environmental effects such as dust control and providing oxygen.

Most respondents were willing to accept pesticides and fertilizers—as long as they were applied properly.

In our experience, it is the people who are neighbors of your clients who have concerns about the safety of the chemicals being used. In other words, even when you have done a good job of explaining your procedures to your client, you'll need to provide information that the client can use if the neighbors are worried or concerned.

Occasionally, whole communities or neighborhoods have become embroiled in controversy regarding community spraying programs. Even when these do not directly involve your company, you might be called into the discussion as a representative of a related industry.

How can you participate in a public debate? Here's a scenario for your consideration:

Recently village workers in Bugsby, Illinois (population 12,578), were spraying for gypsy moths. Observing this, a neighborhood resident became concerned about "widespread use of chemicals in the village" and initiated a campaign to ban all use of chemicals for control of insects, plant diseases, and weeds, including both public and private use. Village board meetings were tied up with testimony and discussion on the issue. Lawn-care companies, arboriculture companies, the garden club, the local environmental association, and individuals all expressed their points of view. The members of the village board were unable to devise a policy that met the needs of their different constituencies.

What led to the controversy? Conflicting goals. The village workers were concerned about stopping a disease that would result in loss of aesthetic value of the trees in the community. The community activist was concerned about effects of the chemicals on children, pets, and other landscape materials. The lawn-care and tree companies were concerned about constraints on their procedures as well as their image in the community. Representatives of the Protect Our Environment association opposed any use of chemicals. Members of the garden club spoke on the value of tree-lined streets to improve the quality of life in Bugsby. The issue became public because the consequences of spraying the trees went beyond the plan to prevent insect damage and resulted in an effort by people in the community to influence the policy.

Why did we find conflicting goals? Because people have different values and are affected differently by the policy. When people are concerned about the effect of a policy on their life, they frequently take the issue public in order to solve the problem through the political process.

Here's a situation where scientific solutions will not work—because we have multiple goals and different values. Also, it's hard to scientifically measure the aesthetic value of tree-lined streets in a community. The inability to measure this value might make it unlikely that those who feel this is the main goal will accept scientific solutions.

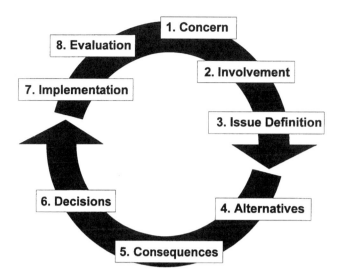

Figure 11.1 ▪ *Phases of issue evolution*

There are no optimal choices in a debate such as this. The public policy process can be an opportunity to bring together these divergent values and objectives to create a policy that satisfies the many viewpoints of the people involved. Through effective use of a "policy development process" (Figure 11.1), people with similar goals will cluster together to increase their political power. Working within the policy development model encourages consensus building in groups with divergent interests to develop policies with which all can be comfortable. Although it might appear cumbersome and time consuming on the front end, this recognition of divergent views early in the process eliminates the potential for groups to stop the policy implementation. Groups involved in creating the policy are not likely to try to "scuttle it."

Getting Involved in the Environmental Debate

First, it is important to acknowledge that your position in the environmental debate will be perceived as biased. Although you certainly are knowledgeable about the science involved in this issue, you also have a financial stake in the outcome. Regardless of how careful you might be to maintain an unbiased approach, people will believe they know what you think based on what they know about your affiliation in the industry. This does not lessen the need for your understanding of the progression of public policy debate.

However, it will be essential that the community locate a neutral facilitator to organize the public discussion. A neutral facilitator will increase the potential for collaborative resolution by including all interested parties in the discussion, facilitating equitable discussion of the alternatives, and developing standards for public discussion of controversial issues.

This issue sprang up when a community resident became concerned about the safety of chemicals being used. The resident contacted neighbors, the media, and organizations that might share this concern to involve them in protesting this practice.

When concern escalates to this level of public discussion, it is helpful to call a public meeting of all interested parties to clarify the parameters of the issue, and, through discussion, agree on what the issue is. A key to developing a workable solution is to include all viewpoints in the discussion. During this stage, the group might decide to conduct a survey to learn citizens' opinions. They might bring in experts from several fields to comment on possible solutions.

It is more than likely that with different viewpoints represented, the issue will become more than "stop spraying." The issue might become, "How can we protect the health and beauty of our community landscape in an environmentally and fiscally sound manner?"

After participants agree on what the issue is, they can begin to identify alternative solutions for dealing with the issue. When alternative solutions are identified, the group should consider the consequences of each alternative. These consequences will affect each point of view differently; open discussion of the consequences encourages participants to look more objectively at the solution of the issue.

If the process has worked effectively, community leaders will adopt a policy that reflects the recommendations of the study committee. The plan is then implemented.

After implementation, the people who are affected by the new policy should be involved, formally or informally, in deciding whether the new policy works. This can result in suggestions for change that cause the process to start over again.

The Importance of Effective Communication

Another important consideration in the deliberation process is the development of a plan to communicate with citizens about the issue and the processes underway to develop a policy.

A communication plan contains some of the same steps as the policy process. First comes a needs assessment (emergence stage). This step identifies the stakeholders who have an interest in the outcome. The second step is to ensure that stakeholders perceive the study group as a credible source of information and action on the policy formation. The third step is to establish communication objectives: What do you want to accomplish as a result of your communication efforts?

Next, you should establish your communication process. Which techniques will you use? Meetings? Newspaper articles? A speakers' bureau? Radio? A community newsletter? Who will be responsible for coordinating the different media? What resources are available to implement the communication plan? How (and at what point) will you involve the public in the plan?

Finally, conduct ongoing evaluation of your communication efforts to determine whether you are meeting your communication objectives.

These steps will be useful to you not only in developing communication strategies during a public controversy but also when you are simply trying to get the message of PHC disseminated in a community. Remember, your communication with the public will be most effective when it is an ongoing process with clearly defined objectives and a system for monitoring its effectiveness.

Hints for Working with the Media

Here are some guidelines developed by the chemical industry's public relations staff that might be helpful:

- Be prepared; review beforehand the questions you think the media will ask.
- Be newsworthy; provide information the media can use.
- Plan the points you want to make.
- Use everyday language, not jargon or technical terminology.
- You're always on the record. There is no legal obligation for the reporter to keep anything off the record, although some will.
- Do not use "no comment." Instead, say, "I don't have enough information to properly answer that question."
- Don't play into traps. If a question includes a hostile or inaccurate remark, say something like, "First, let me correct a misconception that was part of your question."
- Don't argue or get mad.
- Don't speculate. Trying to respond to hypothetical questions can create problems.
- If you don't know the answer to a question, admit it. Offer to get the answer later, if you can.
- Stay on track, and help the interviewer stay on track too.

- Don't assign blame or take potshots at other groups.
- Be available to answer follow-up questions.
- Don't lie or stretch the truth.

Jeri Marxman
Public Policy Specialist
Cooperative Extension Service
University of Illinois

Rex Bastian
Director of Technical Services
Hendricksen the Care of Trees
Wheeling, Illinois

References and Suggested Readings

Dale, D. 1993. *Public Issues Education: A Handbook.* Madison: University of Wisconsin-Extension.

Edelman, M.A., and B.L. Flinchbaugh. 1991. *How to Handle Controversial Issues: Principles of Public Policy Education.* NCR Extension Publication 390. Ames: Iowa State University.

Harwood, R.C., M.J. Perry, and W.G. Schmitt. 1993. *Meaningful Chaos: How People Form Relationships with Public Concerns.* Prepared for the Kettering Foundation. Dayton, Ohio: The Harwood Group.

National Public Policy Education Committee, Cooperative Extension. 1994. *Increasing Competence in Resolving Public Issues.* Farm Foundation, Chicago, IL.

Stevens, G.L. 1992. *How to Impact Public Policy for Families.* Lincoln: University of Nebraska.

Wadley, T.L., ed. 1995. *Plant Health Care Management System Manual.* 2d ed. Savoy, Illinois: International Society of Arboriculture.

Young, A., and V. House. 1987. *Working with Your Publics, Module 6, Public Policy Education.* Raleigh, North Carolina: North Carolina State University.

Appendix A

University-Related Plant Disease and Soil Testing Laboratories in the United States and Canada

This list was compiled in 1996 by Gail Ruhl, Senior Plant Diagnostician, Department of Botany and Plant Pathology, Purdue University.

Note: Contact your local County Extension Office for specific procedures on how to submit soil samples to the diagnostic lab.

State/Province[1]	Department or Institution Performing Soil Test	Department or Institution Performing Plant Problem Diagnosis
Alabama	Soil Testing Laboratory Auburn University 118 Funchess Hall Auburn, AL 36849-5624 Phone: (334) 844-3958 Fax: (334) 844-4001 Contact: Hamilton Bryant E-mail: hhbryant@acenet.auburn.edu *or* Phone: (334) 844-5489 Fax: (334) 844-3945 Contact: Charles Mitchell E-mail: cmitchel@ag.auburn.edu	Plant Disease Clinic 102 Extension Hall Department of Plant Pathology Auburn University Auburn, AL 36849-5624 Phone: (334) 844-5508, 5507 Fax: (334) 844-4072 Contact: Jacqueline Mullen E-mail: jmullen@acenet.auburn.edu
Alaska	Soil Testing Laboratory Agricultural Experiment Station University of Alaska 533 E. Firewood Palmer, AK 99645	Department of Plant Pathology Attn: Jenifer McBeath University of Alaska Agriculture Forestry Experiment Station Fairbanks, AK 99775-0080

[1]Canadian provinces are listed at the end, following Wyoming.

State/Province	*Department or Institution Performing Soil Test*	*Department or Institution Performing Plant Problem Diagnosis*
Arizona	Soil, Water, and Plant Tissue Testing Laboratory Department of Soils, Water and Engineering Shantz (#38), Room 431 University of Arizona Tucson, AZ 85721 Phone: (602) 621-9703 Fax: (602) 621-3516	Information not available.
Arkansas	Soil Testing and Research Laboratory University of Arkansas P.O. Drawer 767 Marianna, AR 72360	Plant Disease Clinic Lonoke Agricultural Center P.O. Drawer D; Hwy 70 East Lonoke, AR 72086 Phone: (501) 676-3124 Fax: (501) 676-7847 Contact: Stephen Vann E-mail: fungus@uaexsun.uaex.arknet.edu
California	No soil testing service is offered by a public agency.	Contact your local County Farm Advisor or Extension Specialist at a university near you.
Colorado	Soil, Water, and Plant Testing Laboratory A319 NESB Colorado State University Fort Collins, CO 80523	Plant Diagnostic Clinic Jefferson County Extension 15200 W. 6th Avenue Golden, CO 80401
Connecticut	Soil Testing Laboratory Plant Science Department University of Connecticut 2019 Hillside Road, U-102 Storrs, CT 06268 Phone: (860) 486-4274 Fax: (860) 486-4562 Contact: Erika Kares E-mail: ekares@canr1.cag.uconn.edu	Consumer Horticultural Center University of Connecticut Storrs, CT 06269-4087 Phone: (860) 486-3437 Fax: (860) 486-0682 Contact: Edmond Marrotte E-mail: emarrott@canr1.cag.uconn.edu *or* Connecticut Ag. Experiment Station Huntington Ave. East Haven, CT 06512
Delaware	Soil Testing Laboratory University of Delaware Department of Plant and Soil Science Newark, DE 19711	Extension Plant Pathologist University of Delaware 136 Townsend Hall Newark, DE 19717-1303
Florida	Soil Testing Laboratory University of Florida Wallace Building P. O. Box 110740 Gainesville, FL 32611-0740 Phone: (352) 392-1950 Fax: (352) 392-1960	Nematode Assay Laboratory Entomology and Nematology Department Building 8, Mowry Road University of Florida Gainesville, FL 32611 Phone: (352) 392-1994 Fax: (352) 392-3438 Contact: Frank Woods E-mail: few@gnv.ifas.ufl.edu

State/Province	Department or Institution Performing Soil Test	Department or Institution Performing Plant Problem Diagnosis
Florida (continued)		Florida Extension Plant Disease Clinic Building 8, Mowry Road University of Florida Gainesville, FL 32611 Phone: (352) 392-1795 Fax: (352) 392-3438 Contact: G.W. Simone/R. E. Cullen E-mail: extppclinic@gnv.ifas.ufl.edu *Three Regional State Labs* 1. Florida Extension Plant Disease Clinic North Florida Research Center Route 3, Box 4370 Quincy, FL 32351 Phone: (904) 627-9236 Contact: D. Chellami/H. Dantars E-mail: doc@gnv.ifas.ufl.edu 2. Florida Extension Plant Disease Clinic SW Florida Research & Education Center P.O. Drawer 5127 Immokalee, FL 33934 Phone: (941) 751-7636 Fax: (941) 751-7639 Contact: R. McGovern/R. Urs E-mail: rjm@gnv.ifas.ufl.edu 3. Florida Extension Plant Disease Clinic Tropical Research and Education Center 18905 SW 280th Street Homestead, FL 33032-3314 Phone: (305) 246-7000 Contact: R. Maxmillan/Wm. Graves E-mail: rtmcm@gvn.ifas.ufl.edu
Georgia	Soil Testing and Plant Analysis Laboratory University of Georgia 2400 College Station Road Athens, GA 30602	Extension Plant Disease Clinic 4-Towers Building University of Georgia Athens, GA 30602
Hawaii	Soil Testing Laboratory Agricultural Diagnostic Service Center 1910 East-West Road Sherman Hall 134 Honolulu, HI 96822	Plant Disease Clinic Agricultural Diagnostic Service Center 1910 East-West Road Sherman Hall 112 Honolulu, HI 96822
Idaho	Plant Pathology/PSES University of Idaho Moscow, ID 83843 Phone: (208) 885-6650 Fax: (208) 885-7760 Contact: Maury Wiese E-mail: mwiese@uidaho.edu	Extension Plant Pathologist University of Idaho Research and Extension Center 3793 N., 3600 E. Kimberly, ID 83341 Phone: (208) 423-6603 Fax: (208) 423-6555 Contact: Bob Forster E-mail: forster@kimberly.uidaho.edu

State/Province	Department or Institution Performing Soil Test	Department or Institution Performing Plant Problem Diagnosis
Idaho (continued)		Extension Plant Pathologist Research and Extension Center Parma, ID 83660
Illinois	No soil testing service is offered by a public agency.	(May–September) Plant Clinic 1401 W. St. Mary's Road Urbana, IL 61801 Phone: (217) 333-0519

(October–March) N-533 Turner Hall 1102 S. Goodwin Avenue University of Illinois Urbana, IL 61801 Phone: (217) 333-2478 Fax: (217) 244-1230 E-mail: PatakyN@IDEA.AG.UIUC.EDU (winter) |
Indiana	No soil testing service is offered to homeowners by a public agency. Contact the Plant and Pest Diagnostic Laboratory for a partial list of private soil testing labs.	Plant and Pest Diagnostic Laboratory Department of Botany and Plant Pathology 1155 Lilly Hall Purdue University West Lafayette, IN 47907
Iowa	Soil Testing Laboratory G501 Agronomy Iowa State University Ames, IA 50011 Phone: (515) 294-3076	Plant Disease Clinic Department of Plant Pathology 323 Bessey Hall Iowa State University Ames, IA 50011 Phone: (515) 294-0581 Fax: (515) 294-9420 Contact: Paula Flynn E-mail: x1flynn@exnet.iastate.edu
Kansas	Soil Testing Laboratory Agronomy Department Kansas State University Manhattan, KS 66506 Phone: (913) 532-7897 Fax: (913) 532-6315 Contact: Kathy Lowe E-mail: klowe@ksuvm.ksu.edu	Plant Disease Diagnostic Laboratory Department of Plant Pathology Throckmorton Hall Kansas State University Manhattan, KS 66506-5502
Kentucky	Soil Testing Laboratory 103 Regulatory Services Building University of Kentucky Lexington, KY 40546 Phone: (606) 257-7355 Fax: (606) 257-7351 Contact: Vern Case E-mail: vcase@ca.uky.edu	*For western Kentucky* Plant Disease Diagnostic Laboratory University of Kentucky Research and Education Center P.O. Box 469 Hwy 91 South Princeton, KY 42445 Phone: (502) 365-7541 Fax: (502) 365-2667 Contact: Paul Bachi E-mail: pbachi@ca.uky.edu

State/Province	Department or Institution Performing Soil Test	Department or Institution Performing Plant Problem Diagnosis
Kentucky (continued)		*For central and eastern Kentucky* Plant Disease Diagnostic Laboratory Department of Plant Pathology University of Kentucky Lexington, KY 40546-0091
Louisiana	Soil Testing Laboratory Department of Agronomy Louisiana State University Baton Rouge, LA 70803 Phone: (504) 388-1219 Fax: (504) 388-1403 Contact: Rodney Henderson E-mail: henderson@lanmail.lsu.edu	Plant Disease Diagnostic Clinic 220 H.D. Wilson Building Louisiana State University Baton Rouge, LA 70803-1900 Phone: (504) 388-6195 Fax: (504) 388-2478 Contact: Charles Overstreet E-mail: coverst@lsuvm.sncc.lsu.edu *or* Clayton Hollier E-mail: chollie@lsuvm.sncc.lsu.edu
Maine	Maine Soil Testing Service 5722 Deering Hall University of Maine Orono, ME 04469-5722 Phone: (207) 581-2945 Fax: (207) 581-2999 Contact: Bruce Hoskins E-mail: RPT910@maine.maine.edu	Pest Management Office Cooperative Extension University of Maine 491 College Avenue Orono, ME 04473-1295 Phone: (207) 581-3880 Fax: (207) 581-3881 Contact: Bruce Watt E-mail: jdill@umce.umext.maine.edu
Maryland	Soil Testing Laboratory Agronomy Department The University of Maryland College Park, MD 20742 Phone: (301) 405-1349 Fax: (301) 314-9049 E-mail: jb97@umail.umd.edu	Plant Diagnostic Laboratory Department of Plant Biology The University of Maryland College Park, MD 20742 Phone: (301) 314-1611 Fax: (301) 314-9082 Contact: Ethel Dutky E-mail: ed16@umail.umd.edu
Massachusetts	Soil Testing West Experiment Station University of Massachusetts Amherst, MA 01003	No disease diagnostic service is offered by a public agency to homeowners. Commercial samples are handled by individual Extension specialists at the University.
Michigan	MSU Soil & Plant Nutrient Laboratory A81 Plant & Soil Sciences East Lansing, MI 48824 Phone: (517) 355-0218 Fax: (517) 355-1732 Contact: Donna Ellis E-mail: ELLIS%staff%cssdept@banyan.msu.edu	Plant Diagnostic Clinic Department of Botany and Plant Pathology Michigan State University East Lansing, MI 48824-1312

State/Province	Department or Institution Performing Soil Test	Department or Institution Performing Plant Problem Diagnosis
Minnesota	Research & Soil Testing Laboratories University of Minnesota 135 Crops Research Bldg. 1903 Hendon Avenue St. Paul, MN 55108 Phone: (2) 625-3101 Fax: (612) 624-3420 E-mail: kuhlx001@maroon.tc.umn.edu	*For homeowners* Dial U Clinic 145 Alderman Hall 1970 Folweel Avenue University of Minnesota St. Paul, MN 55108 *For commercial growers* Plant Disease Clinic Department of Plant Pathology 495 Borlaug Hall, 1991 Upper Buford Circle University of Minnesota St. Paul, MN 55108 Phone: (612) 625-1275 Fax: (612) 625-9728 Contact: Sandra Gould E-mail: sandyg@puccini.crl.umn.edu
Mississippi	Soil Testing Laboratory Cooperative Extension Service Mississippi State University Mississippi State, MS 39762	Plant Pathology Laboratory Room 9, Bost Extension Center Box 9655 Mississippi Cooperative Extension Service Mississippi State, MS 39762 Phone: (601) 325-2146 Fax: (601) 325-8407 Contact: Mukund Patel E-mail: pplab@mces.msstate.edu
Missouri	Soil Testing Laboratory Room 23, Mumford Hall University of Missouri Columbia, MO 65211 Phone: (314) 882-3250 Fax: (314) 882-1467 Contact: Manjula Nathan E-mail: nathanm@ext.missouri.edu	Plant Disease Identification Room 45 Ag. Building University of Missouri Columbia, MO 65211 Fax: (314) 884-5405 Contact: Barb Corwin E-mail: corwinb@ext.missouri.edu
Montana	No soil testing service is offered by a public agency.	Plant Disease Clinic 525 Leon Johnson Hall Department of Plant Pathology Montana State University Bozeman, MT 59717
Nebraska	Soil Testing Laboratory Department of Agronomy University of Nebraska Lincoln, NE 68583	Plant and Pest Diagnostic Clinic Department of Plant Pathology 448 Plant Sciences University of Nebraska Lincoln, NE 68583-0722
Nevada	No soil testing service is offered by a public agency.	Jeff Knight, Entomologist Kathy Kosta, Plant Pathologist Bureau of Plant Industry Division of Agriculture 350 Capital Hill Avenue Reno, NV 89502

State/Province	Department or Institution Performing Soil Test	Department or Institution Performing Plant Problem Diagnosis
New Hampshire	Analytical Services Laboratory Nesmith Hall University of New Hampshire Durham, NH 03824 Phone: (603) 862-3212 Fax: (603) 862-4757 Contact: Stuart Blanchard E-mail: stuartb@christa.unh.edu	Plant Diagnostic Laboratory 241 Spaulding Hall Plant Biology Department University of New Hampshire Durham, NH 03824 Phone: (603) 862-3841 Fax: (603) 862-4757 Contact: Cheryl Smith E-mail: cheryl.smith@unh.edu
New Jersey	Soil Testing Laboratory Department of Environmental Sciences Rutgers University P.O. Box 902 Milltown, NJ 08850 Phone: (908) 932-9292 or 9295 Fax: (908) 932-8644 Contact: Stephanie Murphy E-mail: smurphy@aesop.rutgers.edu	Plant Diagnostic Laboratory Rutgers University P.O. Box 550 Milltown, NJ 08850 Phone: (908) 932-9140 Fax: (908) 932-7070 Contact: Rich Buckley E-mail: clinic@aesop.rutgers.edu
New Mexico	SWAT Laboratory Agronomy and Horticulture New Mexico State University Box 30003 Las Cruces, NM 88003 Phone: (505) 646-4422 Fax: (505) 646-6041 Contact: Andrew Bristol E-mail: abristol@nmsu.edu	Extension Plant Pathologist Box 3AE; Plant Sciences Cooperative Extension Service New Mexico State University Las Cruces, NM 88003
New York	CNA Labs SCAS Department Cornell University Ithaca, NY 14853-1901 Phone: (607) 255-1722 Contact: W. Shaw Reid E-mail: wsr1@cornell.edu	*Homeowner and commercial* Insect and Plant Disease Diagnostic Laboratory Department of Plant Pathology 334 Plant Science Building Cornell University Ithaca, NY 14853 Phone: (607) 255-7850 Fax: (607) 255-0939 Contact: Diane Karasevicz E-mail: diane_karasevicz@cce.cornell.edu *Commercial ornamental samples only* Long Island Horticultural Research Laboratory Cornell University 39 Sound Ave. Riverhead, NY 11901 Phone: (516) 727-3595 Fax: (516) 727-3611

State/Province	Department or Institution Performing Soil Test	Department or Institution Performing Plant Problem Diagnosis
North Carolina	Soil Testing Laboratory Agronomic Division North Carolina Department of Agriculture 4300 Reedy Creek Road Raleigh, NC 27611 Phone: (919) 733-2656, 2657, 2655 Fax: (919) 733-2837 Contact: Ray Tucker E-mail: Ray_Tucker@NCDAmail.agr.state.nc.us	Plant Disease and Insect Clinic Box 7616 Room 1104 Williams Hall North Carolina State University Raleigh, NC 27695-7616 Phone: (919) 515-3619 or (919) 515-3825 Fax: (919) 515-3670 Contact: Tom Creswell E-mail: Tom_Creswell@ncsu.edu
North Dakota	Soil Testing Laboratory Soil Science Department North Dakota State University Fargo, ND 58105	Plant Diagnostic Clinic Department of Plant Pathology Box 5012 North Dakota State University Fargo, ND 58105
Ohio	Information not available.	Plant and Pest Diagnostic Clinic Department of Plant Pathology 2021 Coffey Road The Ohio State University Columbus, OH 43210 Phone: (614) 292-5006 Fax: (614) 292-7162 Contact: Nancy Taylor E-mail: ppdc@agvax2.ag.ohio-state.edu
Oklahoma	SWFAL Agronomy Department 048 Ag. Hall Oklahoma State University Stillwater, OK 74078 Phone: (405) 744-6630 Fax: (405) 744-5269	Plant Disease Diagnostic Laboratory Department of Plant Pathology 110 Noble Research Center Oklahoma State University Stillwater, OK 74078 Phone: (405) 744-9961 Fax: (405) 744-7373 Contact: Betsy Hudgins E-mail: hudgins@vm1.ucc.okstate.edu
Oregon	Central Analytical Laboratory Oregon State University 3017 ALS Building Corvallis, OR 97331 Phone: (503) 737-5716 Fax: (503) 737-5725 Contact: Dean Hanson E-mail: hansond@css.orst.edu	Plant Disease Clinic Extension Plant Pathology Cordley Hall 1089 Oregon State University Corvallis, OR 97331-2903 Phone: (503) 737-3472 Fax: (503) 737-2412 Contact: Melodie Putnam E-mail: putnamm@bcc.orst.edu Plant Pathology Laboratory H.A.R.E.C. Oregon State University P.O. Box 105 Hermiston, OR 97838 Phone: (541) 567-8321 Fax: (541) 567-2240 Contact: Philip Hamm E-mail: EXTPPLAB@EPPL.OES.ORST.EDU

State/Province	*Department or Institution Performing Soil Test*	*Department or Institution Performing Plant Problem Diagnosis*
Pennsylvania	Agricultural Analytical Service Laboratory College of Agricultural Sciences Pennsylvania State University University Park, PA 16802 Phone: (814) 863-0841 Fax: (814) 863-4540 Contact: Ann Wolf E-mail: amw2@psu.edu	Plant Disease Clinic 220 Buckhout Laboratory Pennsylvania State University University Park, PA 16802 Phone: (814) 865-2204 Fax: (814) 863-7217 Contact: John Peplinski E-mail: jdp3@psu.edu
Rhode Island	Soil Testing Laboratory University of Rhode Island Kingston, RI 02881	Homeowner Clinic Cooperative Extension Education Center University of Rhode Island East Alumni Avenue Kingston, RI 02881-0804 Phone: (401) 792-2900 Fax: (401) 792-2259 Contact: Marcia Morreira E-mail: rsherry@uriacc.uri.edu For commercial samples, contact Extension specialists at the University.
South Carolina	Soil Testing Laboratory Agricultural Service Laboratory Clemson University Clemson, SC 29634 Phone: (803) 656-2300 Fax: (803) 656-2069 Contact: Kathy Moore E-mail: kmr@mail.clemson.edu	Plant Problem Clinic Cherry Road Clemson University Clemson, SC 29634-0377 Phone: (803) 656-3125 Fax: (803) 656-2069 Contact: James Blake E-mail: ppclnc@clemson.edu *or* blake@clemson.edu
South Dakota	Soil Testing Laboratory Plant Science Department Box 2207-A, Ag Hall 06 South Dakota State University Brookings, SD 57007-1096 Phone: (605) 688-4766 Fax: (605) 688-4602	Plant Disease Clinic Department of Plant Science South Dakota State University Box 2109 Brookings, SD 57007
Tennessee	Soil and Forage Testing Laboratory University of Tennessee P.O. Box 110019 Nashville, TN 37222-0019	Plant and Pest Diagnostic Center University of Tennessee P.O. Box 110019 Nashville, TN 37222-0019
Texas	Soil Testing Laboratory Room 220 Soil and Crop Sciences Texas A&M University College Station, TX 77843	Texas Plant Disease Diagnostic Laboratory Room 101, L.F. Peterson Building Texas A&M University College Station, TX 77843-2132 Phone: (409) 845-8033 Fax: (409) 845-6499 Contact: Larry Barnes E-mail: Barnes@ppserver.tamu.edu

State/Province	*Department or Institution Performing Soil Test*	*Department or Institution Performing Plant Problem Diagnosis*
Utah	Soil Testing Laboratory Department of Plant Soils and Biometeorology Ag Science Building Utah State University Logan, UT 84322-4830 Phone: (801) 797-2217 Fax: (801) 797-2117 Contact: Jan Kotuby-Amacher E-mail: Jkotuby@mendel.usu.edu	Plant Pest Diagnostic Laboratory Department of Biology Utah State University Logan, UT 84322-5305 Phone: (801) 797-2435 Fax: (801) 797-1575 Contact: Karen Flint E-mail: KarenF@ext.usu.edu
Vermont	Soil Testing Laboratory Department of Plant and Soil Science University of Vermont Hills Building Burlington, VT 05405-0086 Phone: (802) 656-0493	Plant Diagnostic Clinic Department of Plant and Soil Science University of Vermont Hills Building Burlington, VT 05405-0086 Fax: (802) 656-4656 Contact: Ann Hazelrigg E-mail: ahazelrigg@clover.uvm.edu
Virginia	Virginia Tech Soil Testing Lab 145 Smyth Hall P.O. Box 10664 Blacksburg, VA 24062-0664 Phone: (540) 231-9807 or (540) 231-6893 Fax: (540) 231-3431 Contact: Steve Heckendorn E-mail: soiltest@vtvl1.cc.vt.edu *or* shckndrn@vt.edu	Plant Disease Clinic Department of Plant Pathology, Physiology and Weed Science VPI and SU Blacksburg, VA 24061
Washington	No public agency provides soil testing. Contact your local County Extension Agent for a list of local laboratories.	*For eastern Washington* Plant Diagnostic Clinic WSU-Prosser-IAREC Rt. 2 Box 2953-A Prosser, WA 99350-9687 *For western Washington* Plant Diagnostic Clinic WSU-Puyallup Research and Extension Center 7612 Pioneer Way East Puyallup, WA 98371-4998
West Virginia	Soil Testing Laboratory 1090 Ag Sciences Building West Virginia University Morgantown, WV 26506 Phone: (304) 293-6023 Contact: Larry Bennett	Plant Disease Diagnostic Clinic 401 Brooks Hall Downtown Campus West Virginia University Morgantown, WV 26506
Wisconsin	Soil and Plant Analysis Laboratory University of Wisconsin 511 Mineral Pt. Road Madison, WI 53705	Plant Pathogen Detection Clinic Department of Plant Pathology 1630 Linden Drive University of Wisconsin Madison, WI 53706

State/Province	Department or Institution Performing Soil Test	Department or Institution Performing Plant Problem Diagnosis
Wyoming	Soil Testing Laboratory Plant Science Department University of Wyoming Box 3354 Laramie, WY 82071	Plant Disease Clinic Department of Plant, Soil and Insect Sciences University of Wyoming P.O. Box 3354 Laramie, WY 82071-3354
Alberta	Soil and Crop Diagnostic Center University of Alberta #905 OS Longman Building 6909 116 Street Edmonton, Alberta T6H 4P2	Brooks Diagnostics Ltd.[2] Plant Diagnostic Laboratory c/o Crop Diversification Centre–South Brooks, Alberta T1R 1E6 Regional Crop Laboratory Alberta Agriculture Box 10 Olds, Alberta T0M 1P0 Regional Crop Laboratory Alberta Agriculture Provincial Building Box 7777 Fairview, Alberta T0H 1L0 Alberta Environmental Centre Bag 4000 Vegreville, Alberta T0B 4L0
British Columbia	Soil Testing Unit British Columbia Department of Agriculture 1873 Spall Road Kelowna, British Columbia VIY 4R2	Plant Diagnostic Laboratory British Columbia Ministry of Agriculture and Fisheries Abbotsford Agriculture Centre 1767 Angus Campbell Road Abbotsford, British Columbia V3G 2M3
Manitoba	Department of Soil Science University of Manitoba Winnipeg, Manitoba R3T 2N2	Crop Diagnostic Centre 201-545 University Crescent Agricultural Service Complex Winnipeg, Manitoba R3T 5S6
New Brunswick	Agricultural Soils Laboratory New Brunswick Department of Agriculture P.O. Box 6000 Fredericton, New Brunswick E3B 5H1	Pest Diagnostic Laboratory New Brunswick Department of Agriculture and Rural Development P.O. Box 6000 Fredericton, New Brunswick E3B 5H1
Nova Scotia	Soil and Crops Branch Nova Scotia Agricultural College Truro, Nova Scotia B2N 5E3	Plant Diagnostic Laboratory Nova Scotia Department of Agriculture and Marketing Kentville Research Station Kentville, Nova Scotia B4N 1J5 Plant Diagnostic Laboratory Department of Biology Nova Scotia Agricultural College Box 550 Truro, Nova Scotia B2N 5E3 Fax: (902) 895-4547

[2]Brooks Diagnostics Ltd. (a private laboratory) has taken over the testing for Alberta Special Crops and Horticultural Research Center.

State/Province	Department or Institution Performing Soil Test	Department or Institution Performing Plant Problem Diagnosis
Ontario	No provincial soil testing service is offered.	Pest Diagnostic Clinic Agricultural and Food Service Centre P.O. Box 3650 95 Stone Road W., Zone 2 Guelph, Ontario N1H 8J7
Prince Edward Island	Soil and Feed Testing Laboratory Department of Agriculture Box 1600 Charlottetown, Prince Edward Island C1A 7N3	PEIDAFF Plant Health Services Box 1600 Charlottetown, Prince Edward Island C1A 7N3 Phone: (902) 368-5600 Fax: (902) 368-5661 E-mail: mmpeters@gov.pe.ca
Quebec	Canadian Industries Limited Soil Laboratory Beloeil Works McMasterville, Quebec J3G 4S7	Laboratoire de diagnostic Le Service de Recherche en Phytotechnie de Quebec 2700, rue Einstein Ste.-Foy, Quebec G1P 3W8

Appendix B

Tree Selection Guidelines for the Midwestern United States

This information was compiled by David Williams, Department of Natural Resources and Environmental Sciences, University of Illinois at Urbana–Champaign.

Species	Hardiness Zone	Origin
Trees For Acid Soils		
Acer buergeranum (trident maple)	5b–8a	Japan
Acer campestre (hedge maple)	5a–8b	Western Asia, Europe
Acer freemanii cultivars (Freeman hybrid maples)	3b–9a	Hybrid
Acer ginnala (amur maple)	3a–6b	China, Japan, Manchuria
Acer griseum (paperbark maple)	5a–7b	China
Acer miyabei (miyabe maple)	5a–7b	Japan
Acer palmatum (Japanese maple)	5b–9a	Japan, Korea
Acer rubrum cultivars (red maple)	3b–9a	Eastern North America
Acer saccharum (sugar maple)	3–8	Southeastern Canada, eastern U.S.
Acer tataricum (Tatarian maple)	3b–6b	Western Asia, southeastern Europe, Japan
Acer triflorum (three–flowered maple)	5a–7a	China, Korea
*Franklinia alatamaha** (Franklin tree)	6b–7b	Southeastern U.S.
Fraxinus americana cultivars (white ash)	3–9	Eastern North America
Fraxinus pennsylvanicum cultivars (green ash)	3–9	Eastern North America
Fraxinus quadrangulata (blue ash)	4a–8a	Eastern U.S.
*Ilex opaca** (American holly)	6b–9a	Eastern U.S.
*Nyssa sylvatica** (black gum)	5a–9a	Eastern North America
*Oxydendrum arboreum** (sourwood)	5b–9a	Eastern and southeastern U.S.
Picea abies (Norway spruce)	3a–8a	Northern and central Europe
Picea omorika (Siberian spruce)	4b–8a	Southeastern Europe
Picea orientalis (Oriental spruce)	5b–8a	Northern and central Europe
Picea pungens (Colorado spruce)	3a–7b	Northern Mexico, Rocky Mountains, western U.S.
Pinus cembra (Swiss stone pine)	3b–6b	Southern Asia, central Europe

Species	Hardiness Zone	Origin
Pinus flexilis (limber pine)	4b–7b	Mountains of western Canada and U.S.
Pinus ponderosa (ponderosa pine)	3b–8a	Western U.S. and adjacent Canada and Mexico
Pinus resinosa (red pine)	3a–6b	Canada and north-central and northeastern U.S.
Pinus rigida (pitch pine)	4b–7a	East-central U.S. from Maine to Appalachia
Pinus strobus (white pine)	3a–9a	Northeastern and central North America
Pinus sylvestris (Scots pine)	3a–8b	Europe through Siberia
Quercus alba (white oak)	4a–9a	Eastern U.S.
Quercus bicolor (swamp white oak)	4a–8b	Eastern North America
*Quercus coccinea** (scarlet oak)	5a–9a	Eastern North America
*Quercus palustris** (pin oak)	4b–9a	Eastern U.S.
*Quercus phellos** (willow oak)	6a–9a	Mid-Atlantic coast to southern and western U.S.
Quercus prinus (chestnut oak)	5a–9a	Eastern U.S.
Quercus rubra (red oak)	3b–9a	Eastern North America
Quercus shumardii (Shumard oak)	6a–9a	Eastern U.S.

*For these trees, acid soils are a requirement, not a preference.

Trees For Alkaline Soils

Species	Hardiness Zone	Origin
Aesculus glabra (Ohio buckeye)	3a–8b	Central U.S. south to Texas
Alnus glutinosa (European alder)	4a–8b	Northern Africa, western Asia, Europe
Alnus incana (speckled alder)	3a–7b	Europe
Catalpa bignoniodes (southern catalpa)	5a–9a	Southeastern U.S.
Catalpa speciosa (northern catalpa)	4a–9a	Southeastern U.S.
Cercis canadensis (eastern redbud)	5b–9a	Eastern U.S.
Cladrastis lutea (American yellowwood)	4b–8a	Southeastern U.S.
Fraxinus americana (white ash)	4a–9a	Eastern North America
Fraxinus excelsior (European ash)	4b–8b	Europe
Fraxinus pennsylvanicum (green ash)	2a–9a	Eastern North America
Fraxinus quadrangulata (blue ash)	4a–8a	Eastern U.S.
Gleditsia triacanthos var. *inermis* cultivars (thornless honey locust)	4b–9a	Eastern and midwestern U.S.
Gymnocladus dioicus (Kentucky coffee-tree)	4a–7b	Eastern and midwestern U.S.
Juglans cinerea (butternut)	3b–7a	Eastern North America
Juniperus chinensis (Chinese juniper)	4a–9a	China, Japan
Juniperus scopulorum (Rocky Mountain juniper)	3b–6b	Rocky Mountains and west
Juniperus virginiana (eastern red cedar)	3b–9a	Eastern and central U.S.
Thuja occidentalis (American arborvitae)	3a–7b	Eastern North America

Trees For Wet Sites

Species	Hardiness Zone	Origin
Acer freemanii cultivars (Freeman hybrid maples)	3b–9a	Hybrid
Acer rubrum cultivars (red maple)	3b–9a	Eastern North America
Alnus species (alders)	4a–8b	Various
Betula nigra (river birch)	4a–9a	Eastern U.S.
Calocedrus decurrens (California incense cedar)	6b–9a	Western U.S.
Diospyros virginiana (common persimmon)	5b–9a	Southeastern and south-central U.S.
Ilex opaca (American holly)	6b–9a	Eastern U.S.
Liquidambar styraciflua (American sweet gum)	5b–9a	Eastern U.S.
Magnolia virginiana (sweetbay magnolia)	5b–9a	Eastern U.S.
Nyssa sylvatica (black gum)	5a–9a	Eastern North America
Platanus occidentalis (sycamore)	4b–9a	Eastern North America
Populus deltoides (eastern cottonwood)	3a–9a	Eastern North America
Quercus bicolor (swamp white oak)	4a–8b	Eastern North America

Species	Hardiness Zone	Origin
Quercus palustris (pin oak)	4b–9a	Eastern U.S.
Quercus phellos (willow oak)	6a–9a	Mid-Atlantic coast to southern and western U.S.
Quercus shumardii (Shumard oak)	6a–9a	Eastern U.S.
Salix species (willows)	3a–9a	Various
Taxodium distichum (bald cypress)	4a–9a	Southeastern U.S.
Thuja occidentalis (American arborvitae)	3a–7b	Eastern North America

Trees For Dry But Not Arid Sites

Species	Hardiness Zone	Origin
Acer campestre (hedge maple)	5a–8b	Western Asia, Europe
Acer ginnala (amur maple)	3a–6b	China, Japan, Manchuria
Acer negundo (box elder)	2a–8a	Eastern North America
Acer palmatum (Japanese maple)	5b–9a	Japan, Korea
Acer platanoides (Norway maple)	4a–7b	Europe, Caucasus Mountains, escaped in U.S.
Acer saccharum nigrum (black maple)	3b–7b	Central U.S.
Acer spicatum (mountain maple)	2–4	Southeastern Canada, northeastern U.S.
Acer tataricum (Tatarian maple)	3b–6b	Western Asia, southeastern Europe, Japan
Ailanthus altissima (tree of heaven)	5a–9a	China, naturalized in eastern U.S.
Betula lenta (sweet birch)	4a–7b	Northeastern U.S. south to northern Alabama
Betula pendula (European birch)	3a–5b	Northern Europe
Betula populifolia (gray birch)	4a–7a	Northeastern North America
Carya glabra (pignut hickory)	5b–9a	Eastern North America
Crataegus lavallei (Lavelle hawthorn)	4b–7a	Hybrid
Crataegus mollis (downy hawthorn)	3a–6b	Eastern and central North America
Crataegus phaenopyrum (Washington hawthorn)	4b–8b	Southeastern U.S.
Elaeagnus angustifolia (Russian olive)	3a–7b	Central Asia, southern Europe
Fagus grandifolia (American beech)	4a–9a	Eastern North America
Fagus sylvatica (European beech)	5a–9a	Europe
Franklinia alatamaha (Franklin tree)	6b–7b	Southeastern U.S.
Gleditsia triacanthos var. *inermis* cultivars (thornless honey locust)	4a–9a	Eastern and midwestern U.S.
Koelreuteria paniculata (panicled golden-rain tree)	5b–9a	China, Japan, Korea
Populus grandidentata (bigtooth aspen)	4a–7a	Eastern North America
Populus nigra italica (Lombardy poplar)	3a–9a	Italy
Populus tremuloides (quaking aspen)	2b–6b	Northern North America
Prunus serotina (black cherry)	3b–9a	Eastern North America
Quercus coccinea (scarlet oak)	5a–9a	Eastern North America
Quercus phellos (willow oak)	6a–9a	Mid-Atlantic coast to southern and western U.S.
Quercus velutina (black oak)	4b–9a	Eastern U.S.
Robinia pseudoacacia (black locust)	4b–9a	East–central U.S. to Iowa and Georgia
Sassafras albidum (common sassafras)	5b–9a	Southern Ontario, northeastern U.S.
Sorbus aucuparia (European mountain ash)	3b–7b	Northern Europe and Asia
Tilia americana (American linden)	3a–8a	Southern Canada, northeastern and central U.S.
Ulmus pumila (Siberian elm)	2b–9a	Northern China, eastern Siberia

Trees That Will Tolerate Full Sun In Summer

Species	Hardiness Zone	Origin
Acer buergeranum (trident maple)	5b–8a	Japan
Acer campestre (hedge maple)	5a–8b	Western Asia, Europe
Acer ginnala (amur maple)	3a–6b	China, Japan, Manchuria
Acer griseum (paperbark maple)	5a–7b	China
Acer miyabei (miyabe maple)	5a–7b	Japan
Acer platanoides (Norway maple)	3–7	Caucasus Mountains, Europe, escaped in U.S
Acer rubrum (red maple)	3–9	Northeastern North America

Species	Hardiness Zone	Origin
Acer saccharum (sugar maple)	3–8	Southeastern Canada, eastern U.S.
Acer tataricum (Tatarian maple)	3b–6b	Western Asia, southeastern Europe, Japan
Carpinus caroliniana (American hornbeam)	3b–9a	Eastern North America
Celtis laevigata (sugar hackberry)	5–9	Southeastern U.S.
Celtis occidentalis (common hackberry)	2–9	Eastern North America
Cercis canadensis (eastern redbud)	5b–9a	Eastern U.S.
Corylus colurna (Turkish hazelnut)	5a–8b	Southeastern Europe and adjacent Asia
Crataegus crus-galli var. *inermis* (thornless cockspur hawthorn)	4a–6b	Eastern North America
Crataegus phaenopyrum (Washington hawthorn)	4b–8b	Southeastern U.S.
Franklinia alatamaha (Franklin tree)	6b–7b	Southeastern U.S.
Fraxinus americana (white ash)	3–9	Eastern North America
Fraxinus pennsylvanicum (green ash)	3–9	Eastern North America
Ginkgo biloba male clones (maidenhair tree)	4b–8b	China
Gleditsia triacanthos var. *inermis* clones (thornless honey locust)	4b–9a	Central U.S.
Gymnocladus dioicus (Kentucky coffee-tree)	4a–7b	Eastern and midwestern U.S.
Halesia carolina (Carolina silverbell)	5a–9a	West Virginia to Florida to Texas
Ilex aquifolium (English holly)	7a–9a	Northern Africa, southern Europe
Ilex opaca (American holly)	6b–9a	Eastern U.S.
Koelreuteria paniculata (panicled golden-rain tree)	5b–9a	China, Japan, Korea
Liquidambar styraciflua (American sweet gum)	5b–9a	Eastern U.S.
Liriodendron tulipifera (tuliptree)	5a–9a	Eastern U.S.
Magnolia kobus (kobus magnolia)	5a–8b	Japan
Magnolia soulangiana (saucer magnolia)	5a–9a	Hybrid
Magnolia stellata (star magnolia)	5a–9a	Japan
Magnolia virginiana (sweetbay magnolia)	5b–9a	Eastern U.S.
Malus selected cultivars (crabapples)	3–8	Various, some hybrids
Ostrya virginiana (American hophornbeam)	3b–9a	Eastern North America
Phellodendron amurense (amur corktree)	4b–7b	China, Japan
Picea abies (Norway spruce)	3a–8a	Northern and central Europe
Picea omorika (Serbian spruce)	4b–8a	Southeastern Europe
Picea orientalis (Oriental spruce)	5b–8a	Northern and central Europe
Pinus cembra (Swiss stone pine)	3b–6b	Southern Asia, central Europe
Pinus flexilis (limber pine)	4b–7b	Mountains of western Canada and U.S.
Pinus ponderosa (ponderosa pine)	3b–8a	Western U.S. and adjacent Canada and Mexico
Pinus resinosa (red pine)	3a–6b	Canada and north-central and northeastern U.S.
Pinus rigida (pitch pine)	4b–7a	East-central U.S. from Maine to Appalachia
Pinus strobus (white pine)	3a–9a	Northeastern and central North America
Pinus sylvestris (Scots pine)	3a–8b	Europe through Siberia
Prunus padus (European birdcherry)	3b–7b	Asia, Europe
Prunus serrulata cultivars (Japanese cherry)	6a–8b	Japan
Prunus subhirtella 'Pendula' (weeping Higan cherry)	5b–9a	Japan
Quercus alba (white oak)	4a–9a	Eastern U.S.
Quercus bicolor (swamp white oak)	4a–8b	Eastern North America
Quercus muehlenbergii (chinkapin oak)	5a–8b	Eastern U.S.
Quercus palustris (pin oak)	4b–9a	Eastern U.S.
Quercus phellos (willow oak)	6a–9a	Mid-Atlantic coast to southern and western U.S..
Quercus prinus (chestnut oak)	5a–9a	Eastern U.S.
Quercus rubra (northern red oak)	3b–9a	Eastern North America
Quercus shumardii (Shumard oak)	6a–9a	Eastern U.S.
Sophora japonica (Japanese pagoda-tree)	6a–9a	China, Korea
Styrax japonicus (Japanese snowbell)	6b–8b	Japan
Styrax obassia (fragrant snowbell)	6b–8b	China, Japan

Species	Hardiness Zone	Origin
Syringa pekinensis (Pekin lilac)	4a–7a	China
Syringa reticulata (Japanese tree lilac)	3a–7b	Japan
Tilia americana (American linden)	2–8	Southern Canada, northeastern and central U.S.
Tilia cordata (littleleaf linden)	3–7	Europe
Tilia x *euchlora* (Crimean linden)	3–7	Hybrid
Tilia heterophylla (beetree linden)	5–9	Southeastern U.S.
Tilia tomentosa (silver linden)	5a–8a	Southeastern Europe
Viburnum prunifolium (blackhaw viburnum)	3b–9a	Eastern U.S.
Zelkova serrata (Japanese zelkova)	6a–9a	Japan, Korea

Trees For Shady Sites

Species	Hardiness Zone	Origin
Acer ginnala (amur maple)	3a–6b	China, Japan, Manchuria
Acer pensylvanicum (striped maple)	3b–7a	Eastern U.S. and adjacent Canada
Acer platanoides (Norway maple)	4a–7b	Caucasus Mountains, Europe, escaped in U.S
Acer pseudoplatanus (sycamore maple)	5b–7b	Europe
Acer saccharum (sugar maple)	3b–7b	Southeastern Canada, northeastern U.S.
Acer spicatum (mountain maple)	2–4	Canada and northeastern U.S.
Amelanchier arborea (downy serviceberry)	3b–8a	Northeastern U.S. and adjacent Canada
Amelanchier canadensis (shadblow serviceberry)	3b–8a	Eastern and midwestern North America
Amelanchier laevis (Allegheny serviceberry)	3b–8a	Eastern U.S. and adjacent Canada
Betula lenta (sweet birch)	4a–7b	Northeastern U.S. south to northern Alabama
Betula lutea (yellow birch)	3b–6b	Canada and northeastern U.S.
Betula nigra (river birch)	4a–9a	Eastern U.S.
Betula papyrifera (paper birch)	2b–7a	Northern North America
Carpinus caroliniana (American hornbeam)	3b–9a	Eastern North America
Cercis canadensis (eastern redbud)	5b–9a	Eastern U.S.
Cornus alternifolia (pagoda dogwood)	4a–7a	Northeastern U.S. and adjacent Canada
Cornus florida (flowering dogwood)	5a–8b	Eastern U.S.
Cornus kousa (kousa dogwood)	5a–7b	China, Japan, Korea
Cornus mas (Cornelian-cherry dogwood)	5a–8a	Western Asia, southeastern Europe
Crataegus crus-galli (cockspur hawthorn)	4a–6b	Eastern North America
Crataegus phaenopyrum (Washington hawthorn)	4b–8b	Southeastern U.S.
Fagus grandifolia (American beech)	4a–9a	Eastern North America
Fagus sylvatica (European beech)	5a–9a	Europe
Oxydendrum arboreum (sourwood)	5b–9a	Eastern and southeastern U.S.
Populus tremuloides (quaking aspen)	2b–6b	Northern North America
Prunus virginiana (common chokecherry)	3a–5a	Canada and northeastern and north-central U.S.
Ptelea trifolia (hoptree)	4a–9a	Eastern U.S.
Sassafras albidum (common sassafras)	5b–9a	Southern Ontario, northeastern U.S.
Tilia europea (European linden)	3b–8a	Hybrid
Tilia tomentosa (silver linden)	5a–8a	Southeastern Europe
Viburnum prunifolium (blackhaw viburnum)	3b–9a	Eastern U.S.

Trees That Tolerate Windy Conditions

Species	Hardiness Zone	Origin
Acer ginnala (amur maple)	3a–6b	China, Japan, Manchuria
Acer negundo (boxelder)	2a–8b	Eastern North America
Aesculus glabra (Ohio buckeye)	3a–8b	Central U.S. south to Texas
Catalpa speciosa (northern catalpa)	4a–9a	Southeastern U.S.
Cercis canadensis (eastern redbud)	5b–9a	Eastern U.S.
Corylus colurna (Turkish hazel)	5a–8b	Southeastern Europe and adjacent Asia
Fraxinus pennsylvanicum (green ash)	3–9	Eastern North America
Ginkgo biloba (maidenhair tree)	4b–8b	China

Species	Hardiness Zone	Origin
Picea abies (Norway spruce)	3a–8a	Northern and central Europe
Pinus cembra (Swiss stone pine)	3b–6b	Southern Asia, central Europe
Pinus flexilis (limber pine)	4b–7b	Mountains of western Canada and U.S.
Pinus ponderosa (ponderosa pine)	3b–8a	Western U.S. and adjacent Canada and Mexico
Pinus resinosa (red pine)	3a–6b	Canada and north-central and northeastern U.S.
Pinus rigida (pitch pine)	4b–7a	East-central U.S. from Maine to Appalachia
Pinus sylvestris (Scots pine)	3a–8b	Europe through Siberia
Ptelea trioliata (hoptree)	4a–9a	Eastern U.S.
Quercus alba (white oak)	4a–9a	Eastern U.S.
Quercus bicolor (swamp white oak)	4a–8b	Eastern North America
Quercus macrocarpa (bur oak)	3a–9a	Northeastern North America from Nova Scotia to Texas
Quercus muehlenbergii (chinkapin oak)	5a–8b	Eastern U.S.

Trees That Are Usually Pest Free

Species	Hardiness Zone	Origin
Ailanthus altissima (tree of heaven)	5a–9a	China, naturalized in eastern U.S.
Carpinus betulus (European hornbeam)	5a–7a	Asia Minor, Europe
Carpinus caroliniana (American hornbeam)	3b–9a	Eastern North America
Cercidiphyllum japonicum (katsura-tree)	5a–9a	China, Japan
Franklinia alatamaha (Franklin tree)	6b–7b	Southeastern U.S.
Ginkgo biloba (maidenhair tree)	4b–8b	China
Gymnocladus dioicus (Kentucky coffee-tree)	4a–7b	Eastern and midwestern U.S.
Kalopanax pictus (castor-aralia)	5a–8a	China, Japan, Korea
Koelreutaria paniculata (panicled golden-rain tree)	5b–9a	China, Japan, Korea
Liquidambar styraciflua (American sweet gum)	5a–9a	Eastern U.S.
Magnolia acuminata (cucumber magnolia)	4b–8b	Eastern U.S.
Ostrya virginiana (American hophornbeam)	3b–9a	Eastern North America
Phellodendron amurense (amur corktree)	4b–7b	China, Japan
Sophora japonica (Japanese pagoda-tree)	6a–9a	China, Korea
Styrax japonica (Japanese snowbell)	6b–8b	China, Japan
Viburnum prunifolium (blackhaw viburnum)	3b–9a	Eastern U.S.

Trees For Small Properties

Species	Hardiness Zone	Origin
Acer buergeranum (trident maple)	5b–8a	Japan
Acer campestre (hedge maple)	5a–8b	Western Asia, Europe
Acer ginnala (amur maple)	3a–6b	China, Japan, Manchuria
Acer griseum (paperbark maple)	5a–7b	China
Acer miyabei (miyabe maple)	5a–7b	Japan
Acer palmatum (Japanese maple)	5b–9a	Japan, Korea
Acer tataricum (Tatarian maple)	3b–6b	Western Asia, southeastern Europe, Japan
Acer triflorum (three–flowered maple)	5a–7a	China, Korea
Amelanchier arborea (downy serviceberry)	3b–8a	Northeastern U.S. and adjacent Canada
Amelanchier canadensis (shadblow serviceberry)	3b–7	Eastern and midwestern North America
Amelanchier laevis (Allegheny serviceberry)	3b–8a	Eastern U.S. and adjacent Canada
Carpinus caroliniana (American hornbeam)	3b–9a	Eastern North America
Cercis canadensis (eastern redbud)	5b–9a	Eastern U.S.
Cornus florida (flowering dogwood)	5a–8b	Eastern U.S.
Cornus florida x *kousa* hybrids (flowering x kousa dogwood hybrids)	5a–8b	Hybrid
Cornus kousa (kousa dogwood)	5a–7b	Japan, Korea
Cornus mas (cornelian-chery dogwood)	5a–8a	Western Asia, southeastern Europe
Crataegus crus-galli var. *inermis* (thornless cockspur hawthorn)	4a–6b	Eastern North America

Species	Hardiness Zone	Origin
Crataegus phaenopyrum (Washington hawthorn)	4b–8b	Southeastern U.S.
Franklinia alatamaha (Franklin tree)	6b–7b	Southeastern U.S.
Halesia carolina (Carolina silverbell)	5a–9a	West Virginia to Florida to Texas
Ilex aquifolium (English holly)	7a–9a	Northern Africa, southern Europe
Ilex opaca (American holly)	6b–9a	Eastern U.S.
Koelreuteria paniculata (panicled golden-rain tree)	5b–9a	China, Japan, Korea
Magnolia kobus (kobus magnolia)	5a–8b	Japan
Magnolia soulangiana (saucer magnolia)	5a–9a	Hybrid
Magnolia stellata (star magnolia)	5a–9a	Japan
Magnolia virginiana (sweetbay magnolia)	5b–9a	Eastern U.S.
Malus selected cultivars (crabapples)	3–8	Various, some hybrids
Ostrya virginiana (American hophornbeam)	3b–9a	Eastern U.S.
Oxydendrum arboreum (sourwood)	5b–9a	Eastern and southeastern U.S.
Prunus padus (European birdcherry)	3b–7b	Asia, Europe
Prunus serrulata cultivars (Japanese flowering cherry)	6a–8b	Japan
Prunus subhirtella 'Pendula' (weeping Higan cherry)	5b–9a	Japan
Styrax japonicus (Japanese snowbell)	6b–8b	Japan
Styrax obassia (fragrant snowbell)	6b–8b	China, Japan
Syringa pekinensis (Pekin lilac)	4a–7a	China
Syringa reticulata (Japanese tree lilac)	3a–7b	Japan
Viburnum prunifolium (blackhaw viburnum)	3b–9a	Eastern U.S.

Shade Trees Recommended For Street-Tree Use

Acer x *freemanii* 'Marmo' (Marmo Freeman maple)	3–8	Selected in Chicago area
Acer platanoides (Norway maple)	3–7	Caucasus Mountains, Europe, escaped in U.S.
Acer platanoides 'Cleveland' (Cleveland Norway maple)	3–7	Introduced by E. Scanlon, Ohio
Acer platanoides 'Crimson King' (Crimson King Norway maple)	3–7	Selected in Orleans, France
Acer platanoides 'Deborah' (Deborah Norway maple)	3–7	Introduced by J. Mathes, Oregon
Acer platanoides 'Emerald Queen' (Emerald Queen Norway maple)	3–7	Introduced by J. McIntyre, Oregon
Acer platanoides 'Jade Glen' (Jade Glen Norway maple)	3–7	Introduced by McGill Nursery, Oregon
Acer platanoides 'Royal Red' (Royal Red Norway maple)	3–7	Introduced by M. Holmason
Acer platanoides 'Schwedleri' (Schwedler Norway maple)	3–7	Introduced by G. H. Schwedler, Prussia
Acer platanoides 'Summershade' (Summershade Norway maple)	3–7	Introduced by Princeton Nurserymen's Research
Acer rubrum (Red maple)	3–9	Northeastern North America
Acer rubrum 'Bowhall' (Bowhall red maple)	3–8	Introduced by Cole Nursery, Ohio
Acer rubrum 'Northwood' (Northwood red maple)	3–8	Introduced by Minnesota Landscape Arboretum
Acer rubrum 'October Glory' (October Glory red maple)	3–8	Introduced by Princeton Nurserymen's Research
Acer rubrum 'Red Sunset' (Red Sunset red maple)	3–8	Introduced by J. Frank Schmidt Nursery, Oregon
Acer rubrum 'Schlesingeri' (Schlesinger red maple)	3–8	Introduced by C. J. Sargent, New England area
Acer saccharum (sugar maple)	3–8	Southeastern Canada, eastern U.S.
Acer saccharum 'Green Mountain' (Green Mountain sugar maple)	3–8	Introduced by Princeton Nurserymen's Research
Acer saccharum nigrum (black maple)	3–8	Central U.S.
Celtis laevigata (sugar hackberry)	5–9	Southeastern U.S.
Celtis occidentalis (common hackberry)	2–9	Eastern North America

Species	Hardiness Zone	Origin
Corylus colurna (Turkish hazel)	5a–8b	Southeastern Europe and adjacent Asia
Fraxinus americana (white ash)	3–9	Eastern North America
Fraxinus americana 'Autumn Applause' (Autumn Applause white ash)	3–9	Introduced by W. Wandel, Illinois
Fraxinus americana 'Autumn Purple' (Autumn Purple white ash)	3–9	Introduced by McKay Nursery, Wisconsin
Fraxinus americana 'Champaign County' (Champaign County white ash)	3–9	Introduced by W. Wandel, Illinois
Fraxinus americana 'Elk Grove' (Elk Grove white ash)	3–9	Selected in Chicago Area
Fraxinus pennsylvanicum (green ash)	3–9	Eastern North America
Fraxinus pennsylvanicum 'Kindred' (Kindred green ash)	3–9	Selected in North Dakota
Fraxinus pennsylvanicum 'Marshall's Seedless' (Marshall's seedless green ash)	3–9	Introduced by Porter–Walton Co., Utah
Fraxinus pennsylvanicum 'Summit' (Summit green ash)	3–9	Introduced by Summit Nurseries, Minnesota
Ginkgo biloba male clones (maidenhair tree)	4b–8b	China
Gleditsia triacanthos var. *inermis* cultivars (thornless honey locust)	4b–9a	Eastern and midwestern U.S.
Gleditsia triacanthos 'Fairview' (Fairview honey locust)	3b–7b	Introduced by A. McGill and Son Nursery, Oregon
Gleditsia triacanthos 'Green Glory' (Green Glory honey locust)	3b–8b	Introduced by R. Synnestvedt, Illinois
Gleditsia triacanthos 'Halka' (Halka honey locust)	3b–8b	Introduced by C. Halka
Gleditsia triacanthos 'Imperial' (Imperial honey locust)	3b–9a	Introduced by the Cole Nursery Company, Ohio
Gleditsia triacanthos 'Majestic' (Majestic honey locust)	3b–9a	Introduced by the Cole Nursery Company, Ohio
Gleditsia triacanthos 'Moraine' (Moraine honey locust)	3b–9b	Introduced by J. Siebenthaler, Ohio
Gleditsia triacanthos 'Perfection' (Perfection honey locust)	5a–8b	*
Gleditsia triacanthos 'Shademaster' (Shademaster honey locust)	3b–9b	Introduced by Princeton Nurserymen's Research
Gleditsia triacanthos 'Skyline' (Skyline honey locust)	3b–9a	Introduced by the Cole Nursery Company
Gleditsia triacanthos 'Summerlace' (Summerlace honey locust)	4b–7b	*
Gleditsia triacanthos 'True–Shade' (True–Shade honey locust)	4a–8b	Introduced by R. Cultra, Illinois
Gymnocladus dioicus (Kentucky coffee-tree)	4a–7b	Eastern and midwestern U.S.
Koelreuteria paniculata (panicled golden-rain tree)	5b–9a	China, Japan, Korea
Liquidambar styraciflua (American sweet gum)	5b–9a	Eastern U.S.
Liriodendron tulipifera (tuliptree)	5a–9a	Eastern U.S.
Magnolia acuminata (cucumber magnolia)	4b–8b	Eastern U.S.
Nyssa sylvatica (black gum)	5a–9a	Eastern North America
Phellodendron amurense (amur corktree)	4b–7b	China, Japan
Platanus x *acerifolia* 'Bloodgood' (Bloodgood plane tree)	5–8	Hybrid
Quercus alba (white oak)	4a–9a	Eastern U.S.
Quercus bicolor (swamp white oak)	4a–8b	Eastern North America
Quercus muehlenbergii (chinkapin oak)	5a–8b	Eastern U.S.
Quercus palustris (pin oak)	4b–9a	Eastern U.S.
Quercus phellos (willow oak)	6a–9a	Mid-Atlantic coast to southern and western U.S.

Species	Hardiness Zone	Origin
Quercus prinus (chestnut oak)	5a–9a	Eastern U.S.
Quercus rubra (northern red oak)	3b–9a	Eastern North America
Quercus shumardii (Shumard oak)	6a–9a	Eastern U.S.
Sophora japonica (Japanese pagoda-tree)	6a–9a	China, Korea
Tilia americana 'Dakota' (Dakota linden)	2–8	*
Tilia americana 'Redmond' (Redmond linden)	2–8	Introduced by M. Redmond, Nebraska
Tilia cordata (littleleaf linden)	3–7	Europe
Tilia cordata 'Chancellor' (Chancellor littleleaf linden)	3–7	Introduced by Cole Nursery Company, Ohio
Tilia cordata 'Erecta' (upright littleleaf linden)	3–7	*
Tilia cordata 'Glenleven' (Glenleven littleleaf linden)	3–7	Selected in Canada
Tilia cordata 'June Bride' (June Bride littleleaf linden)	3–7	Introduced by Manbeck Nursery, Ohio
Tilia cordata 'Olympia' (Olympia littleleaf linden	3–7	Introduced by J. Frank Nursery, Oregon
Tilia cordata 'Rancho' (Rancho littleleaf linden)	3–7	*
Tilia cordata 'Turesi' (Tures littleleaf linden)	3–7	*
Tilia x *euchlora* (Crimean linden)	3–7	Hybrid
Tilia heterophylla (beetree linden)	5–9	Southeastern U.S.
Tilia tomentosa (silver linden)	5a–8a	Southeastern Europe
Zelkova serrata (Japanese zelkova)	6a–9a	Japan, Korea

*Cultivated variety; selection site unknown to author.

Glossary

Words in this glossary appear in boldface type the first time they appear in a chapter.

abdomen ▪ The hind portion of the insect where digestion and reproduction take place.

abiotic ▪ Nonliving; also refers to plant problems caused by nonliving agents, such as drought, lawn mowers, string-trimmers, and so forth.

abscisic acid ▪ A growth-regulating chemical found in plants that causes the stomata to close during drought stress.

absorption ▪ The process by which a substance is taken into plants, for example, from the soil solution into a plant root cell.

acervulus (acervuli) ▪ A saucer-shaped fungal structure bearing conidia.

activation ▪ The process by which a surface-applied herbicide is moved into the soil, where it can be absorbed by emerging seedlings.

activator ▪ A chemical added to a pesticide to increase its activity.

active ingredient (ai) ▪ The chemical in a pesticide formulation primarily responsible for phytotoxicity to its target and which is identified as the active ingredient on the product label.

adjuvant ▪ Any substance in a pesticide formulation or added to the spray tank to modify pesticidal activity or application characteristics.

adsorption ▪ The process by which a pesticide is held on the surface of a soil particle.

adult ▪ An insect or mite with functional reproductive organs.

adventitious ▪ A plant part that appears in an area where it normally would not, such as adventitious roots emerging from stems.

aecium (aecia) ▪ A cup-shaped spore-bearing structure formed by rust fungi.

aeration ▪ The provision of air to the soil.

aggregate ▪ A close cluster or mix of particles.

aggregation pheromone ▪ A pheromone that attracts insects and causes them to form large groupings. Used by bark beetles to promote mass attack. Multilure is a commercial formulation used for monitoring elm bark beetle activity.

agitation ▪ The process of stirring or mixing in a sprayer.

allelochemicals ▪ Chemical substances produced by plants that protect them from their natural enemies and environmental stress. Examples of allelochemicals include tannins and other phenolic compounds (such as tannin acid), terpenes (such as pine resins and fragrant chemicals in herbs and spices), and alkaloids (such as nicotine and morphine).

allelopathy ▪ The adverse effect on the growth of plants or microorganisms caused by the action of chemicals produced by other living or decaying plants.

antagonism ▪ A situation in which the activity of a combination of pesticides is less than the expected effect of each pesticide applied separately.

antibiotic ▪ A chemical produced by a microorganism that inhibits or kills other microorganisms.

anticoagulant ▪ A rodenticide that kills the mammal by reducing its ability to form blood clots. Poisoned animals usually die by internal bleeding through leakage in capillaries and other blood vessels.

antler ▪ A hornlike ornamental structure made of bone protruding from the skull of a mammal.

apical dominance ▪ A growth pattern in which a plant maintains a strong central stem, or leader, due to inhibition of lateral buds by a chemical signal from the terminal buds.

apothecium ▪ An open or cup-shaped fruiting structure formed by certain fungi and containing spores formed by sexual recombination.

aqueous ▪ A term used to indicate the presence of water in a solution.

area repellent ▪ A chemical that causes a pest to leave once the chemical is smelled.

arthropod ▪ Meaning "jointed appendage," this term refers to a species that is part of a large group of invertebrates including crustaceans, arachnids, insects, millipedes, and centipedes. All members of this group have a segmented body and an exoskeleton. Each segment has (or had) a jointed appendage during its evolutionary development.

auxin ▪ A growth-regulating chemical that can inhibit lateral bud development but that can also stimulate cell enlargement and initiation of roots in other parts of the plant.

avoidance ▪ A disease-management strategy in which using disease-free plants or planting in sites unfavorable for disease development keeps disease problems from occurring.

Bacillus thuringiensis ▪ A bacterium that produces a poison that kills certain insects. Formulations of this poison are commercially available.

bacterium (bacteria) ▪ A normally single-celled microorganism having a cell wall but no organized nucleus.

balled-and-burlapped ▪ A term that describes trees and shrubs harvested with the root system enclosed in a soil ball that is held together with burlap and twine, a wire basket, or both.

band treatment ▪ The application of a pesticide to a linear restricted strip on or along a row rather than continuous over the entire area.

bare-root ▪ Trees and shrubs harvested with an exposed root system and with no soil covering their roots.

basal flare ▪ The transitional area from a tree's stem to its root system. Normally the stem flares out to a larger diameter as it approaches the root area.

basal treatment ▪ The application of a pesticide to encircle the stem of a plant just above the soil surface such that foliage contact is minimal. A term used mostly to describe treatment of woody plants.

biological control ▪ The control or suppression of pests by the action of one or more organisms through natural means or by manipulation of the pest, organism, or environment.

biotic ▪ Alive; caused by living agents. Usually a reference to diseases caused by living microorganisms.

biotype ▪ A population within a species that has a distinct genetic variation.

blight ▪ A symptom or disease in which plant parts such as leaves, flowers, and stems are rapidly killed.

blotch (leaf) ▪ Areas of dead tissue, randomly dispersed on a leaf.

blotch mine ▪ An irregularly shaped discoloration in a leaf caused by the excavation of tissue between upper and lower leaf surfaces.

bonsai ▪ A potted plant dwarfed and trained to an artistic shape by special methods of culture; the art of growing such a plant.

boring ▪ The act of drilling through plant tissue, especially stems, twigs, trunk, and roots.

botanical pesticide ▪ A pesticide made from plants. Also called plant-derived pesticide.

branch bark ridge ▪ A ridge of bark that forms in a branch crotch and partially around the stem, resulting from the growth of the stem and branch tissues against one another.

branch axil ▪ The angle formed where a branch joins another branch or stem of a woody plant.

branch collar ▪ A "shoulder," or bulge, formed at the base of a branch by the annual production of overlapping layers of branch and stem tissues.

broadcast treatment ▪ The application of pesticide in a continuous sheet over an entire field or area.

broadcast rate equivalent ▪ For band treatments, the amount of pesticide applied per unit area when only the band area is considered. All rates for band treatment should be expressed as the broadcast rate equivalent.

broadleaf weed ▪ A plant with broad, rounded, or flattened leaves.

bronze ▪ A brown discoloration of many small, light, or tan spots caused by spider mite feeding.

browse ▪ To feed on plant material. Usually associated with an animal removing and eating leaves and stems.

brush control ▪ The control of woody plants such as brambles, sprout clumps, shrubs, trees, and vines.

buffering capacity ▪ The ability of a soil to maintain its pH.

bulk density ▪ A measurement of the mass of soil per unit volume, usually grams per cubic centimeter.

burrow ▪ An underground tunnel in which a mammal spends much of its time.

callus ▪ A term synonymous with woundwood.

callus tissue ▪ Tissue formed when the plant is wounded by pruning, insects, and other sources of mechanical injury. Callus tissue grows over the wound, isolating it from undamaged tissue and the external environment. Also known as wound periderm tissue.

cambium ▪ The thin layer of cells in the inner bark that gives rise to the conductive tissues, xylem, and phloem.

candle stage ▪ The period of time after budbreak when shoot elongation normally occurs in conifers.

canker ▪ A localized dead area on woody tissue, often sunken, on a twig, branch, or stem, that can enlarge over time.

carbohydrates ▪ Materials (sugar and starch) produced by plants during photosynthesis that serve as an energy source.

carrier ▪ The inert liquid or solid material added to an active ingredient to prepare a pesticide formulation.

cation ▪ A positively charged ion.

cation exchange capacity ▪ The ability of a soil to absorb and hold cations.

caterpillar ▪ A butterfly or moth larva.

causal agent ▪ Either a biotic or an abiotic agent that causes a disruption of a plant's normal growth or physical properties.

cell turgor/turgidity ▪ The internal pressure within a cell that keeps it from shrinking or collapsing.

cell wall ▪ The outermost part of a cell made up of cross-linked cellulose molecules and containing lignin and hemicellulose.

cellular membrane ▪ A thin layer immediately surrounding the body of a cell and inside the cell wall that serves to regulate the movement of water and molecules into or out of the cell.

cellulose ▪ Forms the structural framework of cell walls of plants; cellulose is formed by linking many sugar molecules into long chains.

chelate ▪ A combination of a metal ion and an organic molecule that results in making the metal ion less reactive with other chemicals in water or in a soil solution.

chewing ▪ Refers to the ability of animal mouthparts to chew food. Animals with chewing mouthparts can tear and crush food.

chicken wire ▪ A woven mesh of lightweight wire with 1- to 2-inch openings commonly used in agriculture to confine chickens and other barnyard birds.

chlorophyll ▪ The name given to the green pigment in plant cells that is responsible for absorbing light energy during photosynthesis.

chloroplast ▪ An organelle within a plant cell containing the pigments, enzymes, and other elements required for photosynthesis.

chlorosis ▪ Whitish or yellowish discoloration of normally green plant material due to the lack of chlorophyll.

chlorotic ▪ Plant tissues that appear pale-green to yellow.

chronic ▪ A condition or situation that occurs on a regular or frequent basis.

circular scars ▪ Feeding injury associated with leaf-cutter bees.

cleistothecium (cleistothecia) ▪ A closed, spherical fruiting structure containing sexual spores.

clone ▪ Asexually produced organisms that are genetically identical.

compatible ▪ Describes the ability of two or more chemicals to be mixed without affecting each other's properties.

competition ▪ The active acquisition of limited resources by an organism that results in a reduced supply and consequently reduced growth of other organisms in a common environment.

complete metamorphosis ▪ The pattern of development from egg to adult in which immatures are wormlike.

complex ▪ A variety of symptoms expressed as the result of different causal agents.

concentration ▪ The amount of active ingredient in a given volume or weight of formulation.

conidium (conidia) ▪ An asexual spore.

conk ▪ The large spore-bearing structures of wood-decay fungi.

conspicuous white wax ▪ A waxy excretion that covers insects. A diagnostic feature of many insects.

contact herbicide ▪ A herbicide that causes injury to only the plant tissue to which it is applied, or a herbicide that is not appreciably translocated within plants.

contact repellent ▪ A chemical that causes a pest to leave once the chemical is tasted or touched.

container-grown ▪ Plant material that has been grown in a container, either from seed or from cuttings, before planting and moving.

containerized ▪ Plant material grown in a nursery and placed in a container before shipment.

copper compounds ▪ Pesticides containing copper that are used to manage fungal and bacterial diseases.

cornicles ▪ Bumps on the hind end of an aphid.

crawler ▪ The immature nymph of a scale or a mealybug after egg hatch; the only stage at which many scales are able to walk.

critical root zone ▪ The area of a tree's root system that contains the majority of woody and fine roots. The area is determined by allowing 1 to 1½ feet of root radius for each inch of stem diameter at breast height (dbh).

crochet ▪ Hooklike protrusion on the base of an insect proleg. Common on caterpillars.

crown raising ▪ A method of pruning to provide clearance for pedestrians, vehicles, buildings, lines of sight, and vistas by removing lower branches.

crown thinning ▪ A method of pruning in which lower branches are removed to increase light penetration and air movement through the crown of a tree.

crown-reduction pruning ▪ A method of pruning used to reduce the height of a tree. Branches are cut back to laterals that are at least one-third the diameter of the limb being removed.

cultivar ▪ A cultivated variety of a plant. A named plant selection from which identical or near-identical plants can be produced, usually by vegetative reproduction or cloning.

curl ▪ A leaf or shoot distortion associated with lack of water or sucking injury.

cytokinin ▪ A growth-regulating chemical found in plants that promotes bud growth and development.

damage ▪ An injury that is extensive enough to cause economic loss.

deciduous ▪ Perennial plants that lose their leaves during the winter.

decline syndrome ▪ A progressive decline in health (vitality) of a plant, usually from a combination of causes and commonly occurring over a lengthy period.

decurrent ▪ A major tree form resulting from weak apical control. Trees with this form have several to many lateral branches that compete with the central stem for dominance resulting in a spherical or "globose" crown. Most hardwood trees have decurrent forms.

defoliate ▪ To lose leaves.

degradation ▪ The process by which a chemical is reduced to a less complex form.

desiccation ▪ Drying out.

diagnosis ▪ The process of determining the cause of a disorder.

diameter at breast height (dbh) ▪ Stem diameter measured at a point 4½ feet above the ground.

diapause ▪ A slowing down or delay in insect or mite development.

dieback ▪ The gradual death of tissues beginning at the tips of branches that can kill part of or entire branches or groups of branches.

diluent ▪ Any liquid or solid material used to dilute or carry an active ingredient.

directed application ▪ Precise application to a specific area or plant organ, such as to a row or bed or to the leaves or stem of a plant.

disease ▪ Any disturbance of a plant over some period of time that interferes with its normal structure, function, or economic value and that induces symptoms.

disorder ▪ Any disease caused by a noninfectious (nonliving) agent.

dispersible granule ▪ A dry granular formulation that will separate or disperse to form a suspension when added to water.

dispersing agent ▪ A material that reduces the attraction between particles.

distortion ▪ Abnormal shape.

dormancy ▪ A state of inactivity between periods of growth often associated with the ability to withstand low temperature.

dormant ▪ A state in which growth of seeds or other plant organs stops temporarily.

drop-crotch pruning ▪ A method of pruning to reduce the size of the tree's crown. Cuts are made to lateral branches.

elytra ▪ The hardened forewing of a beetle.

emulsifier ▪ A chemical that aids in suspending one liquid in another.

emulsion ▪ A mixture in which one liquid is suspended as tiny drops in another liquid, such as oil in water.

encircling roots ▪ Roots that grow in a circular manner rather than radiating out from a plant's root collar area.

energy reserves ▪ The excess photosynthates that a tree or shrub stores in various tissues for later use as a source of energy for growth, repair, and recovery.

epicormic sprout ▪ A shoot that arises from latent or adventitious buds—also known as watersprouts—that occurs on stems and branches and on suckers produced from the base of trees. In many plants, a symptom of stress; in a few species, a natural trait.

epinasty ▪ The state in which more rapid growth on the upper side of a plant organ or part (especially leaf) causes it to bend or curl downward.

eradication ▪ Removal and destruction of diseased plants or plant parts.

eriophyoid mites ▪ A group of three closely related mite families characterized by a cigar-shaped body and four visible legs.

espalier ▪ A plant trained to grow flat against a support (as a wall).

essential elements ▪ Any of the sixteen minerals essential to the growth and development of trees.

eutrification ▪ Increased nutrient load in bodies of water; a result of garden and crop overfertilization, pet excreta, and sewage overflow.

exclusion ▪ The erection of barriers or sealing of openings so that pests are unable to enter an area.

excurrent ▪ A major tree form resulting from strong apical control. Trees with this form have a strong central stem and pyramidal shape. Lateral branches rarely compete for dominance. Most conifers and a few hardwoods, such as sweetgum and tulip poplar, have excurrent forms.

exoskeleton ▪ The hardened exterior shell of an insect that gives structural support to the insect body.

fatty acid ▪ Long-chain carbon molecules commonly used in soaps and similar products.

fawn ▪ A young deer.

feces ▪ Manure; food waste, usually solid, that is expelled from the body.

field capacity ▪ Soil moisture content remaining after the drainage of gravitational water.

fixation (nitrogen) ▪ The metabolic assimilation of atmospheric nitrogen into ammonia by soil microorganisms.

flagellum (flagella) ▪ A tail-like structure projecting from a bacterial cell or from certain types of fungal spores.

flagging ▪ A disease or disorder symptom manifested by the leaves on a branch wilting, turning brown, and clinging to the branch for an extended period instead of falling off immediately.

flowable ▪ A two-phase formulation containing solid pesticide suspended in liquid and forms a suspension when added to water.

flush cuts ▪ Pruning cuts that originate inside the branch bark ridge or the branch collar, causing unnecessary injury to stem tissues.

form ▪ A nest on the ground.

friable ▪ Easily crumbled or pulverized.

frill treatment ▪ The placement of a pesticide into a series of overlapping ax cuts made through the bark in a ring around the trunk of a tree.

frost cracks ▪ Longitudinal cracks in the stems of trees and shrubs that run parallel to the wood grain and extend to the center of stems and branches. Usually associated with extremely cold temperatures and previous wounds.

fruiting structure, or **fruiting body** ▪ A fungal structure made of mycelium and containing spores.

fumigant ▪ A pesticide gas that is able to penetrate pest hiding places through very small spaces. Many fumigants are general poisons that kill animals or plants that they contact.

fungicide ▪ A chemical compound that is toxic to fungi.

fungus (fungi) ▪ A multicellular lower plant without chlorophyll. The fungus normally consists of strands called mycelium and reproduces through the dispersal of spores.

gall ▪ An abnormal swelling or growth of plant tissue that is initiated by a pathogen, insect, or mite.

gall making ▪ The inducement of gall production by an insect, mite, or pathogen.

genus ▪ A group of species having similar fundamental traits.

geotextile fabric ▪ A permeable fabric often used to stabilize soil and as a weed barrier.

germination ▪ The process of initiating growth in seeds.

gestation ▪ Pregnancy. The length of time in mammals that occurs from mating to birth.

girdle ▪ To remove the bark and cambium, exposing the inside of a plant stem. Plants that are girdled completely without any intact bark connecting the roots to the shoots usually die.

girdler ▪ Any insect that severs a twig or leaf by feeding on the outside.

girdling

   girdling root syndrome (GRS) ▪ A collection of symptoms produced by roots that either partially or completely compress sapwood tissues near or above the root collar flare, or result in phloem girdling.

   mulch girdling ▪ A situation in which the stem caliper below the mulch line does not increase as the caliper does above the mulch line, resulting in a pinched appearance. Associated with excessive depths of mulches against the stems of young trees and shrubs.

   phloem girdling ▪ Caused by the disruption of phloem tissues; this can be the physical removal of stem bark tissues or the death of said tissues caused by wires, ropes, chemicals, encircling roots, insects, or diseases.

girdling root ▪ A plant root that encircles the plant rather than spreads out radially from the plant.

GPA ▪ Gallons per acre.

GPM ▪ Gallons per minute.

gravitational water ▪ Water that will drain from the soil under the force of gravity.

grub ▪ A beetle larva.

guard hair ▪ The external hair or fur of a mammal.

hardiness ▪ Ability of a plant to survive low temperatures.

hardiness zones ▪ Distinct geographic regions delineated by isotherms of average minimum winter temperature.

hardpans ▪ Layers of soil that are impenetrable by roots, oxygen, or water.

hardware cloth ▪ Screen wire; an open mesh made of wire.

head ▪ The front section of the insect responsible for ingesting food, seeing, and, in part, tasting. Eyes and antennae are attached here.

heartwood ▪ Nonliving xylem cells forming a core of wood in the center of the stem; provides structural strength to a tree.

heat island effect ▪ The tendency of urban areas to be several degrees warmer in temperature than the surrounding areas.

hemicellulose ▪ A material made up of chainlike molecules that combines with cellulose to increase the strength of the cell wall.

herbaceous ▪ A vascular plant that does not develop persistent woody tissue above ground.

herbicide ▪ A chemical substance or cultured biological organism used to kill or suppress the growth of plants.

herbicide resistance ▪ The trait or quality of a population of plants within a species that have a tolerance for a particular herbicide that is substantially greater than the average for the species. Herbicide resistance develops through selection for naturally occurring tolerance by exposing the weed to the same herbicide for several reproductive cycles.

herbivore ▪ An animal whose diet consists of plant material.

hibernaculum ▪ A winter shelter constructed by an insect. Often shallow pits dug into twig crotches, limbs, or trunks.

hibernate ▪ When an animal's temperature drops close to that of its surroundings, and its heartbeat and breathing is much less than that of an active animal. Many mammals hibernate to avoid adverse conditions, particularly those in winter.

honeydew ▪ The sugary liquid excrement of sucking insects.

horticultural oil ▪ A highly refined petroleum oil with an ability to kill insects by smothering them and disrupting membranes.

humus ▪ A material resulting from partial decomposition of plant or animal matter and forming the organic portion of soil.

hydrogen ion concentration ▪ A measure of acidity or alkalinity, expressed in terms of the pH of the solution.

hypha (hyphae) ▪ A single filament of a fungus.

incisors ▪ The front teeth of mammals used primarily for cutting off a mouthful of food.

included bark ▪ Bark enclosed between branches with narrow angles of attachment, forming a wedge between the branches.

incorporate ▪ To mix or blend; for example, when pesticides are mixed into the soil.

infectious ▪ Able to spread from plant to plant. For example, disease caused by living pathogenic microorganisms is infectious.

infiltration ▪ Downward entry of water into the soil.

infiltration rate ▪ Speed at which water soaks into the soil.

injury ▪ Physical removal, discoloration, or distortion of a plant part.

inoculum ▪ The part of a pathogen, or collection of individual pathogens, that can cause disease.

instar ▪ The stage of an insect between successive molts.

interface ▪ The transition area between native, undisturbed soil and soil loosened by digging operations.

ion ▪ Molecule that carries an electrical charge.

jute rope ▪ Rope made from a coarse, natural fiber.

larva (larvae) ▪ An immature insect with complete metamorphosis.

latent (buds) ▪ Refers to buds that are buried under bark during shoot growth in woody plants. Latent buds remain dormant until released by pruning.

lateral movement ▪ Movement of a pesticide through soil, generally in a horizontal plane, from the original site of application.

leach ▪ Tendency for elements and chemical compounds to wash down through the soil.

leaf scorch ▪ Leaf browning associated with rapid water loss.

leaf mining ▪ The act of feeding between leaf surfaces.

leaf notching ▪ The removal of leaf tissue from leaf edge.

leaf spot ▪ A discrete dead area on a leaf.

lenticels ▪ Tiny pores in the leaf that open and close to regulate the rate of transpiration and the diffusion of gases into and out of the leaf.

light compensation point ▪ The point at which the rate of photosynthesis equals the rate of respiration, which stops plant growth.

lignify ▪ To convert into wood or woody tissue.

lignin ▪ A chemical substance that makes the cell walls of plants rigid and strong; lignin is the typical component of wood.

live trap ▪ A trap that captures an animal but doesn't harm it. This allows the animal to be released unharmed in an area where its presence will not be a problem or to be killed in a humane manner.

macronutrient ▪ An essential element required by plants in relatively large quantities.

macropore ▪ Larger spaces between soil particles, usually air filled.

maggot ▪ A fly larva.

marginal necrosis ▪ Browning (death) of green tissue around the outer edges of a leaf.

meristem ▪ A group of undifferentiated cells that gives rise to plant tissues by rapid cell division. Meristems are located at the tips of the stems and roots and in the cambium.

mesophyll ▪ The soft tissue in a leaf, underneath the epidermis and palisade layers, that allows for diffusion of gases and water vapor within the leaf.

metamorphosis ▪ The series of changes an insect passes through in its growth from egg to adult.

microclimate ▪ Environmental conditions of a specific limited area.

micronutrient ▪ An essential element required by plants in relatively small quantities.

micropore ▪ The space between soil particles that is relatively small and likely to be water filled.

mildew ▪ A plant disease in which white mycelium and spores of the causal fungus are visible on the plant surface.

mitochondria ▪ Organelles in the cells where respiration occurs.

mitosis ▪ Cell division leading to the formation of identical daughter cells, each with a copy of the same genetic information as the original cell.

molting ▪ The process of shedding the skin between developmental stages.

mortality spiral ▪ A series of interrelated, stress-inducing events leading to the gradual death of a tree.

mosaic ▪ A pattern of yellow-and-green tissue intermingled on a leaf; typical of many virus diseases.

mulch ▪ Any material—such as straw, sawdust, leaves, plastic film, or loose soil—that is spread on the surface of the soil to protect the soil and plant roots from the effects of raindrops, soil crusting, freezing, or evaporation, or to control weeds.

mushroom ▪ The fruiting structure of many wood-decay fungi, consisting of a rounded cap on a cylindrical stalk.

mycelial mat ▪ A thickened mycelium visible to the unaided eye.

mycelial fan ▪ Fan-shaped pattern of hyphal growth of some wood-decay fungi, visible between the bark and wood of infected trees.

mycelium (mycelia) ▪ The body of a fungus, consisting of many hyphae.

mycorhizae ▪ Fungal organisms that form beneficial associations with plant roots, increasing the effective surface area of the roots for absorption of water and nutrients from the soil.

necrosis ▪ Localized death of tissue, usually characterized by browning and desiccation.

necrotic ▪ Showing varying degrees of dead areas or spots. Often used to describe brown spots left by insects or diseases that kill leaf tissue.

nematode ▪ A microscopic, wormlike animal that can be parasitic on plants.

noninfectious ▪ Unable to spread from plant to plant. For example, nutritional disorders are noninfectious.

nonselective herbicide ▪ A herbicide that is generally toxic to all plants treated. Some selective herbicides can become nonselective if used at very high rates.

nontarget species ▪ Species not intentionally affected by a pesticide.

notches ▪ Areas on a leaf edge where leaf tissue has been removed. A characteristic of feeding by some weevil adults.

noxious weed ▪ A plant regulated or identified by law as being undesirable, troublesome, and difficult to control. Precise definition varies according to legal interpretations.

nymph ▪ An immature insect with incomplete metamorphosis.

oospore ▪ A sexual spore formed by some fungi that has thickened walls and can act as a survival structure.

ooze ▪ A sticky liquid composed of bacterial cells and the polysaccharides they produce.

organic matter, soil ▪ The organic fraction of the soil. Includes plant and animal residues at various stages of decomposition, cells and tissues of soil organisms, and substances synthesized by the soil population.

osmotic adjustment ▪ The process by which some plants maintain high turgor pressure in their cells during periods of drought by increasing the concentration of dissolved substances in the cell, causing more water to enter the cell.

outrigger ▪ A strand of wire extending out from a fence to provide support or to restrict the approach of animals to the fence.

oviposition ▪ The act of depositing an egg.

ovipositors ▪ Specialized structures on the abdomen of an adult female that are used for depositing eggs. Some ovipositors responsible for gluing eggs to plants are relatively inconspicuous. Other ovipositors responsible for drilling into wood or cutting into leaf tissues are more obvious. Ovipositors such as those on adult sawflies provide good diagnostic characteristics.

oxygen-diffusion rate ▪ A measurement of the movement of oxygen through soils. Low oxygen-diffusion rates have been associated with poor plant health (vitality) and are common in compacted clay soils or waterlogged soils.

palisade ▪ The layer of cells near the upper surface of a leaf where most of photosynthesis occurs.

passive absorption ▪ Movement of water and nutrients into plant roots in which transpiration of water by leaves acts like a wick, pulling water into the roots.

pathogen ▪ A microorganism capable of causing disease.

periderm ▪ The outer bark of a tree made up of corky cells produced by a tissue called phellogen located outside of the phloem. Secondarily developed protective bark tissue that replaces the epidermis in woody plant parts.

perithecium (perithecia) ▪ A rounded, flask-shaped fruiting structure containing sexually produced spores with an opening or pore where spores are released.

permeability ▪ The measure of the ability of water and gases to move through the soil over a period of time.

pH ▪ A logarithmic measure of acidity or alkalinity. A pH level of 7 is neutral. A pH level of 1 through 6 is acidic, and 8 through 14 is alkaline.

pH, soil ▪ The negative logarithm of the hydrogen-ion activity of a soil. The degree of acidity (or alkalinity) of a soil.

phellogen ▪ A meristematic tissue that produces the outer, corky bark on a tree.

pheromone ▪ A chemical secreted by an organism for the purpose of communication with other individuals of the same species.

phloem ▪ The living vascular tissue in plants, located outside the cambium, that functions primarily to transport metabolic compounds sugars produced during photosynthesis from the site of synthesis leaves or storage to the site of utilization (other parts of plant).

photosynthate ▪ A product that results from photosynthesis; a source of chemically stored energy.

photosynthesis ▪ The process of capturing light with chlorophyll pigment and using its energy to convert carbon dioxide and water into sugar that is used as an energy source directly or converted to starch for storage and later use.

phytoplasma ▪ A microorganism without a cell wall or organized nucleus that causes yellows diseases in plants.

phytotoxic ▪ Harmful to plants.

plant growth regulator ▪ A substance used for controlling or modifying plant growth processes without severe phytotoxicity.

pollarding ▪ The annual removal of all of the previous year's growth, resulting in a flush of slender shoots and branches each spring.

polymorphic ▪ Capable of many forms. For example, aphid adults can be winged or wingless.

positive feedback ▪ When one event stimulates a second event that in turn stimulates the first event (for example, Dutch elm disease and elm bark beetles).

postemergence ▪ Refers to pesticides or herbicides applied after emergence of the specified crop or weed.

prebaiting ▪ The practice of placing food or other attractant in areas where pests will find it and get used to it before mixing it with a pesticide or placing it in a set trap.

preemergence ▪ Refers to pesticides or herbicides applied before emergence of the specified crop or weed.

pressure pad ▪ The mycelial mats formed by *Ceratocystis fagacearum*, the causal agent of oak wilt.

prolegs ▪ The fleshy, unsegmented legs on the body of an immature insect, which are used for walking. The number and position of prolegs, as well as presence of crochets, are used to distinguish between sawflies and caterpillars.

pronotum ▪ A distinctive piece of exoskelton that lies between the head and the attachment of the first pair of wings on the first segment of the thorax.

pruner ▪ Any insect that severs a twig or leaf by feeding from the inside.

pubescent ▪ Having hairy leaves or stems.

pupa (pupae) ▪ The intermediate stage between a larva and an adult with complete metamorphosis. Does not feed.

pycnidium (pycnidia) ▪ An asexual rounded or flask-shaped fruiting structure.

rachis (rachises) ▪ An extension of the petiole of a compound leaf that bears the leaflets.

raptor ▪ The group of predatory birds including hawks, eagles, and owls.

relocation ▪ The release of a live animal in an area other than its home area.

repellent ▪ A pesticide that does not kill the pest but, rather, causes it to leave the area.

residual toxicity ▪ The amount of time after pesticide application when the material is toxic to the pest.

residual herbicide ▪ A herbicide that persists in the soil and injures or kills germinating weed seedlings for a relatively short period of time after application.

resistance ▪ The ability to overcome or to slow the development of disease.

respiration ▪ The series of reactions, occurring in the mitochondria, by which sugar is broken down to provide energy for plant functions. Oxygen is consumed and carbon dioxide released during respiration.

rhizomorph ▪ A dark brown, shoestringlike structure formed from bundled hyphae of *Armillaria mellea.*

ringspot ▪ A circular area of chlorosis or necrosis with a green, healthy-appearing center.

rodent ▪ A small mammal with two front teeth suited for gnawing that continue to grow throughout the animal's life.

rodenticide ▪ A pesticide used to kill mice, rats, and other rodents.

root ball ▪ The containment of roots and soil of a tree.

root-bound ▪ Refers to container-grown or containerized plants that have produced roots that grow in a circular manner in the container and take up most of the available rooting space. Also known as pot-bound.

root collar flare ▪ The transitional area connecting the stem tissues and root tissues, usually exhibiting a larger diameter as the stem approaches the root system.

root graft ▪ A situation in which roots of two or more trees grow together, sharing parts of the same vascular system.

root hair ▪ Modified epidermal cells of a root that aid in the absorption of water and minerals.

rot ▪ Tissue breakdown.

runway ▪ A path that an animal commonly uses to travel from one point to another. The vegetation is usually trampled or removed, and there may be a depression in the soil, appearing as a tunnel without a ceiling.

rut ▪ The breeding season of a hooved mammal.

sanitation ▪ The process of removing and destroying old or dead plants or plant parts from a site.

saprophytic ▪ Describes any organism that lives on dead or decaying matter.

sapsucker ▪ A woodpecker whose diet largely consists of plant sap.

sapwood ▪ Functional, conductive xylem positioned next to the bark tissues.

scion ▪ A detached living portion of a plant joined to a stock in grafting.

scorch (leaf) ▪ Dead (necrotic) tissues on the margins of leaves or between veins that results in browning and shriveling of foliage.

selective herbicide ▪ A chemical that is more toxic to some plant species than to others.

serpentine ▪ A snakelike form associated with serpentine leaf mines.

sex pheromone ▪ A scent released by a female that is carried downwind to attract males. Commercially available formulations are used to trap insects and time insect activity.

shrew ▪ A small, very active, predatory mammal with an elongate face and usually a short tail.

sign ▪ The physical evidence of a causal agent.

simple metamorphosis ▪ The pattern of development from egg to adult in which the young superficially resemble adults, with the exception of the size of wings.

skeletonization ▪ The removal by insects of tissue between leaf veins.

slime flux ▪ A liquid, composed of bacteria and their byproducts, that oozes out of wounds in trees.

slime layer ▪ The polysaccharide layer around a bacterial cell that protects the cell from extremes in the environment.

soil amendment ▪ Material added to soil to alter its physical or chemical properties.

soil compaction ▪ The reduction of the total pore space in a soil, especially the macropores.

soil interface ▪ The zone between the modified and unmodified soil in the planting hole. The soil surface in a planting hole where undisturbed soil meets soil backfilled into the hole during planting or transplanting.

soil pH ▪ See pH, soil.

soil structure ▪ The degree to which soil particles are aggregated.

soil texture ▪ The size distribution of soil particles.

soluble ▪ Will dissolve in a liquid.

solution ▪ A mixture of one or more substances in another, in which all ingredients are completely dissolved.

solvent ▪ A liquid that will dissolve a substance to form a solution.

sooty mold ▪ One of several species of fungi with black fruiting bodies that grow on the sugary liquid excrement of sucking insects.

spore ▪ The reproductive or propagative unit of a fungus, which can be formed from sexual recombination or from cell division.

spot treatment ▪ Application of pesticide to restricted area or areas of a whole unit. For example, the treatment of spots or patches within a larger field.

spray drift ▪ The movement of airborne spray from the intended area of application.

spreader ▪ A chemical that increases the area that a given volume of liquid will cover on a solid.

stagheading ▪ Large, dead branches or leaders in a tree that have no dead leaves attached to the branches or stems.

stem caliper ▪ The diameter of a stem, measured either 6 inches or 12 inches above ground, according to the standards established by the American Association of Nurserymen.

sticker ▪ A material added to a pesticide to increase its adherence.

stipple ▪ White flecks on green leaves caused when chlorophyll is removed by a sucking insect. Common for lace bugs.

stomate (stomata) ▪ An opening in the leaf surface through which carbon dioxide used in photosynthesis enters and through which water escapes during transpiration. Stomata can be opened and closed to regulate the amount of water lost to the atmosphere.

stress factor ▪ An external force, such as drought, nutrient deficiency, air pollution, pathogen, or insect defoliation, that limits the ability of plants to acquire essential nutrients, such as water and carbon dioxide, from the environment.

stroma (stromata) ▪ A compact mass of hyphae that usually contains fruiting structures.

stub cuts ▪ Pruning cuts made too far outside the branch bark ridge or branch collar, which leave branch tissue attached to the stem.

stunt ▪ To abnormally reduce growth of stems, branches, leaves, flowers, fruit, or roots of plants.

stunting ▪ Abnormally small size, dwarfing.

suberin ▪ A waxy substance found in the bark of older stems and roots, making them somewhat waterproof.

suckers/suckering ▪ Vigorous shoots located at the base of plants, near or at the ground line.

sucking ▪ Refers to the ability of insect mouthparts to remove food from a plant or insect by piercing tissue and ingesting food as if through a straw.

suet ▪ Meat scraps consisting of fat.

sunscald ▪ The term applied to dead or injured bark and cambial tissues. Sunscald results from cold bark temperatures followed warm bark temperatures. This condition usually occurs when thin bark tissues are warmed well above air temperatures in the winter months due to bright, sunny exposures. When temperatures suddenly drop from passing clouds or the onset of evening, freezing injury to the warmed tissues occurs. Also called frost cankers.

surfactant ▪ A material that improves the emulsifying, dispersing, spreading, wetting, or other properties of a liquid by modifying its surface characteristics.

susceptible ▪ Capable of being injured or killed.

suspension ▪ Finely divided solid particles mixed in a liquid.

symptom ▪ A plant's reaction to a disorder resulting from a causal agent.

synergism ▪ The joint action of two or more pesticides that is greater than the sum of their activity when used alone.

systemic ▪ Describes the property of insecticides or fungicides that penetrate and disperse throughout a plant; synonymous with translocated herbicide.

tar spot ▪ A black spot of plant-bug excrement found on leaf underside.

target pest ▪ The pest at which a particular pesticide or other control method is directed.

telial gall ▪ A swollen mass of host and fungal tissue formed by certain rust fungi on which spores are produced.

test ▪ The waxy shell produced by an armored scale. Made of wax and waste products.

thorax ▪ The middle part of the insect responsible for locomotion. Wings and legs are attached here.

tipping ▪ A poor maintenance practice used to control the size of tree crowns; involves the cutting of branches at right angles, leaving long stubs.

tolerance ▪ The ability of a living thing to withstand adverse conditions, such as pest attacks, weather extremes, or pesticides. The amount of pesticide that may legally remain in or on raw farm products at time of sale.

topiary ▪ The pruning and training of a plant into a desired geometric or animal shape.

topping ▪ A poor maintenance practice often used to control the size of trees; involves the indiscriminate cutting of branches and stems at right angles, leaving long stubs. Synonymous with "rounding-over," "heading-back," "dehorning," "capping," and "hatracking." Topping is often improperly referred to as pollarding.

toxicant ▪ A poison; a chemical that will kill an animal or plant.

trade name ▪ Brand name.

translocated herbicide ▪ A herbicide that is moved within the plant. Translocated herbicides can be either phloem-mobile or xylem-mobile, but the term is frequently used in a more restrictive sense to refer to herbicides that are applied to the foliage and move downward through the phloem to underground parts.

transpiration ▪ The process by which water is lost from the leaf to the atmosphere through leaf pores, or stomata, caused by evaporation. Transpiration serves to draw water and nutrients into the plant from the soil and to cool the leaf surface.

transplant shock ▪ A physiological condition occurring over an extended period of time of stress in woody ornamental plants brought about by the loss of fibrous roots and root hairs or drastic changes of growing environments during the transplanting process.

true leg ▪ A jointed appendage that is attached to the insect thorax and used for walking.

turgor pressure ▪ The force exerted on cell walls by water contained under pressure within the cell (similar in concept to the force exerted by water contained within a water tower or water balloon). A loss of turgor pressure results in wilting.

underfur ▪ The soft, insulating fur of a mammal closest to the skin. It is commonly a different color than the overlying guard hairs.

ungulate ▪ Hooved, plant-feeding mammal.

vapor drift ▪ The movement of pesticides as vapor from the area of application after the spray droplets have impinged on the target.

variety ▪ A subdivision of a species having a distinct difference and breeding true to that difference.

vascular system ▪ The circulatory system of plants; consists of xylem and phloem that conducts water and nutrients.

vascular tissue ▪ Network of phloem and xylem tissue through which water, sugar, nutrients, and other substances are transported throughout the plant.

vascular-wilt fungi ▪ Fungi that colonize and grow within vascular tissue, thereby blocking the transport of water, sugar, nutrients, and other substances and resulting in wilting or even death of the plant.

vertebrate ▪ An animal with a backbone. Fish, amphibians, reptiles, birds, and mammals are vertebrates.

virus ▪ A submicroscopic pathogen consisting of a nucleic acid surrounded by a protein coat.

vitality ▪ The relative health of a plant, usually a function of the growing environment.

volatile ▪ Evaporates at ordinary temperatures when exposed to air.

vole ▪ A field mouse or meadow mouse that is larger than a house mouse, and that has a more rounded face and a short tail.

water table ▪ The depth underground at which free-standing water can be found.

water-holding capacity ▪ Ability of a soil to hold moisture.

waterfowl ▪ Ducks, geese, and other birds that spend much of their time in or on lakes, ponds, and other bodies of water.

weaning ▪ The point at which a young mammal ceases to rely on mother's milk as part of its diet.

web ▪ Structure formed from silk excretion of insects.

weed ▪ Any plant that is objectionable or interferes with the activities or welfare of humans.

weed control ▪ The process of reducing weed growth or infestation to an acceptable level.

wetting agent ▪ A chemical that causes a liquid to contact surfaces more thoroughly.

whorl ▪ The radial joint of tree branches produced during a single growth flush. Used to describe branching of pines at the trunk.

wilt ▪ The loss of water turgor pressure in a leaf, causing it to droop or curl or to lose a degree of its normal color.

wilting point ▪ The point at which enough water is lost from the soil that a plant's roots can no longer extract it.

wind-tunnel effect ▪ An increase in the velocity of wind caused by the channeling or restriction of air flow due to artificial structures in urban areas.

wind-throw ▪ The uprooting of trees and shrubs, usually during wind storms.

winterkill ▪ Plant material fatally affected by adverse or extreme winter conditions.

witches' brooms or **witches' brooming** ▪ The broomlike growth or mass proliferation of buds and shoots caused by a dense clustering of branches formed by simultaneous development of side shoots. Results from many causal agents, ranging from de-icing salts, to insects, to fungi.

wound periderm tissue ▪ Tissue formed when the plant is wounded by pruning, insects, or other sources of mechanical injury. Callus tissue grows over the wound, isolating it from undamaged tissue and the external environment. Also known as callus tissue.

woundwood ▪ Lignified, differentiated tissues produced on woody plants as a response to wounding (also know as callus tissue).

xylem ▪ The nonliving vascular tissue in plants through which water, nutrients, and other substances are transported from the roots to the canopy.

yard ▪ (v.) When deer band together in dense cover, especially in winter. (n.) An area where deer and similar animals band together in winter.

yellow ▪ A leaf discoloration that occurs when the green chlorophyll pigment degrades. Associated with sucking injury or leaf aging.

yellows ▪ A plant disease caused by a phytoplasma that results in chlorosis and stunting of the affected plant.

Index

Page numbers in **boldface** refer to tables. Figures are not indexed separately, with one exception.

A

Erratum

The heading for column 3 of the table in Annex E was incorrectly printed (listed as weight, lb per foot). This sheet contains the correct heading, weight, lb per ft^3.

ANNEX E
(Informative)
Weight of Green Logs

Scientific name	Common name	Weight, lb per ft^3	Weight of a 1-foot section, based on average diameter							
			10″	12″	14″	16″	18″	20″	22″	24″
Abies concolor	white fir	47	25	37	50	66	83	102	124	148
Abies procera	noble fir	29	16	23	31	41	51	63	77	91
Acer rubrum	red maple	50	27	39	53	70	88	109	132	157
Acer saccharinum	silver maple	45	25	35	48	63	79	98	119	141
Acer saccharum	sugar maple	56	31	44	60	78	99	122	148	176
Aesculus hippocastanum	horsechestnut	41	22	32	43	57	72	89	108	129
Alnus rubra	red alder	46	25	36	49	64	81	100	121	144
Betula papyrifera	paper birch	50	27	39	53	70	88	109	132	157
Calocedrus decurrens	incense-cedar	45	25	35	48	63	79	98	119	141
Carya illinoensis	pecan	61	33	48	65	85	108	133	161	192
Carya ovata	shagbark hickory	64	35	50	68	89	113	140	169	201
Celtis occidentalis	hackberry	50	27	39	53	70	88	109	132	157
Diospyros virginiana	persimmon	63	34	49	67	88	111	137	166	198
Eucalyptus camaldulensis	red gum	50	27	39	53	70	88	109	132	157
Fagus spp.	beech	54	29	42	58	75	95	118	142	169
Fraxinus americana	white ash	48	26	38	51	67	85	104	126	150
Fraxinus latifolia	Oregon ash	48	26	38	51	67	85	104	126	150
Fraxinus pennsylvanica	green ash	47	25	37	50	66	83	102	124	148
Gleditsia triacanthos	honeylocust	61	33	48	65	85	108	133	161	192
Juglans nigra	black walnut	58	32	45	62	81	102	126	153	182
Larix spp.	larch	51	28	40	54	71	90	111	135	160
Liquidambar styraciflua	sweetgum	55	30	43	58	77	97	120	145	173
Liriodendron tulipifera	yellow poplar, tuliptree	38	21	30	40	53	67	83	99	199
Melia azedarach	Chinaberry	50	27	39	53	70	88	109	132	157
Nyssa sylvatica	black gum	45	25	35	48	63	79	98	119	141
Picea rubens	red spruce	34	19	27	36	47	60	74	90	106
Picea sitchensis	Sitka spruce	32	17	25	34	45	56	70	84	100
Pinus contorta	lodgepole pine	39	21	30	41	55	69	85	103	122
Pinus elliottii	slash pine	58	32	45	62	81	102	126	153	182
Pinus lambertiana	sugar pine	52	28	41	55	72	92	113	137	163
Pinus monticola	western white pine	36	20	28	38	50	64	78	95	113
Pinus palustris	longleaf pine	55	30	43	58	77	97	120	145	173
Pinus ponderosa	ponderosa pine	46	25	36	49	64	81	100	121	144
Pinus strobus	eastern white pine	36	20	28	38	50	64	78	95	113
Pinus taeda	loblolly pine	53	29	41	56	74	93	116	140	166
Platanus occidentalis	sycamore	52	28	41	55	72	92	113	137	163
Populus spp.	cottonwood	49	27	38	52	68	86	107	129	154
Populus tremuloides	quaking aspen	43	23	34	46	60	76	94	114	135

©2006, International Society of Arboriculture

Scientific name	Common name	Weight, lb per ft^3	Weight of a 1-foot section, based on average diameter							
			10″	12″	14″	16″	18″	20″	22″	24″
Prunus serotina	black cherry	45	25	35	48	63	79	98	119	141
Pseudotsuga menziesii	Douglas-fir	39	21	30	41	55	69	85	103	122
Quercus alba	white oak	62	34	48	66	86	109	135	163	194
Quercus coccinea	scarlet oak	64	35	50	68	89	113	140	169	201
Quercus kelloggii	California black oak	66	36	51	70	92	116	144	174	207
Quercus palustris	pin oak	64	35	50	68	89	113	140	169	201
Quercus robur	English oak	52	28	41	55	72	92	113	137	163
Quercus rubra	red oak	63	34	49	67	88	111	137	166	198
Quercus stellata	post oak	63	34	49	67	88	111	137	166	198
Quercus virginiana	live oak	76	41	60	81	106	134	166	200	238
Robinia pseudoacacia	black locust	58	32	45	62	81	102	126	153	182
Salix spp.	willow	32	17	25	34	45	56	70	84	100
Sequoia sempervirens	coast redwood	50	27	39	53	70	88	109	132	157
Taxodium distichum	baldcypress	51	28	40	54	71	90	111	135	160
Thuja plicata	western red cedar	28	15	22	30	39	49	61	74	88
Tilia americana	basswood	42	23	33	45	59	74	92	111	132
Tsuga canadensis	eastern hemlock	49	27	38	52	68	86	107	129	154
Tsuga heterophylla	western hemlock	41	22	32	43	57	72	89	108	129
Ulmus americana	American elm	54	29	42	58	75	95	118	142	169